Does He know a mother's heart?
How suffering refutes religions

Does He know
a mother's heart?

How suffering refutes religions

ARUN SHOURIE

HarperCollins *Publishers* India
a joint venture with

New Delhi

First published in India in 2011
by HarperCollins *Publishers* India
a joint venture with
The India Today Group

Copyright © Arun Shourie 2011

ISBN: 978-93-5029-091-0

2 4 6 8 10 9 7 5 3

Arun Shourie asserts the moral right
to be identified as the author of this work

HarperCollins *Publishers*
A-53, Sector 57, Noida 201301, India
77-85 Fulham Palace Road, London W6 8JB, United Kingdom
Hazelton Lanes, 55 Avenue Road, Suite 2900, Toronto, Ontario M5R 3L2
and 1995 Markham Road, Scarborough, Ontario M1B 5M8, Canada
25 Ryde Road, Pymble, Sydney, NSW 2073, Australia
31 View Road, Glenfield, Auckland 10, New Zealand
10 East 53rd Street, New York NY 10022, USA

Typeset in Palatino 11/14
by Aditya K. Goel, 2/18, Ansari Road, New Delhi 110 002

Printed and bound at
Thomson Press (India)Ltd.

For mothers
who have had to bring up
special children

CONTENTS

1

Taat maat guru sakhaa tu . . .

Your neighbours have a son. He is now thirty-five years old. Going by his age you would think of him as a young man, and, on meeting his mother or father, would ask, almost out of habit, 'And what does the young man do?' That expression, 'young man', doesn't sit well as he is but a child. He cannot walk. Indeed, he cannot stand. He cannot use his right arm. He can see only to his left. His hearing is sharp, as is his memory. But he speaks only syllable by syllable . . .

The father shouts at him. He curses him: 'You are the one who brought misery into our home . . . We knew no trouble till you came. Look at you—weak, dependent, drooling, good for nothing . . .' Nor does the father stop at shouting at the child, at pouring abuse at him, at cursing the child. He beats him. He thrashes him black and blue . . . As others in the family try to save the child from the father's rage, he leaps at them. Curses them, hits out at them.

What would you think about that damned father? Wouldn't you report him to the police or some such authority that can lock him up? Wouldn't you try everything you can to remove the child from the reach of the father?

But what if the father is *The Father*—the 'T' and 'F' capital, both words italicized? That is, what if the 'father' in question is 'God'?

Why does the perspective of so many of us change at once? Suddenly, they exclaim, 'There must be some reason God has done this.' Suddenly, they shift the blame to that poor child: 'Must have done something terrible in his previous life to deserve such hardship . . .'

And yet the child loves. He laughs. He is filled with joy at the littlest things—a tape of Talat Mahmood, lunch at a restaurant, the visit of an aunt or a cousin . . . What are we to conclude? That the cruelties rained upon him by his father have 'built his character'? That they have instilled forbearance? Are we to infer, 'See, while to us the father seems cruel, in fact he never inflicts more hardship on the son than the son can bear'?

Were we to say and infer as much, that would be not just obnoxious, it would be perverse. And yet those are the *exact* things that, as we shall see, a revered religious text says about God: He inflicts hardship upon us to build our character; He never imposes more hardship on a person than the latter can bear.

But that child is our son—Aditya, our life. Adit is thirty-five now. He cannot walk or stand. He can see only from the left side of his eyes. He cannot use his right arm or hand. He speaks syllable by syllable. Yet he laughs—you can hear his laughter three houses away. He enjoys going out to restaurants. He loves the songs of Talat Mahmood, Mohammed Rafi and Kishore Kumar. There are some songs, though, the moment they commence, we have to rush and turn off the tape—he is so moved by them that he starts sobbing. There are others which he identifies with himself:

Tu aake mujhe pehchaan zaraa
Main dil hoon ik armaan bharaa . . .
. . .
Muskaan lutaataa chal
Tu deep jalaataa chal
Khud bhi sambhal
Auron ko bhi raah dikhlaa . . .

'*Mere baare mein*,' he declares with joy—and laughs even more as in our rendering the last line has been altered to '*Papa ko bhi raah dikhlaa* . . .'

He loves these singers and their songs. He loves even more the tapes that his grandparents made for him, and the tapes that his uncles and cousins make for him now. He doesn't watch television—moving images bother him. But he does listen to the news over the radio. The newspaper is read to him—among the things he calls himself is the '*ghar kaa samvaad-daataa*'. He loves poems being read to him. Seeing Adit's spirit, and how many of his poems Adit knew by heart, Ashok Chakradhar has gifted him many of his books, and even dedicated one to him. Every time you read the books, you have to begin at the very first page, not just the title page, but the very first, blank page—for on them Ashok Chakradhar has written many an endearment—'*Pyaare, ati pyaare Aditya ke liye* . . .' And if, while reading the poems, you pronounce even a syllable wrong, he hoots with joy, '*Galti*'. That was one of my father's favourite games with Adit. He would deliberately make a little mistake, and Adit would catch him out—hoot, and laugh, beaming with triumph . . . He loves everyone. Everyone in the family loves him. His maternal grandmother, Malti Shukla, was his life. He is ours.

And that God just does not stop pounding this helpless, defenceless child. The last two months have been traumatic—again. Adit has a very high threshold of pain. He has the forbearance of Job, as the devout would say. He sleeps with us. There is a routine to his waking up: he will open his eyes and get us to join in repeating things that his favourites say: 'Adit is my best friend. Adit is absolutely my best friend . . . *Main nahin*, Adit is the top tiptop, Adit is top tiptop Number *One* . . .' So we were alarmed when he woke up one morning almost crying. By the evening a blue-white cloud had formed over his right pupil. We rushed from one hospital to the other . . . from one eye specialist to the other . . . The membrane of his right eye had ruptured. Fluid from inside the eye had oozed out—that was the cloud over his pupil . . . He was in extreme pain . . . 'Keratoconus with resolving acute hydrops,' the doctors pronounced—the cornea, instead of being spherical has become conical, they said, it may have been so for a long time. This has stretched the membrane, and has eventually ruptured it . . . We keep being taught these new words, Manju[1] remarks as we come out of the doctor's clinic one day. Adit's vision, already limited, has been impaired further—we cannot say how much: it cannot be tested by asking him to read those eye-charts that you and I take for granted. 'He must be in excruciating pain,' the doctor says, surprised that Adit is not even complaining.

It isn't just that Adit has a very high threshold of pain, like his two grandmothers he has taught himself to bear an unbelievable amount of it.

'You have to go in for a cornea transplant,' the doctors say. Will that require general anaesthesia? we ask, full of dread. Yes, of course. For how long? O, just half an hour for each eye.

An *hour* under general anaesthesia? We can't bring ourselves to put Adit under sedation for that long. For how long may we defer the decision? I inquire.

Well, indefinitely, says the doctor. But if you want his vision to improve, if you want to reduce the chances of this problem recurring . . .

We are paralysed.

ANITA COMES

I had not known Anita. Our aunts knew each other. We are

---

[1] Manjulika Dubey, my wife Anita's elder sister.

looking for a nice girl for my nephew, my aunt must have said. We are looking for a good boy for my niece, Anita's aunt must have said. So, one evening—an evening that is naturally so vivid that it is as if it were last evening—my parents and I drove up to Anita's aunt's place.

We didn't need the forty-five minutes for which the tea lasted. Anita was dazzlingly beautiful. As we got into the car, I looked back to get another glimpse of her. My father started the car. My mother asked, 'Arun, *pehle General Sahib nu mil aayiye, yaa ghar chalke enaanoon* phone *kar dayee e ki saadhi valon taan haan hi hai?'*—'Arun, should we first go and look up General Sahib'—my uncle, Major General U.C. Dubey, who had taken ill that morning and was in the Army Hospital—'or should we first go home and ring them up that from our side the answer is of course "Yes"?' I said, *'Mama, pehle ghar hi chalo!'*—'Mummy, let us first go home!'

By the time my mother rang up, Anita had already taken the bus back to the university where she was studying. I thought we had lost the prize of my life. Later, she was to tell me, 'I told myself, "If he looks back, I will say Yes . . ."' Since that day, I always look back as I leave.

We had the happiest, carefree nine years. I had a job at the World Bank in Washington DC. We were just two of us. The salary wasn't as sumptuous as it had seemed from India, but it was enough—that was one of the many things Anita taught me then: 'We have to learn to be satisfied with enough,' she said. 'And, at any time, "enough" is whatever we have at that time.'

Years passed. Happy carefree years. But I lost all interest in the World Bank. I wanted to work in India, on matters that concerned India. Soon, there was another pull, a compulsive one. Mrs Indira Gandhi had imposed the Emergency, thrown the entire Opposition into jail and snuffed out all freedoms. I wanted to join the fight against it. But Anita had conceived. We decided that we would return

to India soon after the birth of our child. Accordingly,
I resigned my job at the World Bank.

ADIT COMES

Anita had been under the care of a wonderful doctor. Seven
months into her pregnancy, he went on a vacation. She kept
up the visits—this time to his associate. The vacation over,
the senior doctor was back. The moment Anita entered his
office, he exclaimed, 'But, my dear girl, something doesn't
seem right . . .' He examined her. 'We must take the baby out
at the earliest.'

We did not know what had hit us. Anita's mother had
just reached Washington to be with us for the delivery.
We turned up at the hospital not knowing what was in
store.

A premature child. Barely four pounds. In distress.
Placed in an incubator. As they could not locate a vein in
his tiny arms, the doctors had stuck needles through his
scalp . . . A horrible sight for us . . . His sugar level is not
stabilizing, some nurse came and said to us. 'Will you please
sign these forms for a blood transfusion?' . . .

Three days went by. A Pakistani lady doctor used to visit
Anita to check up on her. I am not supposed to tell you, she
said, and I will lose my job if they come to know I have told
you, but something has happened. Insufficient supply of
oxygen in the incubator . . .

Anita came back to our home in Alexandria. Adit stayed
on in that incubator. For an entire month. A horrible month.

'The child will finish your life as you have known it, may
finish your life altogether,' a senior at the World Bank said
to me one day. He was a cheerful, warm-hearted person,
but was speaking from first-hand knowledge as he had been
bringing up a mentally handicapped son. 'The doctors may
well tell you, "We can do little more for the child." And ask
you, "Are you desperate that he lives?" When they do so,
don't let your emotions come in the way. Do you know

what you will have to go on doing for the boy—not just now or for a few years but for as long as the child lives? . . .'

That evening I reported the conversation to Anita and my mother-in-law. A person of iron-will, my mother-in-law said, 'That is just not the case. Handicapped children live perfectly useful lives these days . . .'

Three months later we were advised to take the child to the head of pediatric neurology at the Georgetown University Hospital. We were exhausted, felled. The doctor was a kind, elderly gentleman. 'I am going to use a word that you would have heard—it is used a lot these days to raise money. The word is cerebral palsy. It only means that the baby's brain has suffered an injury . . .'

We were too stunned to ask what exactly this was going to mean for our Adit's future. I told the doctor, 'We had planned to return to India. But if you feel that, for the sake of the child, we should stay on in Washington, of course we will. I will take back my resignation from the World Bank.'

'I have not been to your country, young man,' that kind doctor said. 'If you are here, all that we will be able to do will be to tell you how your son is faring against the milestones. But as observant parents you will notice that yourselves . . .'

'I have not been to your country, as I said,' he continued. 'But from what I have heard, you have strong, well-knit families there. That is what this child will need as he grows up—a net of love and security. So, if I were you, I would stick to your decision, return to your country, and bring him up in the embrace of your family.'

Among the wisest bits of advice we ever received.

We returned to India. We stayed with my parents. Soon, Anita's mother came to stay with us . . . Adit became the centre of many lives.

ANGELS FROM NOWHERE

Just as difficulties would burst out of the blue, angels would

appear in the nick of time. One day a lady turned up at the
gate. She had worked at Loreto Convent in Lucknow, and
had known Anita's mother and aunts when they studied
there, and Anita and her sisters when they studied there
later. '*Arey*,' she said as she came in and saw Anita, 'You are
one of the Shukla sisters. I know your entire family. I hear
your son is not well. I will look after him . . .'

Adit began to be seized by tremors—they would strike
fifteen/twenty times a day. You have to get him into the
Medical Institute at once, we were told. But you won't
get a room unless you can approach some Kashmiri high up
to put in a word to the Director. Mr P.N. Haksar got us the
room.

Adit was put on sedatives of all kinds. He became listless
as a handkerchief. And yet, even at that depth, he would be
seized by convulsions . . . You must take him to the
Children's Hospital at Great Ormond Street in London at
once . . . Mrs Gandhi's Emergency had ended. Mr Atal
Behari Vajpayee had become the Foreign Minister—I had
got to meet him during the Emergency after his release. He
invited me to join the delegation to the UN General
Assembly which he was going to lead. We were able to take
Adit to London.[2]

'What in the name of God have your doctors been doing?'
the doctors in London exclaimed upon examining Adit and
his medical records. They have been stuffing the child with

---

[2] This was the one occasion that I had gone abroad after our return
to India during the Emergency. When, three years later, I exposed the
misdeeds of A.R. Antulay, the then Chief Minister of Maharashtra,
a magazine attempted to shield Antulay by insinuating that I was a CIA
plant, that I had written what I had at the behest of the CIA because
Antulay had spoken out against US arms aid to Pakistan, that I had been
using 'the pretext' of my son's illness as an 'excuse' to 'regularly visit'
my 'foreign bosses abroad'. On the top of the page, it had carried
a photograph of little Adit laughing away in my arms, a photograph
taken by my father.

five sedatives—some in doses large enough for adults. They have nearly blinded him . . . He is suffering from myclonic epilepsy. This will not be suppressed by these medicines. Stop all of them. It will fade away in due course as he grows up. Don't, *don't* give him any medicines. Give nature a chance . . .'

We returned. I had joined the *Indian Express*. We were in Bangalore for the summer, in the house of Mr Ram Nath Goenka. Suddenly Adit developed high fever. But we had been warned not to give him any medicines. We were frantic.

At the time, the Bangalore edition of the paper had as its manager one of the old-world gentlemen, Mr K. Sankaran Nayar. He saw our plight. 'If you do not mind,' he said, 'I will call Panikkar. He is the doctor in the local branch of the Arya Vaidya Pharmacy of Coimbatore—just opposite our office.'

What is the problem with the child? Panikkar asked. He has high fever . . . No, no. The fever will go in any case, with or without medicines. What is the *problem* with him? The seizures . . . Any sudden sound—the horn of a bus on the road, a clap—any of these can trigger it off . . .

No problem, he said. I will prescribe medicines. I will do the puja tomorrow. We will begin the day after, it is an auspicious day. The tremors will go in three months. They will return once for a fortnight or so. But after that they will go forever.

And that is what happened.

The same sort of thing happened a few months ago. As if overnight, Adit began to have difficulties passing urine. We took him to one hospital, and then to another, to the best specialists. An obstruction has grown around the opening of his bladder . . . A catheter has to be put, one of the best-known urologists pronounced.

A catheter at thirty-four? we thought in dread. How will he live the rest of his life?

It so happened that, as Anita's symptoms had been getting worse, we had earlier scheduled to go to the Arya Vaidya Pharmacy in Coimbatore for her treatment. Once there, we naturally took up Adit's problem also with Dr Ravindran, the chief physician.

No problem, he said. I will send medicines this evening. An obstruction has grown around the opening of the bladder? No problem. We have medicines that will corrode that away. Sure enough, that is what happened. The problem was over by the second day.

Had we not come to Coimbatore for an altogether different purpose, we might have subjected Adit to a catheter for the rest of his life.

So, difficulties would pounce on the hapless child from nowhere. And angels would arrive from nowhere. The biggest angel, of course, was Maltiji, his maternal grandmother. A person, as I said, of iron-will, she was always focused on doing whatever had to be done at that particular moment. Accustomed to the hardships of army life, she had not a want of her own . . . She set aside everything and stayed with us for twenty-five years. She looked after Adit every waking moment. She ran our household. And we were all staying with my parents. We could not have survived without Maltiji's steel, nor without my parents' love and home and sustaining support. That is why we just don't understand where today's TV serials get their conceptions of evil, scheming mothers-in-law, of families at each other's throats.

When Adit was seven and already the darling of the family, Anita started the practice of having all our relatives and friends come over to celebrate his birthday. That remains the most important day of the family to this day. Everyone comes out of their love for Adit. They sing his favourite songs. One thing has changed—his grandparents are all gone. And that is a huge change—Nani used to arrange everything; Anita's two sisters do so now. But one thing hasn't: Adit's favourite songs are the same, and his joy at his favourite persons singing the same songs year after year—that hasn't changed.

THE SCHOOL

Adit was growing up. Shanti-amma, his maid, would sing to him, tell him stories, take him to the park. She was ever so possessive of him—always ticking off anyone who expressed the slightest doubt about Adit's condition, or who uttered a word of pity or condescension. My mother-in-law would teach him—from news, to stories, to rhyming games, to poems, to arithmetic. 'But why *arithmetic*, Mummy?' I would remonstrate. 'Why make him do *sums*? Why make him learn *tables*? He is never going to use them.' 'But just see his sense of achievement when he gets the answer right,' she would teach me. 'And he learns fast. He has excellent memory.'

In these and other ways, Adit was fully occupied. He was happy. But there had been no school for spastic children in India.

Malini was born to Mithu Chib—now Mithu Alur. She and her husband were in London at the time. Malini too had been struck by cerebral palsy.

They had returned to India. Mithu is another of those ladies who just won't give up or give in. She set up the first school for spastic children. Her sister, Mita Nundy, set up the second one in Delhi. It was in all of two or three rooms.

Anita would drive Adit to the school. Soon, she joined it.

Again, so many helped. Mrs Nargis Dutt had helped raise funds for the school in Bombay. For the school in Delhi, Mr Rajiv Gandhi, then the Prime Minister, sanctioned governmental assistance. Mr Jagmohan, then the Lieutenant Governor of Delhi, sanctioned land at institutional rates. Mr N.A. Palkhivala got TISCO to send

steel at a concessional rate . . . A building specially designed
for wheelchair-bound children came up. Adit's world
swelled—his teachers became parts of his family. The
school—now the Centre for Special Education—became
one of the most innovative institutions of its kind. Seeing
how great the need was, and how many more schools
would be required, Mita and her associates began to train
teachers. By now there are schools for spastic children in
several parts of the country.

Many helped, as I said. Many placed impediments.
One casteist minister, who contributed to ruining several
institutions, demanded to know the caste-wise breakdown
of students and teachers and the reasons why the school
was not implementing the reservations' edicts of
government . . .

Anita continued to work at the school. One day, as she
was driving Adit and herself to school, a jeep coming in the
opposite direction lost control. It rammed into Anita's little
Fiat. She and Adit were tossed inside the car. They were
shaken, of course, but neither seemed to be badly hurt.

Soon after the accident, however, Anita began to feel
peculiar sensations on her left side. We thought the problem
was a 'frozen shoulder'. But soon, the stiffness and pain
developed into tremors . . . One doctor after another . . .
Eventually she was diagnosed as having developed
Parkinson's disease. She was just about forty-two at the
time—another one of those 'one in ten million' blows.

By now the tremors have spread to the right side also.
Every time Anita does something with her hands—for
instance, when she eats—her legs flail uncontrollably. That
is dyskinesia, another one of those words with which our
circumstances have enlarged our vocabulary. The
symptoms become worse every winter. This winter—of
2009, in which I begin working on this book about Adit and
her—Anita has fallen four times . . .

With my parents having passed away, with Maltiji also having gone, I am now the servant-in-chief, not just of Adit but of the two of them. The help of many friends and relatives sees us through the day. But more than anything, Anita's strength and equanimity keep us afloat. 'I had another toss today,' I heard her tell her sister the other day, describing a fall so bad that we were lucky she had not fractured her skull. And so helpless and shocked was she that, while there was an alarm bell next to where she lay, she could not reach out to it. She now wears another alarm on her wrist . . . Even though this is her own condition, she manages the entire household; she husbands our savings; she runs everything so that every need of Adit is met—at once; and so that I am absolutely free to do my work.

'We have to be thankful for an ordinary, boring, eventless day,' Anita taught me long ago.

Her fortitude is a daily, ever-present example of another one of the lessons she taught me once: 'You have to remember, there are many types of courage.'

My father's courage as he evacuated Hindus in July-August 1947 out of Lahore—where he was City Magistrate at the time. The courage with which he settled, comforted and on occasion quelled the raging refugees in camps across Punjab. My mother's courage as she comforted *her* mother and father when they lost a young son, as husbands deserted two of their daughters. My mother-in-law's courage as she went on looking after all of us even as rheumatoid arthritis twisted and turned and crippled her hands and feet. Malini's[3] courage, Veena's[4] courage evident in the dignity and fortitude with which they have borne

---

[3] Anita's younger sister, Malini Saran, who lost her husband to cancer when he was so young and at the peak of his abilities.

[4] Veena Devasher who lost her husband, Vijay Devasher, my cousin and the jewel of our family, when he was just thirty-four.

blows of unimaginable severity, faced life, brought up their children single-handed, and, on top of it, continued working . . . Here we are: we get so puffed up just because we have stood up to some authority-of-the-moment. And here are these girls: they have stood up to life itself.

'But I will never get over what God has done to Adit,' Anita says. How true:

Ghaayal ki gati ghaayal jaane
Jauhar ki gati jauhar . . .

MY TEACHER

Adit has taught us lessons upon lessons. He has given us a sense of proportion. I am dismissed from the *Indian Express?* But he hasn't had and isn't going to have a job at all. In losing my place at the *Express,* I feel that my tongue has been yanked out? But Adit can scarcely speak at all. At every turn of this kind, I have but to look at him—he is laughing away, almost breathless, with someone over some little joke, happy in his little world. The medication works just as well the other way round. Another award? Some new post? Another book published? That none of these is of the slightest significance to Adit keeps the head from swelling.

We cannot afford something? We have to only look at how Adit derives the greatest joy from the littlest things— his Nani's tape, another lunch at Sagar Restaurant . . . He loves going to restaurants, actually—where he will eat the very same, simple dishes. In turn, our choice of restaurants has come to depend on how they treat our darling Adit. He loves fragrances: he would take his Nani's handkerchief to his face as she would have put two/three drops of some delicate fragrance on it. Adit's cousins and aunts and uncles are always bringing him shirts and the like, and he loves wearing the brightly coloured ones. . . With his recent eye trouble, so as to shield his eyes from glare and dust we have had to make him wear sunglasses when he goes out to the park in the evening. 'Hero, Adit *to bilkul* hero *lagta hai*' we said to encourage him to keep them on. 'How is Adit?' I asked Anita over the phone the other day as I was on tour. 'He has just left for the park,' she said, 'wearing his goggles—looking sharp left, and sharp right to make sure that I have noticed how smart he is looking . . .' Made my day. For a moment I could think of him seeing himself as a hero rather than be consumed by that damned rupture in his eye that had made us put those glasses on him.

Someone pastes another calumny? I have just to ask, 'Does Adit care? Is his love going to be the slightest bit less because of this nonsense?'

No text or teacher could have taught us that virtue on which Gandhiji placed such significance—*aparigraha*, non-possession—as Adit has. Nothing sticks to his hand. You hand him a ten-rupee note—it gets crumpled as he clenches his hand. You give him a hundred-rupee note, and ask him to give it away. He does so without a thought. 'But he will never give up his tape recorder,' said a cousin. Adit was a child. The cousin was living with us. He saw how avidly Adit listened to his tapes. They were his life. The cousin was not sharing something with another child. Anita said, 'But one must share, one must give. Look at Adit . . .' Before she had finished, the cousin said, 'But he will never give up his tape recorder.' 'Why not ask him?' Anita said. 'Ask Adit even for his tape recorder.' The cousin turned to Adit, 'Adit, *tum mujhe apna* tape recorder *de doge?*' Adit pushed it away towards him . . .

Adit has a wonderful ear, and deep appreciation of our classical music. To raise funds, the school for spastic children would organize concerts. Anita would request the great artists to come. One year, Mrs M.S. Subbulakshmi had come. The concert was in the evening. She came to visit the school in the forenoon—the school was still in those two/

three rooms. The children had been gathered in one room. Like the others, tiny Adit was sort of locked into a chair with a table affixed to it. Subbulakshmi began a song, *Yaad aave, Vrindavan mein Krishna ki leelaa* . . . She had just sung a stanza or two, Adit pursed his lip and began to cry . . . I immediately took him out of his chair and lifted him on to my shoulder and pressed him to my heart . . . 'Adit *tum royo mat, yeh to gaanaa hi hai* . . .' 'No, no,' Subbulakshmi said. 'That shows how much he understands music. I have a granddaughter. She too, on this very song, at this very line, begins crying . . .' Adit loves recalling the incident, as he does others. *'To papa nein kya kahaa?'* he will ask, and you have to begin from the very beginning—the school, Mama inviting Subbulakshmi, what Gandhiji had written to her, how Panditji had once introduced her to the audience in Delhi—'Who am I to introduce Subbulakshmi?' he had said. 'I am just the Prime Minister of India. Subbulakshmi is Subbulakshmi'—the song she sang, how he began to cry, what Subbulakshmi said . . .

Thirty years later, a role reversal. We are in Chennai. Adit is to be examined at the Sankar Nethralaya. We are staying at the house of dear friends. Recitations and bhajans are often going on in their home. Early morning. Having completed my pranayama and asanas, I come out of our room. Subbulakshmi's voice. She is singing Meera's bhajans.

I rush back, bring Adit out—for he knows this set of bhajans. He is all attention—he has his head lowered as he does when he is concentrating. I am stroking Adit's shoulders and back. Subbulakshmi sings:

Ansuan jal seench seench prem bel boyee . . .

I just cannot hold tears back. I try, but I just cannot, though no sound escapes my lips. The song over, I take Adit back to our room. I have deliberately kept myself behind him, out of his sight, gently pushing the wheelchair. But he turns, pulls me to himself. Takes my head to his chest, holds

it there, and, as he often does, twirls my ear. *Tum royo mat,*
he says . . .

The dire choices put to us by doctors in Delhi repressed in
our minds, we reach the Sankar Nethralaya. The kindest
and most skilful doctors examine Adit. One test after
another. One measurement after another. Two-and-a-half
hours go by. Anita and I scarcely look at each other. I busy
myself cajoling Adit to go on with the tests, propping his
back, holding his head to the machines.

'All the things I am going to tell you are good ones,' the
kind doctor begins. The left eye is the one he uses for seeing,
she explains. There is some irregularity in it, and the cornea
is slightly thinner than normal, but there is no imminent
danger. As for the right eye, the cornea is much thinner
than it should be. The recent rupture has settled. It has left a
scar, but that is not entirely over the pupil. There is opacity
in one portion of the lens—but this is not what is preventing
the light going in, nor is the cataract of a kind that threatens
the eye. The optic nerve is much weakened—but in cerebral
palsy cases, we come across this condition almost 50 per
cent of the time: perhaps when the main injury to the brain
took place there may have been insufficient supply of
oxygen to this part also . . . Over the years, his brain has
selected the left eye. That is what he uses to see. In sum,
there is so little potential for sight in the right eye that we
will gain little by a transplant . . . To make him use his left
eye to the best advantage, spectacles . . . The number is
minus five . . .

In a word, once again, the unexpected relief, the relief we
dared not wish for: no operation. Anita and I exhale.

*Namumkin to nahin, maujon mein kahin behtaa hua saahil
aajaaye* . . .

I send smses to Adit's aunts. Excellent news, they answer.
Oof, what a relief, they say. All of us are relieved—even as
each of us realizes that the relief is based on the fact that

there is so little sight, and so little potential for sight in one of Adit's eyes that an operation will be of little help . . . But even I can see the positive side at the moment, and request our friends to repeat the line that follows in Meera's bhajan:

Ab to bel phail gayee, ananda phal hoyee . . .

To derive joy from simple things; to derive joy from beautiful, giving persons; to give back, indeed to give away; to be thankful, as we are so often told we must be, for small mercies.

Every turn reminds us how things could have been so much worse. Another phase in which Anita's condition has dipped frighteningly. We go to the neurologist to see if the medication should be adjusted. He examines her, asks her to describe her symptoms. As is the case always, she is very precise, indeed clinical and detached as she does so. The exchanges go on. Beginning his diagnosis, the doctor says, 'Mrs Shourie you must remember you are very lucky . . .' Lucky? *Lucky?* We couldn't have thought of the word that day. 'You have had this condition now for close to twenty years. Believe you me, by now things could have been much, much worse . . .'

Adit himself. After all, he need not have been such a loving and lovable child. He had every reason to have been, every *right* to have been full of resentment and anger and frustration. But he is the opposite. And that travels. I am in Mumbai for a lecture, and am having lunch at the restaurant. A gentleman approaches, 'May I join you?' We get talking. 'May I say something personal?' he asks. 'You will not mind?' Of course not—I think he is going to say how something I have written has caused him offence. 'You wouldn't know what you have done for us,' he continues. 'You see, my wife and I have a handicapped child like your son. We always thought that it was all our fault, that we were to blame. We were ashamed of taking him anywhere. . . But then one day, we saw you on television with your son. You were walking him in a park. He was laughing. Later they showed you with him in a restaurant. You seem to take him everywhere. That opened our eyes. Now we take our child out also.' But surely, that change had little to do with me. It was all due to Adit. Locked in his wheelchair, how far into the distance has Adit sprinkled his *Ganga-jal!*

And our material circumstances. I am in Pune for a lecture, and am having breakfast at the hotel's restaurant. The sequence is repeated. A gentleman comes over and asks if he can sit and talk things that concern us both. I resign myself to another of those inconclusive conversations about corruption and other ills, one in which I will hear and repeat the same lines. He turns out to be a professor at one of our leading educational institutions. His wife and he have not one but two grown-up boys with multiple handicaps to look after. They cannot afford much help. In fact, both of them have to have jobs to meet their expenses. But what is to be done about the young boys when they leave for work? . . . But that is nothing, I learn when I am back in Delhi. At the school for spastic children, they come across—not a husband and wife who, all on their own, have to care for handicapped children; they come across single mothers who have to do so. In a case they tell me about, the mother has no income except what she earns by slogging herself. She feeds the child in the morning, and has to leave him alone in the locked house till she returns from work . . .

Adit has taught me to be grateful. He loves the helpers who assist him, his *bajrang dal*, as we call them to his delight. Ever so often, you will see him take their heads into his hand and draw them to his face so that he may plant a kiss. He loves, he just loves handing out gifts to each of them. That is what Holi and Diwali and every other festival means to him. And therefore to us.

Indeed, that he is thanking someone even in the circumstances in which he is stupefies us. The school had just been set up. We did not know, the saintly staff of the school did not know the importance of always having seat belts buckled. Adit was in his wheelchair. He leaned forward, and toppled, face down. Two of his front teeth broke. Blood gushed out from his mouth. He was rushed to the dentists' clinic. The doctor pulled out what was left of those two teeth. Adit was crying, blood was all over his shirt. In *that* condition, Adit blew a kiss to the doctor to thank him. The doctor was stunned . . . Such incidents and Adit's love and gratitude that we see every day have changed us also—they have made us see every single moment that we cannot get through the day without the love and time of our relatives, of the assistance of attendants who help take care of him.

He has taught me—and Anita's difficulties have reinforced the lesson—to focus only on the task at hand. If Adit has to be toileted, then only on lifting him out of bed, and toileting him. If Anita has to be helped change her clothes, then only on that. Nothing but nothing can be gained by brooding, 'If this is how things are now, how will we manage ten years hence?' So, nothing but 'the here and now'—that lesson Adit teaches me every moment. But isn't that exactly what the great meditation masters want us to do, to learn to focus on the here and now alone?

Anita and Adit have together taught me how merely looking at things another way can change them. Adit had grown up, I could no longer lift him up and carry him on my own. As Anita was finding Delhi winters progressively more difficult, we were to go south by plane. But how can we afford to take an attendant *by plane?* I was wondering— not just the money that doing so would cost, but *the idea* that we should be taking a helper by air as if we were millionaires . . . Anita said, 'We have just to think that we have two children . . .'

Adit has bonded us closer together. I have often noticed the contrast between couples who have drifted apart as the children have grown up and left home, and between couples who have had an Adit to look after day and night. Of course, that is not always so. In just as many cases, the parents, more often the father, have not been able to cope, and the marriage has fallen apart. But we have been lucky. Not just Adit's tasks, his love has held us together.

By the way he bears every difficulty and waits for it to pass, Adit has prepared for us what the Buddhists prize, 'the armour of patience'.

And he has been a buoy. Even when he was a little child, he had exceptional sensitivity. When we would be particularly discouraged and downcast about our circumstances, about his condition, he would do something, some little thing—utter a word, say something that we did not know he knew, smile—to lift us up, to let us know that he understood more than we thought he did. Adit was lying in Anita's lap. She was humming to him, talking to him. He stuck out his tongue—a feat for him. She went on singing and talking. He put his tongue out again. 'Adit, *tumhari zubaan mein kuch mushkil hai?*' Anita asked. He took his hand—the only one he could raise—up to his head. A hair had got into his mouth. Anita's heart leapt with joy. We hadn't realized that Adit could communicate that much just with his hand. Just as unexpectedly, one day when everybody around him was debating what had to be done next, he read out the time—we had not known till then that, far from reading it, he could even see the clock: the clock had been put up only because his Nani, a disciplinarian, was very particular about his routine being maintained to the dot . . . A Diwali of years ago is as if it were yesterday. Far from standing and all, Adit could not even sit up on his own or, even if helped to sit up, keep sitting unaided. We had put Adit to bed. Anita and I were getting ready to sleep. We were upset about the noise in the colony—firecrackers going off on all sides. We turned, and there was Adit sitting up in bed. He had raised himself on the only arm he could use and was sitting cross-legged . . . We were as astonished as we were delighted. We didn't utter a sound, lest we startle him, and he lose balance. We just stood—frozen, silent, gazing, holding each other's hand. We had never had, nor have we since had a Diwali gift like that one.

Of course, now that Adit is grown up and his legs are longer, he is not able to draw them up and sit up on his own.

How ordinary these things sound—that a child should touch his hair, that he should read time of the clock, that he should sit up. How we take these things for granted. Yet for these children, to do any of these simple things is to scale K2. Lessons that we would not have learnt, a world that we would not have known but for Adit.

Hence did Meera sing:
Taat maat guru sakhaa tu
Sab vidihi he tu mero . . .

LIFE-LESSONS

Indeed, by making us enter his world and feel his deprivation, he may have lifted us a bit. Did Gandhiji not teach us through one of his favourite hymns:

Vaishnav jan to taine kahiye peer paraaee jaane rey . . .

Nor is it just by himself that Adit has taught us lessons. He has taken us to other great teachers.

'Since the Mahatma's time there is not a leader; since Ramana's time and Sri Aurobindo's time, there is not a godman that I have not known on intimate terms, not one with whom I have not cracked jokes,' Ram Nathji[5] would say, and then regale us with stories about his encounters with them.

---

[5] Ram Nath Goenka, founder of the *Indian Express*, a formidable fighter.

Sai Baba of Puttaparthi was visiting Delhi. He knew the troubles Ram Nathji had been through during the Emergency—how Mrs Indira Gandhi had taken over the paper, and the rest. She had been ousted. Sai Baba was going to come over to the Express building to bless Ram Nathji.

'Bring your son, Baba will bless him' Ram Nathji said. 'Everything will be all right. You will yourself see.'

My mother holding Adit, Anita and I were waiting in Ram Nathji's room as Sai Baba and he walked in. Ram Nathji introduced us to him. Sai Baba blessed Adit, of course. I don't remember exactly what Sai Baba said. What I remember about the occasion is my mother. Anita and I were standing to a side. My mother had Adit in her arms. 'Please bless him, please bless him, Baba,' she implored. She was trembling—in desperate hope that a miracle would lift Adit as much as in awe of being in Sai Baba's presence.

Years later, however, Sai Baba was to teach me a life-lesson. As I mentioned above, Mita Nundy had set up the school for spastic children in Delhi. A woman with steel for determination and with *sevaa-bhaava* to match, she had been, and is today the main impulse behind the school. Because of Adit, she and her husband, the distinguished surgeon, Samiran Nundy, had become among our, and Adit's, dearest friends. For all her saintly work, Mita too was struck by a blow—cardiac amyloidosis, the doctors pronounced. The heart gets filled up with protein cells, much like a reservoir were to get filled up with sediment. The doctors gave her little time.

But she has done so much for children like our Adit, we thought. What is it that we can do for her? Knowing that she was an ardent devotee of Sai Baba, I decided to go to him and entreat him for something that would help Mita.

An uncle and aunt of mine had left Delhi and settled in Puttaparthi after their son, barely twenty years old and in

the pink of health, had suddenly and for no apparent
reason died. Through them I got to meet Sai Baba in a room
with just five/six other persons. We were seated in a small
circle. Baba was moving from person to person. A watch for
a General. Something else for the brother of a former Prime
Minister of Italy . . . 'Baba, I have come to seek your blessings
and something special for Mita Nundy,' I said as he turned
to me. 'She has done so much for handicapped children. She
is utterly devoted to you . . .' 'Haan, haan, jaantaa hai, jaantaa
hai,' Baba cut me short. And moved on.

He came again. My hands were stretched out still. I began
about Mita. He poured vibhuti into my hands, and moved
ahead.

As he came round a third time, I became a bit insistent.
'Main apne liye nahin, Mita Nundy ke liye, aap se maangne
aayaa hun,' I said.

Sai Baba looked at my palms, filled as they were with
vibhuti. 'Kaise de saktaa hai,' he remarked, 'jab haath khaali hi
nahin hai?'—'How am I to give when the hands are not
empty?'

Another life-lesson: until our minds are emptied, how
will we receive?

I put the vibhuti in a handkerchief, and held out my
hands. He gave a shivlinga—'Is par paani daalna, aur paani ko
pina. Achcha hoga.'

I brought the shivlinga and gave it to Mita. That was
twenty-five years ago. Mita has suffered strokes, and much
else. Her right side is severely impaired. But where the
doctors had given her little time, she is here. And her spirit is
firm as ever.

A MOTHER'S HEART

Years passed. J. Krishnamurti, the great philosopher and
teacher, was visiting Delhi. As usual, Ram Nathji had met

him in the past, and had a way to get to him now. Krishnaji
was staying at the house of Mrs Pupul Jayakar—a lady who
had done great service to Indian handicrafts, a close friend
of Mrs Indira Gandhi and one of Krishnaji's closest
disciples.

Ram Nathji sent me to interview Krishnaji. We talked of
the state of affairs, and the rest. Krishnaji's point was
responsibility. Unless each of us owned responsibility for
what he as an individual was doing, the state of affairs
would just go one hurtling the way it was doing. Krishnaji
asked me about Anita. The conversation turned to Adit.

Bring the young man around, Krishnaji said as I got up to
take leave of him. His mother is as welcome, but she will not
come.

I was to go back two days later. I asked Anita to come
along also. She refused—nothing happens, she had
concluded, our hopes are raised again and again, and again
and again they are shattered.

I went with Adit. Krishnaji talked. Adit was in my lap.
From time to time, Krishnaji would fondle his hair and smile
at him. A noble child, he said.

'Your wife did not come?'

'No, Sir. She had work at school.'

Krishnaji just looked at me.

'Come again. Bring the child. Ask your wife to come too.'

This sequence was repeated twice. Krishnaji was most
kind to Adit. Sometime during the conversation, he would
remark, 'So, your wife didn't come?' I would repeat some
transparently cooked-up excuse.

'Well, I am going to Benares day after. As you know, I
have spent my life debunking godmen. I do not believe in
miracles. But some people say they have been healed by
these hands'—he looked at his elegant hands and turned
them out. 'Come to Benares. We have a good place there—

completely peaceful. Stay with us. Bring the child along. Your wife too is welcome, if she will come. If I can do anything at all for this child, I would love to. In any case, come again before I go.'

I was truly touched. Such a great man. One of the greatest teachers of our times. Prepared to go so far out of his way for our little Adit.

As I used to do after every visit, I told Anita what had transpired. I implored her, 'Please come along. Every time he asks about you. He is such a kind and such an elegant man . . . Come, for my sake.'

The three of us went to meet Krishnaji.

This time Krishnaji made me sit on a chair opposite him— holding Adit in my lap. He made Anita sit on the sofa with him. He took her hand in his, and kept it in his hand.

The conversation proceeded. Suddenly, one moment, Krishnaji turned fully to Anita and asked, 'How do you feel about your son?'

'He is a happy child,' Anita replied.

'I didn't ask what kind of a child he is. I asked "*How do you feel about your child?*"' Krishnaji said with some emphasis.

'He is our life.'

'I didn't ask what he is to you,' Krishnaji said in a raised voice, almost scolding Anita, 'I ASKED YOU WHAT DO YOU FEEL ABOUT YOUR CHILD,' his voice even higher, the pauses between each word, minatory, stern, unyielding.

Anita, who had not cried even once in the years since Adit's birth, burst into tears. It was as if a missile had pierced a dam. She wept uncontrollably. Krishnaji kept her hand in his, and let her continue crying.

'See?' Krishnaji turned to me, still holding her hand. 'I told you, you don't know a mother's heart.'

And here I was—thinking that I had my mother's caring heart.

A life-lesson, a *live*-lesson that I have never forgotten.

BY SOMEONE'S DESIGN?

'But don't you see what this tragedy has done for you? Your friends will at this very moment be wasting their time at the movies and parties, and here you are discussing these deep questions'—that was a well-known Maulana, without the slightest doubt a deep scholar, and, more than that, a pious and kind gentleman. We were seated next to each other on a flight. The conversation had turned to Adit, and from him to the general question of suffering. The age-old question: how can such things happen if there is an All-knowing, All-powerful, compassionate God? Either He does not know. Or He knows, and is powerless to do anything about it. Or He knows and *has* the power to prevent suffering, but cares not to do so.

Recall what the Maulana was saying about my going into questions. Take his statement at face value, and ask with me, 'Could He not have found an easier way to teach me?' Similarly, when we look at the way Mithu Alur and Mita Nundy and Anita and so many other mothers have transmuted their suffering into service of others, should we give credit to God—that He inflicted brain injuries on Malini and Adit and so many other children, and thereby ensured that schools would come up for spastic children in India? Or should we give thanks to and reserve our admiration for these wonderful women who have put their personal suffering to work for others? May we not ask as has been asked in other contexts, when these mothers and aunts struggle to help those who have been afflicted, are they carrying out God's will or opposing it? If they fail, is God asserting His will and punishing them for being so audacious as to have presumed that they could relieve the suffering of the children in spite of what He had decreed? If they succeed, have they succeeded in the face of God's decree or because He has turned around and now willed that they succeed?

Years later, I wanted to pursue this matter with the Maulana as I had done with others. I telephoned his son. He discusses such topics once a week with a small group, his son told me. Send your questions. I will record his discourse on them.

I did so. When I heard the tape, new questions arose. I listed these and sent them again to the son. In the second tape, you can distinctly hear the Maulana get angry . . . We should see things in perspective. Allah has created the universe, the stars and galaxies . . . He has created the entire magnificent firmament . . . The food for us to eat . . . To remain obsessed because one child is not perfect is to lose the sense of proportion. This shows the ego at work—that the person cannot see beyond his son . . .

Firstly, of course, it is not just one child. Millions and millions of children suffer, as do millions and millions of adults. That has to be explained.

That apart, does the argument not work the other way? Assume that only one child is suffering, our Adit alone. As Allah has the power to create this magnificent and infinite universe, can't He help that single child?

It is one of the questions that assail every parent who has to bring up a handicapped child. Why do such horrible things happen? Why did this happen to this innocent child? Who will lift him out of bed as I weaken with age? Who will look after him when we are gone?

Yes, yes, I know what I just wrote—that Adit has taught me to focus only on the here and now. But,

Laut jaati hai udhar ko bhi nazar kya keejey . . .

Hence, this book.

2

His concerns, His test

God puts a hundred-year-old devotee through the most cruel trauma just to test whether the old man is sufficiently devoted to Him, whether he is devoted enough to Him so that he will sacrifice even his only child just because He asks him to do so.

The story is narrated in the book of *Genesis* in the Old Testament. It is set out in the Quran also. As a result we get not just an explanation for suffering, we get in addition a preliminary glimpse into the sorts of things over which religions fall out.

THE ORIGINAL VERSION

Abraham is one of the most revered figures both in the Bible and the Quran. So important a figure is he that each of the Middle Eastern religions claims its origin from him. They are often referred to as Abrahamaic religions.

We start with the account set out in *Genesis*.

Abraham[1] and his wife Sarah[2] have not had a child. They have grown old. Sarah says to Abraham,

'See now, the Lord has refrained me from bearing children. Please go in to my maid; perhaps I shall obtain children by her.' And

---

[1] Referred to as Abram in verses up to 17.5 in *Genesis*. All references in this section are to verses in *Genesis*. In the next section we turn to the Quran. Throughout this book, unless otherwise stated, italics have been added. Words within square brackets, [ ], have been added by me; those within curled ones, ( ), have been added by the translator or commentator whose text has been used.

[2] Referred to as Sar'ai up to verse 17.15.

Abram heeded the voice of Sar'ai.

Then Sar'ai, Abram's wife, took Ha'gar her maid, the Egyptian; and gave her to her husband Abram to be his wife...

So he went in to Ha'gar, and she conceived. And when she saw she had conceived, her mistress became despised in her eyes.[3]

Seeing this, Sar'ai is enflamed. 'My wrong be upon you,' she says to Abram. 'I gave my maid into your embrace; and when she saw that she had conceived, I became despised in her eyes. The Lord judge between you and me.'[4]

Abram, through whom the maid has become pregnant, says to Sar'ai, 'Indeed your maid is in your hand; do to her as you please.'

Sar'ai deals so harshly with Ha'gar that the latter flees. Exchanges take place between her, an angel and God. She bears a son, Ishmael.[5]

Abram is eighty-six years old at this time.[6]

Another thirteen years pass. Abraham is ninety-nine. God appears to him. Henceforth you will be called Abraham, God tells him, that He, God, shall make him a father of many nations and 'exceedingly fruitful'.[7] God tells Abraham that, in return, he must ensure that he and all the males in his family are circumcised, that this shall be the covenant between God and Abraham, that anyone who is not circumcised 'shall be cut off from his people' as that one 'would have broken My covenant'.[8] Ostensibly, He has created the entire universe—time, space, galaxies; He is to manage all that. And yet, *this* is His concern—whether

[3] 16.2-4.
[4] 16.6.
[5] 16.6-15.
[6] 16.16.
[7] 17.5-6.
[8] 17.10-14.

332232323

males are circumcised or not. No wonder the world is in the condition in which it is!

God next tells Abraham that He shall bless Sarah with a son from Abraham. Abraham is incredulous as by now he is one hundred years old and Sarah is ninety.[9]

God dismisses the astonishment. He tells Abraham that the son shall be called Isaac.

Isaac is born. He is duly circumcised. God appears along with three men. Abraham runs to his herd of cattle. He takes 'a tender and good calf', gives it to a young man who hastens to prepare it.[10]

God and His three companions are treated to a meal. An exchange that is important for our present concern now takes place. God confides that He will be proceeding to Sodom and Gomorrah and destroy them for they have sinned. Abraham asks, 'Would You also destroy the righteous and the wicked? Suppose there were fifty righteous within the city; would you also destroy the place and not spare it for the fifty righteous that were in it? Far from You be it to do such a thing as this, to slay the righteous with the wicked, so that the righteous be as the wicked; far be it from You. Shall not the Judge of all the earth do right?'[11]

God assures Abraham, 'If I find in Sodom fifty righteous within the city, then I will spare all the place for their sakes.'

Suppose there are forty-five righteous persons, Abraham asks. Will You spare the city then?

God assures him, I will spare it . . .

If there are forty? Thirty? Twenty? What if there are *ten*?

Each time God says 'I will not destroy it for the sake of forty/thirty/twenty/ten.'[12] The same argument could be

---

[9] 17.15-17.
[10] 18.7.
[11] 18.23-25.
[12] 18.26-32.

taken to there being just one righteous person in the city.
And God would have to promise not to go ahead with His
resolve to destroy the cities. But Abraham does not press the
point. Set those two cities aside for a moment. And think of
Hiroshima, Nagasaki, the coastal settlements that were hit
by the tsunami, think of the regions in POK in which nearly
90,000 people were killed by the earthquake. *Could it be that
God did not find a single righteous person or ten or twenty in
any of them?*

The narrative proceeds, and we get to see how death and
destruction are rained down—on the righteous as much as
on the sinful.

Two angels come to Sodom in the evening. They reach
Lot's house. He prostrates before them, invites them to
spend the night in his home.[13]

Men from Sodom surround the house. 'Where are the
men who came to you tonight?' they demand. 'Bring them
out to us that we may know them carnally.'[14]

Lot begs them to spare the men. 'See now, I have two
daughters who have not known a man; please, let me bring
them out to you, and you may do to them as you wish; only
do nothing to these men, since this is the reason they have
come under the shadow of my roof.'[15] *What have the poor
daughters done that their father should be so ready to make an
offering of them to the lust and vengefulness of the Sodom men?*

The men try to force their way into the house. The angels
pull Lot in. They blind the men.

Next morning, the angels urge Lot to hurry out of town
with his wife and daughters, warning them not to look
back. Then God 'rained brimstone and fire on Sodom and
Gomorrah. So He overthrew those cities, all the plain, all the
inhabitants of the cities, and what grew on the ground.'[16]

---

[13] 19.1-4.
[14] 19.5.
[15] 19.8.
[16] 19.24-25.

What happened to His assurance that He would spare the cities if there were even ten righteous men? Were there not even that many? Or was God now so enraged that He freed Himself of that assurance?

Lot and his family leave. Lot's wife looks back and is turned into a pillar of salt.[17] Reflect for a moment: *Why has this fate been visited upon her? Because she disobeyed a command? Because a longing for what she was leaving behind lingered in her heart?*

Lot and his two daughters take refuge in a cave in the mountains. The two daughters make him drink wine, and sleep with him successively over two nights so that 'we may preserve the lineage of our father'. They conceive children by their father.[18] *Why is God allowing them to violate His law? So that they may be set up for subsequent punishment?*

Abraham journeys south. He passes his wife, Sarah, off as his sister. And gives her to the ruler. Fortunately, the latter, before he has got into bed with her, realizes that she is not the sister but the wife of Abraham. Abraham's explanation is that though Sarah is his wife, she is also his sister: 'She is the daughter of my father, but not the daughter of my mother; and she became my wife.'[19]

Soon enough, Isaac is born to Sarah.

She now goads Abraham, 'Cast out this bondwoman and her son; for the son of this bondwoman shall not be heir with my son, namely with Isaac.'[20]

Abraham puts bread and a skin of water on Hagar's shoulder and sends her and Ishmael away. The bread and water are soon used up. God comes to her rescue. A well appears.[21]

God now turns to test Abraham and says, 'Take now

---

[17] 19.26.
[18] 19.32-36.
[19] 20.12.
[20] 21.10.
[21] 21.14-20.

your son, your only son Isaac.' This is the very son that God
Himself has enabled Abraham to have after a life of longing;
and Abraham also has another son, Ishmael, through
Hagar, a point, as we shall soon see, that shall come up for
stern comment from Islamic scholars; but presumably, for
the moment, Ishmael does not count, for God commands,
'Take now your son, your *only* son Isaac', 'whom you love,
and go to the land of Moriah, and offer him there as a burnt
offering on one of the mountains of which I shall tell you.'[22]

Obedient, Abraham rises early, saddles his donkey, takes
two young men and Isaac, and sets off.

After trudging a while, he reaches the spot. The party
halts. He splits wood. Imagine the trauma that Abraham is
going through as he prepares to gather the material that he
shall use to burn his son.

Abraham tells the other two young men to stay back with
the donkey.

Innocent of what God has demanded, the young boy
Isaac asks his father, 'My father . . . look, the fire and the
wood, but where is the lamb for a burnt offering?'[23]

Abraham gives a parliamentary answer, one that, though
not an outright lie, misleads. Though he knows that Isaac is
the one he has to burn as offering, he says, 'My son, God will
provide for Himself the lamb for a burnt offering.' Then we
read with horror:

> Then they came to the place of which God had told him.
> And Abraham built an altar there and placed the wood in order;
> and bound Isaac his son and laid him on the altar, upon the
> wood.
> And Abraham stretched out his hand and took the knife to
> slay his son.[24]

---

[22] 22.2.
[23] 22.7.
[24] 22.9-10.

Imagine the tumult in his, the father's mind. Imagine the panic in Isaac at the sudden turn of events. And why has God subjected the two to this extreme cruelty? Just so that He can reassure Himself that Abraham is obedient enough to Him. *What if you were a grandfather, and you subjected your son and grandchild to such trauma just to ascertain whether they love you enough?*

At the penultimate moment, an angel calls out and tells Abraham to stop. And God tells Abraham not to lay a hand on the son, saying, 'for now I know that you fear God, since you have not withheld your son, your only son, from Me'. *An important enough objective? Or an obsession that He must be loved and obeyed? Indeed, in any other person, this constant apprehension that even his most devoted kin do not love him would be called paranoia.*

Abraham looks around and finds 'a ram caught in a thicket by its horns'. He offers it up as a burnt offering.[25] *What wrong has the poor ram done? Is it not by this very precedent that animals are killed to this day to appease the supposedly merciful God?*

NOT JUST ON AN INDIVIDUAL, ON THE WHOLE LOT

Nor is His obsession about being revered limited to individuals. Pestilence, destruction, death are brought down on entire peoples—including, and especially on the people He has Himself chosen. Entire cities are obliterated for faltering in their reverence of Him.

'If there is a calamity in a city,' we read in the *Book of Amos*, 'will not the Lord have done it?'[26] God sets out how He will bring down cities and empires because they have had the audacity to browbeat the people He has chosen.[27] Then he turns on the chosen people themselves. In part this

---

[25] 22.13.
[26] *The Book of Amos*, 3.6.
[27] Ibid., Chapters 1 and 2.

is because of what might be seen as personal sins and wrongdoings:

> . . . because they sold the righteous for silver, and the poor for a pair of sandals;
> That they pant after the dust of the earth on the head of the poor, and turn aside the way of the meek: and a man and his father will go in unto the same maid, to defile My holy name:
> And they lie down by every altar on clothes taken in pledge, and drink the wine of the condemned in the house of their god . . .[28]

But then comes His fundamental concern, and the fundamental reason for visiting pestilence and worse on His chosen people. He has hurled one calamity after another on them, He thunders, so that they may at last heed Him and return to Him. Yet they have not done so. Hence shall they be subjected to further and even harsher thrashing. Read what God thunders and see what is His real obsession:

> Hear this word that the Lord has spoken against you, O children of Israel, against the whole family which I brought up from the land of Egypt, saying:
> 'You only have I known of all the families of the earth;
> Therefore I will punish you for your inequities.'
> . . .
> The Lord God hath sworn by His holiness: 'Behold, the days shall come upon you, when He will take you away with hooks, and your posterity with fishhooks . . .'

Continue your transgressions for which you have fallen, He challenges them, and behold what shall befall you. He reminds them of what He sent down on them and why:

> Also I gave you cleanness of teeth in all your cities [that is, famine], and want of bread in all your places: *yet have ye not returned unto Me*, says the Lord.

---

[28] Ibid., 2.6-8.

I also withheld the rain from you, when there were still three months to the harvest: and I caused it to rain upon one city, and caused it not to rain upon another city: one part was rained upon, and the part whereupon it rained not withered.

So two or three cities wandered into another city to drink water; but they were not satisfied: *yet have ye not returned unto Me,* says the Lord.

I have smitten you with blasting and mildew: when your gardens and your vineyards and your fig trees and your olive trees increased, the locust devoured them: *yet have ye not returned unto Me,* says the Lord.

I have sent among you the plague after the manner of Egypt: your young men have I slain with the sword along with your captive horses; and I made the stench of your camps to come up into your nostrils: *yet have ye not returned unto Me,* says the Lord.

I overthrew some of you, as God overthrew Sodom and Gomorrah, and ye were as a firebrand plucked out of the burning: *yet have ye not returned unto Me,* says the Lord.

Therefore thus will I do to you, O Israel: and because I will do this to you, prepare to meet your God, O Israel.

For, behold, He who forms the mountains, and creates the wind, and declares to man what his thought is, and makes the morning darkness, who treads upon the high places of the earth, The Lord God of hosts, is His name.[29]

Famine; plague; young men being put to the sword; their blameless horses too; the people being deprived of water even to drink; blight and mildew to ruin crops; locusts to devour crops—one calamity after another.

All this for what? Simply because 'Yet you have not returned to Me'.

'I will make Jerusalem a heap of ruins, a den of jackals,' God thunders. 'I will make the city of Judah desolate, without an inhabitant.' I will punish all—the circumcised as

---

[29] Ibid., 4.6-13.

much as the uncircumcised, He declares, because the former—'all the house of Israel'—'are uncircumcised in the heart'. Through His prophet, Jeremiah, He decrees calamity upon calamity, and declares that, though the people, hammered thus, shall cry out for relief, He shall not relent. 'They shall die gruesome deaths,' Jeremiah reports God as having told him. 'They shall not be lamented nor shall they be buried, but they shall be like refuse on the face of the earth. They shall be consumed by the sword and by famine, and their corpses shall be meat for the birds of heaven and for the beasts of the earth . . .' 'Behold, I will bring such a catastrophe on this place, that whoever hears of it, his ears will tingle,' God vows. The days are coming when this place shall not be known by its name but as 'the Valley of Slaughter'. I shall cause the cities and their inhabitants to suffer defeat and destruction at the hands of their enemies and of those who seek their lives. I shall break the cities 'as one breaks a potter's vessel which cannot be made whole again'. 'I will make the city desolate and a hissing; everyone who passes by it will be astonished and hiss because of all its plagues. And I will cause them to eat the flesh of their sons and flesh of their daughters, and everyone shall eat the flesh of his friend in the siege and in the desperation with which their enemies and those who seek their lives shall drive them to despair.' 'Their infants shall be dashed in pieces,' God declares, 'And their women with child ripped open . . .'[30] All this for what? Because they have 'committed prostitution with pagan gods'! 'Because they have forsaken Me and made this an alien place, because they have burned incense in it to other gods . . . and filled this place with the blood of innocents.'

A good father? A 'perfectly good' God? What would we

---

[30] *The Book of Jeremiah*, 9.11, 9.25, 16.4, 19.3, 19.4, 19.6-9; *The Book of Hosea*, 13.16.

say of a person who teaches everyone to be humble, and is so proud and full of conceit himself?

Notice that God pulverizes entire cities. He puts all the youth to the sword. He destroys everyone's crops. In a word, He does not spare even the innocent. And there is a purpose to that. To strike real terror in everyone's heart, violence has to be random. When a terrorist group acts on that principle, we say they are cruel—'They don't spare even women and children, for God's sake!' And when God doesn't spare them? We say, 'His ways are mysterious.'

All this is visited upon the people because, going solely on God's word, they 'filled this place with the blood of innocents'. And when God 'fills this place with the blood of innocents'?

And does the fact that He just has to go on hurling one calamity on the people after another testify to His capacity to hurl calamities or to His powerlessness—to the fact that, in spite of His hurling so many calamities at them, the people still do not fall in line? They still keep turning to those pagan gods. Do these repeated failures not suggest that the pagan gods are stronger?

He sends down His own Son. The Son dies for our sins. We continue to sin. He dies to redeem us. We continue unredeemed.

God drowns all—except a few who can be accommodated on a small craft. He repopulates the world after the cataclysmic flood. Even after so complete a purge, almost everyone who lives turns out to be a sinner.

All-powerful? All-wise? Is He even effective?

He lets the evil ruler—Manasseh—continue heaping evil and suffering on the people for half a century. Much of the evil is evil from the particular point of view of God: Manasseh rebuilds temples and idols. He resumes practices which God despises. He practises soothsaying and consults 'spiritists and mediums'. 'Moreover Manasseh shed very much innocent blood, till he had filled Jerusalem from one end to another . . .' All this God lets continue for 55 years.

And Josiah? He is the one of whom the Bible tells us, 'Now before him there was no king like him, who turned to the Lord with all his heart, with all his soul, and with all his might, according to all the Law of Moses; nor after him did any arise like him.' He does God's work with spectacular thoroughness. God's work that Josiah accomplishes, of course, includes banishing and burning all articles made in honour of other gods; removing priests who have helped venerate other gods; burning to ashes the wooden image of another god 'and throw[ing] its ashes on the graves of the common people'; tearing down 'the ritual booths of the perverted persons that were in the house of the Lord, where women wove hangings for the wooden image'; defiling the places where incense had been burned before the images; breaking down and pulverizing the altars and throwing their dust into a brook; and defiling the places that Solomon had built to honour gods that are 'abominations'; and '[breaking] in pieces the sacred pillars and cut[ting] down the wooden images, and fill[ing] them with the bones of men'; and breaking and crushing to powder and then burning another wooden image; and defiling the altar by burning on it bones taken out of tombs; and executing 'all the priests of the high places who were there, on the altars, and burn[ing] men's bones on them'; and putting away 'those who consulted mediums and spiritists, the household gods and idols, and all the abominations that were seen in the land of Judah and in Jerusalem' . . .

And what does God do to this foremost and virtuous of kings? God has Josiah killed by a Pharaoh!

Josiah's reign—though the fact is admittedly of little consolation to us pagans—is cut short. Manasseh is allowed to continue doing evil for 55 years. Does God know even His own interest?

Why? you ask. Why is the man who does what is the worst evil in God's eye allowed to continue doing it and why is the one who does nothing but what is good in God's eye finished off? Yes, Josiah did so much for God. Yes, there never was a king before or after him who did as much for God. 'Nevertheless,' the Bible tells us, 'the Lord did not turn from the fierceness of His great wrath, with which His anger was aroused against Judah, because of all the provocations with which Manasseh had provoked Him.'[31]

Manasseh provokes, and Josiah is engineered to be killed.

THE LENGTHS TO WHICH HE WILL GO

After a lecture in Bangalore in which I had recounted the lengths to which God goes in the Old Testament to glorify Himself, a learned priest came up and said, 'You forgot to mention the *New* Testament. You could start with Jesus restoring sight to the blind; you could start with his reviving Lazarus—to say nothing of God sacrificing His Son to convince us how much He cares for us. The same point leaps through.' And so it does.[32]

Out on a journey, Jesus and his disciples see a man who has been blind from birth. 'Rabbi,' his disciples ask Jesus, 'who sinned, this man or his parents, that he was born blind?'

'Neither this man nor his parents sinned,' Jesus responds, *'but that the works of God should be revealed in him.'* Soon, Jesus 'spat on the ground and made clay with the saliva; and he anointed the eyes of the blind man with the clay'. That done, Jesus asks the man to go and wash his eyes in the pool of Siloam. The man does so, and comes back seeing.

---

[31] 2 *Kings,* 21 and 22.

[32] I later learnt that these instances are often noted by Biblical scholars. Bart Ehrman, for instance, highlights the embarrassing features in the narratives of curing blindness and reviving Lazarus in his *God's Problem, How the Bible Fails to Answer Our Most Important Question, Why We Suffer,* HarperCollins, New York, 2008.

The people are astonished. They ask the man how his sight has come to him. He narrates what Jesus said and did. Soon the Pharisees arrive. They are not interested in the miracle, but in the sacrilege that Jesus has committed by working the miracle on a Sabbath! And the narrative takes off in that direction.[33] For us, however, the point is the averment of Jesus that the man was born blind not because either he or his parents had sinned, *'but that the works of God should be revealed in him'*. That is, so that an opportunity may arise for a miracle to be worked which will convince everyone of God's powers and that Jesus is the Son of God. And God is compassionate? And what of the millions who are born blind and remain blind throughout their lives? The compassionate God does not think it worth His while to demonstrate His power by giving sight to them!

A while later, Lazarus, the brother of Mary and Martha, falls grievously ill. They are in Bethany. Mary is the one who had anointed Jesus with fragrant oil and wiped his feet with her hair. The sisters rush to Jesus and tell him that one he loves is sick. Jesus says, *'This sickness is not unto death, but for the glory of God, that the Son of God may be glorified through it.'*

Jesus loves Mary, Martha, their brother. He does not proceed to Bethany. He stays back for two days. Lazarus dies. Jesus tells his disciples that Lazarus is dead. *'And I am glad for your sakes that I was not there, that you may believe. Nevertheless let us go to him.'* In a word, Lazarus has been left to die so that Jesus may resurrect him and thereby once again establish in the eyes of onlookers the power of God and the fact that he is the Son of God.

He and the disciples reach Bethany, which is just two miles from Jerusalem. Martha rushes to meet Jesus. She says, 'Lord, if you had been here, my brother would not have

---

[33] *John*, 9.1-41. The exchanges with the Pharisees continue in *John*, 10.

died,' and adds, 'But even now I know that whatever you ask God, God will give you.'

'Your brother will rise again,' Jesus assures her. 'I know that he will rise again at resurrection on the last day,' Martha says. Jesus corrects her, 'I am the resurrection and the life. He who believes in me, though he may be dead, he shall live. And whoever lives and believes in me shall never die.' 'Do you believe this?' Jesus asks Martha. Martha affirms that she does.

Martha returns to the house—a number of Jews are at the house, consoling the sisters—and tells Mary that Jesus has arrived. Mary rushes to meet him. Seeing him, she falls down and says, 'Lord, if you had been here, my brother would not have died.' Seeing her distress, Jesus too breaks down.

'Where have you laid him?' he asks. Some of the onlookers remark, 'Could not this man who opened the eyes of the blind, also have kept this man from dying?'

They proceed to the tomb, a cave the opening of which has now been blocked with a stone. 'Take away the stone,' Jesus commands. Martha tells him that by now the body has been lying there for four days and there is a stench. *'Did I not say to you,'* Jesus asks her, *'that if you would believe you would see the glory of God?'*

The stone is removed. Jesus raises his eyes and addresses God: 'Father, I thank You that You have heard me. And I know that You always hear me, but because of the people who are standing by I said this, that they may believe that You sent me.'

He then commands in a loud voice, 'Lazarus, come forth!'

'And he who had died came out bound hand and foot with grave-clothes, and his face wrapped with a cloth.' Jesus tells the people to loosen him and let him go.

Many of the Jews who had come to console Mary and Martha begin to believe in Jesus. The Pharisees are incensed even more, and become more than ever convinced that unless this man is stopped, hordes will desert them and begin to follow him.[34]

A man is made to fall grievously ill. He is left to die. So that he may be revived. So that people may believe in the power of God and in the fact that Jesus is indeed His Son. A compassionate God?

But to get back to the story of Abraham.

AN ADDITIONAL VIRTUE

Abraham is mentioned sixty-nine times in the Quran. 'He was a man of truth,' Allah tells us. 'A prophet.'[35] In fact, he is the one who is said to have constructed the Kabbah. It is from him that the religion of Muhammad is said to originate.

Abraham of the Quran has one special virtue that Job, for instance, does not. He is forever campaigning against idolatry. He breaks idols. He even misleads so as to fix blame for breaking the idols on the principal idol-god himself. In a word, Abraham is as virtuous as one can get, and yet he is put to a test similar to the one in *Genesis*.

There also are several key differences from the account in the Old Testament. In the Quran, Abraham has a vision. It is in this vision that he receives God's command—that he sacrifice his son to Him. While in *Genesis,* Abraham proceeds to fulfil God's command keeping the son in the dark, in the Quran, Abraham seeks the son's view of what he should do about the command he has received in his vision—that he sacrifice his son. The son—Isaac in some accounts, Ishmael in others—concurs enthusiastically.

Let us go through the narrative in the Quran a bit as, in addition to giving us another glimpse into God's concerns

---

[34] *John*, 11.1-57.
[35] The Quran, 19.41. Henceforth, in this section all citations are from the Quran.

and His test, it will introduce us to a vital question about the Books that God has sent down.

Like other members of the tribe, Azhar, the father of Abraham, worships idols. Abraham remonstrates with him. Why do you worship that which does not see or hear, and cannot profit you in any way? Do not serve Satan, Abraham tells his father. A great punishment will befall you if you continue to worship idols. His father in turn presses Abraham not to revile their gods. He threatens Abraham: 'If thou forbear not, I shall stone thee.' He tells Abraham, 'Now get away from me for a good long while.'[36]

Abraham distances himself from his father and his tribesmen, telling the father that he, Abraham, will beseech Allah to forgive him, the father, 'For He is to me most gracious.' Seeing all this, Allah is pleased.[37]

Abraham continues to strive to wean his father and people away from worshipping idols. They maintain that they shall continue to do so as that is what their ancestors used to do. As they persist, Abraham declares, 'And by Allah, I have a plan for your idols—after ye go away and turn your backs.' On one of their festivals, the people go to a gathering. Abraham smashes the idols with an axe. He breaks all the idols, except the principal one. He hangs the axe on to that idol. When the people return, they see that their idols have been smashed. Who has done this? they demand. Some among them say that they had heard Abraham speak ill of their gods and idols.

Abraham is fetched. Are you the one who has done this to our gods? they ask him. No, he says. The principal idol destroyed them, he says; ask them 'if they can speak intelligently'. The tribesmen reflect. 'Then were they [the tribesmen] confounded with shame: [they said] "Thou knowest full well that these [idols] do not speak." How can we ask them?'

---

[36] 19.42-46.
[37] 19.47.

Why do you then worship those who cannot speak or hear? Abraham asks them. Why do you worship those who can neither benefit you if you worship them nor harm you if you don't? You should worship the one and only God.

The people are enraged. They cry out, 'Burn him and protect your gods.' They gather wood. They tie Abraham up. They light the fire.

God intervenes. The fire becomes a source of cool comfort for Abraham. Nothing of him is singed—save the bonds with which the tribesmen had tied him.[38]

God tests Abraham—commanding him to fulfil certain assignments, and to abide by some prohibitions. As Abraham fulfils them, God tells him, 'I will make thee an Imam to the Nations.' Abraham constructs the Kabbah. Having laid the foundations of the Kabbah, Abraham and his son Ismail beseech Allah:

Our Lord! Make of us
Muslims, bowing to Thy (Will),
And of our progeny a people
Muslim, bowing to Thy (Will) . . .
Our Lord! Send amongst them
A Messenger of their own,
Who shall rehearse Thy Signs
To them and instruct them
In scripture and wisdom,
And sanctify them . . .[39]

It is in response to this prayer that Allah eventually sends Muhammad. That is a familiar sequence. Passages in the Old Testament were stretched to constitute prophecies that foretold the coming of Jesus—to the extent that the word which means 'a young woman' to whom Jesus was to be born came to be translated as 'a virgin'. In the Quran, the prayer and its fulfilment are directly stated.

---

[38] 21.52-72.
[39] 2.128-29.

It turns out that Abraham is in fact a devout Muslim even though Islam is to be revealed and codified many centuries later.[40] 'Ye People of the Book,' Allah admonishes:

Why dispute ye
About Abraham, When the Law and the Gospel
Were not revealed
Till after him?
Have ye no understanding?
Ah! Ye are those
Who fell to disputing
(Even) in matters of which
Ye had some knowledge!
But why dispute ye
In matters of which
Ye have no knowledge?
It is Allah who knows,
And ye know not!
Abraham was not a Jew
Nor yet a Christian;
But he was true in faith.
And bowed his will to Allah's
(Which is Islam),
And he joined not gods with Allah.[41]

It is this Abraham, so virtuous in the eyes of God Himself, whom God blesses with two sons—that Sarah, Abraham's wife, is ninety-nine years old, and Abraham himself is a hundred or a hundred and twenty years old is no problem as Allah can will anything.[42]

Abraham is 'gentle, compassionate, repentant'. The sequence that we have encountered earlier about Abraham asking the angels whether God will not spare the accursed cities if there are even a few righteous men in them, that

40 3.58-60.
41 3.65-67.
42 11.72-78.

sequence recurs—though the numbers are different. Allah's
messengers tell Abraham that the city of Lot will be erased.
Will you destroy a city wherein are 300 believers? Abraham
asks the angels—a difference right there: for in the original
Old Testament account, Abraham asks this of God directly,
and it is God who gives the answers and the assurance.
In any event, in the Quran the angels too say, No, in that
event the city will not be destroyed. Abraham proceeds:
And will you destroy a city wherein are 200 believers?
They answer, No. He says, And will you destroy a city
wherein are forty believers? They answer, No. He says, And
will you destroy a city wherein are fourteen believers? They
answer, No. He says, And tell me, if there be in it one
believer? They answer, No.

Abraham exclaims, Well, in the city is Lot, virtuous
without a doubt.

By now the angels have become impatient with
Abraham's questions. His disputation has become tedious.
We know best who is in the city, they say. Abstain from
such disputation, they tell Abraham. The command of
Allah has already come for the destruction of the city, and
the punishment cannot be averted.[43]

The cities are turned 'upside down'. Stones are rained
down on them—on each stone is inscribed the name of the
person who the stone is to smother.[44]

Abraham goes to an area that is in what is today Syria or
Palestine. There he asks God for a son who shall be
righteous. 'Whereupon We gave him the good news of a boy
ready to suffer and forbear.'[45] And then God directs the
same Abraham in a dream to sacrifice the son.

When the son has attained the age at which he could
work with Abraham—some put this at seven years, and

[43] 11.74-76.
[44] 11.84.
[45] 37.100-01.

some, thirteen—Abraham tells the son that, in a vision, he has been commanded to sacrifice the son. What do you think I should do? he asks the son. Without the slightest hesitation, the son tells Abraham to proceed with the sacrifice:

> O my father! Do
> As thou art commanded:
> Thou wilt find me,
> If Allah so wills one
> Practising Patience and Constancy![46]

The two submit themselves to carrying through the sacrifice. Abraham lays the son down 'prostrate on his forehead', and draws a knife across his throat—the sacrifice is to be carried out by slitting the son's throat; not by burning him as in *Genesis*. God calls out to him 'O Abraham! Thou hast already fulfilled the vision!' 'Thus indeed,' Allah tells us, 'Do We reward those who do right. For this was obviously a trial.' In place of the son, Allah has substituted 'a momentous sacrifice'. This turns out to be a ram directly from Paradise, the same ram, we learn, that Abel had offered. Gabriel has brought it down, we are told. Abraham sacrifices it, proclaiming, 'God is most great!'

For his fidelity, Allah says, He has decreed that later generations shall offer salutations to Abraham, by declaring 'Peace and salutation to Abraham!' 'Thus indeed do We reward those who do right: for he was one of Our believing servants.'[47]

Fine, there is no doubt about the fealty of Abraham and his son. But what about Allah? *Why did He need to put either to the test? It isn't just that Allah has Himself certified to the righteousness of Abraham from the very beginning. The fact is*

---

[46] 37.102.
[47] 37.103-11.

*that, on the telling of the Quran and other Books of revelation,
Allah already knows what is in everyone's heart, whether
mortals conceal it or reveal it.* Does the Quran not proclaim:

> To Allah belongeth all
> That is in the heavens
> And on earth. *Whether*
> *Ye show what is in your minds*
> *Or conceal it, Allah*
> *Calleth you to account for it.*
> He forgiveth whom He pleaseth,
> And punisheth whom He pleaseth.[48]

And again,

> Say: *'whether ye hide*
> *What is in your hearts*
> *Or reveal it,*
> *Allah knows it all:*
> *He knows what is*
> *In the heavens,*
> *And what is on earth.*
> And Allah has power over all things . . .[49]

And yet again,

> *From Allah, verily*
> *Nothing is hidden*
> *On earth or in the heavens.*[50]

And again,

> And He is Allah
> In the heavens
> And on earth. *He knoweth what ye*
> *Hide, and what ye reveal,*
> And He knoweth

---

[48] 2.284.
[49] 3.29.
[50] 3.5

The (recompense) which
Ye earn (by your deeds).[51]

And yet again,
Lord knoweth best
Who strayeth from His Way:
He knoweth best
Who they are that receive
His guidance.[52]

Again,
Allah doth know what
Every female (womb) doth bear.
By how much the wombs
Fall short (of their time
Or number) or do exceed.
Every single thing is before
His sight, in (due) proportion.
It is the same (to Him)
Whether any of you
Conceal his speech or
Declare it openly;
Whether he lie hid by night
Or walk forth freely by day.[53]

And yet again,
Undoubtedly, Allah doth know
What they conceal.
And what they reveal:
Verily He loveth not the arrogant.[54]

Again,
Say: *'My Lord*
Knoweth (every) word (spoken)

---

[51] 6.3.
[52] 6.117.
[53] 13.8-10.
[54] 16.23.

In the heavens and on earth:
He is the One that heareth
And knoweth (all things).'[55]

And again,

Verily the knowledge
Of the Hour is
With Allah (alone).
It is He Who sends down
Rain, and He Who knows
What is in the wombs.
Nor does anyone know
In what land he is
To die. *Verily with Allah*
Is full knowledge and He
Is acquainted (with all things).[56]

And yet again,

He knows all that goes
Into the earth, and all that
Comes out thereof: all that
Comes down from the sky
And all that ascends thereto
And He is the Most Merciful.
The Oft-Forgiving.[57]

Again,

He knows what is
In the heavens
And on earth;
And He knows what
Ye reveal: yea. Allah
Knows well the (secrets)
Of (all) hearts.[58]

---

[55] 21.4.
[56] 31.34.
[57] 34.2.
[58] 64.4.

He knows everything, every hidden thought, He witnesses every deed of everyone and whatever happens to everything:

> In whatever business thou
> Mayest be, and whatever portion
> Thou mayest be reciting
> From the Quran—and whatever
> Deed ye (mankind) may be doing—
> We are Witnesses thereof
> When ye are deeply engrossed
> Therein. Nor is hidden
> From the Lord (so much as)
> The weight of an atom
> On the earth or in heaven.
> And not the least
> And not the greatest
> Of these things but are recorded
> In a clear Record.[59]

This being the case, why does Allah need to test Abraham or his son? Why does He need to put them through such extreme trauma?

WHAT SHOULD WE BELIEVE?

Who was the one whose throat Abraham tried to slit with the knife? Isaac, says the *Genesis*. Not at all, say Islamic commentators. That is how the Jews and Christians have perverted the scripture, they declare.

In a passage typical of religious contentions, Abdullah Yusuf Ali comments, 'Our version [that is, the Islamic version as contained in the Quran] may be compared with the Jewish–Christian version of the present Old Testament,' and ascribes a motive.

> The Jewish tradition, in order to glorify the younger branch of the family, descended from Isaac, ancestor of the Jews, as against the

---

[59] 10.61.

elder branch descended from Ismail, ancestor of the Arabs, refers
this sacrifice to Isaac (*Gen.* xxii.1–18). Now Isaac was born when
Abraham was 100 years old (*Gen.* xxi.5) while Ismail was born to
Abraham when Abraham was 86 years old (*Gen.* xvi.16). Ismail
was therefore 14 years older than Isaac. During his first 14 years
Ismail was the *only* son of Abraham; at no time was Isaac the *only*
son of Abraham. Yet, in speaking of the sacrifice, the Old
Testament says (*Gen.* xxii.2) 'And he said, Take now thy son, thine
only son, whom thou lovest, and get thee into the land of Moriah:
and offer him there for a burnt offering . . .' This slip shows at any
rate which was the older version, and how it was overlaid like the
present Jewish records, in the interests of the tribal religion. The
'land of Moriah' is not clear: it was three days journey from
Abraham's place (*Gen.* xxii.4). There is less warrant for identifying
it with the hill of Moriah on which Jerusalem was subsequently
built than with the hill of Marwah which is identified with the
Arab tradition about Ismail.[60]

So,

- ❑ Which son? Isaac or Ismail?
- ❑ Hagar? Was she, as the *Genesis* affirms, the maid of
  Sarah whom Abraham, at Sarah's asking,
  impregnated? Or his *wife*, as the Quran affirms?
- ❑ What kind of a person was Ismail himself? When the
  infant is abandoned in the desert, in *Genesis* an
  angel, addressing Hagar, says of him, 'Behold, you
  are with child, And you shall bear a son . . . He will
  be a wild man, his hand against all, and every man's
  hand against him . . .'[61] But in the Quran, Allah
  speaks of him as a *rasul*, a messenger of Allah, and a
  nabi, a prophet.[62] Indeed, it is from him—through
  Qaidar, one of his twelve sons—that Prophet

---

[60] Abdullah Yusuf Ali, *The Meaning of the Glorious Quran*, Dar Al-Kitab
Al-Masri, Cairo, no date, footnote 4101, p. 1205.

[61] *Genesis*, 16.12.

[62] Quran, 19.54-55

Muhammad himself is said to have descended. It is because of the desperation of his mother, Hagar, to not see him thirst to death that the waters of Zamzam begin to flow. He is the one who, along with his father, Abraham, builds the Kabbah, and institutes the pilgrimage to it.[63]

❑ Was the consent of the son taken or not for sacrificing him?

❑ Was the wood gathered and the fire lit? Or was the knife wielded across the throat?

❑ Where did all this occur? In Palestine, say the Jewish and Christian traditions. In the Hejaz, insist the Islamic traditions.

❑ Was the ram from Paradise? Was it brought down by Gabriel?

❑ Was Abraham a true Muslim even though centuries were to pass till Prophet Muhammad was to codify Islam?

SYMPTOMATIC

Such are the differences over which religions split and come to blows. And they are symptomatic.

But there is also a creative appropriation that is just as characteristic, one that is almost worth admiring! In this particular case, Sir William Muir drew attention to it in a way that can scarcely be improved. In his *The Life of Mahomet*, recalling how, with the drying up of the southern trade, the opulence and mercantile importance of Mecca had decayed, and yet 'the Kaaba continued as the national temple of the Peninsula', Muir noted and inquired, '. . . how shall we account for the tradition current among the Arabs, that the temple owed its origin to Abraham?' After recounting how Jewish legends had got grafted upon local

---

[63] Quran, 2.119, 121.

worship and rites, and the legends of Abraham and Ishmael had got 'superimposed upon the superstition of Mecca', Muir wrote of the second narrative that was grafted:

> By a summary adjustment, the story of Palestine became the story of the Hejaz. The precincts of the Kaaba were hallowed as the scene of Hagar's distress, and the sacred well Zemzem as the source of her relief. The pilgrims hasted to and fro between Safa and Marwa in memory of her hurried steps in search of water. It was Abraham and Ishmael who built the temple [Kaaba], placed in it the black stone, and established for all mankind the pilgrimage to Arafat. In imitation of him it was that the stones were flung at Satan; and sacrifices were offered at Mina in remembrance of the vicarious sacrifice by Abraham instead of his son. *And so, although the indigenous rites may have been little if at all altered, by the adoption of the Israelitish legends, they came to be viewed in a totally different light, and to be connected in the Arab imagination with something of the sanctity of Abraham, the friend of God. The gulf between the pure idolatry of Arabia and the pure theism of the Jews was bridged over. Upon this common ground Mahomet took his stand, and proclaimed to his people a new and spiritual system, in accents to which all Arabia could respond. The rites of the Kaaba were retained, but stripped of all idolatrous tendency, they still hang, a strange unmeaning shroud, around the living theism of Islam.*[64]

Rites of the very world that is being condemned and reviled and crushed—pagan polytheism, in this case—are appropriated, and 'meanings', 'significance'—supposedly, in this case, of uncompromising monotheism—are pasted on them. Genealogies are read into the distant past—both to show how ancient the particular religion is and to appropriate the legitimacy that those figures of the distant past had at the time this new religion was being formed.

And not just in the Middle East, nor just in Islam, Malini

---

[64] William Muir, *The Life of Mahomet, From Original Sources*, 3rd edition, 1894, Smith, Elder, and Co., London. Reprinted, Voice of India, Delhi, 1991. pp. c-cvii.

Saran, the Ramayana scholar, instructs me. In Hinduism, our gods are always reincarnating, after all. Rama is Lakshmana's elder brother in one round; in the other, he becomes the younger brother, Krishna, while Lakshmana becomes the elder brother, Balaram. Bharata and Shatrughana, the brothers of Rama and Lakshmana in one round, become the son and grandson respectively, Pradyumna and Aniruddha, in the other . . .[65] As are the Dalai Lamas and Rinpoches in Tibet. Nor is the purpose merely to acquire legitimacy, she says. The real purpose of reincarnating is to acquire the secret knowledge, and the *wahyu*, the mystical power that the original figure possessed. Indonesia constitutes an example that combines all the constituents—reincarnation, Hinduism, Islam.

---

[65] Cf. Bhagavan Das, *Krishna, A study in the theory of Avataras,* Bharatiya Vidya Bhavan, Bombay, 1962, in passing: the examples are mentioned at pp. 22, 51. Reincarnations and acquisition of this kind are accepted as nothing strange, indeed as a normal, frequent occurrence in our tradition. To continue with the example from the study by Bhagavan Das, later on he remarked that 'possibly not only one but many' incarnations embodying vestiges of Krishna's attributes and form have appeared after him: ' . . . Possibly portions of the super-physical sheaths, the *sukshma-sharir* etc., of the glorious vesture worn by the original Krishna, were preserved, and were "inherited" and used by some of these later manifestations, as the robes of state and crown jewels and weapons and throne made for and used by a great sovereign may be used by his successors. Sections xliii and xliv of *The Secret Doctrine,* Volume III, on "The Mystery of the Buddha" and "The Reincarnation of the Buddha", mention such utilization of "astral remains" and "principles"; and the *Mahabharata* and the *Bhagwata* and other Puranas mention many other similar "mystical" facts . . . Thus, the cases of Arjuna and Karna, whose bodies were compounded out of several previous "personae" . . . So Krishna too was an "incarnation" of Rishi Narayana, as well as "a hair from the head of Aditya-Narayana". His contemporary Vyasa was also a partial manifestation of Narayana. Yudhishthira was a previous Indra, and also the son of Dharma; and Vidura was an incarnation of Yama, and quitted his physical body by standing up against a tree and "looking fixedly into Yudhishthira's eyes, till he (Vidura) *passed into* Yudhishthira," Yama being Dharmaraja . . .' Ibid., pp. 162-63 [italics in the original].

The Indonesians believe that the Ramayana is actually *their* epic, an epic that travelled *westward* to India and places beyond. Tales of the Mahabharata and Ramayana that we in India learn as being different have, in Indonesia, commingled. Characters from one appear seamlessly in the other—and they turn out to be the ancestors of the Javanese kings: in this way, the latter come to be descendants of Hindu gods—Vishnu, Shiva—on the one side and of Baba Adam, and thence of the founders of Islam, on the other.

Arjuna is the one who is believed to have brought Islam to Indonesia. And he did so through a secret corridor. And there is a cave in the northern coast of Java to testify to this fact. It is through this cave that Arjuna brought the secret knowledge, the Indonesians affirm—the Quran, as well as other pillars of Islam. Located at Cirebon, the cave is now a holy place . . .[66]

---

[66] Cf. Malini Saran and Vinod C. Khanna, *The Ramayana in Indonesia*, Ravi Dayal, New Delhi, 2004.

3

And who do you think is responsible?

Genetic engineering has advanced. A firm guarantees not just a beautiful and perfectly formed child, but also a genius-of-a-child for your daughter. You have apprehensions. But your daughter is a *believer*—in the new sciences. And her friend has already had an angelic child through this firm's new technique. You give in.

But the firm has one condition. Your daughter must follow their prescriptions to the dot. She must accept every implant, she must take every potion they prescribe, she must do all the exercises they prescribe. She must think positive, she must entertain no doubt about their technique and medications. She must have total faith in them. In a word, she must *surrender* herself totally to their direction.

She does. An angelic child is born to her. The firm claims success. It appropriates all credit. It uses your daughter's experience and that beautiful child in its advertising campaigns to convert others to its implants and drugs.

No problem. The child is your joy. The happiness of your daughter is your reward.

But what if the child turns out to be blind? What if he is born with an injured brain?

We are in no way responsible, declares the firm. So many other young girls have had perfectly angelic children using our new implants. Your daughter must not have followed the regimen. She must not have had full faith. In any case, we did not compel her to take the treatment. *She* did so on her own. If anyone is responsible, it is you: *you* are the one

who gave in and agreed to have her undergo our
procedures and drugs . . .

How justified would that somersault of the firm be?

Now consider God. He says in His Book that He knows,
that He alone knows what is in the womb, and how it is
progressing:

> 13:8: God doth know what every female (womb) doth bear, by how
> much the wombs fall short (of their time or number) or do exceed.
> Every single thing is before His sight, in (due) proportion.
>
> 16:78: It is He Who brought you forth from the wombs of your
> mothers when you knew nothing; and He gave you hearing and
> sight and intelligence and affections: that you may give thanks (to
> God) . . .
>
> 31:34: Verily the knowledge of the Hour is with God (alone). It is He
> Who sends down rain, and He Who knows what is in the wombs.
> Nor does any one know what it is that he will earn on the morrow:
> Nor does any one know in what land he is to die. Verily with God
> is full knowledge and He is acquainted (with all things).

So, He knows what is happening in the womb. He knows in
time—so that, in case He is so inclined, He can easily
prevent any infirmity that may handicap the child in future.
But, most important, we are told in the Book:

> 3:6: *He it is Who shapes you in the wombs as He pleases.* There is no
> god but He, the Exalted in Might, the Wise.

Accordingly, when the angelic child is born, everyone is
obliged to give thanks to Him Who has 'shaped' the child.
To Him go the credit and the glory. And when the child is
born without sight?

Furthermore, in the latter case, do we find it easier to
blame Him if the 'God' who has advanced this claim is
Yahweh? If He is the One whose son is Jesus? If He is Allah?
If He is Brahma-Vishnu-Mahesh? Does the identity of the
claimant make a difference to the validity of the claim, and
hence the assigning of responsibility?

There is a mighty earthquake. Over a lakh of people are crushed to death. In the excruciating days that follow, a few score are pulled from the debris. Eventually, the rescue efforts are called off. Maddened by the loss of her child, a mother persists. She just goes on digging and searching through the rubble of the building in which they lived. Five days after the devastation, the child is recovered. Battered, exhausted, but alive, all her faculties intact. We exclaim, 'The child is blessed. God has saved her.'

But, as scholars like Ehrman ask, *by the very same reasoning,* has God not *killed* the others? We do not dare say as much. Is it because we are culturally conditioned to believe one thing and not the other? Is it out of fear—lest God get offended and rain down another calamity on us?

Mir sighs:

Naahaq hum majbooron par yeh tohmat hai mukhtaari kee
Chaahtein hain so aap karen hain humko abas badnaam kiya . . .

But first, what do we know about this God? What does the Book He has sent down say about Him? What does He want of us? Why does He want *that thing,* and not some other? Why does He send calamities down? Do others instigate Him to inflict the calamities? Does the Devil? Do persons for whom He has a special regard? Do we ourselves? Does He send them down on some and not on others? Why do so many do the things that will offend Him and thus bring down His wrath?

Let us do a further experiment. While recording the precise source of each affirmation/assertion, let us not identify the Book from which the passages are taken. As we read them, and as we weigh the argument, let us ask ourselves: 'Would this proposition merit greater belief if the Book turns out to be the Book that we revere in our religion? Would it merit derision if it turns out that the Book from which the passage is taken is one that is revered by the religion we despise?

HIS POWER

The first thing about Him, of course, is His power. It is absolute. It encompasses everything, everybody, every event that happens or is kept from happening. He has created everything and everybody. Everything and everybody fall within His dominion:

> *3:189:* To God belongeth the dominion of the heavens and the earth; and God hath power over all things.
> *4:126:* But to God belong all things in the heavens and on earth: And He it is that Encompasseth all things.
> *5:120:* To God doth belong the dominion of the heavens and the earth, and all that is therein, and it is He Who hath power over all things.
> *67:1:* Blessed be He in Whose hands is Dominion; and He over all things hath Power . . .

In particular, He is the One who has the Power to send hardship crashing down on us or to deliver us from it:

> *6:17:* If God touch thee with affliction, none can remove it but He; if He touch thee with happiness, He hath power over all things.
> *6:18:* He is the Irresistible . . .
> *6:63:* Say: 'Who is it that delivereth you from the dark recesses of land and sea, when ye call upon Him in humility and silent terror: "If He only delivers us from these (dangers), (we vow) we shall truly show our gratitude"?'
> *6:64:* Say: 'It is God that delivereth you from these and all (other) distresses: and yet ye worship false gods!'

And He is the One who has the Power to rain down calamities:

> *6:65:* Say: 'He hath power to send calamities on you, from above and below, or to cover you with confusion in party strife, giving you a taste of mutual vengeance—each from the other' . . .

NO DISTANT OBSERVER

Second, He most assuredly uses this Power. He most assuredly intervenes in human affairs. He is the One who created the universe in the first place. And the earth. And man. And everything that man needs. Each step being an active intervention:

> 16:78: It is He Who brought you forth from the wombs of your mothers when ye knew nothing; and He gave you hearing and sight and intelligence and affections: that ye may give thanks (to God).
>
> 16:79: Do they not look at the birds, held poised in the midst of (the air and) the sky? Nothing holds them up but (the power of) God. Verily in this are signs for those who believe.
>
> 16:80: It is God Who made your habitations homes of rest and quiet for you; and made for you, out of the skins of animals, (tents for) dwellings, which ye find so light (and handy) when ye travel and when ye stop (in your travels); and out of their wool, and their soft fibres (between wool and hair), and their hair, rich stuff and articles of convenience (to serve you) for a time.
>
> 16:81: It is God Who made out of the things He created, some things to give you shade; of the hills He made some for your shelter; He made you garments to protect you from heat, and coats of mail to protect you from your (mutual) violence. Thus does He complete His favours on you, that ye may bow to His Will . . .

From life to death; from laughter to tears; from wealth and satisfaction to their opposite, He gives what He wills, and takes away what He wills:

> 53:42: That to thy Lord is the final Goal;
>
> 53:43: That it is He Who granteth Laughter and Tears;
>
> 53:44: That it is He Who granteth Death and Life;
>
> 53:45: That He did create in pairs—male and female;
>
> 53:46: From a seed when lodged (in its place);
>
> 53:47: That He hath promised a Second Creation (Raising of the Dead);

53:48: That it is He Who giveth wealth and satisfaction;
53:49: That He is the Lord of Sirius (the Mighty Star) . . .

And He uses the Power all the time. To teach and warn and admonish and discipline; to punish and reward; to destroy and save . . . He says that He divided the sea for those He wanted to save from the Pharaoh's marauders [2:50]. But in the other instance, convinced that they had provoked Him, He 'exacts retribution from them, and We drowned them all' [43:55]. He joined the hearts in love of those He favoured even as they were on the brink of the pit of Hell's eternal Fire [always with a capital 'F', so fierce is it]. He reminds us again and again that He has wiped out countless generations. [6:6. Again, 10:13. And yet again, 17:17. And yet again, 19:74. And yet again, 19:98. And yet again, 20:128. And yet again, 36:31. And yet again, 38:3. And yet again, 50:36 . . .] That He has completely erased from the face of the earth entire populations. [18:59. Again, 21:6. And yet again, 22:45. And yet again, 28:58. And yet again, 46:27 . . .] Convinced that some have plotted against His Way, He 'took their structures from their foundations, and the roof fell down on them from above; and the Wrath seized them from directions they did not perceive' [16:26]. He hurls earthquakes [7:78, 7:91]. He rains showers of brimstone down on those whose conduct He disapproves [7:84]. He inflicts droughts and famines on entire peoples 'that they might receive admonition' [7:130]. Convinced that they have not imbibed the admonition, ' . . . We sent (plagues) on them; wholesale death, locusts, lice, frogs, and blood . . .' [7:133].

In a word, He is no distant, detached observer. He is not One who, having once created the universe, has since let it roll which way it will, and take the consequences. On the contrary,

53:50: And that it is He Who destroyed the (powerful) ancient Ad (people),

53:51: And the Thamud nor gave them a lease of perpetual life.

53:52: And before them, the people of Noah, for that they were (all) most unjust and most insolent transgressors,

53:53: And He destroyed the Overthrown Cities (of Sodom and Gomorrah).

53:54: So that (ruins unknown) have covered them up.

85:12: Truly strong is the Grip (and Power) of thy Lord.

85:13: It is He Who creates from the very beginning, and He can restore (life) . . .

85:15: Lord of the Throne of Glory,

85:16: Doer (without let) of all that He intends.

Indeed, He claims:

57:22: No misfortune can happen on earth or in your souls but is recorded in a decree before We bring it into existence: That is truly easy for God.

KNOWS, AND WATCHES, AND HEARS EVERYTHING, AND EVERYONE

The good and ill fortunes come upon us because we do things He likes or detests. He knows. Everything. He watches. Everyone.

2:284: To God belongeth all that is in the heavens and on earth. *Whether ye show what is in your minds or conceal it, God Calleth you to account for it.* He forgiveth whom He pleaseth, and punisheth whom He pleaseth, for God hath power over all things.

3:29: Say: 'Whether ye hide what is in your hearts or reveal it, God knows it all: He knows what is in the heavens, and what is on earth. And God has power over all things.'

6:13: ' . . . To him belongeth all that dwelleth (or lurketh) in the night and the day. *For He is the one who heareth and knoweth all things.'*

10:61: In whatever business thou mayest be, and whatever portion thou mayest be reciting from the [Book]—and whatever deed ye (mankind) may be doing—*We are witnesses thereof when ye are deeply*

engrossed therein. Nor is hidden from thy Lord (so much as) the weight of an atom on the earth or in heaven. And not the least and not the greatest of these things but are recorded in a clear record . . .

Several inferences follow. For the moment, we may take note of just one of them. It isn't just that He knows the evil that a person does after he does it. He knows it even before the deed is done—He knows it the instant the person so much as *intends* to do it. In a word, He knows the evil before it is done—well in time to prevent the person from doing it, and thus igniting His wrath. And yet He lets it be done— with consequences for the immediate target of the deed as well as for the doer.

SINGULAR, OVERRIDING CONCERN

Now, there are many things He regards as wrong, even evil. But He is most forgiving. On occasion, He even pardons direct disobedience of His command. He warned Adam and Eve, for instance, not to heed Satan. He will mislead you, God warned them. Yet they allowed themselves to be beguiled by Satan into eating the forbidden fruit. God banished them from the garden. But He spared them from further punishment. [God recounts the episode many times in the Book. For instance, in *2:37; 7:16-23; 20:120-26,* etc.]

But there is one thing He never lets pass—and that is if anyone venerates anyone along with Him or beside Him. That is literally the cardinal sin. There is no forgiveness for that.

That this is the one unpardonable sin, of course, is the running theme of the Book, and we would have to reproduce almost the entire Book if we were to recount the passages in which God declares this overriding concern of His. But here are four or five passages that will give a glimpse of the seriousness with which He views this matter, and the contrast that He countenances between this lapse and others:

> 4:48: God forgiveth not that partners should be set up with Him; but He forgiveth anything else, to whom He pleaseth; to set up partners with God is to devise a sin most heinous indeed.
>
> 4:110: If anyone does evil or wrongs his own soul but afterwards seeks God's forgiveness, he will find God Oft-forgiving, Most Merciful.
>
> 4:116: God forgiveth not (the sin of) joining other gods with Him; but He forgiveth whom He pleaseth other sins than this: one who joins other gods with God, hath strayed far, far away (from the right).
>
> 39:53: Say: 'O my Servants who have transgressed against their souls! Despair not of the Mercy of God. For God forgives all sins: for He is Oft-Forgiving, Most Merciful.'
>
> 53:32: Those who avoid great sins and shameful deeds, only (falling into) small faults—verily thy Lord is ample in forgiveness. He knows you well when He brings you out of the earth, and when ye are hidden in your mothers' wombs. Therefore justify not yourselves: He knows best who it is that guards against evil.
>
> 57:21: Be ye foremost (in seeking) Forgiveness from your Lord, and a Garden (of Bliss), the width whereof is as the width of heaven and earth, prepared for those who believe in God and His apostles: that is the Grace of God, which He bestows on whom He pleases: and God is the Lord of Grace abounding.

Why this is so, why He attaches so much importance to whether we revere Him and Him alone remains a complete mystery. After all, we are told that He created the universe, the galaxies, the sun and the planets. Having created these innumerable and magnificent bodies, having created space and time, asked Tom Paine over two hundred years ago in *The Age of Reason*, how come He is so concerned whether this speck of a man on this speck of an earth in this speck of a solar system in this speck of a galaxy in this one among an unknown number of universes reveres Him or not, whether, in addition to Him, he reveres anyone else or not? The Book gives no answer. Nor do the advocates of this particular Book or any other Holy Book. And what does this obsession do to His stature? Josh Malihabadi's irrefutable barb:

> *Ghulam Hasan Khan badlaa nahin letaa*
> *Ghulam Hasan Khan se bhi chotaa hai Khuda . . .*

RECORDS

And it isn't just that He watches everyone; that He sees everything and everyone; that He makes sure that He hears every whisper. It isn't just that He knows everything—including, and especially, the regard you may have in the recesses of your heart for something or someone other than Him, a regard that you may try to conceal. *He records.* He records *everything*—every deed, every intention, every thought of yours:

> *10:61:* In whatever business thou mayest be, and whatever portion thou mayest be reciting from the [Book]— and whatever deed ye (mankind) may be doing—We are witnesses thereof when ye are deeply engrossed therein. Nor is hidden from thy Lord (so much as) the weight of an atom on the earth or in heaven. And not the least and not the greatest of these things but are recorded in a clear record.
>
> *17:13:* Every man's fate We have fastened on his own neck: On the Day of Judgement We shall bring out for him a scroll, which he will see spread open.
>
> *17:71:* One day We shall call together all human beings with their (respective) (leaders): those who are given their record in their right hand will read it (with pleasure), and they will not be dealt with unjustly in the least.
>
> *19:77:* Hast thou then seen the (sort of) man who rejects Our Signs, yet says: 'I shall certainly be given wealth and children?'
>
> *19:78:* Has he penetrated to the Unseen, or has he taken a contract with (God) Most Gracious?
>
> *19:79:* Nay! We shall record what he says, and We shall add and add to his punishment.

22:70: Knowest thou not that God knows all that is in heaven and on earth? Indeed it is all in a Record, and that is easy for God.

36:12: Verily We shall give life to the dead, and We record that which they send before and that which they leave behind, and of all things have We taken account in a clear Book (of evidence).

27:75: Nor is there aught of the unseen, in heaven or earth, but is (recorded) in a clear Record.

The Record is written up for a reason, of course—indeed, for two related reasons. The first of these is that, as God affirms repeatedly in the Book, everyone will be rewarded or punished according to what he does:

3:30: 'On the Day when every soul will be confronted with all the good it has done, and all the evil it has done, it will wish there were a great distance between it and its evil. But God cautions you (to remember) Himself. And God is full of kindness to those that serve Him.'

4:40: God is never unjust in the least degree: If there is any good (done), He doubleth it, and giveth from His own presence a great reward.

6:70: Leave alone those who take their religion to be mere play and amusement, and are deceived by the life of this world. But proclaim (to them) this (truth): that every soul delivers itself to ruin by its own acts: it will find for itself no protector or intercessor except God. If it offered every ransom, (or reparation), none will be accepted: such is (the end of) those who deliver themselves to ruin by their own acts: they will have for drink (only) boiling water, and for punishment, one most grievous: for they persisted in rejecting God.

6:132: To all are degrees (or ranks) according to their deeds: for thy Lord is not unmindful of anything that they do.

14:51: That God may requite each soul according to its deserts; and verily God is swift in calling to account.

16:111: One Day every soul will come up struggling for itself, and every soul will be recompensed (fully) for all its actions, and none will be unjustly dealt with.

52:16: 'Burn ye therein: the same is it to you whether ye bear it with patience, or not: Ye but receive the recompense of your (own) deeds.'

74:38: Every soul will be (held) in pledge for its deeds.

74:39: Except the Companions of the Right Hand.

74:40: (They will be) in Gardens (of Delight): they will question each other,

74:41: And (ask) of the Sinners:

74:42: 'What led you into Hell Fire?' . . .

Of course, there is a tale to the exception. But that need not detain us for the moment.

The second, related reason for writing everything meticulously down in a Record is that no one is to be made to bear the burden of another—that is, no one is to be made to suffer the consequences for what someone else has done or neglected to do:

6:164: Say: 'Shall I seek for (my) Cherisher other than God, when He is the Cherisher of all things (that exist)? Every soul draws the meed of its acts on none but itself: no bearer of burdens can bear the burden of another. Your goal in the end is towards God. He will tell you the truth of the things wherein ye disputed.'

53:38: Namely, that no bearer of burdens can bear the burden of another;

53:39: That man can have nothing but what he strives for;

53:40: That (the fruit of) his striving will soon come in sight:

53:41: Then will he be rewarded with a reward complete . . .

Several lemmas follow. For the moment, listing just one will do. Three hundred thousand people were killed by the tsunami. A hundred thousand get killed routinely in an earthquake. A few score are blown up every other week when some suicide bomber detonates his belt in a market. In view of what God has just told us, we must believe—must we not?—that each of them has been punished with death because of the evil that he has himself done. It is, of course, a miracle that all three hundred thousand of them were positioned exactly where and at the precise moment when they would be drowned by the tsunami, that those hundred thousand who perished in the earthquake, those scores in the market were gathered together to die simultaneously of the same blow. A miracle of coincidences—but then miracles are the stuff of God. The evil they had done may have varied but the punishment they merited—death by drowning, by being buried alive or by being blown up—and the moment they deserved to have that punishment visited upon them was identical. What precise accounting!

Incidentally, does God, on His own telling, adhere to this limitation—namely, that no one shall be made to pay for the transgressions of another? Consider what He Himself declares. Some persons offend God by worshipping some others even as they worship Him. He crushes not just those persons, He crushes their wives too:

> 37:22: 'Bring ye up', it shall be said, 'The wrong-doers and their wives, and the things they worshipped—
> 37:23: Besides God, and lead them to the Way to the (Fierce) Fire!'

Not just solitary wives. When a few privileged persons do not heed His directions, He pulverizes not just them. He erases entire populations, entire generations:

> 17:16: When We decide to destroy a population, We (first) send a definite order to those among them who are given the good things of this life and yet transgress; so that the word is proved true against them: then (it is) We destroy them utterly.
> 17:17: How many generations have We destroyed after Noah? And enough is thy Lord to note and see the sins of His servants.

And yet, He is always just, and we must believe that.

ALWAYS JUST

The improbability in the sequence—that all who had sinned were standing right where they did, and that too at the very moment at which they could all be killed by one blow—does not bother either God or His advocates. The Book tells us, and He Himself claims repeatedly that He is just, that He is always just—always rewarding those who believe in Him, and punishing those who don't. And always in strict proportion to the good and the evil they have done.

Even if we accept this narrowest of narrow criteria of virtue—that those and those alone are virtuous who revere Him and Him alone—we must remember that God is 'always just' only in a very special sense. After all, the faithful also die in battle, and, ever so often, those who do not believe in Him prosper. Where is the justice in this? the sceptic may wonder.

Consider the ones who go out to fight in His cause as commanded by Him and die. In what sense has He been just to them? In the sense, as He explains in regard to a famous 'battle' recounted often in the Holy Book, that, first of all, they are *not* dead. Second, they are being rewarded with bounties and are joyous in heaven:

> 3:169: Think not of those who are slain in God's way as dead. Nay, they live, finding their sustenance in the presence of their Lord;
> 3:170: They rejoice in the bounty provided by God. And with regard to those left behind, who have not yet joined them (in their bliss), the (Martyrs) glory in the fact that on them is no fear, nor have they (cause to) grieve.
> 3:171: They glory in the Grace and the bounty from God, and in the fact that God suffereth not the reward of the Faithful to be lost (in the least).
> 3:172: Of those who answered the call of God and the Messenger, even after being wounded, those who do right and refrain from wrong have a great reward;
> 3:173: Men said to them: 'A great army is gathering against you': And frightened them: But it (only) increased their Faith: They said: 'For us God sufficeth, and He is the best disposer of affairs.'
> 3:174: And they returned with Grace and bounty from God. No harm ever touched them: for they followed the good pleasure of God. And God is the Lord of bounties unbounded.

And how is He just in the case of unbelievers who, in spite of every command that has issued from Him, still do not follow the path of truth, and yet prosper? God is just in the sense that He has merely postponed their punishment:

> *3:177:* Those who purchase Unbelief at the price of faith, not the least harm will they do to God, but they will have a grievous punishment.
>
> *3:178:* Let not the Unbelievers think that Our respite to them is good for themselves: We grant them respite that they may grow in their iniquity: But they will have a shameful punishment.

An obvious question arises. How just, not to ask 'how compassionate', is a judge who, knowing full well that the accused will commit further crimes if he gives them the time to do so, 'grant[s] them respite that they may grow in their iniquity' so that in the second round he can torture them all the more?

THE DANGER OF EMPTYING THE EARTH

But there is a reason, God explains, for not lifting all unbelievers to Hell at once. So many do so much wrong, God explains, that if He were to punish here and now each for his wrongdoing, no one would be left on the earth. That is why He defers punishment to 'the day appointed':

> *16:61:* If God were to punish men for their wrong-doing, He would not leave, on the (earth), a single living creature: but He gives them respite for a stated Term: When their Term expires, they would not be able to delay (the punishment) for a single hour, just as they would not be able to anticipate it (for a single hour).

Several questions arise. One just has to be mentioned. How does this fact—that so many do so much wrong that if God were to punish them here and now, the earth would be emptied—square with the claim—a claim that is made repeatedly by God Himself—that His creation is 'perfect'?

> *67:3:* He Who created
> The seven heavens

One above another:
No want of proportion
Wilt thou see
In the creation
Of (God) Most Gracious
So turn thy vision again:
Seest thou any flaw?

How does the fact that, were God to punish here and now all who sin, the earth would be emptied square with God's own affirmation that He has made man 'in the best of moulds', that He has created man as His 'vicegerent on earth'? '"Behold," thy Lord said to the angels,' the Holy Book tells us: '"I will create a vicegerent on earth."' The angels had their doubts, for, the Book records them asking, 'Wilt Thou place therein one who will make mischief therein and shed blood?—whilst we do celebrate Thy praises and glorify Thy holy (name)?' God said: 'I know what ye know not' [2.30]. So, a vicegerent it is.

How does the fact that all earth would be instantly emptied if God were to punish all who do wrong square with His own declaration,

95:4: We have indeed created man in the best of moulds . . .

Yes, yes, I know what you will say: 'What is the problem? God *has* created man in "the best of moulds". It is man who then does wrong, and thereby sets himself up for the wrath of God.' Then how come God Himself says in the next verse:

95:5: Then do *We* abase him (to be) the lowest of the low,
95:6: Except such as believe and do righteous deeds: For they shall have a reward unfailing.

Who abases man? God Himself—'Then do *We* abase him (to be) the lowest of the low . . .'—not man!

But we are running ahead of the story. For the moment we have to note merely the claim of God and of His Book that He is 'always just'. Believers when they are killed while fighting in the cause of God are not really dead. Unbelievers who prosper have merely had their deserts postponed for a while. And for good reason: they clamoured for the good things in this life, they grasped at them greedily, they enjoyed them to the full. They did not value the truly important life, the life of the Hereafter. Hence, their recompense:

> 46:20: And on the Day that the Unbelievers will be placed before the Fire, (it will be said to them): 'Ye received your good things in the life of the world, and ye took your pleasure out of them: but today shall ye be recompensed with a Penalty of humiliation: for that ye were arrogant on earth without just cause, and that ye (ever) transgressed.'

We shall soon see why they do not believe in the first place. But for the moment, read this verse, and picture Jesus being crucified, Mansur being put to death, Sri Ramakrishna dying of cancer, Gandhiji as he is being assassinated, Sri Ramana Maharshi dying of cancer . . . Can the torment they had to pass through be justified on the ground that they hankered after 'the good things of life', and to the fact that they 'took your pleasure out of them', that they valued this life rather than the life Hereafter?

SCALE OF THE BURDEN

There is a related assurance that God holds out. We might as well glance at it before we proceed further. No one shall be burdened with a burden greater than what he can bear, God assures us repeatedly:

> 2:286: On no soul doth God Place a burden greater than it can bear. It gets every good that it earns, and it suffers every ill that it earns. (Pray:) 'Our Lord! Condemn us not if we forget or fall into error; our Lord! Lay not on us a burden like that which Thou didst lay on those before us; our Lord! Lay not on us a burden greater than we

have strength to bear. Blot out our sins, and grant us forgiveness.
Have mercy on us. Thou art our Protector; Help us against those
who stand against faith.'
7:42: But those who believe and work righteousness— no burden
do We place on any soul, but that which it can bear—they will be
Companions of the Garden, therein to dwell (for ever).
23:62: On no soul do We place a burden greater than it can
bear: before Us is a Record which clearly shows the truth: they
will never be wronged.

At the moment one is being crushed by trauma, this
assurance, of course, is a great buoy: one makes believe that,
though at that moment the burden seems unbearable, in
view of the assurance given by God Himself, in fact it *just
cannot be* beyond one's capacity to bear. But is the purpose of
God's assurance to boost morale; or is the statement—
'On no soul do We place a burden that is greater than it can
bear'—a statement of fact? Is the assurance not a mere
tautology? Does the fact that the Jews who were being
driven into the gas chambers did not commit suicide, does
the fact that a person suffering from leukemia does not
commit suicide mean that the burden which has been
inflicted on them is not greater than they can bear? For they
do 'bear it' till they are extinguished, do they not?

UNSURE OF US? OR OF HIMSELF?

Now, it is not just that He watches, He hears, He records our
innermost thoughts and intention to make sure that we
revere Him and none beside Him. He is so unsure of the very
men whom He has created and chosen that He repeatedly
and continually tests even those who believe in Him:

3:140: If a wound hath touched you, be sure a similar wound hath
touched the others. Such days (of varying fortunes) We give to men
and men by turns: that God may know those that believe, and that
He may take to Himself from your ranks Martyr-witnesses
(to Truth). And God loveth not those that do wrong.

3:142: Did ye think that ye would enter Heaven without God testing those of you who fought hard (in His Cause) and remained steadfast?

6:53: Thus did We try some of them by comparison with others, that they should say: 'Is it these then that God hath favoured from amongst us?' Doth not God know best those who are grateful?

29:2: Do men think that they will be left alone on saying, 'We believe', and that they will not be tested?

57:25: We sent aforetime our apostles with Clear Signs and sent down with them the Book and the Balance (of Right and Wrong), that men may stand forth in justice; and We sent down Iron, in which is (material for) mighty war, as well as many benefits for mankind, that God may test who it is that will help, Unseen, Him and His apostles: For God is Full of Strength, Exalted in Might (and able to enforce His Will).

67:2: He Who created Death and Life, that He may try which of you is best in deed: and He is the Exalted in Might, Oft-Forgiving . . .

2:155: Be sure We shall test you with something of fear and hunger, some loss in goods or lives or the fruits (of your toil), but give glad tidings to those who patiently persevere . . .

3:186: Ye shall certainly be tried and tested in your possessions and in your personal selves; and ye shall certainly Hear much that will grieve you, from those who received the Book before you and from those who worship many gods. But if ye persevere patiently, and guard against evil—then that will be a determining factor in all affairs.

47:31: And We shall try you until We test those among you who strive their utmost and persevere in patience; and We shall try your reported (mettle).

'He is so unsure of us,' we said. The fact is that if someone other than God displayed such nervousness, we would say, 'He is so unsure of *himself.*' In either event, the question naturally arises, 'Why does He need to test when He already knows?' The conventional answer is that He tests us not so that *He* may get to know who is true to Him and who is not. But so that *we* may, through seeing how we conduct ourselves during these trials, get to know ourselves—that

we may see for ourselves whether We believe in Him and
His message or not. And thereby learn, and grow. But that
only opens up another question: 'Why must He employ such
roundabout methods, especially ones that entail such
terrible suffering for persons who are altogether innocent?'
Does He really need to put millions to death in wars and
famines and at the hands of tyrants to make them see
whether or not they lose faith in Him, whether they
turn to others in the extreme circumstances in which
He has deliberately put them? Assume that those who were
faithful to Him—in whichever guise He made His message
known to them: as Yahweh, as God, as Allah, as
Bhagwan—retained their faith in Him to the end. They did
die. What use was it to them; what use is it to us; indeed,
what use is it to Yahweh-God-Allah-Bhagwan that the ones
who were killed learnt that their faith in Him did not
waver? Or that it did?

LENGTHS TO WHICH HE GOES TO FULFIL HIS OVERRIDING CONCERN

To ensure that we believe in Him and in no one else, God
sends Messengers. He sends a Message with each of them.
He displays and sends Signs. The sun, stars (with which He
stones the Devil), seasons, birds suspended in mid-air . . .
one and all are Signs from Him, if only we would heed
them.

Some heed them. Most don't. Recalling the unremitting
efforts of one of His Messengers and their meagre fruit, God
exclaims:

> 12:103: Yet no faith will the greater part of mankind have, however
> ardently thou dost desire it.

He purges the believers of doubters and hypocrites who are
lurking among them. He purges the true believers of any
residual doubts in their hearts. He deprives those who do
not believe of blessings:

3:141: God's object also is to purge those that are true in Faith and to deprive of blessing those that resist Faith . . .

At a critical moment, He lets doubts assail some among those who have gathered to fight in His cause. 'Why should we expose ourselves to this slaughter? What have we to do with this affair?' they tell each other. God instructs His Messenger to tell them:

3:154: . . . 'Even if you had remained in your homes, those for whom death was decreed would certainly have gone forth to the place of their death'; but (all this was) that God might test what is in your breasts and purge what is in your hearts. For God knoweth well the secrets of your hearts.

He hates those who do not believe the Signs. He hates them more than they hate themselves and each other:

40:10: The Unbelievers will be addressed: 'Greater was the aversion of God to you than (is) your aversion to yourselves, seeing that ye were called to the Faith and ye used to refuse.'

He punishes them—converting many of them, for instance, into apes:

2:65: And well ye knew those amongst you who transgressed in the matter of the Sabbath: We said to them: 'Be ye apes, despised and rejected.'

2:66: So We made it an example to their own time and to their posterity, and a lesson to those who fear God.

And again,

7:164: When some of them said: 'Why do ye preach to a people whom God will destroy or visit with a terrible punishment?', said the preachers: 'To discharge our duty to your Lord, and perchance they may fear Him.'

7:165: When they disregarded the warnings that had been given them, We rescued those who forbade Evil; but We visited the wrong-doers with a grievous punishment because they were given to transgression.

7:166: When in their insolence they transgressed (all) prohibitions, We said to them: 'Be ye apes, despised and rejected.'

7:167: Behold! thy Lord did declare that He would send against them, to the Day of Judgement, those who would afflict them with grievous penalty. Thy Lord is quick in retribution, but He is also Oft forgiving, Most Merciful.

He takes revenge:

3:4: ... Then those who reject Faith in the Signs of God will suffer the severest penalty, and God is Exalted in Might, Lord of Retribution.

32:22: And who does more wrong than one to whom are recited the Signs of his Lord, and who then turns away therefrom? Verily from those who transgress We shall exact (due) Retribution.

He destroys. As we have seen, He completely erases generations after generations, He pulverizes heaps upon heaps of unbelievers.

For them, He creates Hell. He personally hurls countless numbers into it. He personally supervises their torment, ensuring, among other things, that it never ends:

17:97: ... On the Day of Judgement We shall gather them together, prone on their faces, blind, dumb, and deaf: their abode will be Hell: every time it shows abatement, We shall increase for them the fierceness of the Fire.

By His Command, unbelievers are 'seized by their forelocks and their feet', they are led into Hell in hordes [*39:71-72; 55:41*]. He commands, 'Seize ye him, bind ye him, and burn ye him in the blazing fire. Further, make him march in a chain, whereof the length is seventy cubits. This was he that would not believe in God Most High' [*69:30-33*]. Their skins are roasted. And renewed. And roasted. Over and over again [*4:56*]. They are made to drink boiling, fetid water, molten brass and other boiling fluids [*14:16-17; 18:29; 38:55-58; 56:42-44; 88:2-7*]. Their faces are held to the blazing fire [*14:49-50*]. .... They shriek that they be killed and the torture be brought to an end. But they are not allowed either to live or to die [14:17; 20:74; 25:13-14; 35:36; 78:21-25; 87:13].

But, of course, for none of this is God to blame. He is Just and Merciful, always so. The unbelievers are the ones who have been unjust and cruel to themselves:

43:74: The sinners will be in the Punishment of Hell, to dwell therein (for aye):

43:75: Nowise will the (Punishment) be lightened for them, and in despair will they be there overwhelmed.

43:76: Nowise shall We be unjust to them: but it is they who have been unjust themselves.

43:77: They will cry: 'O Master! would that thy Lord put an end to us!' He will say, 'Nay, but ye shall abide!'

43:78: Verily We have brought the Truth to you: but most of you have a hatred for Truth.

Recalling what was visited upon entire peoples and generations who did not heed the Signs and Messages, God reiterates yet again:

11:99: And they are followed by a curse in this (life) and on the Day of Judgement: and woeful is the gift which shall be given (unto them)! ...

11:101: It was not We that wronged them: They wronged their own souls ...

Such is His concern for being venerated, such is His determination to be the only one who is venerated.

THE CENTRAL EXPLANATION

The principal explanation for suffering thus is that, in spite of the countless Signs He sends for our edification, in spite of the Messengers He sends and the Message that they deliver, we do not venerate God; or that, in spite of His countless warnings, even as we venerate Him, we revere others also.

What would you say of the father—the ordinary, mortal father—who went to these lengths to ensure that his children honour him, and him alone?

It is, of course, true that most verses that talk of reward or punishment talk of these being meted out on the Day of Judgement—and taking the form of staying in the gardens of heaven or in Hell and its fire. But on occasion, God tells us that the sufferings of this world are also visited upon unbelievers and those who join others to Him:

> 13:34: For them is a penalty in the life of this world, but harder, truly, is the penalty of the Hereafter: and defender have they none against God.

So, the explanation holds not just for the suffering to come after the Day of Judgement. It holds as much for sufferings encountered here and now.

That, of course, leaves three questions open. For one thing, those who believe in Him unstintingly also suffer here and now. They also suffer setbacks. What accounts for these? Second, has the infant who suffers brain damage during birth suffered the injury because he has, in the womb or in those few moments as he came out of it, already joined others with God? Third, why is it that, though God has created man 'in the best of moulds', though His creation is 'perfect', on the very matter that concerns Him the most— namely, that everyone must venerate Him and Him alone— His creation is so deficient? Why do the unbelievers not believe? Why are there so many of them?

God has ready answers. Two contrasting events bring out vividly His answer to the first of these questions.

WHEN DEVOTEES PREVAIL, WHEN THEY ARE VANQUISHED

God's devotees hear of a group from among their adversaries that is on its way home. The group is laden with valuables. Waylaying it will bring huge winnings. But by the time the believers reach within pouncing distance, the band carrying valuables has already gone out of reach. Some among the believers argue that the expedition be abandoned. God steels His chosen one. Under his leadership, the remaining believers confront and vanquish the main force—one that is said to be thrice as large. 'In this is a warning for such as have eyes to see,' God declares. 'God doth support with His aid whom He pleaseth' [3:13]. God lists the stratagems He deployed to bring about this unexpected outcome—His chosen one throws a little sand in the direction of the adversaries, for instance; it blinds them as a dust storm would. God sends in a thousand angels to aid His devotees [8:9]. Dispatching them, He exhorts the angels, 'I am with you: give firmness to the Believers: I will instill terror into the hearts of the Unbelievers: smite ye above their necks and smite all their fingertips off them' [8:12]. He sends rain to bog down the cavalry of the opponents. He makes His chosen one underestimate the numbers arrayed against his much smaller force—so as to embolden him [8:43–44] . . . A minor lemma: as God is the One who says He is responsible for the victory of the believers, He is ipso facto responsible for the deaths of the unbelievers. In fact, the Book puts the matter beyond doubt:

8:17: It is not ye who slew them; it was God . . .

Why are the unbelievers killed? For a reason, says God: 'to justify the truth according to His words and to cut off the roots of the unbelievers, that He may justify Truth and prove Falsehood false':

8:7: Behold! God promised you one of the two (enemy) parties, that it should be yours: Ye wished that the one unarmed should be yours, but God willed to justify the Truth according to His words and to cut off the roots of the Unbelievers;

8:8: That He might justify Truth and prove Falsehood false, distasteful though it be to those in guilt.

And because the unbelievers dared to contend against the Will of God and His chosen one:

8:13: This because they contended against God and His Apostle: If any contend against God and His Apostle, God is strict in punishment.

He engineers victory for the believers as a message of hope and assurance to their hearts:

8:9: Remember ye implored the assistance of your Lord, and He answered you: 'I will assist you with a thousand of the angels, ranks on ranks.'

8:10: God made it but a message of hope, and an assurance to your hearts: (in any case) there is no help except from God: and God is Exalted in Power, Wise.

Furthermore, He does all this to test the believers on the one hand, He tells us in His Book, and because one of His attributes is that He nullifies the plans of unbelievers:

8:17: It is not ye who slew them; it was God: when thou threwest (a handful of dust), it was not thy act, but God's: in order that He might test the Believers by a gracious trial from Himself: for God is He Who heareth and knoweth (all things).

8:18: That, and also because God is He Who makes feeble the plans and stratagem of the Unbelievers.

He repeatedly claims that He is the One who brought about the victory. Here then are a series of reasons on account of which suffering to the point of death is brought down on one lot—those who do not believe in Him: rather on those who do not believe in one version of Him.

But within the shortest possible time, a second encounter takes place between the believers and the same set of opponents. The victory over the far larger force had convinced the believers that God was indeed on their side. But now suddenly, the believers are vanquished. One of the reasons is that several do not come out to fight alongside the chosen one. Even so, the faithful, being more disciplined and zealous, are about to prevail. But suddenly a handful who have been stationed to guard a flank; and who have been directed not to leave their post come what may, in fact rush to fall upon the booty. That gives the enemy an opportunity to launch a counter-attack, and this vanquishes the faithful.

The defeat traumatizes the faithful—as any blow might the one who has placed his entire trust in God. But it is no problem for God. The defeat too has been by leave of, indeed by the design of God. The ones who stayed away from the fight, the ones who disobeyed the commander and thereby caused the defeat also did so by the Will of God. He has reasons for this also. He has engineered all this, we learn, so as to test the believers on the one hand and to expose the hypocrites on the other:

> 3:166: What ye suffered on the day the two armies met, was with the leave of God, in order that He might test the believers,
> 3:167: And the Hypocrites also. These were told: 'Come, fight in the way of God, or (at least) drive (the foe from your city).' They said: 'Had we known how to fight, we should certainly have followed you.' They were that day nearer to Unbelief than to Faith, saying with their lips what was not in their hearts but God hath full knowledge of all they conceal.

God says that He deliberately varies the fortunes of men so as to test them, as we have seen, to take to Himself martyr-witnesses, and to deprive the unbelievers of blessings:

> 3:140: If a wound hath touched you, be sure a similar wound hath touched the others. Such days (of varying fortunes) We give to men and men by turns: that God may know those that believe, and that He may take to Himself from your ranks Martyr-witnesses (to Truth). And God loveth not those that do wrong.
> 3:141: God's object also is to purge those that are true in Faith and to deprive of blessing those that resist Faith.

Death and maiming as the instrument to ascertain what He already knows? What if some ordinary mortal—a Stalin, a Hitler, a Mao, or a Pol Pot—inflicted death and maiming on millions just to satisfy himself that they revere him and him alone?

'OTHERS MADE ME DO IT'

So, it is all settled. If those who believe in Him win, He has brought about the victory—to give them heart, to prove His word to be true, to finish those who denied His Message. If those who believe in Him lose, He has contrived that also—to teach them humility, to remind them to keep Him in mind all the time, to test whether they would lose faith in Him, to expose the hypocrites, to swell the non-believers with false confidence. If the cancer is cured, that is because of His mercy. It is because He wanted to show how He fulfils His Word—that He *will* answer the prayers of His devotees. If it continues to spread, and eventually kills the devotee, that is because deep down in his heart the devotee had doubts. That is because God desired to instill humility and fear in all—that they should not presume that just because they think they are devoted to Him, He will do as they want. No, no, He saves whom He will and He lets die whom He will . . .

On occasion, of course, suffering is hurled—in the cases we are about to list, suffering to the point of death itself is hurled—in response to the prayers of someone God cherishes.

I repeatedly exhorted them—loudly, in private, in public—to believe, Noah tells God. I reminded them of Your might, of the grandeur of Your creation. I listed for them the boons that You have conferred on all of us.

I recalled the warnings You have sent down. I warned them of the wrath that would most assuredly befall them if they do not obey Your command.

71:6: 'But my call only increases (their) flight (from the Right).

71:7: 'And every time I have called to them, that Thou mightest forgive them, they have (only) thrust their fingers into their ears, covered themselves up with their garments, grown obstinate, and given themselves up to arrogance.'

71:21: Noah said: 'O my Lord! They have disobeyed me, but they follow (men) whose wealth and children give them no increase but only Loss.

71:22: 'And they have devised a tremendous Plot . . .'

Therefore, Noah beseeches God:

71:26: And Noah, said: 'O my Lord! Leave not of the Unbelievers, a single one on earth!

71:27: 'For, if Thou dost leave (any of) them, they will but mislead Thy devotees, and they will breed none but wicked ungrateful ones.

71:28: 'O my Lord! Forgive me, my parents, all who enter my house in Faith, and (all) believing men and believing women: and to the wrong-doers grant Thou no increase but in perdition!'

And so God drowns everyone in a mighty flood, save that handful on the ark.

So, 'Noah made Me do it.' Were the millions of animals who must have perished in the flood, were they also given to untruth? What about the fact that God has so arranged matters that animals kill each other for food or sport, and we kill them all? Is this also a manifestation of benevolence?

And then Moses. He preaches, 'There is no God but God.' His people believe him. But for fear of the Pharaoh and because of the prohibitions that the Pharaoh imposes, they are not able to live and pray openly by their belief. 'Deliver us by Thy Mercy from those who reject Thee . . .' they implore. And Moses prays:

10:88: 'Our Lord! Thou hast indeed bestowed on Pharaoh and his chiefs splendour and wealth in the life of the present, and so, our Lord, they mislead (men) from Thy Path. Deface, our Lord, the features of their wealth, and send hardness to their hearts, so they will not believe until they see the grievous penalty.'

Notice the prayer. Moses does not beseech God that He should make the Pharaoh and his men see the light. On the contrary, he prays, ' . . . send hardness to their hearts, so they will not believe until they see the grievous penalty'— that is, till they are securely in Hell. This is what God proceeds to do. He leads the people of Moses through the parted sea to safety. The Pharaoh and his hosts follow them. God closes the sea. They are drowned in the flood. As he is being drowned, the Pharaoh exclaims, 'I believe there is no God except Him Whom the Children of Israel believe in. I am of those who submit . . .' [10:90]. Too late, announces God [10:90-91; also 4:18]. The Pharaoh dies by drowning. God grants one posthumous mitigation: his body survives, and is embalmed—and that for a purpose: 'This day shall We save thee in thy body,' God declares, 'that thou mayest be a sign to those who come after thee!' Of course, that is not much help for, as God explains, 'But verily, many among mankind are heedless of Our Signs' [10:92].

So, 'Moses made Me do it.'

But the one who most frequently makes Him hurl suffering upon mankind is the Devil.

'THE DEVIL MADE ME DO IT'

Everyone is abiding in eternal bliss. God has created the angels, including Satan, out of fire. He creates man—out of clay. Having created man 'in the best of moulds', God directs all the angels to bow down to him, that is to man. All do except Satan. Why don't you also bow? God demands.

Of course, if only Satan had had a lawyer, he would have covered up his disobedience with fidelity. 'Because I am a monotheist,' he would have told God. 'I bow to You and to You alone.'

Uninstructed by lawyers, he tells God, 'But how can I bow to man? He is my inferior. You made me out of fire. You have made him out of mere clay' [2:30-34; 15:26-33; 38:75-76]. And thereby leads God to see him, Satan, as haughty and arrogant.

'Then get thee out from here,' God decrees, 'for thou art rejected, accursed. And the curse shall be on thee till the Day of Judgement' [15:34-35; 38:76-77]. And thus begins a winding tale.

The moment Satan is cursed, two occurrences transpire. First, Satan requests some respite. God can refuse it. He can send Satan forthwith into Hell, and thus keep him from working mischief on earth. But God does the opposite:

> 38:79: (Satan) said: 'O my Lord! Give me then respite till the Day the (dead) are raised.'
> 38:80: (God) said: 'Respite then is granted thee—
> 38:81: 'Till the Day of the Time Appointed.'

It is during this interval that Satan works his evil. But who has given Satan the opportunity to execute his plans?

And no one can have any doubt about what Satan intends to do during the respite he is being given—least of all, God, who, in any case, always knows everything that is in anyone's and everyone's heart. The moment Satan is granted respite till the Day we are all to be taken up, he tells God,

> 38:82: (Satan) said: 'Then, by Thy power, I will put them all in the wrong,
> 38:83: 'Except Thy Servants amongst them, sincere and purified (by Thy Grace).'

Notice both things.

- ❑ Satan states his plan explicitly—'*I will put them all in the wrong . . .*'
- ❑ And he acknowledges what is enabling him to waylay people: 'Then, *by Thy Power . . .*'

Even if God was not paying attention when He granted
Satan respite till the Day of Judgement, He has certainly
been alerted to what Satan is going to do. He can nip it in
the bud: by a sort of anticipatory nullification, or, better still,
by cancelling the bail He has granted Satan. He does
nothing of the kind. All He does is,

> 38:84: (God) said: 'Then it is just and fitting—and I say what
> is just and fitting—
> 38:85: 'That I will certainly fill Hell with thee and those that
> follow thee—every one.'

Why cast them into Hell *after* Satan has misled them and
made them do what You detest? Why not prevent any of
that from happening in the first place?

In another telling of the same sequence, God is even more
explicit in granting Satan leave to do what he will to waylay
people. In this telling, the exchanges take place as follows.
God reports:

> 17:61: Behold! We said to the angels: 'Bow down unto Adam':
> They bowed down except Satan: He said, 'Shall I bow down
> to one whom Thou didst create from clay?'
> 17:62: He [that is Satan] said: 'Seest Thou? this is the one whom
> Thou hast honoured above me! If Thou wilt but respite me
> to the Day of Judgement, I will surely bring his descendants
> under my sway—all but a few!'

That is, Satan is telling God explicitly, 'If You give me the
time, I will surely bring his descendants under my sway—all
but a few!' God does not direct Satan to cease and desist. On
the contrary,

> 17:63: (God) said: 'Go thy way; if any of them follow thee, verily
> Hell will be the recompense of you (all)—an ample recompense.
> 17:64: 'Lead to destruction those whom thou can among them, with thy
> (seductive) voice; make assaults on them with thy cavalry and thy
> infantry; mutually share with them wealth and children; and make
> promises to them.' But Satan promises them nothing but deceit.

Not culpable?

Of course, here as well as in other places in the Book that record the exchange, God adds a caveat—one that we will have occasion to consider more fully in a moment:

17:65: 'As for My servants, no authority shalt thou have over them': Enough is thy Lord for a Disposer of affairs.

Notice that God Himself leaves Satan free to waylay and mislead, and thus lead into Hell, all whom He does not take to be His servants. This restriction is stated more than once in the Book—the result of the precise words is such that lawyers assisting Satan will be able to drive a truck through the restriction.

When God curses Satan, the latter, on the recounting of God Himself, tells Him straight out that he will take His servants also, except some of them. God does not bar Satan totally from touching even His servants. He merely declares that whoever follows Satan shall come to an unhappy end:

4:118: God did curse him, but he said: 'I will take of Thy servants a portion marked off;
4:119: I will mislead them, and I will create in them false desires; I will order them to slit the ears of cattle, and to deface the (fair) nature created by God.' Whoever, forsaking God, takes Satan for a friend, hath of a surety suffered a loss that is manifest.
4:120: Satan makes them promises, and creates in them false desires; but Satan's promises are nothing but deception.
4:121: They (his dupes) will have their dwelling in Hell, and from it they will find no way of escape.

When the incident of bowing to man or not bowing to him is next reported, again God does not exclude His servants from Satan's reach ipso facto. The matter turns into another tautology. In declaring his intention to lead people away from God, Satan himself lays down a rule of self-limitation:

15:39: (Satan) said: 'O my Lord! because Thou hast put me in the wrong, I will make (wrong) fair-seeming to them on the earth, and I will put them all in the wrong,

15:40: 'Except Thy servants among them, sincere and purified (by Thy Grace).'

God responds:

15:41: (God) said: 'This (way of My sincere servants) is indeed a way that leads straight to Me.

15:42: 'For over My servants no authority shalt thou have, *except such as put themselves in the wrong and follow thee.'*

15:43: And verily, Hell is the promised abode for them all!

And God proceeds to describe Hell—its seven gates and the rest.

Thus, Satan is left free to get at a chunk of God's servants also—those 'as put themselves in the wrong and follow thee'. Yet the limitation stated elsewhere—that Satan has no authority over the servants of God—is said to hold. For, *by definition,* those of the servants of God who relapse and fall for Satan's guile are not sincere servants of God. As the Book says,

16:99: No authority has he over those who believe and put their trust in their Lord.

16:100: His authority is over those only, who take him as patron and who join partners with God.

Satan has authority over all except 'those who believe and put their trust in their Lord'—those who fall under Satan's authority and sway are *by definition* not ones who believe and put their trust in God.

22:4: About the (Evil One) it is decreed that whoever turns to him for friendship, him will he lead astray, and he will guide him to the Penalty of the Fire.

Notice also what it is that originally propelled Satan to mislead people. Satan is careful to put it on record, so to say. The Book records him telling God,

> *7:16:* He said: *'Because Thou hast thrown me out of the way,* lo! I will lie in wait for them on thy straight way:
> *7:17:* 'Then will I assault them from before them and behind them, from their right and their left: Nor wilt Thou find, in most of them, gratitude (for Thy mercies).'

And again,

> *15:39:*(Satan) said: 'O my Lord! *because Thou hast put me in the wrong,* I will make (wrong) fair-seeming to them on the earth, and I will put them all in the wrong . . .'

In a word, it isn't just that God is the One who has given him—Satan—the time—till the Day of Judgement—to work his evil. God is the One who has provided the initial shove—by asking Satan to prostrate himself before mere man; and then by casting him out and putting him in the wrong.

The same thing holds for the individual who ultimately falls for Satan's guile and follows him. The initiative to do so may be that of the individual—he may be the one who 'turns to the Evil One for friendship'—but the opportunity has been provided by God—both in the respite He gave Satan to hang around and do his worst, and in leaving man free to befriend Satan should the individual so desire.

But is even that last bit true? Is the individual befriending Satan entirely on his own? At the least, are all the individuals befriending Satan on their own? Look at what God Himself says:

> *7:27:* O ye Children of Adam! Let not Satan seduce you, in the same manner as He got your parents out of the Garden, stripping them of their raiment, to expose their shame: for he and his tribe watch you from a position where ye cannot see them: *We* made the Evil Ones friends (only) to those without faith.

The '(only)', of course, is added by the translator! In any case, even if we confine ourselves to 'those without faith', who has 'made the Evil Ones friends' of this lot? God, on the acknowledgment of God Himself.

The position regarding those who do not believe, of course, is even clearer. God asks, almost impatiently:

19:83: Seest thou not that *We* have set the Evil Ones on against the unbelievers, to incite them with fury?

Even after He sets the Evil One free to molest individuals, so to say, God has the Power to nullify whatever it is that Satan may have done—and He *does* use this Power on occasion. For instance, see what God tells His Messenger:

22:52: Never did We send an apostle or a prophet before thee, but, when he framed a desire, Satan threw some (vanity) into his desire: *but God will cancel anything (vain) that Satan throws in, and God will confirm (and establish) His Signs:* for God is full of Knowledge and Wisdom...

But most often, God leaves the poison that Satan has injected to work its way, and He leaves it working for a purpose:

22:53: That He may make the suggestions thrown in by Satan, but *a trial for those in whose hearts is a disease and who are hardened of heart:* verily the wrong-doers are in a schism far (from the Truth): *22:54:* And that *those on whom knowledge has been bestowed may learn that the (Book) is the Truth from thy Lord, and that they may believe therein, and their hearts may be made humbly (open) to it:* for verily God is the Guide of those who believe, to the Straight Way.

When you are present at the scene; when it is within your power to stay the hand of the murderer, and you do nothing, are you not at the least an accessory to the crime? But not God. He holds back His Hand for a purpose. And He must be judged only by the norms He wrote.

Satan also passes off the responsibility to the individual. God warns the people that, when they are arrayed before Him on the Day of Judgement and are asked to account for their crime—that of associating another with God—and they point to Satan, Satan, says God, will disown all responsibility:

> *14:22:* And Satan will say when the matter is decided: 'It was God Who gave you a promise of Truth: I too promised, but I failed in my promise to you. I had no authority over you except to call you *but ye listened to me: then reproach not me, but reproach your own souls.* I cannot listen to your cries, nor can ye listen to mine. I reject your former act in associating me with God. For wrong-doers there must be a grievous penalty.'

BARQ GIRTI HAI TO BECHAARE INSAAN PAR . . .

Even though everyone is, and everything is at His beck and call, even though no one does anything or even can do anything but at His Command and by His leave, going by the way that God puts the matter, the individual is the one who has to reap the consequences of what he does.

'On the Day when every soul will be confronted with all the good *it* has done, and all the evil *it* has done . . . ' God warns us in His Book [*3:30*]; ' . . . every soul delivers itself to its ruin *by its own acts . . .* ' He tells us [*6:70*]; 'There will every soul prove (the fruits of) the deeds *it* sent before: they will be brought back to God their rightful Lord, and their invented falsehoods will leave them in the lurch,' we are warned [*10:30*]; 'At length will be said to the wrong-doers: "Taste ye the enduring punishment! Ye get the recompense of what *ye* earned,"' God proclaims [*10:52*]; affairs have been so arranged, we learn, 'that God may requite each soul according to *its* deserts; and verily God is swift in calling to account' [*14:51*]; 'Burn ye therein,' God declares, 'the same is it to you whether ye bear it with patience, or not: ye but receive the recompense of *your* (own) deeds' [*52:16*]. We are to be called to account for and be rewarded or punished for what we alone have done or failed to do, but for that we are certainly going to be rewarded or punished: in a word, 'that no bearer of burdens can bear the burden of another; that man can have nothing but what *he* strives for; that (the fruit of) his striving will soon come in sight: then will he be rewarded with a reward complete; that to thy Lord is the final Goal . . .' [53:38-42]. 'Every soul will be (held) in pledge for *its* deeds, except the Companions of the Right Hand . . .' [74:38-39]. And so on.

God specifies a long list of transgressions, and an equally long list of acts that the individual must do. And when the individual departs from doing the prescribed thing, even when God explicitly declares that it is He who made the individual commit that transgression—for instance, not join the righteous battle, or desert the battlefield, or join others to Him—He maintains, 'It was not We that wronged them: they wronged their own souls . . .' [for instance, 11:101-04].

When doing so will help paste responsibility on some particular group, God makes a vital distinction: *'their souls'* were convinced that they should heed His Signs, He says, yet *'they'* rejected them—'And they rejected those Signs in iniquity and arrogance, though their souls were convinced thereof: so see what was the end of those who acted corruptly!' [27:14].

The same inference—namely, that the individual is the one who is responsible—is driven in from other angles. We sent you a Warner, God says, and We gave you enough time to heed our Signs; *you* did not heed them. So, now, suffer the consequences [35:36-37]. We summon, God says. The believers exclaim, 'We hear and we obey,' and come rushing. The unbelievers, the ones with a disease in their hearts—we will hear much more about this disease in a moment—decline. Do they doubt the summons? Or are they in fear that We will deal unfairly with them? God asks. In either event, 'It is *they themselves* who do wrong' [24:48-51].

The implication is the same when God says that He never

changes the condition of men until they themselves change what is in their hearts, namely, that what is in their hearts is of their own doing, that whether to change that or not is a matter for their own volition, and changing it also is within their own capacity [for instance, 8:53; 13:11]. Similarly, God assures that He will *not* mislead people once He has guided them [for instance, 9:115]. The inference is ineluctable: if, after He has guided them, they go astray, they do so of their own accord and out of their own perversity.

The lapse is a major one in the case of believers. God says time and again that He has blotted out all evil from them [for instance, 29:7]. Clearly then, if, even after all evil has been blotted out from him, the believer does wrong, he is the one who is responsible. Why and how he does evil even though all evil has been blotted out from him is, of course, not explained.

On occasion it seems that there is something inherent in man's nature, and something inevitable in his circumstances that propels him to evil:

17:11: The prayer that man should make for good, he maketh for evil; for man is given to hasty (deeds).

And again,

16:36: For We assuredly sent amongst every People an apostle, (with the Command), 'Serve God, and eschew Evil': of the People were some whom God guided, and some on whom error became inevitably (established) . . .

Sometimes though, there is a tiny step towards culpability— God acknowledges that He does a bit, rather that He does *not* do what He could, that He holds back and does not prevent the individual from doing what is wrong and thereby falling into an abyss:

7:175: Relate to them the story of the man to whom We sent Our Signs, but he passed them by: so Satan followed him up, and he went astray.

7:176: If it had been Our will, We should have elevated him with Our signs; but he inclined to the earth, and followed his own vain desires. His similitude is that of a dog: if you attack him, he lolls out his tongue, or if you leave him alone, he (still) lolls out his tongue. That is the similitude of those who reject Our Signs; so relate the story; perchance they may reflect.

THE EXTREME CASE

We can catch hold of the thread of each of these instances, follow it and determine who actually is to blame for the wrong that the individual does, and, therefore, for the consequences that befall him. Much of the answer follows from what we have already been taught about the attributes of God—that He has power to do everything, that He knows everything even before it happens, that He knows the innermost thoughts and intentions of everyone even before the person knows them, that Satan works under His authority and by His leave . . . To put the answer beyond doubt, however, we can skip to the extreme case.

As we have seen earlier, while God is prepared to pardon every other transgression, the one sin for which He never forgives anyone is that of revering any entity besides Him. This sin sometimes takes ancillary forms—of not acknowledging His Signs; of denying that there is an afterlife, and Hell: both of which—Hell and the afterlife—are strictly necessary to make people surrender to His Will and Message.

The question that can, therefore, pinpoint culpability is this: why is it that, even after God has admonished them so many, many times, and that too so very clearly; why is that even after He has threatened them with such dire consequences; why is that even though He has sent them His Message and messengers ever so often, why is it that these unbelievers still do not believe?

God sets the answer out repeatedly throughout His Book. The answer is twofold:

- ❑ They do not believe because there is 'a disease in their hearts';
- ❑ And He—that is, God—is the One who has planted that disease in their hearts.

As *I* have planted the disease in their hearts, He tells His Messenger time and again, and yet again; as *I* have made them blind; as *I* have made them deaf; as *I* have put yokes around their necks so that they just cannot lower their necks to look, there is nothing that even you can do to make them heed My Message and My Signs.

Scores and scores of declarations of God can be cited. And they should all be read—if for no other reason then so that God does not escape by claiming, as so many of His followers invariably attempt to do, that this is just some one-off comment that is being 'torn out of context'. It is an affirmation that is put beyond all reasonable doubt—by reiteration if nothing else. And as you read each successive reiteration, ask, 'If some run-of-the-mill, ordinary don had said as much, would his mere agent who pulled the trigger be held responsible for the crime?'

Here then are just a few of the affirmations as stated by God Himself and recorded in His Book itself:

2:6: As to those who reject Faith, it is the same to them whether thou warn them or do not warn them; they will not believe.

2:7: God hath set a seal on their hearts and on their hearing, and on their eyes is a veil; great is the penalty they (incur).

2:10: In their hearts is a disease; *and God has increased their disease:* And grievous is the penalty they (incur), because they are false (to themselves).

2:17: Their similitude is that of a man who kindled a fire; when it lighted all around him, *God took away their light and left them in utter darkness.* So they could not see.

2:18: Deaf, dumb, and blind, they will not return (to the path).

4:168: Those who reject Faith and do wrong, *God will not forgive them nor guide them to any way—*

4:169: Except the way of Hell, to dwell therein for ever. And this to God is easy.

5:41: O Messenger, let not those grieve thee, who race each other into unbelief: (whether it be) among those who say 'We believe' with their lips but whose hearts have no faith; or it be among the Jews—men who will listen to any lie—will listen even to others who have never so much as come to thee. They change the words from their (right) times and places: they say, 'If ye are given this, take it, but if not, beware!' *If any one's trial is intended by God, thou hast no authority in the least for him against God. For such—it is not God's will to purify their hearts.* For them there is disgrace in this world, and in the Hereafter a heavy punishment.

6:25: Of them there are some who (pretend to) listen to thee; but *We have thrown veils on their hearts, so they understand it not, and deafness in their ears;* if they saw every one of the Signs, not they will believe in them; in so much that when they come to thee, they (but) dispute with thee; the Unbelievers say: 'These are nothing but tales of the ancients.'

6:113: To such (deceit) let the hearts of those incline, who have no faith in the Hereafter: let them delight in it, and let them earn from it what they may.

6:125: Those whom God (in His plan) willeth to guide—He openeth their breast to [the true religion]; those whom He willeth to leave straying— He maketh their breast close and constricted, as if they had to climb up to the skies: thus doth God (heap) the penalty on those who refuse to believe.

6:137: Even so, in the eyes of most of the pagans, their 'partners' made alluring the slaughter of their children, in order to lead them to their own destruction, and cause confusion in their religion. *If God had willed, they would not have done so:* but leave alone them and their inventions.

13:33: Is then He who standeth over every soul (and knoweth) all that it doth (like any others)? And yet they ascribe partners to God. Say: 'But name them! is it that ye will inform Him of something he knoweth not on earth, or is it (just) a show of words?' Nay! to those who believe not, their pretence seems pleasing, but they are kept back (thereby) from the path. *And those whom God leaves to stray, no one can guide.*

13:34: For them is a penalty in the life of this world, but harder, truly, is the penalty of the Hereafter: and defender have they none against God.

17:97: It is he whom God guides, that is on true Guidance; *but he whom He leaves astray—for such wilt thou find no protector besides Him.* On the Day of Judgement We shall gather them together, prone on their faces, blind, dumb, and deaf: their abode will be Hell: every time it shows abatement, We shall increase for them the fierceness of the Fire.

17:98: That is their recompense, because they rejected Our Signs, and said, 'When we are reduced to bones and broken dust, should we really be raised up (to be) a new Creation?'

18:57: And who doth more wrong than one who is reminded of the Signs of his Lord, but turns away from them, forgetting the (deeds) which his hands have sent forth? *Verily We have set veils over their hearts lest they should understand this, and over their ears, deafness. If thou callest them to guidance, even then will they never accept guidance.*

19:83: Seest thou not that *We* have set the Evil Ones on against the unbelievers, to incite them with fury?

27:4: As to those who believe not in the Hereafter, *We have made their deeds pleasing in their eyes; and so they wander about in distraction.*

27:5: Such are they for whom a grievous Penalty is (waiting); and in the Hereafter theirs will be the greatest loss.

30:59: Thus does *God seal up the hearts of those who understand not.*

31:23: But if any reject Faith, let not his rejection grieve thee: to Us is their return, and We shall tell them the truth of their deeds: for God knows well all that is in (men's) hearts.

31:24: We grant them their pleasure for a little while: in the end shall We drive them to a chastisement unrelenting.

33:64: Verily *God has cursed the Unbelievers and prepared for them a Blazing Fire,*

33:65: To dwell therein for ever: no protector will they find, nor helper.

36:8: *We have put yokes round their necks right up to their chins,* so that their heads are forced up (and they cannot see).

36:9: And *We have put a bar in front of them and a bar behind them,* and further, *We have covered them up;* so that they cannot see.

36:10: The same is it to them whether thou admonish them or thou do not admonish them: they will not believe.

40:74: 'In derogation of God.' They will reply: 'They have left us in the lurch: Nay, we invoked not, of old, anything (that had real existence).' *Thus does God leave the Unbelievers to stray.*

42:44: For any whom God leaves astray, there is no protector Hereafter. And thou wilt see the wrongdoers, when in sight of the Penalty, Say: 'Is there any way (to effect) a return?'

42:46: And no protectors have they to help them, other than God. And *for any whom God leaves to stray, there is no way (to the Goal).*

47:23: Such are the men whom God has cursed for He has made them deaf and blinded their sight . . .

74:31: And We have set none but angels as Guardians of the Fire; and We have fixed their number only as a trial for Unbelievers, in order that the People of the Book may arrive at certainty, and the Believers may increase in Faith, and that no doubts may be left for the People of the Book and the Believers, and that those in whose hearts is a disease and the Unbelievers may say, 'What symbol doth God intend by this?' *Thus doth God leave to stray whom He pleaseth, and guide whom He pleaseth: and none can know the forces of thy Lord, except He and this is no other than a warning to mankind.*

And God affirms this many, many times more. As He puts it:

10:99: If it had been thy Lord's will, they would all have believed, all who are on earth! wilt thou then compel mankind, against their will, to believe!

10:100: No soul can believe, *except by the will of God,* and He will place doubt (or obscurity) on those who will not understand.

In another typical acknowledgement:

6:112: Likewise did We make for every Messenger an enemy, evil ones among men and jinns, inspiring each other with flowery discourses by way of deception. If thy Lord had so planned, they would not have done it: so leave them and their inventions alone.

6:113: To such (deceit) let the hearts of those incline, who have no faith in the Hereafter: let them delight in it, and let them earn from it what they may.

Who then is responsible? The one who has committed the one sin that cannot be pardoned? Or the One who so blinded and deafened him that he could not but commit that sin? The one who does not believe or the One who has made sure that he will never heed? The one who opposes a Messenger or the One who Himself acknowledges, 'Likewise did We make for every Messenger an enemy . . .' ?

Nor is it just that He puts a veil across the eyes of the unbelievers. He actively sets persons among them to mislead them. Thus, to cite just one instance,

6:122: Can he who was dead, to whom We gave life, and a light whereby he can walk amongst men, be like him who is in the depths of darkness, from which he can never come out? Thus to those without faith their own deeds seem pleasing.

6:123: Thus have We placed leaders in every town, its wicked men, to plot (and burrow) therein: but they only plot against their own souls, and they perceive it not.

6:124: When there comes to them a Sign (from God), They say: 'We shall not believe until we receive one (exactly) like those received by God's apostles.' God knoweth best where (and how) to carry out His mission. Soon will the wicked be overtaken by humiliation before God, and a severe punishment, for all their plots.

God places wicked leaders among men to plot and mislead. And then punishes them because they have been misled and have plotted!

In exactly the same way, consider what God Himself says about the cruelties of the Pharaoh and the Egyptians, and ask, 'Who is responsible?'

On His own telling, God deliberately hardens the heart of the Pharaoh so that the Egyptian ruler will inflict extreme cruelties on the Jews, and so that their slavery is prolonged. He hardens the heart still more so that the Pharaoh will not let the Jews go. Why?

You go back to Egypt and do all the wonders before the Pharaoh which I have equipped you to do, God tells His prophet in the parallel scripture. 'But I will harden his heart,' God tells him, *'so that he will not let the people go.'* 'Go in to Pharaoh,' God tells His prophet, 'for I have hardened his heart and the hearts of his servants, *that I may show these signs of Mine before him, and that you may tell in the hearing of your son and your son's son the mighty things I have done in Egypt, and My signs which I have done among them, that you may know that I am the Lord.'* And then God hardens the hearts of the Egyptians so that they will plunge into the sea chasing the Jews—where God will get the opportunity to drown them and thus 'I will gain honour over Pharaoh and over all his army, his chariots, and his horsemen. Then the Egyptians will know I am the Lord, when I have gained honour for Myself over Pharaoh, his chariots, and his horsemen.'[1] Such devious plotting, and prolonging the suffering of people devoted to Him alone—just so that He can show the Egyptians who is boss. And the thing of it is that, even now, millennia later, most of the Egyptians have not seen the light!

FREE WILL?

But has man not been endowed with free will? Is he not free to believe or disbelieve? And, thus, is he not accountable for committing the cardinal crime when he does not believe? The Book provides the conclusive answer. Yes, man can believe or not believe, it proclaims, *but . . .*

> *74:49:* Then what is the matter with them that they turn away from admonition?
> *74:50:* As if they were affrighted asses,
> *74:51:* Fleeing from a lion!
> *74:52:* Forsooth, each one of them wants to be given scrolls (of revelation) spread out!

---

[1] 4.20, 10.1-2, 14.14-18 in the second book of that Scripture.

> 74:53: By no means! But they fear not the Hereafter,
> 74:54: Nay, this surely is an admonition:
> 74:55: Let any who will, keep it in remembrance!
> 74:56: *But none will keep it in remembrance except as God wills:* He is the Lord of Righteousness, and the Lord of Forgiveness.
> 76:27: As to these, they love the fleeting life, and put away behind them a Day (that will be) hard.
> 76:28: It is We who created them, and We have made their joints strong; but, when We will, We can substitute the like of them by a complete change.
> 76:29: *This is an admonition: Whosoever will, let him take a (straight) Path to his Lord.*
> 76:30: *But ye will not, except as God wills;* for God is full of Knowledge and Wisdom.
> 76:31: He will admit to His Mercy whom He will; But the wrongdoers, for them has He prepared a grievous Penalty.

Strange, to say the least. He grants you free will—except that you will not will other than what He wills you to will. He prevents people from doing right, and then prepares a 'grievous penalty' for them for not doing right!

And again, after assuring the people that the Messenger amidst them has indeed been sent by Him, and that the Message he is delivering is indeed the Message that He, God, intends for them, God asks, as if in surprise, 'When whither go ye?', and answers:

> 81:27: Verily this is no less than a Message to (all) the Worlds:
> 81:28: (With profit) to whoever among you wills to go straight:
> 81:29: *But ye shall not will except as God wills,* the Cherisher of the Worlds.

The believer, of course, sees great wisdom in this arrangement. Had God not given man free will, he reasons, had God made everyone a believer to begin with as He certainly had the power to do, coming to believe would not have been an attainment. By leaving the option to man, God has made it possible for him to earn the reward. But naturally, as God is the One who has the ultimate and overriding Power, the will of man is necessarily subject to the Will of God . . . God retains the ultimate Power but, as for the ultimate responsibility, He delegates that to man! And so that some select ones—selected by God 'as He wills'—may earn the great boon through attainment, countless others must suffer the torments of Hell forever.

And the believer is satisfied with such an explanation. Were he to doubt, he would be an unbeliever 'for whom is the grievous penalty'!

NOR IS IT JUST THAT THE UNBELIEVERS DO NOT BELIEVE

But, God has so designed affairs that it isn't just that unbelievers do not believe in Him, that they deny the Hereafter, that they deny there are Hell and its fierce tortures in wait for them. God has made them perfidious in the extreme. To recall just one of His warnings to the faithful:

> 3:118: O ye who believe! Take not into your intimacy those outside your ranks: They will not fail to corrupt you. They only desire your ruin: Rank hatred has already appeared from their mouths: What their hearts conceal is far worse. We have made plain to you the Signs, if ye have wisdom.
>
> 3:119: Ah! ye are those who love them, but they love you not, though ye believe in the whole of the Book. When they meet you, they say, 'We believe': But when they are alone, they bite off the very tips of their fingers at you in their rage. Say: 'Perish in your rage; God knoweth well all the secrets of the heart.'
>
> 3:120: If aught that is good befalls you, it grieves them; but if some misfortune overtakes you, they rejoice at it. But if ye are constant and do right, not the least harm will their cunning do to you; for God Compasseth round about all that they do.

Consider two incidental questions before we proceed. Could it be that only the primary defect—of not believing—

has been planted in them by God, and not these subsidiary/ consequential traits? Second, has He implanted these subsidiary/consequential traits and does He list them in His Book so that believers fight unbelievers all the more zealously? For that is the instrument—the hatred and suspicion and passionate hostility of believers towards unbelievers—by which He spreads His empire on earth.

ALL FOR A PURPOSE

Nor is any of this done inadvertently. God plants the disease for a purpose, and He states the purpose again and again— the stated purpose varies with the occasion, but there always is a purpose.

Sometimes the purpose is to strengthen the faith of the believers, and to provide yet another occasion for the unbelievers to harbour and express their faithlessness:

> 74:31: And We have set none but angels as Guardians of the Fire; and We have fixed their number *only as a trial for Unbelievers, in order that the People of the Book may arrive at certainty, and the Believers may increase in Faith, and that no doubts may be left for the People of the Book and the Believers, and that those in whose hearts is a disease and the Unbelievers may say, 'What symbol doth God intend by this?'* Thus doth God leave to stray whom He pleaseth, and guide whom He pleaseth: and none can know the forces of thy Lord, except He and this is no other than a warning to mankind.

Sometimes, having made persons blind so that they will just not see His Signs, having made them deaf so that they just will not hear His Message, God puts them in the way of the faithful—to test the latter. How far will those devoted to Me go? He wonders. Will they put these deniers out—fully and finally—or will they demur? Will My devotees fight and slaughter to the bitter end, or will some of them desert midway? In a word, as He puts the matter, He tests some by others:

47:4: Therefore, when ye meet the Unbelievers (in fight), smite at their necks; At length, when ye have thoroughly subdued them, bind a bond firmly (on them): Hereafter (is the time for) either generosity or ransom: Until the war lays down its burdens. Thus (are ye commanded): *but if it had been God's Will, He could certainly have exacted retribution from them (Himself); but (He lets you fight) in order to test you, some with others.* But those who are slain in the Way of God, He will never let their deeds be lost.

THE TEST CASE

Here then is the test case—the one crime for which there is no forgiveness:

- ❏ God, Himself, and directly, ensures that some— indeed, the majority of mankind—will commit that crime;
- ❏ He then holds the hapless individuals responsible for it;
- ❏ And punishes them with the never-to-end tortures of Hell and its Fire.

Sounds less than just? Less than what a compassionate one would do? But that is what faith is all about. Who would have difficulty in venerating the One who is obviously beneficent? Who would have difficulty in believing what is manifestly true? But you love God truly only when you know for certain that He is being cruel! You believe in Him truly only when all evidence points the other way!

THE DIVISION OF LABOUR

Hence, we must believe that all good is from Him:

16:52: To Him belongs whatever is in the heavens and on earth, and to Him is duty due always: then will ye fear other than God?
16:53: *And ye have no good thing but is from God:* and moreover, when ye are touched by distress, unto Him ye cry with groans;
16:54: Yet, when He removes the distress from you, behold! some of you turn to other gods to join with their Lord—

16:55: (As if) to show their ingratitude for the favours We have bestowed on them! Then enjoy (your brief day): but soon will ye know (your folly)!

And all misfortune is because of us:

42:30: Whatever misfortune happens to you, is because of the things your hands have wrought, and for many (of them) He grants forgiveness.

Proof definite that the author of the Book is God. Who else could have conjured up a doctrine so convenient to Him?

THE SOVEREIGN REMEDY

But how is one to bring oneself to believe all this? The way to do so is not to reason. Not to ask too many questions! Think of His bounties, we are told, not of His reasons, not of His essence:

5:101: O ye who believe! Ask not questions about things which, if made plain to you, may cause you trouble. But if ye ask about things when the [Book] is being revealed, they will be made plain to you, God will forgive those: for God is Oft-forgiving, Most Forbearing.

5:102: Some people before you did ask such questions, and on that account lost their faith.

A LITTLE EXERCISE BEFORE WE PROCEED

Now, the religious authorities would be perfectly in order were they stressing that the quest for the Ultimate Truth is not a matter of reasoning, not one in which ratiocination is to be the touchstone. It is not even an exercise of the mind—the mind taken in a more comprehensive sense; that is, not just its reasoning faculty but one including emotions and other mental means of perception. The search is a spiritual exercise. Some teachers may indeed mean this when they cite such passages. But ever so often, the passages are deployed to put an end to the searching question, to shut out reason altogether.

The question is: does our assessment of the proposition—that it is unreasonable to shut out reason by such peremptory diktat—change once we get to know which text directs us to shut reason out? That it is the Quran, say, rather than the Old Testament?

As an exercise, consider the following dialogue between one of the greatest seers of a tradition, and his equally percipient interlocutor.

> The great sage has just explained that 'all this here is woven, like warp and woof, on water.' The interlocutor asks, then in what is water woven, warp and woof?
> On wind.
> Then on what is wind woven, warp and woof?
> On the worlds of the sky.
> Then on what are the worlds of the sky woven, warp and woof?
> On the world of [a particular class of deities].
> Then on what is the world of [that class of deities] woven, warp and woof?
> On the worlds of the sun.
> Then on what are the worlds of the sun woven, warp and woof?
> On the worlds of the moon.
> Then on what are the worlds of the moon woven, warp and woof?
> On the worlds of the stars.
> Then on what are the worlds of the stars woven, warp and woof?
> On the worlds of gods.
> Then on what are the worlds of the gods woven, warp and woof?
> On the worlds of [a much greater deity].
> Then on what are the worlds of [that great deity] woven, warp and woof?
> On the worlds of [an even more encompassing deity].
> Then on what are the worlds of [that even more encompassing deity] woven, warp and woof?
> On the worlds of [the all-encompassing deity, the ground of all being].

Then on what are the worlds of [that all-encompassing deity, that ground of all being] woven, warp and woof?

The great sage remonstrates, '[the name of the interlocutor] do not question too much lest your head fall off. Verily, you are questioning too much about a divinity about which we are not to ask too much. Do not O [the name of the interlocutor], question too much.'

Thereupon, the text tells us, '[the interlocutor] held her peace/kept silent.'

Does it, indeed *should* it make any difference to the veracity of the proposition—'do not question too much lest your head fall off'—when we learn that the text is not the Quran or the Old Testament but the *Brihadaranyaka Upanishad*?[2] That the sage is not some Muslim or Christian cleric but Yajnavalkya? That the intrepid interlocutor is not some obstinate undergraduate but Gargi herself?

In fairness, and just to get the answer straight: Gargi might have fallen silent at that moment. But she does not remain silent for long. And the texts in question—the Upanishads—are based on incessant and endless questioning.

---

[2] *Brihadaranyaka Upanishad*, III.6.

4

Are these *'explanations'* ?

In the reckoning of God Himself, Job is 'a blameless and upright man, who fears God and shuns evil', so much so that God declares 'there is none like him on the earth.'[1]

Satan tells God that Job is virtuous only because You, God, have been good to him. Were any misfortune to befall Job, Satan says, God will Himself see how he, Job, will blame and curse Him for it.[2]

God allows Satan to inflict what he will on Job's possessions. But do not lay hand on Job's person, God says.

Pause right here for a moment. Why has God agreed to have Job lose his possessions, and, as we see immediately, so much more? Just because Satan has taunted Him and cast doubt on the devotion of a humble person, of 'a blameless and upright man' so dedicated to Him that 'there is none like him on the earth'.

Wouldn't you expect an All-knowing, compassionate God to find some other way to shut Satan up? In any case, why would He need to prove a point to Satan?

As for satisfying Himself, as God knows everything and the innermost being of everybody, doesn't He know in advance whether Job will or will not curse Him were sufferings to be rained down on him?

Satan jumps at the opportunity. The oxen, sheep, camels, servants as well as Job's sons and daughters are killed.[3]

---

[1] *The Book of Job*, 1.8. Unless otherwise indicated, references in this chapter up to page 131 are to *The Book of Job*.

[2] 1.9-10.

[3] 1.12-19

Pause again for a moment. What would you think of a father who allows severe pain and trauma and death to be inflicted on his children just because a neighbour has cast doubt on their devotion to him?

And there is the pain and suffering of the children and the livestock too. What wrong have they done that they should lose their very lives as 'collateral damage'? They are not the ones whom Satan is putting to the test. They are not the ones who are to gain anything whether God's premise turns out to be right or wrong.

Job is driven to grief. He tears up his robe. He shaves off his head. He collapses on to the ground. Even so Job exclaims:

Naked I came from my mother's womb
And naked shall I return there.
The Lord gave, and the Lord has taken away;
Blessed be the name of the Lord.[4]

At this, we are told: 'In all this Job did not sin nor charge God with wrong.'[5]

Satan now tells God, but wait till pain and suffering touch Job's own person. He will curse You then. God allows Satan to inflict pain and torment on Job's person, saying only that he should not take Job's life. Satan rushes to inflict the severest pain and distress with relish. He inflicts on Job 'painful boils from the sole of his foot to the crown of his head'. Job's wife taunts him—Do you still hold to your faith in God? In spite of the pain, Job still says, 'Shall we indeed accept good from God, and shall we not accept adversity?'

'In all this Job did not sin with his lips,' we are told.[6]

Three friends of Job hear of the troubles that have befallen him. They come to sympathize and console.

---

[4] 1.20.
[5] 1.22.
[6] 2.1-10.

So disfigured is he with the boils and eruptions that they do not recognize him.[7]

Job curses the day he was born. In such pain is he that he wishes that he had died at birth.[8]

The first friend acknowledges the extreme suffering that has befallen Job. He acknowledges that Job has been good in every way—that he has helped the weak, that he has guided those who did not know, that he has upheld those who stumbled. But, says the friend, and this is the first explanation that is proffered for the suffering that befalls the virtuous:

> Remember now, whoever perished being innocent?
> Or where were the upright ever cut off?
> Even as I have seen,
> Those who plow iniquity
> And sow trouble reap the same.
> By the blast of God they perish,
> And by the breath of His anger they are consumed.[9]

Are these assertions true even as fact? Have the innocent not perished? Have the upright not been cut off for no reason? Do those who inflict iniquity on others—starting with God Himself—reap the troubles they sow? Are they actually made to perish and be consumed?

This is 'explanation' by definition. The implication of what the friend is saying is that Job *must have been* iniquitous and sown trouble and therefore these sufferings have come upon him. This must be the case, the friend reasons. For

> Can a mortal be more righteous than God?
> Can a man be more pure than his Maker?[10]

But the record of God's deeds as set out in the other Books

---

[7] 2.11-13.
[8] 3.1-26.
[9] 4.7-9.
[10] 4.17.

of the Bible itself leads to but one answer: a most emphatic, 'Yes, many, many mere mortals have certainly been more righteous than God.' The friends, however, stick to their proof-by-definition:

> For affliction does not come from the dust;
> Nor does trouble spring from the ground;
> Yet man is born to trouble.
> As the sparks fly upwards.[11]

In the last two lines, we have the second 'explanation': suffering is inherent in the very fact of being born a man. Our ordinary experience tells us that that is indeed the case, just as joy is inherent in the very fact of being born a man. But that certainly does not explain why the All-powerful, All-knowing, compassionate God makes suffering an inherent ingredient of being born.

'But', says the friend, 'as for me, I would seek God, and to God I would commit my cause:

> Who does great things, and
> unsearchable,
> Marvellous things without number . . .[12]

Here we have the third and fourth 'explanations'. As He does great and marvellous things, we must trust Him, we must be in awe of Him. Therefore, we must not dare to doubt Him. Fourth, as what He does is 'unsearchable'—that is, as it is beyond our understanding—we must believe that, when He inflicts suffering on us, He must have good reason to do so.

And then comes the fifth reason for suffering:

> Behold, happy is the man whom God corrects;
> Therefore do not despise the chastening of the Almighty.

---

[11] 5.6-7.
[12] 5.8-9.

> For the bruises, but He binds up;
> He wounds, but His hands make whole.[13]

That is, be happy for God has chosen you—to be improved. And while you are in pain at the moment, God will heal the wounds which He has inflicted.

Job wails: the unbearable pain he is in; the troubles that have befallen him—the death of his children, for one. He moans about the scorn in which he is now held. If only God would crush me, he exclaims in agony; if only He would cut me off completely and kill me. His flesh is 'caked with worms and dust', he groans, 'my skin is cracked and breaks out afresh.'[14] ' . . . So that my soul chooses strangling and death rather than my body. I loathe my life . . .'[15] He recalls how he has served and helped all, that he has never bargained with God or man for any favour[16] and yet . . .

His second friend answers:

> Does God subvert judgement?
> Or does the Almighty prevent justice?

We are back to the 'by-definition' explanation. As God, by definition, does not subvert what is due, as He does not, by definition, prevent justice, the afflictions that have come upon you, *must have* a reason.

> If your sons have sinned against Him,
> He has cast them away for their transgression.[17]

But how do we know that Job's sons have sinned against God? From the fact that He has cast them away! And what about the poor daughters, and all those camels and oxen and sheep and servants?

---

[13] 5.17-18.
[14] 7.5.
[15] 7.9
[16] 6.22-23.
[17] 8.3-4.

We come now to the next 'explanation-cum-cure'.

If you would earnestly seek God
And make your supplication to the Almighty,
If you were pure and upright
Surely now He would awake for you
And prosper your dwelling place . . .[18]

The inference is direct and immediate. As He has not turned to ease your suffering, as He has not turned to make your home prosperous,

❑ *you* are not earnestly seeking Him;
❑ *you* are not pure and upright.

For those who 'forget God' shall perish.[19]

Instead of explaining the reasons on account of which the victim has been subjected to such torment in the first place, the Book dangles a *subz baagh* that lies in wait for the poor fellow—albeit in the indefinite future:

Behold, God will not cast away the blameless
Nor will He uphold the evildoers.
He will yet fill your mouth with laughing,
And your lips with rejoicing.
Those who hate you will be clothed with shame,
And the dwelling place of the wicked will come to nothing.[20]

Job is humility personified. 'God is wise in heart and mighty in strength,'[21] he declares, and enumerates the many marks of God's might as well as the splendours He has wrought: His mighty blows, the heavens He has created . . . In view of such might and works, Job resigns himself,

How then can I answer Him,
And choose my words to reason with Him?

---

[18] 8.5-6.
[19] 8.13.
[20] 8.20-22.
[21] 9.4

> For though I were righteous, I could not answer Him;
> I would beg mercy of my Judge . . .[22]

'If it is a matter of strength indeed He is strong,' Job reminds himself. 'And if of justice, who will appoint my day in Court?' he asks.[23]

Job points to the obvious fact—the fact that stares us every day in the face, the fact that is counter to the assertions of his friends—the innocent suffer, the wicked prosper, by *God's* hand: 'If it is not He, who else could it be?' Job inquires.[24]

He has no intention of contesting God's verdict, Job says. He will merely ask God

> Do not condemn me;
> I will say to God, show me why You contend with me.
> Does it seem good to You that you should oppress,
> That you should despise the work of Your hands
> And smile on the counsel of the wicked?[25]

That is a telling point: on the say-so of theistic religions, after all, man has been made by God Himself. Not just that. God has made man in His own image.

> Your hands have made me and fashioned me
> An intricate unity:
> Yet You would destroy me.[26]

'Why then have You brought me out of the womb?' Job beseeches God.[27]

Job's third friend steps in. He cannot talk away the suffering that has been inflicted on Job. That suffering is as manifest as it is extreme. Yet, he says, God is merciful:

---

[22] 9.14-16.
[23] 9.19-20.
[24] 9.24.
[25] 10.1-3.
[26] 10.8.
[27] 10.18.

> Know therefore that God exacts from you
> Less than your iniquity deserves.[28]

But this too is just an assertion, an after-the-fact assertion. How do we know that Job deserves even crueller punishment? Has God Himself not testified to the contrary? Has He not acknowledged at the very outset that Job is 'a blameless and upright man, who fears God and shuns evil'? Has He not pronounced that 'there is none like him on the earth'?

The friend falls back on the usual, 'God's ways are mysterious, they are beyond our reach.'

> Can you search out the deep things of God?
> The limits of the Almighty?
> They are higher than heaven—what can you do?
> Deeper than She'ol—what can you know?
> Their measure is longer than the earth
> And broader than the sea.[29]

We are now back to the argument, 'As He is so mighty, so lofty, we cannot, therefore we *should not* try to fathom His reasons.' Is this an explanation? Or a ban on striving for an explanation?

Job acknowledges that everything is in and by God's hand.

> In whose hand is the life of every living thing,
> And the breath of all mankind?[30]
> With Him are wisdom and strength
> He has counsel and understanding . . .[31]
> With Him are strength and prudence . . .[32]

Even so, innocent and trusting in God as he is, Job tells his friends:

---

[28] 11.6
[29] 11.7-9.
[30] 12.10.
[31] 12.13.
[32] 12.16.

> Though He slay me, yet I will trust Him.
> Even so, I will defend my own ways before Him.[33]

That last affirmation—though it springs from Job's faith in God, from his unyielding faith that God *is* just—is what will soon be held against Job. That he thinks he can defend himself, it will be said, shows that he thinks what has befallen him at God's Hand is not just.

But the innocent Job is confident. 'He also shall be my salvation,' he says. 'For a hypocrite could not come before Him.'[34]

Job asks of God:

> How many are my iniquities and sins?
> Make me know my transgression and my sin.
> Why do you hide Your face,
> And regard me as Your enemy?

Does it behoove You who are Almighty?

> Will You frighten a leaf driven to and fro?
> And will You pursue dry stubble?[35]

His friend admonishes Job for remonstrating 'with empty knowledge', for reasoning 'with unprofitable talk'.[36]

> Yes, you cast off fear,
> And restrain prayer before God.
> For your iniquity teaches your mouth.
> And you choose the tongue of the crafty.
> Your own mouth condemns you, not I.
> Yes, your own lips testify against you.[37]

But what has Job done to cause offence? May a victim not inquire, what are my transgressions? May the helpless not

---

[33] 13.15.
[34] 13.16.
[35] 13.23-25.
[36] 15.2-3.
[37] 15.4-6.

wonder, does it behoove You who are the mightiest of all to 'frighten a leaf driven to and fro'? Yet, as we shall see, this is the refrain which will soon be made specific and be converted into a charge.

The friend continues:

> Are you the first man who was born?
> Or were you made before the hills?
> Have you heard the counsel of God?

The answer is, 'No'. But how does the fact that others had been born before Job, that Job is not older than the hills, that he has not indeed received any direct revelation from God— how does any of this answer Job's question? The friend is not done. He demands:

> Do you limit wisdom to yourself?

If Job says 'No, I certainly do not think that I am the only one who has wisdom,' the conclusion will be, 'So, how do you know that others may not have the answer, how do you presume that there is no answer?' If Job says, 'Yes, I do think I have a point here that others may or may not have,' he will be condemned for conceit, arrogance, pride. The friend asks:

> What do you know that we do not know?
> What do you understand that is not in us?[38]

'Both the gray-haired and aged are among us,' the friend continues, 'Much older than your father.'[39] So what? What is their answer to Job's questions?

Next,

> Are the consolations of God too small for you
> And the word spoken gently with you?[40]

---

[38] 15.7-9.
[39] 15.10.
[40] 15.11.

Again, damned if you do, and damned if you don't. If Job answers 'No, they are *not* too small for me,' the conclusion immediately is, 'In that case, you shouldn't be asking questions of God.' If he answers, 'Yes, compared to what has been inflicted on me without any cause, they *are* small,' the charge immediately becomes, 'That answer itself shows that you are one of little faith, and, therefore deserve severe punishment.' The friend is now accusatory:

> Why does your heart carry you away;
> And what do your eyes wink at;
> That you turn your spirit against God
> And let such words go out of your mouth?[41]

The pain that is wracking his body, the death of his children should not affect his heart!

To ask simple, obvious questions is to 'turn your spirit against God'!

Then, just as God is just by definition, man is impure by definition:

> What is man, that he could be pure?
> And he who is born of a woman, that he could be righteous?[42]

This after God Himself has said at the outset that Job is 'blameless and upright', that he shuns evil, that there is none like him on earth! The friend is undeterred:

> If God puts no trust in saints
> And the heavens are not pure in his sight,
> How much less man, who is abominable and filthy, . . .

Why did God, making man in His own image, make him 'abominable and filthy'?

> Who drinks iniquity like water![43]

---

[41] 15.12-13.
[42] 15.14.
[43] 15.15.

Job is beset:

> Though I speak, my grief is not relieved;
> And if I remain silent, how am I eased?[44]

He describes his condition in harrowing passages:

> ... I have sewn sackcloth over my skin,
> And laid my head in the dust.
> My face is flushed from weeping,
> And on my eyelids is the shadow of death,
> Although no violence is in my hands
> And my prayer is pure.[45]

The friend taunts him:

> You who tear yourself in anger,
> Shall the earth be forsaken for you?

Job's wail-in-pain is dubbed 'anger'. And when has Job said that the earth should be forsaken for him? On the contrary, all—including God—acknowledge that Job is the one who puts himself out for others.

> Or shall the rock be removed from its place?[46]

In a word, God has laid out a particular order for the world. Is this entire order to be forsaken and overturned just for an individual? But that is precisely the question. Why has God, while decreeing His order, provided for such enormous suffering to be visited upon the innocent?

If you persist, warns the friend, a string of calamities leading to complete extinction shall be visited upon you. Job pleads and pleads that they not add to his misery with hurtful words, that all he is praying for is justice . . . The friend remonstrates,

---

[44] 16.6.
[45] 16.15-17.
[46] 18.4.

> Did you not know this of old,
> Since man was placed on earth,
> That the triumphing of the wicked is short,
> And the joy of the hypocrite is but for a moment?[47]

Which we can take as a consolation—if we assume Job to be blameless and truthful; or as a warning—if we assume Job to be wicked and hypocritical.

Job resumes his lament. He asks again the question for which he has not received an answer,

> Why do the wicked live and become old,
> Yes, become mighty in power?
> Their descendents are established with them in their sight,
> And their offspring before their eyes.[48]

In contrast to his own children who have been suddenly torn away to death.

The friend turns on Job: do you think God needs you? Do you think that if you are corrected and improved, God benefits?

> Can man be profitable to God,
> Though he who is wise may be profitable to himself?
> Is it any pleasure to the Almighty that you are righteous?
> Or is it gain to Him that you make your ways blameless?[49]

That is, whatever is happening to you is for *your* good, not for God's profit. In any case, you are guilty and have done all sorts of wrongs—in complete contrast to God's certificate, this friend manufactures a long list of wrongs of which, he maintains, Job is guilty.[50] God knows everything—from high heaven to every crevice of His creation.[51]

---

[47] 20.4-5.
[48] 21.7-8.
[49] 22.2-3.
[50] 22.5-11.
[51] 22.12-22.

Do you think that He does not know what you are trying to argue?

Hence, the only way for you is to submit to God:

Now acquaint yourself with Him, and be at peace
Thereby good will come to you.
Receive, please, instruction from His mouth,
And lay up His words in your heart.
If you return to the Almighty, you will be built up . . .[52]

In a word, *you* are the one who is responsible for your plight. You have not submitted yourself to Him.

Job is on the verge of collapse. He bows to the cruelties that have been heaped on him:

But He is unique, and who can make Him change?
And whatever His soul desires, that He does.
For He performs what is appointed for me . . .[53]

Yet he protests his innocence. He recalls the sins of others and observes, 'yet God does not charge them with wrong.'[54] The friend's answer simply is

Dominion and fear belong to Him;
He makes peace in His high places.[55]

That is, His ways are beyond our ken. And we are back to the argument-by-definition:

How then can man be righteous before God?
Or how can he be pure who is born of a woman?[56]

As Job is but a man, as he has been born of a woman, he *must* not be pure and righteous. And what had God Himself acknowledged about Job?

---

[52] 22.21-23.
[53] 23.13-14.
[54] 24.12.
[55] 25.2-3.
[56] 25.4.

Job recounts the help he rendered to the helpless:

Because I delivered the poor who cried out,
The fatherless and the one who had no helper.
The blessing of a perishing man came upon me,
And I caused the widow's heart to sing for joy.
I put on righteousness, and it clothed me:
My justice was like a robe and a turban.
I was eyes to the blind,
And I was feet to the lame.
I was a father to the poor,
And I searched out the case that I did not know.
I broke the fangs of the wicked,
And plucked the victim from his teeth.[57]

And he sets out what has been inflicted upon him in return.
He recalls how he is mocked by those whom he once guided.
He recalls the perfidy of the wicked, and how he has been
made into 'their taunting song; Yes, I am their byword . . .'

They abhor me, they keep far from me;
They do not hesitate to spit in my face.

Nor is the reason any mystery:

Because He has loosed my bowstring and afflicted me,
They have cast off restraint before me . . .[58]

His plight is extreme:

I go about mourning, but not in the sun;
I stand up in assembly and cry out for help.
I am a brother of jackals,
And a companion of ostriches;
My skin grows black and falls from me;
My bones burn with fever . . .[59]

---

[57] 29.12-17.
[58] 29.21-25; 30.1-11.
[59] 30.27-31.

All he prays for is justice. It isn't that he shirks condign chastisement. Job says he is prepared for whatever punishment his wrongs deserve:

> ... Let me be weighed on honest scales ...
> Then let me sow, and another eat,
> Yes, let my harvest be rooted out ...[60]

Friends now cease answering Job, and the Book summarizes what is to be the charge against Job, explaining that they have done so 'because he was righteous in his own eyes ... because he justified himself rather than God'.[61]

And then another counsellor, so to say, comes upon the scene—Elihu. He explains that *this* is the wrong of which Job is guilty: that he has tried to set the good deeds he has done against the pain that has befallen him; that he has thought and claimed and gone about recounting the good he has done.

> Look, in this you are not righteous.
> I will answer you,
> For God is greater than man.
> Why do you contend with Him?
> For He does not give an accounting of any of His words.
> For God may speak in one way, or another
> Yet man does not perceive it.[62]

That is, as God is greater than man,

- ❑ He does not have to explain what He does;
- ❑ He *must* have His reasons which man cannot perceive.

Elihu lists what he says are Job's transgressions:

---

[60] 31.6,8.
[61] 32.1-2.
[62] 33.12-14.

> For Job has said, 'I am righteous,
> But God has taken away my justice;
> Should I lie concerning my right?
> My wound is incurable, though
> I am without transgression.'[63]

Job's lament is entirely justified. The question he has been asking is entirely justified. But Elihu declares that even to inquire is a transgression, even to point to the injustice is an offence. Doing so implies that you have done right, and God has done wrong.

And the proof of this, once again, is in the definition!

> Therefore listen to me, you men of understanding:
> Far be it from God to do wickedness,
> And for the Almighty to commit iniquity.
> For He repays man according to his work,
> And makes man to find a reward according to his way.
> Surely God will never do wickedly,
> Nor will the Almighty pervert justice.[64]

Therefore, is it fitting to cast doubt on Him?

> Should one who hates justice govern?
> Will you condemn Him who is most just?
> Is it fitting to say to a king,
> 'You are worthless,'
> And to nobles, 'You are wicked'?

But how do we know He is just? Because, and here is the other element of the definition, He is All-seeing!

> For His eyes are on the ways of man,
> And He sees all his steps . . .[65]

But those precisely are the questions:

---

[63] 34.5-6.
[64] 34.10-12.
[65] 34.21.

- ❏ Does He see everything?
- ❏ Alternatively, seeing everything, how does He still inflict such torment?

Jigar is unanswerable:

Yeh jaantaa hoon jaante ho meraa haal-e-dil
Yeh dekhtaa hoon dekhte ho kis nazar se . . .

As one would expect, Elihu quickly shifts ground: God is just because He is powerful:

He breaks in pieces mighty men without inquiry,
And sets others in their place.
Therefore, He knows their works,
He overthrows them in the night,
And they are crushed.[66]

God breaks the mighty and puts others in their place, *therefore*, He knows their works and acts justly?

And in what way are those who have been struck down wicked? Elihu answers:

He strikes them as wicked men
In the open sight of others,
Because they turned their back on Him
And would not consider any of His ways . . .[67]

From this upside-down reasoning, Elihu concludes that Job deserves the punishment that has been rained down on him:

Because his answers are like those of wicked men
For he adds rebellion to his sin.[68]

What is the rebellion of which Job is guilty? That he has dared to beseech God for the reason on account of which

---

[66] 34.24-25.
[67] 34.26-27.
[68] 34.36-37.

the suffering has been inflicted on him, the reason his children have been killed. Elihu just keeps proving-by-repeated-assertion! That God *is* just, that He *is* powerful, that He *is* All-seeing . . . and the cure is for *you* to see that this is so.

> Although you say you do not see Him,
> Yet justice is before Him, and you must wait for Him . . .[69]

Those who suffer have acted 'defiantly'. They are 'hypocrites in heart.'[70] For,

> Behold, God is great, and we do not know Him.[71]
> He does great things which we cannot comprehend.[72]

Then follows a filibuster, an irrelevant harangue on the mighty works that God has wrought—heavens, light . . . Exactly along the lines of the learned Maulana we encountered in the beginning.

The implications for Job and for us are:

- ☐ As *you* did not make the earth, stars, light and the rest, He *is* just and you must believe that.[73]

- ☐ As you cannot understand the workings of the heavens, as you cannot even comprehend the breadth of the earth, how can you presume to comprehend the ways of the One who created these?[74]

How can you, therefore, doubt His justice? Next, you are powerless before Him—when you cannot stand up even to the behemoth He created, how can you stand up

---

[69] 35.14.
[70] 36.9, 13.
[71] 36.26.
[72] 37.5.
[73] Much of 37.
[74] Much of 38.

to Him?⁷⁵ *Therefore* you must submit and accept what He does. You must not just resign yourself to it, you must *accept it to be just,* and you must do so *with veneration in your heart.* Job collapses. He succumbs. He submits. He grovels.

I have uttered what I did not understand,
Things too wonderful for me, which I did not know . . .
Therefore, I abhor myself,
And repent in dust and ashes.⁷⁶

God comes down on the friends—He declares that they have spoken of Him what is not right, that Job is the one who has remained truthful to Him. Once Job has surrendered in these abject terms, God restores his animals and riches; He gives Job a new set of children—in fact, double the number that Job had originally. Job's fortunes multiply. He eventually has fourteen thousand sheep, six thousand camels, one thousand yoke of oxen, and one thousand female donkeys. He also gets seven sons and three daughters. He lives for 140 years, and sees his children and grandchildren up to the fourth generation. 'So Job died, old and full of days' . . .⁷⁷

A Bollywood ending, no doubt. But, as we shall just see, it leaves all the questions unanswered.

DOES THE QURAN EXPLAIN THE MATTER?

Job appears again—this time in the Quran, as Ayyub.

He is mentioned as a Prophet four times—in particular, in verses 21.83-84, and 38.41-44.

In the Quran also Job is as virtuous as he is in the Bible. In fact, as Allah is said to inflict suffering in accordance with one's capacity to bear it; and as the hardships that He

---

⁷⁵ Much of 40 and 41.
⁷⁶ 42.1-6.
⁷⁷ 42.7-17.

rained down on Job are greater than those rained down on any other prophet; and as, throughout these, Job remains steadfast in his devotion to Allah, Job is taken to have been more steadfast than other prophets. At the conclusion of the narrative, Allah says, 'Truly we found him full of patience and constancy, How excellent in Our service! Ever did he turn (to Us)!'[78]

There are some embellishments in the account and some differences from the account in the Old Testament. For instance, God relieves the distress of Job after the latter calls out to him in prayer. He alleviates Job's suffering with cold water in which he asks him to cool and refresh himself. We learn from Islamic lore that on the Day of Judgement, Job will intercede on behalf of those who have suffered persecution.

But, as far as our immediate quest is concerned—to glean some explanation for the miseries that are heaped on Job—we learn nothing new. In verse 21.83, no reason is given as to why distress and suffering have fallen upon Job. Job simply exclaims, 'Truly distress has seized me.' However, in 38.41, he cries out to Allah, 'The Evil One has afflicted me with distress and suffering.' The Quran does not tell us why the Evil One has rained down such distress on Job.

Like the Old Testament, the Quran is clearer on why Allah decides to relieve the suffering of Job. In verse 21.83, Job says, 'Truly distress has seized me. But thou are the Most Merciful of those that are merciful.' Allah in turn gives two reasons. In 21.84, He says, 'So we listened to him'—that is, He relieved Job of pain and tribulation in response to the prayer of a faithful devotee. Allah goes on to record that 'We removed the distress that was on him, and We restored his people to him, and doubled their number—*as a grace from Ourselves, and a thing for commemoration, for all who serve us.*'

---

[78] Quran, 38.44.

That is, (1) as a grace from Him; and (2) so that those who serve Him may remember.[79]

THE QUESTIONS REMAIN

❑ Do any of the explanations hold? That they do not apply to Job is certified by God Himself when He scolds the friends. This itself is of fundamental import for it means that Job was subjected to such torment, pain, loss, humiliation just because God could find no other way, at the least He did not find any other way to deal with the taunt of Satan.

❑ And what of the children, servants and animals who were killed in the first instance? What wrong had they done?

❑ But the immediate case of Job and his kin aside, do the explanations hold even for the suffering to which we ordinary mortals are subjected? In particular, does the argument that He does such mighty things,

---

[79] As we saw, at one point in the Old Testament account, Job loses his peace of mind. He curses the day he was born. Muslim commentators make it a point to note that 'The account given in the biblical sources and the image that it projects of Prophet Job is decidedly different from that found in the Quran and the Hadith, which present him as a Prophet and a brilliant example of dignified patience becoming of a great Prophet of Allah ever trustful in Him and His promises. Nothing could be further from the truth than saying that he lost his peace of mind or resorted to curses during the period of his trial.' (Abdullah Yusuf Ali, *The Meaning of the Glorious Quran,* 1934, reprint Dar al-Kitab al-Masri, Cairo, no date, footnote 2739, p. 813.) That of course leads to a slight problem just a little later. At the height of the torment, their possessions and children gone, Job's wife exhorted him to cast aside his faith in God, he lost his patience with her and berated her. In 38.44 of the Quran, we read, 'and take in thy hand a little grass, and strike therewith; and break not (thy oath).' The same commentator is now forced to note that, 'he [Job] must have said in his haste to the woman [his wife] that he would beat her; he is asked now to correct her with only a wisp of grass, to show that he was gentle and humble as well as patient and constant.' (Ibid., footnote 4202, p. 1171.)

that He created the universe, light and the rest, not work the other way? As He can do such grand things, why has He left this little thing undone, namely, why has He not removed the suffering of a little child? Why has He not devised ways to accomplish His purposes without imposing suffering on helpless creatures?

❑ To say 'Satan did it' or 'The Evil One did it' is no explanation. In Job's case, manifestly Satan acts only after God permits him to act. And in each round, he acts only up to the limit specified by God. In any event, to claim, 'O, Satan did it', only shifts the responsibility to another unknown—for who knows that Satan exists any more than anyone knows that God exists?

But the power of the prose in this particular *Book* is such that it sweeps all discernment aside. Is that the proper response to argument and assertion? Should we not look through the veil of eloquence, and see that, in fact, the 'explanations' are no explanations at all?

5
If, 'Not a leaf falls but by His Will, and not a leaf falls but it subserves His purpose...'

Untouchability has been the curse of our society. Gandhiji is revolted by it. He is strenuously opposed by the orthodox. They say that the shastras mandate it. Gandhiji asks for the shastra they have in mind. They do not come up with any. In any case, Gandhiji says, a shastra that is contrary to reason ought to be burnt. What you are doing and saying will weaken Hinduism, the critics charge. ' . . . I am wholly indifferent whether Hindu religion is strengthened or weakened or perishes,' Gandhiji declares. 'I have so much faith in the correctness of the position I have taken up that, if my taking up that position results in weakening Hinduism, I cannot help it and I must not care. I tell you what I want to do with Hindu religion. I want to purify it of the sin of untouchability. I want to exorcise the devil of untouchability which has today distorted and disfigured Hinduism out of all recognition . . .'[1] The tussle rages.

Gandhiji takes his campaign to the regions of the country, Madras province, Malabar, Travancore and Cochin, where the evil is most virulent.

15 January 1934: Gandhiji is in Calicut. He has addressed a public meeting the previous day, attended functions of the Malabar Merchants Association, the municipality, and

---

[1] *The Collected Works of Mahatma Gandhi,* Publications Division, Government of India, New Delhi, Volume 57, 1974, p. 17.

others. On the sixteenth, he is to meet the Zamorin and urge him to have untouchability erased from the region under his influence and have the temples opened to Harijans. The Zamorin is going to tell him that shastris will be prepared to discuss the issue with Gandhiji if Gandhiji is prepared to discuss the question in Sanskrit, and over several days![2]

2.13 in the afternoon: A devastating earthquake strikes Bihar. It measures 8.4 on the Richter scale. Entire towns are flattened. Around 30,000 people are killed.

Gandhiji receives heart-rending accounts from Dr Rajendra Prasad who has rushed to mobilize relief upon being released from jail. Gandhiji sees statements and accounts issued by the Viceroy and other authorities.

24 January 1934: Twenty-thousand people have turned up at the Municipal Market in Tinnevelly to hear Gandhiji. He refers to the devastation; to the accounts and communications he has received. 'All these communications show what puny mortals we are,' he tells the audience. *'We who have faith in God must cherish the belief that behind even this indescribable calamity there is a divine purpose that works for the good of humanity. You may call me superstitious if you like; but a man like me cannot but believe that this earthquake is a divine chastisement sent by God for our sins. Even to avowed scoffers it must be clear that nothing but divine will can explain such a calamity. It is my unmistakable belief that not a blade of grass moves but by the divine will.'*

This being his basic belief, the deduction is ineluctable.

'For me there is a vital connection between the Bihar calamity and the untouchability campaign,' Gandhiji says. 'The Bihar calamity is a sudden and accidental reminder of what we are and what God is; but untouchability is a calamity handed down to us from century to century. It is a

---

[2] C.B. Dalal, *Gandhi: 1915-1948, A Detailed Chronology*, Gandhi Peace Foundation and Bharatiya Vidya Bhavan, New Delhi, 1971, p. 105.

curse brought upon ourselves by our own neglect of a portion of Hindu humanity. Whilst this calamity in Bihar damages the body, the calamity brought about by untouchability corrodes the very soul. Therefore, let this Bihar calamity be a reminder to us that, whilst we have still a few more breaths left, we should purify ourselves of the taint of untouchability and approach our Maker with clean hearts.'[3]

There are two separate points in what Gandhiji says: one proposition is that the sin of untouchability has caused God to inflict the earthquake; the other is that the earthquake is yet another occasion to erase the sin of untouchability. In the ensuing days, as Gandhiji returns to the earthquake again and again, the two propositions will get conflated.

Gandhiji reaches Tuticorin. Twenty-five thousand people turn up to hear him. Gandhiji speaks about untouchability—the curse, the imperative need to erase it. But he begins with Bihar: it is the land where Sita grew up, the land where Gautama found 'divine knowledge', he reminds the audience, but today that fair land lies desolate. 'This divine calamity has suddenly reminded us that all humanity is one . . .' Government, the Congress, the people have all come together . . . And then the proposition with which we are concerned: *I want you to be "superstitious" enough with me to believe that the earthquake is a divine chastisement for the great sin we have committed and are still committing against those whom I describe as Harijans.* Let us derive the lesson from this calamity that this earthly existence is no more permanent than that of the moths we see every night dancing round lights for a few minutes and then being destroyed . . . Therefore, whilst we have yet breathing time, let us get rid of the distinctions of high and low, purify our hearts, and be ready to face our Maker

---

[3] *The Collected Works of Mahatma Gandhi*, Volume 57, op. cit., pp. 44-46.

when an earthquake or some natural calamity or death in the ordinary course overtakes us . . .'[4]

The next day, he addresses a public meeting at Rajapalayam. Ten thousand people attend. Purses, addresses, a gold medal with Gandhiji's likeness are presented. They are auctioned, and the funds collected for Harijan welfare. 'Now why should this calamity come upon us?' Gandhiji asks during his speech. 'I request you to think with me. Is this great calamity a punishment for our sin? What is the great sin we are committing and have committed? Why should we not take this as a warning to us? The wrong we have done is staring us in the face. We believe, in the name of religion, that thousands of our own countrymen are born "untouchables". Is it right? It is an insolence that we must get rid of, at all costs. I would like you, even as you have paid to the Harijan cause, to contribute your mite for the poverty-stricken citizens of Bihar . . .'[5]

By the next day, 26 January 1934, he has reached Madurai. The merchants organize the meeting . . . Gandhiji turns to the calamity that has befallen Bihar. 'Our forefathers have taught us to think that *whenever a calamity descends upon a people, that calamity comes because of our personal sins*' he tells the assembly. 'You know that when the rains do not come in time we perform sacrifices and ask gods to send us rains and forgive us our sins owing to which rains are detained.' Nor are we the only ones who have this belief, he continues. In England, in South Africa . . . 'I want you to believe with me that for this absolutely unthinkable affliction in Bihar your sins and my sins are responsible. And then when I ask myself what can be that atrocious sin that we must have committed to deserve such a calamity

---

[4] Ibid., pp. 46-47.
[5] Ibid., p. 49.

which staggers us and which today probably has staggered
the whole world—within living memory there is no record
of an earthquake of this magnitude in India—I tell you the
conviction is growing on me that this affliction has come to
us because of this atrocious sin of untouchability.'

He is conscious of the fact that many may scoff at what he
is saying: 'I beseech you not to laugh within yourself and
think I want to appeal to your instinct of superstition.
I don't. I am not given to making any appeal to the
superstitious fears of people. I may be called superstitious,
but I cannot help telling you what I feel deep down in me.'

'I do not propose to take up your time and my time by
elaborating this,' Gandhiji says. 'You are free to believe it or
to reject it. If you believe with me, then you will be quick and
think there is no such thing as untouchability as we practice
it today in the Hindu *shastras*. You will think with me that it
is a diabolical sin to think of any human being as an
untouchable. It is man's insolence that tells him that he is
higher than any other. I tell you, the more I think of it the
more I feel that there cannot be a greater sin than for a man
to consider that he is higher than any single being . . .'[6]

That evening, Gandhiji addresses a public meeting. He is
conscious of what his critics will say about his linking the
earthquake with untouchability. He is just a bit more
circumspect: 'I have not hesitated to say that most probably
the calamity which has come to India through the
earthquake in Bihar is a fit punishment awarded to us
by God for this great sin of untouchability,' he tells the
audience.

But he is not interested in entering into an argument
about the matter, he says. 'But whether it is so or not,' he
tells the gathering, 'it is necessary that you should go to the
alleviation of the sufferings of the people of Bihar.'

---

[6] Ibid., pp. 50-51.

He reverts to the linkage: 'I might say that when we have visitations of this character they have not only a physical reason, but they carry with them also spiritual consequences'—consequences, of course, but also 'causes': that, after all, has been his thesis. Gandhiji invokes numbers: ' . . . and *if it is a superstition, it is a superstition which I share in common with practically all mankind.*' But would that make the superstition any more valid? His concern is not whether anyone thinks that his belief is well founded or not, but what needs to be done. 'You may, if you like, reject this belief of mine,' he says. 'But if we would but rise from the inertia which has overtaken us and has paralysed our vision, we would at once see as clearly as daylight that untouchability as it is practiced today cannot be defended on any ground whatsoever . . .'[7]

The next day, a public meeting at Karaikudi. He tells his audience not to let the following day pass without expressing their sympathy for the people of Bihar by making tangible contributions to the fund that is being collected for their relief. But 'Let us not delude ourselves into the belief that when we have paid a few rupees or given a few bangles towards alleviating this suffering, we shall have discharged our obligations.' 'I would like you tomorrow to enter into the sanctuary of your hearts and examine the causes of this calamity,' he says.

'Geologists and such other scientists will undoubtedly give us physical and material causes of such calamities,' Gandhiji says. 'But the belief has been entertained all the world over by religiously minded people, especially by the Hindus, that *there are spiritual causes for such visitations. I entertain the honest and deep conviction that such visitations are due to the great sin that we have committed towards humanity and to God.* For long, long years, we have not been

---

[7] Ibid., pp. 54-55.

treating our fellowmen properly as our own brethren and should we not take this as a warning sent to us to correct our way of life? . . .' The devastation caused by untouchability is by far greater than the enormous devastation that has been inflicted by this earthquake . . . 'Whilst therefore you are, as I wish you will be, thinking over your duty towards the afflicted people of Bihar, I do hope that you will understand that *there is an invariable connection in a way between this untouchability designed by man and this calamity.* God could never design that one class of men should suppress another class of men. I would therefore like you tomorrow to send your subscriptions to the afflicted men in Bihar with a determination that henceforth you are not going to maintain untouchability and consider a single human-being lower than yourself . . .'[8]

Will you not set your campaign against untouchability aside, and go to Bihar? Will the Mahatma fiddle as Bihar burns? Such are the telegrams he receives. Gandhiji answers by writing 'Bihar and untouchability' in the *Harijan.* He points to the intimate connection between the work he is doing to rid India of a curse and what needs to be done in reconstructing Bihar: apart from the buildings and lives that have to be reconstructed, he says, Bihar must set its face against evil customs and beliefs.

'I share the belief with the whole world—civilized and uncivilized—that calamities such as the Bihar one come to mankind as chastisement for their sins,' Gandhiji writes. 'When that conviction comes from the heart, people pray, repent and purify themselves. I regard untouchability as such a grave sin as to warrant divine chastisement.'

But there are obvious questions: 'Why has the punishment been inflicted now for a sin that is centuries

---
[8] Ibid., p. 60.

old?' 'Why has the punishment been inflicted on Bihar and
not on the South where untouchability is so much more
extreme?' 'Why an earthquake—that kills and maims
indiscriminately—and not some other form of punishment
which would target the chastisement to those who actually
indulge in this sin?'

'I am not affected by such posers,' Gandhiji writes.
*'My answer is: I am not God. Therefore I have but a limited
knowledge of His purpose.* Such calamities are not a mere
caprice of the Deity or Nature. They obey fixed laws as
surely as the planets move in obedience to laws governing
their movement. Only we do not know the laws governing
these events and, therefore, call them calamities or
disturbances.'

But the belief, even though the reason for it cannot be
fathomed, serves a purpose, he maintains. *'It is an ennobling
thing for me to guess that the Bihar disturbance is due to the sin
of untouchability. It makes me humble, it spurs me to greater
effort towards its removal, it encourages me to purify myself, it
brings me nearer to my Maker. That my guess may be wrong
does not affect the results named by me.* For what is guess to the
critic or the sceptic is a living belief with me, and I base my
future actions on that belief. Such guesses become
superstitions when they lead to no purification and may
even lead to feuds. But such misuse of divine events cannot
deter men of faith from interpreting them as a call to them
for repentance for their sins.'

He generalizes the operational message: *'I do not interpret
this chastisement as an exclusive punishment for the sin of
untouchability. It is open to others to read in it divine wrath
against many other sins . . .'* and exert to rid themselves of
the sins they have selected. On the other hand, 'Let anti-
untouchability reformers regard the earthquake as a
Nemesis for the sin of untouchability. They cannot go

wrong, if they have the faith that I have. They will help Bihar more and not less for that faith. And they will try to create an atmosphere against reproduction of untouchability in any scheme of reconstruction.'[9]

Gandhiji repeats the same belief and draws the same operational message at subsequent meetings in his tour of the south.

THE GURUDEV WEIGHS IN

No less a person than Gurudev Rabindranath Tagore weighs in against what Gandhiji has been saying. It has 'caused me painful surprise', he says in a written statement. 'It is all the more unfortunate because this kind of unscientific view is too readily accepted by a large section of our countrymen . . .' Those opposed to Gandhiji's campaign would assert that the connection is the other way round, Tagore points out. 'What is truly tragic about it is the fact that the kind of argument that Mahatmaji used by exploiting an event of cosmic disturbance far better suits the psychology of his opponents than his own, and it would not have surprised me at all if they had taken this opportunity of holding him and his followers responsible for the visitation of Divine anger.'

'Our sins and errors, however enormous, have not enough force to drag down the structure of creation to ruins,' Tagore says.

But we also get a glimpse of why the linkages that Gandhiji has drawn become a problem for a believer in God. ' . . . Physical catastrophes have their inevitable and exclusive origin in certain combination of physical facts,' Tagore writes. '*Unless we believe in the inexorableness of the universal law in the working of which God Himself never*

---

[9] Ibid., pp. 86-87.

interferes, we find it impossible to justify His ways on occasions like the one which has sorely stricken us in an overwhelming manner and scale.'

But maybe the ways *are* unjustifiable. Maybe there is no justification simply because there is no God to ordain all this retribution or to desist from interfering with the working of 'His' laws. The matter is a problem only because we first posit a God, and then have to account for what we see all round us.

To say, as the Gurudev has said, *'Unless we believe in* the inexorableness of the universal law in the working of which God Himself never interferes, we find it impossible to justify His ways on occasions like the one which has sorely stricken us,' and, then to infer, *therefore,* it must be the case that God has set up the universal law and decided never to interfere in its working, is to beg the question—twice over. First, we have to set out the evidence on the basis of which we maintain that He has set up the universal law; and next we have to set out the reason on account of which He has decided never to interfere in its working—even when He sees the catastrophic consequences that His law is inflicting on so many.

Tagore limits himself to setting out the problem that arises when, as Gandhiji has done, we read ethical chastisements or rewards into events like earthquakes. 'If we associate ethical principles with cosmic phenomena,' Tagore says in his statement, 'we shall have to admit that human nature is morally superior to Providence that preaches its lessons in good behaviour in orgies of the worst behaviour possible.' But that again begs the question: why may it not be the case that human nature *is in fact* superior to the Providence that humans have conjured up?

But to continue with Tagore, 'For we can never imagine any civilized ruler of men making indiscriminate examples of casual victims, including children and members of the untouchable community, in order to impress others dwelling at a safe distance who possibly deserve severer condemnation.' Iniquities and evil of the darkest kind continue in the world, Tagore points out; he enumerates some of them, and concludes, ' . . . It only shows that the law of gravitation does not in the least respond to the stupendous load of callousness that accumulates till the moral foundation of our society begins to show dangerous cracks and civilizations are undermined.'[10]

Tagore's statement has an important clue. An insuperable problem arises—namely, that God turns out to be inferior to ordinary human nature 'if we associate ethical principles with cosmic phenomena'. But the problem arises only because we posit a God. If we do not, the evil we see continuing, the injustices that stare us in the face—none of them is a problem that has to be accounted for. Earthquakes occur only as earthquakes.

GANDHIJI REITERATES HIS PROPOSITIONS IN EVEN STRONGER TERMS

Gandhiji writes a full response, 'Superstition versus faith'. To me he is Gurudev, Gandhiji says. But we differ.

When I linked untouchability and the earthquake, he writes, 'I spoke with the greatest deliberation and out of the fullness of my heart. I spoke as I believed. I have long believed that physical phenomena produce results both physical and spiritual. *The converse I hold to be equally true.*'

'To me the earthquake was no caprice of God nor a result of a meeting of mere blind forces. We do not know all the laws of God nor their working . . .' 'I do believe with Gurudev in "the inexorableness of the universal law in the working of which God Himself never interferes". For God is

---

[10] Tagore's critique is reproduced in *The Collected Works of Mahatma Gandhi*, Volume 57, op. cit., pp. 503-04.

the Law. But I submit that we do not know the Law or the laws fully, and what appear to us as catastrophes are so only because we do not know the universal laws sufficiently.'

'If God is not a personal being for me like my earthly father, He is infinitely more. *He rules me in the tiniest detail of my life. I believe literally that not a leaf moves but by His will.* Every breath I take depends upon His sufferance.'

Gandhiji reasons as follows. As not a leaf moves but by His command, phenomena like earthquakes cannot occur but by His command. And as He does not act capriciously, He must have reason to order such devastation. And that reason can only be our sin. Which sin? You can choose. But whichever one you think has propelled God to visit such suffering on thousands, get rid of that sin. I cannot prove the existence of God. I cannot prove that the earthquake is indeed punishment for untouchability or any other sin. But we cannot be certain that it is not the case for we do not understand the laws of God fully. In any event, no harm can come even if the entire chain of my suppositions is wrong. On the contrary, good shall come of it. You would have gained by ridding yourself and society of that evil practice. That is Gandhiji's chain of reasoning. He writes,

Visitations like droughts, floods, earthquakes and the like, though they seem to have only physical origins, are, for me, somehow connected with man's morals. Therefore, I instinctively felt that the earthquake was a visitation for the sin of untouchability. Of course, *sanatanists* have a perfect right to say that it was due to my crime of preaching against untouchability. My belief is a call to repentance and self-purification. I admit my utter ignorance of the working of the laws of Nature. But, even as I cannot help believing in God though I am unable to prove His existence to the sceptics, in like manner I cannot prove the connection of the sin of untouchability with the

Bihar visitation even though the connection is instinctively felt by me. If my belief turns out to be ill-founded, it will still have done good to me and those who believe with me. For we shall have been spurred to more vigorous efforts towards self-purification, assuming, of course, that untouchability is a deadly sin. I know fully well the danger of such speculation. But I would be untruthful and cowardly if, for fear of ridicule, when those that are nearest and dearest to me are suffering, I did not proclaim my belief from the housetop. The physical effect of the earthquake will be soon forgotten and even partially repaired.

And then Pascal's wager:

But it would be terrible if it is an expression of the Divine wrath for the sin of untouchability and we did not learn the moral lesson from the event and repent of that sin. I have not the faith which Gurudev has that 'our own sins and errors, however enormous, have not got enough force to drag down the structure of creation to ruins'. On the contrary, I have the faith that our own sins have more force to ruin that structure than any mere physical phenomenon. There is an indissoluble marriage between matter and spirit. Our ignorance of the results of the union makes it a profound mystery and inspires awe in us, but it cannot undo them. But a living recognition of the union has enabled many to use every physical catastrophe for their own moral uplifting ... With me the connection between cosmic phenomena and human behaviour is a living faith that draws me nearer to my God, humbles me and makes me readier for facing Him ... [11]

'NOT A LEAF FALLS WITHOUT HIS WILL, AND NOT A LEAF FALLS BUT IT SUBSERVES HIS PURPOSE'

Gandhiji's tour continues. He reiterates the propositions, the deductions, the lesson at every stop. At Mercara, he suggests that Bihar has been selected for the chastisement

[11] Ibid., pp. 164-66.

precisely because it is sacred. 'You may know that Bihar is a sacred land because of the birth of both Sita and Gautama Buddha,' he tells the thousands who have gathered to hear him. 'Our countrymen in Bihar believe that every particle of the soil in that land is sacred. And to a man like me, it would almost appear that God has selected that sacred land for castigation for the sin of untouchability. It does not matter to me in the least degree that my imagination may be wrong. But let us cherish the thought and make greater effort to purify ourselves . . .'[12]

Gandhiji has reached Bihar. He has been collecting and forwarding funds for relief. He has been in regular touch with Dr Rajendra Prasad and others who have been exerting themselves to rebuild lives.

A terrible calamity has overwhelmed all of us, Gandhiji tel's the people at Chapra. It has devastated all alike— irrespective of religion, or position, the so-called high- or low-born. We do not fully understand God's ways. And that for good reason: 'God in His wisdom has circumscribed man's vision, and rightly too, for, otherwise man's conceit would know no bounds.'

'But whilst I believe that God's ways cannot be comprehended fully by man, I have firm faith that *not a leaf falls without His will, and not a leaf falls but it subserves His purpose.*' The obstacle to realizing this, and thereby seeing the connection between our sin and the calamity seems to be that we lack humility. Gandhiji says, 'If only we had enough humility, we would have no hesitation in accepting the recent earthquake as a just retribution for our sins.' But how do we know that it is untouchability that has invited this calamity? 'This is not to say that we can with certainty attribute a particular calamity to a particular human action', Gandhiji says. 'Very often we are unconscious of

---

[12] Ibid., p. 206.

our worst sins. All that I mean to say is that every visitation of Nature does and should mean to us Nature's call to introspection, repentance and self-purification. Today, more than ever, our hearts need a thorough cleansing and I would go so far as to say that even the recent earthquake would not be too great a price to pay, if it enabled India to cast out the canker of untouchability.'[13]

But why Bihar? Why us? Gandhiji is assailed everywhere by such questions. 'It is not that Bihar has incurred this punishment because it is more wicked,' Gandhiji says. 'Bihar is part of India. It is a part of the world'—here is an aperture that will be widened soon to argue that a person may be punished for the sins of another, unknown though that sinner may be to all of us and though he may be far, far away!

Gandhiji returns to what will today be called the Argument from Ignorance: 'God alone knows His ways.' And then the tautology: 'We only know that God is full of compassion, love and kindness, so the punishment he metes out *must have been based on justice*. It is beyond my power to comprehend how. It is beyond the power of anyone.'

Vicarious visitation of calamities now becomes a cure: 'We should consider the calamity as an outcome of our sins—not your sins but mine. Everyone should consider Bihar's calamity as his own and should feel as sad for those who died there as he might have felt at the death of his own relatives. One would be called a human being only if he did that and only then could he claim to know God. We should try to wash off our sins—individual and social—while this tragedy is fresh in our minds.'[14]

The discourse is always shifting. Is it the case that the Biharis have been killed by God for sins that may have been committed by others? Or is it the case that all who have

[13] Ibid., p. 318.
[14] Ibid., pp. 351-52.

survived *should* think that *their* sins have brought death to the Biharis, and thereby feel impelled to rid themselves of their particular evils?

A SCIENCE STUDENT

But the people are not convinced. A student, a science student writes to Gandhiji. Earthquakes have physical causes, he says. How could untouchability have caused this one?

Gandhiji reprimands him. 'A science student has no right to disbelieve what is beyond his comprehension,' he begins. 'A science student should be humble. Instead of brushing aside whatever he hears, he must give it some thought. There are very few things in this world which we are able to understand. Many things are beyond our understanding. That is exactly why the learned become more humble as they acquire more knowledge, for the knowledge of the learned man consists in realising his immense ignorance. The deeper he goes, the more he realises that he knows nothing. Moreover, most of what he knows is just surmise. I have no intention of running down science by writing this. Though infinitesimal, the knowledge we acquire has its uses. But compared to what remains to be acquired, what is already acquired is less than a drop in the ocean.' The Argument from Ignorance at full charge.

But the question still remains, 'Why Bihar?' 'Why specially the ones who have died and been maimed?' 'All life in this world originates from the same root,' Gandhiji says. 'Hence all are fundamentally one. These include all things from vegetable life to human life . . . We see this rule working in a family. Everyone is unhappy if the father is unhappy. And everyone is affected by his sinful ways. Hence, if this student accepts the oneness of all living creatures, everyone would be included in the punishment of

Bihar. Those who have not felt the earthquake have not remained untouched. If they do not directly experience, they should be considered ignorant to that extent.' The import of this is that, while the earthquake may have killed people in Bihar alone, it must have caused pain to everyone elsewhere also. And that is how it is chastisement for them also.

'So, the science student would probably agree that there is not much sense in asking: "Why only Bihar?"'— I wouldn't come to that conclusion if I were the science student.

'Why only Bihar and no other province?' Gandhiji proceeds. '*Who are we to put this question to God? His ways are inscrutable.* Hence, where reason cannot function, it is faith that works . . .' Gandhiji next invokes the argument that we have encountered earlier: that there has been no period in human history when countless people did not believe that earthquakes and the like were not caused by the sins of man.

But untouchability is far more virulent in the south. Why has the punishment been inflicted on the poor Biharis? Gandhiji shifts back to the prescriptive: 'It can never be known for which sins of ours such calamities overtake us. The golden rule is for each one of us to regard them as punishment for one's individual and social sins. It is pride and ignorance if one says, "This happened because of your sins"; but it is humility, it is wisdom, if one says, "It happened because of my sins." I have never tried to convince those who do not consider untouchability a sin that the earthquake is the result of it. They may well believe that it is the result of my sin. Imperfect man can never finally determine what is right and what is wrong in such matters. My job is over if I could convince the reader that the earthquake is the result of our sins. Then the people who

regard untouchability as a great sin are bound to connect it
with the earthquake and endeavour to expiate and wipe out
the blot as soon as possible.'[15]

A FEW QUESTIONS

Without doubt, untouchability was a great sin. It was the
curse of our society. Gandhiji was outraged by it. He regarded
it as a blot on our religion and history. He was determined
to uproot it. Few did more to erase it than he did.

At the time Bihar was struck, he was campaigning
against this evil in the region where the curse was most
virulent. Could it then be that, when he heard of the
earthquake, his mind yoked it to the cause he was pursuing?

Gandhiji himself refers to his belief in the earthquake
being divine chastisement as a 'superstition', albeit one he
shares with the vast majority of mankind.

Nor is he particular about the association that he has
formulated—between the earthquake in Bihar and
untouchability. You can regard it as chastisement for
whichever sin you choose, he says, and use the tragedy to
rid yourself of that sin. That is how such a belief can be
ennobling, Gandhiji says.

His proposition thus is instrumental. His singular interest
is not in persuading people that they share this particular
belief, this 'superstition' with him, just that they themselves
give up untouchability and help erase it from our society.

Few will insist that, if such prescription works to rid
a society of such an enormous injustice, a great teacher may
still not use it. I recoil at the next proposition that we should
assume that the calamity has occurred because of our sin, as
this would teach us humility. It could just as well internalize
unwarranted guilt. With all the hardship that he already
has to bear, should my son believe that any calamity that

---

[15] Ibid., pp. 391-92.

befalls *me* is also because of some sin *he* has committed, as this belief will make him even more humble and sensitive than he already is? Such considerations weigh heavily with me. But on this question of what will work with our people, I am prepared to defer to the assessment of a person who knew our people infinitely better than the rest of us are liable to ever know them.

Granting all that, the basic premise—that the tragedy has been brought down upon the people by God and that He has sent it down on them because of something they have done—follows inescapably from the fundamental belief that nothing happens, that not a leaf falls but by the will and command of God, and not a leaf falls but it subserves His purpose.

Several questions arise.

If the Bihar earthquake was chastisement for untouchability, what was the earthquake that devastated Quetta just sixteen months later, and which killed anywhere between 30,000 and 60,000 people, punishment for? And the earthquake in Pakistan-occupied Kashmir in 2005 which killed nearly 80,000? For not enforcing the shariah? What of the series of earthquakes that have been shaking Indonesia? Was the country's Minister of Communication and Information, Tifatul Sembiring, right when he declared in November 2009 that the disasters were being caused by the immorality of the Indonesians? An immorality caused by their watching so many TV shows that undermined morals, an immorality proven by the ready availability of Indonesia-made pornographic CDs? And what of the earthquake that devastated Haiti and killed over 1,50,000 in January 2010? Did God send it down, as the American televangelist Pat Robertson declared, because the Haitians had sworn a pact with the Devil early in the nineteenth century to drive out the French? Or did He send it down because the Haitians continue to practise voodoo? And what about the thesis of the Iranian cleric who, in April 2010, declared that earthquakes in Iran are being caused by women who are promiscuous and dress immodestly? 'Many women who do not dress modestly lead young men astray and spread adultery in society which increases earthquakes,' the BBC reported the cleric, Hojatosalem Kazem Sedighi as telling worshippers in a sermon. Now, Tehran is said to be located at the intersection of several tectonic plates. Even President Ahmadinejad, the BBC reported, has been urging the city's twelve million residents to relocate to safer sites.[16] What would make residents of Tehran safer vis-à-vis the earthquakes that devastate Iran periodically—strengthening the moral police to curb promiscuity among women and to ensure that they adhere to the Islamic dress code, or, as Ahmadinejad has urged, relocating to safer places?

We have but to set such assertions side by side and we see the flaw: anyone can ascribe a catastrophe to his favourite aversion, and deploy it as an argument for giving up that particular practice.

Those declarations of the Indonesian minister and the evangelist, and the immediacy with which we see how absurd they are, hold an important clue. When the person suggesting such a cause is not someone we revere; when the cause that is suggested—in these cases, the sin that has been picked up: TV-induced immorality, the pact with the Devil, voodoo—is not from our cultural milieu, we immediately see that the theses are absurd. That is an important lesson: we must learn to see a proposition independently of the person who advances it; we must see it without the spectacles which we have been conditioned to wear.

The Bihar student asked Gandhiji, 'Untouchability is practised much more in the south than in Bihar, why have

---

[16] BBC News, 20 April 2010.

the Biharis been punished for the crime and not those in the south?' We saw Gandhiji's answer. Going by Gandhiji's logic, could it not be argued that, humanity being one, the Haitians have been punished for the sins we, on the other side of the world, have been committing? Moreover, that student's question applies across time also. Untouchability had come to be practised over the preceding centuries. Why were the Biharis who happened to be living in 1934 punished for the sin? Assume that there really is a Devil. Assume further that in the early nineteenth century, the Haitians made a pact with him. Why were those living in January 2010 killed for what was done by their ancestors 200 years earlier?

By what logic is it justified to kill infants who have just been born, some who are still in the wombs of their mothers, to avenge a wrong that they definitely have not committed? Or have they been killed because God, as is said in the fables, being omniscient, knows that, had He let them live, they would have grown up and sinned? But that opens up the other question: were there no adult sinners among the 1,50,000 who were smothered by the earthquake? If there were, why did the same God then let the sinners grow up till the only punishment that could compensate for their pile of sins was death by drowning in the tsunami or burial under the rubble of the earthquake? God's responsibility in the matter cannot be evaded. After all, as philosophers and Biblical scholars like Bart Ehrman point out, when everyone in a crash dies except an infant, and we exclaim, 'She is blessed. God saved her,' do we not, by that very 'logic', mean that God killed the rest?

Have the lakhs who died in the tsunami been killed so that the technologists among us learn not to neglect devising an early warning system? Have the lakhs who died in the POK and Haiti earthquakes been killed so that governmental authorities and architects may not neglect to devise ways to build earthquake resistant structures?

Why not punish only the government servants who had not enforced the building codes? Or the architects and engineers who did not develop and deploy building technologies and principles that could have withstood earthquakes? Why kill lakhs of others so that these few do their duty? Even if only indirect methods of instruction are to be employed, was it really necessary to kill so many to teach the rest?

Or have these catastrophes been inflicted so that the rest of us get the occasion to serve the ones who have been hit? Has all that death and maiming and suffering been caused so that the rest of us may learn to be kind? But that would bring up the question that was asked of Baba Amte, one to which we will soon turn, and for which, as we shall see, there is no answer.

Another difficulty arises, one that goes way beyond individuals—be the individual Gandhiji or the Indonesian minister or the televangelist—who advance such explanations. While we may have little difficulty in setting aside the proposition *of one who believes in God* that the calamity is the result of God's wrath over something that humans have done or not done, what are we to do *when God Himself declares* that *He* causes the earth to 'swallow up' those who do not pay full obeisance to Him and to Him alone, who devise evil plots?[17] When He Himself reminds us more than once how *He* made the earth swallow up Qaaroon, his palace and his incalculable treasures because of the latter's pride and swagger?[18] When He exhorts us to remember the fate that *He* visited upon Qaaroon, the Pharaoh and Haamaan for their insolence:

Each of them We seized
For his crime: of them,

[17] Quran, 16.45.
[18] Quran, 28.76-81.

Against some We sent
A violent tornado (with showers
Of stones); some were caught
By a (mighty) Blast; some
We caused the earth
To swallow up; and some
We drowned (in the waters) . . .

Of course, we must always bear in mind two distinct things.
First, God has the power to do all this, and He *did* send and
sends the violent tornados, the mighty blasts, He did and
does cause earthquakes and the earth to split and swallow
those who transgress. But, and this is the second point, He is
not the one who has caused the suffering that results!
To continue the verses:

It was not Allah Who
Injured (or oppressed) them:
They injured (and oppressed)
Their own souls.[19]

If earthquakes, why not floods also? At several places in the
Quran, Allah reminds the Prophet about the masses of men
He has drowned in floods. 'So We inspired him (with this
message): "Construct the Ark within Our sight and under
Our guidance: then when comes Our Command, and the
fountains of the earth gush forth, take thou on board pairs
of every species, male and female, and thy family—except
those of them against whom the Word has already gone
forth: And address Me not in favour of the wrong-doers; for
they shall be drowned (in the Flood)."'[20] Allah gives the
reason on account of which He has drowned the whole lot
in the waters. He declares,

(Remember) Noah, when
He cried (to Us) aforetime:

---

[19] Quran, 29.39-40.
[20] Quran, 23.27.

> We listened to his (prayer)
> And delivered him and his
> Family from great distress.
> We helped him against
> People who rejected Our Signs:
> *Truly they were a people*
> *Given to Evil: so We*
> *Drowned them* (in the Flood)
> *All together.*[21]

Was each and everyone alive then—other than Noah, his family and the singular pairs of animals—evil? What of the poor animals, save the pairs that were taken into the ark? Were they also 'truly . . . a people given to Evil'? Were all who were alive at that time, each and every one of them, 'most unjust and most insolent transgressors'?[22] For not one of them was allowed to survive.

What then of the 3,00,000 who were killed by the tsunami recently? Was each and every one of them—including countless infants, women, children—also 'given to evil'? And what was the evil of which they were guilty? Allah instructs us:

> We sent Noah to his people.
> He said: 'O my people!
> Worship Allah! Ye have
> No other god but Him.
> I fear for you the Punishment
> Of a dreadful day! . . .
> But they rejected him.
> And We delivered him,
> And those with him
> In the Ark:
> But We overwhelmed

---

[21] Quran, 21.76-77.
[22] Quran, 53.52

In the flood those
Who rejected Our Signs.
They were indeed a blind people![23]

But so many among those who perished in the tsunami
were Muslims. Did not even one among the Muslims believe
in the signs of Allah? And was the rest of humanity not
drowned because it was *not* 'given to evil', because it
believed the Signs of Allah? Or because He has made other
arrangements to deal with them?

Third, now that we have God in our sights, recall
Gandhiji's characterization of his belief as a 'superstition'.
Does this superstition or any other become valid because
I share it with millions of others? What about *a belief*? What
about *belief in God*? Does the fact that 'mankind has always
believed and still believes that He is there,' make it any more
likely that He is there, any more than the fact that mankind
has always believed that natural calamities are
chastisement for our sins make them so?

And, fourth, if what Gandhiji and the believers hold is
indeed true—that we sin and, therefore, God rains
calamities on us—God has to explain how we may attribute
excellence, or even superiority, to Him. My Persian-
knowing friend recites a couplet in which the poet inquires,

I do evil and You punish me with evil
Pray, what is the difference between You and me?

AS NATURAL DISASTERS ARE DIVINE CHASTISEMENT, ARE MAN-MADE
ONES ALSO GOD'S CHASTISEMENT?

Given that not a leaf moves but by the will and command of
God; given that even in the collective suffering of
thousands—as in natural disasters—there is a 'divine

---

[23] Quran, 7.59-64.

chastisement'; given that the Divinity inflicts the
chastisement because of our sins, how would a believer like
Gandhiji view man-made suffering? What did he have
to say about the persecution of Jews in Hitler's Germany,
for instance?

. By the late 1930s, facts about the brutality to which the
Jews are being subjected in Germany are known across the
world. In India, Gandhiji is the undisputed leader. He is the
great moral voice of the times. He is fighting for the freedom
of his people, but not only for their freedom. Suffering
anywhere, of anyone is of equal concern to him. Leading
Jewish thinkers and activists have been following his
writings and statements diligently. They are attracted to
him because he is manifestly a man of conscience. They
study his methods to discern what they should themselves
be doing in the face of persecution. Hence, as more and
more evidence about what Hitler and the Germans are
doing makes its way into the world, they eagerly, and
impatiently wait to hear when the Mahatma will speak out
about the atrocities, and what he would say and counsel.

'WITHOUT PARALLEL'

Naturally, Gandhiji is revolted by what is being done to the
Jews. Anti-Semitism is barbarism, he says. 'My sympathies
are all with the Jews,' he writes. He had known them
intimately in South Africa, Gandhiji says. Some of them had
become life long companions. 'Through these friends I came
to learn much of their age-long persecution.' He sees a
parallel, one that is conclusive in his eyes. 'They have been
the untouchables of Christianity,' he says. 'The parallel
between their treatment by Christians and the treatment of
untouchables by Hindus is very close. Religious sanction has
been invoked in both cases for the justification of the
inhuman treatment meted out to them.' Apart from the

friendships, therefore, Gandhiji says, 'there is the more common universal reason for my sympathy for the Jews.'[24]

Moreover, in the instance at hand, that of Hitler's Germany, the persecution has reached a scale and ferocity that 'seems to have no parallel in history'. 'The tyrants of old never went so mad as Hitler seems to have gone,' Gandhiji writes. 'And he is doing it with religious zeal. For he is propounding a new religion of exclusive and militant nationalism in the name of which any inhumanity becomes an act of humanity to be rewarded here and hereafter. The crime of an obviously mad but intrepid youth is being visited upon his whole race with unbelievable ferocity . . .' 'If there ever could be a justifiable war in the name of and for humanity, a war against Germany, to prevent the wanton persecution of a whole race, would be completely justified,' Gandhiji declares. He adds a clause to which we shall soon revert, 'But I do not believe in any war. A discussion of the pros and cons of such a war is therefore outside my horizon or province . . .'[25]

COUNSEL

Given the inexcusable scale of the persecution, given its ferocity, given the nature of Hitler's regime, what should the Jews be doing? How should they respond? Apart from the moral support that a statement from the conscience of his times would give, this is the question upper most in the minds of Jews all over the world.

---

[24] *The Collected Works of Mahatma Gandhi*, Volume 68, Publications Division, Government of India, New Delhi, 1977, p. 137. There were two aspects to his observations—the persecution of Jews, and whether they were entitled to a homeland in Palestine. As the latter is not germane to the subject of this book, I shall not pursue the exchanges and arguments on it between Gandhiji and leading Jewish thinkers.
[25] Ibid., p. 138.

By the late 1930s, Gandhiji just has to confront this question. It is, after all, the pre-eminent humanitarian problem of the time. And the circumstances are such that they constitute a real test for the instrument he has forged, of non-violent resistance. Does it have any relevance when confronted by a Hitler? Or is it relevant only when it confronts adversaries like the British—that is, adversaries who are committed, at least at home and in public, to democratic norms?

'Can the Jews resist this organized and shameless persecution? Is there a way to preserve their self-respect, and not to feel helpless, neglected and forlorn?' Gandhiji asks in November 1938, in an article, 'The Jews', which will ignite comments far and wide. 'I submit there is,' he writes. And immediately God comes in. 'No person who has faith in a living God need feel helpless or forlorn,' he says, pointing out that 'Jehovah of the Jews is a God more personal than the God of the Christians, the Mussalmans or the Hindus, though, as a matter of fact in essence, He is common to all and one without a second and beyond description. But as the Jews attribute personality to God and believe that He rules every action of theirs, they ought not to feel helpless.'

'If I were a Jew and were born in Germany and earned my livelihood there, I would claim Germany as my home even as the tallest gentile German may'—but that is precisely what the Jews of Germany are not just 'claiming', they genuinely and tenaciously believe that to be the case— 'and challenge him to shoot me or cast me in the dungeon; I would refuse to be expelled or to submit to discriminating treatment.' 'And for doing this,' he maintains, 'I should not wait for the fellow Jews to join me in civil resistance but would have confidence that in the end the rest are bound to follow my example. If one Jew or all the Jews were to accept the prescription here offered, he or they cannot be worse off than now'—that they are still at least alive and, if they follow his prescription, would be snuffed out in a moment does not seem to make a difference.

In fact, Gandhiji maintains that they would be better off: 'And suffering voluntarily undergone will bring them an inner strength and joy which no number of resolutions of sympathy passed in the world outside Germany can.' But wouldn't their interest be served better if the other Powers were to intervene and rein in Germany? 'Indeed,' Gandhiji maintains, 'even if Britain, France and America were to declare hostilities against Germany, they can bring no inner joy, no inner strength.' On the contrary, the recoil could inflict infinitely greater suffering on them: 'The calculated violence of Hitler may even result in a general massacre of the Jews by way of his first answer to the declaration of such hostilities.'

Gandhiji presses his proposition further: 'But if the Jewish mind could be prepared for voluntary suffering, even the massacre I have imagined could be turned into a day of thanksgiving and joy that Jehovah had wrought deliverance of the race even at the hands of the tyrant. For to the godfearing, death has no terror. It is a joyful sleep to be followed by a waking that would be all the more refreshing for the long sleep.'

We begin to see where the line of reasoning impelled by faith and belief in God leads.

Nor should one forget that the Jews are in a much better position to melt the heart of their oppressors through voluntary suffering than others have been, Gandhiji maintains. They can offer satyagraha 'under infinitely better auspices'. 'It is hardly necessary for me to point out that it is easier for the Jews than for the Czechs to follow my prescription. And they have in the Indian *satyagraha* campaign in South Africa an exact parallel,' Gandhiji writes. *An exact parallel?*

Notice the parallels Gandhiji lists—for they shall come up for comment soon by one of the greatest of Jewish philosophers. (i) 'There the Indians occupied precisely the same place that the Jews occupy in Germany.' (ii) 'The persecution had also a religious tinge. President Kruger used to say that the white Christians were the chosen of God and Indians were inferior beings created to serve the whites.' (iii) 'A fundamental clause in the Transvaal Constitution was that there should no equality between the whites and colored races including Asiatics.' (iv) 'There too the Indians were consigned to ghettos described as locations.' 'The other disabilities were almost of the same type as those of the Jews in Germany.' What would the Jews who were being crushed by Hitler's jackboots and who knew anything at all about South Africa have thought of such an enumeration?

And see what the Indians there were able to do, Gandhiji says: 'The Indians, a mere handful, resorted to *satyagraha* without any backing from the world outside or the Indian Government. Indeed the British officials tried to dissuade the *satyagrahis* from their contemplated step. World opinion and the Indian Government came to their aid after eight years of fighting. And that too was by way of diplomatic pressure not of a threat of war. But the Jews of Germany can offer *satyagraha* under infinitely better auspices than the Indians of South Africa. The Jews are a compact, homogeneous community in Germany. They are far more gifted than the Indians of South Africa. And they have organized world opinion behind them. I am convinced that if someone with courage and vision can arise among them to lead them in non-violent action, the winter of their despair can in the twinkling of an eye be turned into the summer of hope. And what has today become a degrading man-hunt can be turned into a calm and determined stand offered by unarmed men and women possessing the strength of suffering given to them by Jehovah. It will be then a truly religious resistance offered against the godless fury of dehumanized man.'

Nor will the Jews be delivering themselves alone: 'The German Jews will score a lasting victory over the German gentiles in the sense that they will have converted the latter to an appreciation of human dignity. They will have rendered service to fellow-Germans and proved their title to be the real Germans as against those who are today dragging, however unknowingly, the German name into the mire.'

Hence, 'Let the Jews who claim to be the chosen race prove their title by choosing the way of non-violence for vindicating their position on earth. . . They can add to their many contributions [to civilization, contributions to which his interlocutors have drawn attention] the surpassing contribution of non-violent action.'[26]

Thus far, not the Jews but the gentile Germans are the ones who react with anger. They come down on Gandhiji for his remarks about the treatment of Jews in Germany. He did not have, and he need not have accurate knowledge of European politics, Gandhiji says in reply, in order to commend his prescription to the Jews. 'The main facts about the atrocities are beyond dispute,' and for the purpose at hand that is enough. But the spate of criticism does have one effect: Gandhiji re-emphasizes what the Jews should be doing in stronger words. 'Have I not repeatedly said that active non-violence is unadulterated love—fellow-feeling?' he asks while responding to the German critics—does a certain defensiveness show through? *'And if the Jews, instead of being helplessly and of necessity non-violent, adopt active non-violence, i.e., fellow-feeling for the gentile Germans deliberately, they cannot do any harm to the Germans and I am as certain as I*

---

[26] Ibid., pp. 138-41.

am dictating these lines that the stoniest German heart will melt.
Great as have been the Jewish contributions to the world's
progress, this supreme act of theirs will be their greatest
contribution and war will be a thing of the past.'[27]

'But what more do you expect of us?' several Jewish
leaders ask. Are the Jews in Germany being violent? Are
they not bearing the blows in silence? Non-violently? Have
they not been practising non-violence for two thousand
years? Gandhiji's answer comes as close to blaming the
victim as one can come. He writes:

> The Jews, so far as I know, have never practiced non-violence as an
> article of faith or even as a deliberate policy. Indeed, it is a
> stigma against them that their ancestors crucified Jesus.
> Are they not supposed to believe in an eye for an eye and a tooth for
> a tooth? Have they no violence in their hearts for their oppressors?
> Do they not want the so-called democratic powers to punish
> Germany for her persecution and to deliver them from oppression?
> If they do, there is no non-violence in their hearts. Their non-
> violence, if it may be so called, is of the helpless and the weak.
> What I have pleaded for is renunciation of violence of the heart and
> consequent active exercise of the force generated by the great
> renunciation . . .[28]

But the one crushing them is Hitler. Gandhiji reverts to faith
in the efficacy of non-violence: 'Sufferings of the non-violent
have been known to melt the stoniest hearts. I make bold to
say that *if the Jews can summon to their aid the soul power that
comes only from non-violence, Herr Hitler will bow before the
courage which he has never yet experienced in any large measure
in his dealings with men, and which, when it is exhibited, he will
own is infinitely superior to that shown by his best storm
troopers.* The exhibition of such courage is only possible for
those who have a living faith in the God of Truth and Non-
violence, i.e., Love.'[29]

---

[27] Ibid., p. 189.
[28] Ibid., p. 191.
[29] Ibid., p. 192.

How many today would agree with that confidence in the malleability of Hitler's heart?

Gandhiji is expressing this confidence in December 1938. Soon, the gas chambers will be commissioned. Would having love in the heart, even with the capital 'L' that Gandhiji uses, have prevented them? Why did the enormous suffering borne by the Jews between 1938 and the firing up of the gas chambers not prevent the extermination campaign? Gandhiji's answer, as we shall soon see, is the circular one in which all scriptures ultimately take refuge—an answer that drives the blame even deeper into the victim.

On one point, Gandhiji says, he has been misunderstood—and there is a lesson in what he says on that also. 'I see, however, that my remarks are being misunderstood to mean that because I advise non-violent resistance by the persecuted Jews, by inference I expect or would advise non-interference by the democratic powers on behalf of the Jews,' Gandhiji writes. 'I hardly need to answer this fear. Surely there is no danger of the great powers refraining from action because of anything I have said. They will, they are bound to, do all they can to free the Jews from the inhuman persecution. My appeal has force in the face of the fact that the great powers feel unable to help the Jews in an effective manner.'

Would that mean that when and if the Great Powers muster courage to intervene, the prescription would lapse? Not entirely, it seems, for Gandhiji continues, 'Therefore it is that I have offered the prescription which I know to be infallible when taken in the right manner.'[30]

That last bit—*'when taken in the right manner'*—is true, of course. Even the best remedy applied in the wrong manner will recoil. But it is also the basis for explaining away a contrary result. Did the blessing of the guru not work? That is because our faith in the guru was insufficient. Did the

---

[30] Ibid., p. 192.

pilgrimage yield little? That is because we undertook the pilgrimage with an impure heart. Did the patient die in spite of our prayers? That is because our prayers were not fervent enough; because, even as we prayed, at the back of our minds we harboured doubt, 'Will God listen this time?' Failure of the device, therefore, does not prove that the device is inefficacious. It proves that *we* are inadequate.

'IF EVEN ONE JEW ACTED THUS . . .'

Three days later, Gandhiji is talking to Christian missionaries who have come to meet him. The conversation turns to pacifism—the difficulties in adopting it, its true content. Gandhiji elaborates his conception by recalling what he has written about the Jews. 'No Jew need feel helpless if he takes to the non-violent way,' he tells the missionaries. 'A friend has written me a letter objecting that in that article I have assumed that the Jews have been violent. *It is true that the Jews have not been actively violent in their own persons. But they called down upon the Germans the curses of mankind, and they wanted America and England to fight Germany on their behalf. If I hit my adversary, that is of course violence, but to be truly non-violent, I must love him and pray for him even when he hits me. The Jews have not been actively non-violent or, in spite of the misdeeds of the dictators, they would say, "We shall suffer at their hands; they know no better. But we shall suffer not in the manner in which they want us to suffer."* If even one Jew acted thus, he would salve his self-respect and leave an example which, if it became infectious, would save the whole of Jewry and leave a rich heritage to mankind besides.'[31]

But these days, killing is done from great distances. Someone just presses a button, a bomb is released, thousands die. How will non-violent suffering forestall this

---

[31] Ibid., pp. 202-03.

kind of—impersonal, distant—killing? 'Behind the death-dealing bomb,' Gandhiji says, 'is the human hand that releases it, and behind that still, is the human heart that sets the hand in motion.' Moreover, he continues, 'at the back of the policy of terrorism is the assumption that terrorism if applied in a sufficient measure will produce the desired result, namely, bend the adversary to the tyrant's will. But supposing a people make up their mind that they will never do the tyrant's will, nor retaliate with the tyrant's own methods, the tyrant will not find it worth his while to go on with his terrorism. If sufficient food is given to the tyrant, a time will come when he will have had more than surfeit. If all the mice in the world held conference together and resolved that they would no more fear the cat but all run into her mouth, the mice would live . . .'

'THE UNFAILING ASSISTANCE OF GOD'

But you don't know Hitler and Mussolini, one of the visitors remarks. 'They are incapable of any kind of moral response. They have no conscience and they have made themselves impervious to world opinion . . .'

Gandhiji is not persuaded one bit. He replies, 'Your argument presupposes that the dictators like Mussolini or Hitler are beyond redemption. But belief in non-violence is based on the assumption that human nature in its essence is one and therefore unfailingly responds to the advances of love. It should be remembered that they have up to now always found ready response to the violence that they have used. Within their experience, they have not come across organized non-violent resistance on an appreciable scale, if at all. Therefore, it is not only highly likely, but I hold it to be inevitable, that they would recognize the superiority of non-violent resistance over any display of violence that they may be capable of putting forth. Moreover, the non-violent technique that I have presented to the Czechs does not depend for its success on the goodwill of the dictators, *for, a non-violent resister depends upon the unfailing assistance of God which sustains him throughout difficulties which would otherwise be considered insurmountable. His faith makes him indomitable.*'[32]

The main points, of course, concern 'active non-violence'; Gandhiji's faith in the ultimate efficacy of non-violence being rooted in his faith in the 'unfailing assistance of God'; his faith that if even one Jew acts in the way he has set out, he would not just save his own self-respect, in all probability his example would prove infectious and save all Jews— though, in this instance Gandhiji puts the faith conditionally, 'an example which, *if* it became infectious . . .' But one minor point before we proceed further with these.

FAITHFULLY REPORTED

A typical correspondent writes that he just cannot believe that Gandhiji has spoken the remarks that have been attributed to him about Jews calling down curses on the Germans and wanting the Americans and the British to wage war on their behalf. He requests Gandhiji for reassurance that he has been misreported. Gandhiji writes that he can provide no reassurance in the matter as he had, in fact, said as much. And that is because he believes it to be the case. The Jews are not angels. It would be natural for them to react in that way. He himself would, if he were in their place. And he has a case at hand:

> I happen to have a Jewish friend living with me. He has an intellectual belief in non-violence. But he says he cannot pray for Hitler. He is so full of anger over the German atrocities that he cannot speak of them with restraint. I do not quarrel with him over his anger. He wants to be non-violent, but the sufferings of

---

[32] Ibid., pp. 204-05.

fellow-Jews are too much for him to bear. What is true of him is true of thousands of Jews who have no thought even of 'loving the enemy'. With them as with millions 'revenge is sweet, to forgive is divine.'[33]

That bit about their having 'called down upon the Germans the curses of mankind, and they wanted America and England to fight Germany on their behalf' wouldn't go away. For one thing, it could easily be used by Hitler's goons as yet further proof that justifies what they are doing to the Jews. The statement is taken up and challenged by several Jewish thinkers and publications. 'On what evidence do you say this?' they ask Gandhiji.

Gandhiji responds in the way that sets him apart. He reproduces their query and charge. He says that he had asked Pyarelal, and then Mahadev Desai to locate the publications and statements on the basis of which he had formed this impression. As more letters arrived, including from friends for whom he had high regard, 'I put greater diligence in my search.' But the searchers have not been able to lay hands on any conclusive writing, he reports. Therefore, 'I must withdraw it [the statement about Jews having called curses down upon the Germans and wanting America and Britain to fight on their behalf] without any reservation. I only hope that my observation has not harmed any single Jew.'[34]

IS GOD SETTING EVERYONE UP?

But on the main points Gandhiji remains firm. In the same exchange with missionaries, we find him counselling non-violence as the remedy that China should adopt in the face of Japanese aggression. It is 'unbecoming', he says, for a

---

[33] Ibid., pp. 381-82.
[34] *The Collected Works of Mahatma Gandhi*, op. cit., Volume 69, 1977, pp. 291-92.

nation of 400 million to try and resist the Japanese by adopting Japanese methods. 'If the Chinese had non-violence of my conception, there would be no use left for the latest machinery of destruction which Japan posses. "Bring all your machinery, we present half of our population to you. But the remaining two hundred millions won't bend their knee to you." If the Chinese did that, Japan would become China's slave.'[35]

Would it have become 'China's slave'? But, in the context of our present concern, that is the minor question. If, as Gandhiji believed and said again and again—we have just seen him reiterate the belief repeatedly in the context of the Bihar earthquake—that nothing happens but by the will of God, the question naturally would have arisen, 'Why did God put the Japanese up to the terrible atrocities that they inflicted upon the Chinese?' Was He, perchance, setting them up to be repaid for their bad karma with barbarism in return, the obliteration of Hiroshima and Nagasaki? And in Hiroshima and Nagasaki, was He setting up the Americans so that they could be made to suffer in Korea, and then Vietnam, and then Iraq, and then Afghanistan? And what of the millions of Koreans, Vietnamese, Iraqis and Afghans who got killed so that God could balance the Americans' ledger?

These questions are in the future. At the time, observers are exercised about the claim of Gandhiji that non-violent resistance would melt the stoniest heart in Germany, even of a Hitler. *The Statesman* writes a trenchant editorial. What has been the net result of the sufferings that Pastor Niemoeller and his associates have borne in concentration camps for standing up to the Nazis? They have stood up with utmost nobility, with not a trace of resistance or resentment. 'And what change of heart is there in

---

[35] *The Collected Works of Mahatma Gandhi*, op. cit., Volume 68, 1977, p. 203.

Germany?' For five years, members of Bible Searchers'
Leagues who rejected Nazi militarism as being contrary to
the teachings of Jesus have been buried in prisons and
concentration camps. 'And how many Germans know of
them or, if they know, do anything about it?' 'Non-violence,
whether of the weak or of the strong, seems, except in very
specific conditions, rather a personal than a social
gospel . . . Christ is the supreme example of non-violence
and the indignities heaped upon Him and His tortured
death prove once and for all that in a worldly and temporal
sense it can fail hopelessly.'

Characteristically, Gandhiji reproduces the critical
editorial in *Harijan*. He thinks it important enough to
respond at length. The sufferings of Pastor Niemoeller and
others have not been in vain, he dictates in a train. 'They
have preserved their self-respect intact. They have proved
that their faith was equal to any suffering'—were these the
objectives that they had intended to achieve? 'That they
have not proved sufficient for melting Herr Hitler's heart
merely shows that it is made of a harder material than
stone,' Gandhiji says, and repeats his faith, 'But the hardest
metal yields to sufficient heat. Even so must the hardest
heart melt before sufficiency of the heat of non-violence.
And there is no limit to the capacity of non-violence to
generate heat.'

Hence, almost by definition, if in a particular instance, the
heart of the oppressor has not melted, that is only because
an insufficient number has suffered non-violently.

Moreover, Gandhiji says, every action is a result of, and in
turn occasions 'a multitude of forces'. Many of these,
especially in the case of human action, are forces of which
we have no knowledge. 'But our ignorance must not be
made to serve the cause of disbelief in the power of these
forces. Rather is our ignorance a cause for greater faith,' he
maintains. 'And non-violence being the mightiest force in

the world and also the most elusive in its working, it demands the greatest exercise of faith. Even as we believe in God in faith, so have we to believe in non-violence in faith.'

Hence, if God does not relieve our suffering, we must believe all the more in Him. If non-violence does not work, we must reinforce our faith that ultimately it will. From that inevitably follows the deduction: if our suffering has not been relieved, we are at fault—our faith in God is insufficient, a fact that is proven by the fact that our suffering has not been relieved.

'I PLEAD FOR MORE SUFFERING AND STILL MORE'

Gandhiji then turns to some practical reasons for having faith that non-violence would work in the German case. 'Herr Hitler is but one man enjoying no more than the average span of life.' Moreover, 'He would be a spent force if he had not the backing of his people. I do not despair of his responding to human suffering even though caused by him. But I must refuse to believe that the Germans as a nation have no heart or markedly less than the other nations of the earth.' Of course, Gandhiji does not then know what later research will establish, namely, that legions upon legions of common, ordinary Germans collaborated in one way or the other—in looking up property records, genealogical data, censuses to identify Jews and those having even a trace of Jewish blood; in storming their establishments; in rounding them up; in making arrangements for their transport . . . 'They will some day or other rebel against their own adored hero, if he does not wake up betimes. And when he or they do, we shall find that the sufferings of the Pastor and his fellow-workers had not a little to do with the awakening. . .'

Victory achieved through violence in the First World War produced a Hitler and his vengeance, Gandhiji points out. 'And what a vengeance it is! My answer, therefore, must be the answer that Stephenson gave to his fellow-workers who had despaired of ever filling the deep pit that made the first railway possible. He asked his co-workers of little faith to have more faith and go on filling the pit. It was not bottomless, it must be filled. Even so I do not despair because Herr Hitler's or the German heart has not yet melted. On the contrary *I plead for more suffering and still more till the melting has become visible to the naked eye.* And even as the Pastor has covered himself with glory, a single Jew bravely standing up and refusing to bow to Hitler's decrees will cover himself with glory and lead the way to the deliverance of the fellow Jews . . .'

As for the allusion to Jesus' suffering having yielded little, Gandhiji cites his personal faith as evidence: 'Though I cannot claim to be Christian in the sectarian sense, the example of Jesus' suffering is a factor in the composition of my undying faith in non-violence which rules all my actions, worldly and temporal. And I know that there are hundreds of Christians who believe likewise.' Gandhiji's conclusion is instructive: 'Jesus lived and died in vain if he did not teach us to regulate the whole of life by the eternal Law of Love.'[36] But maybe, and history surely shows that, humanity has *not* got converted to regulating its life by the Law of Love, the 'Ls' capitalized or not, and that Jesus *did* die in vain.

THE JEWISH RESPONSE

By now, Jewish thinkers and leaders are completely bewildered. How could the Mahatma, with his commitment to truth, be so completely oblivious of the situation in Germany? It is not just that his advice is impractical. He is just refusing to see what is being done to the Jews in Germany; he is shutting his eyes to the circumstances in

---

[36] Ibid., pp. 276-78.

which they would have to, if they would, offer resistance of the kind he is recommending.

One of the great Jewish philosophers, Martin Buber, who, like so many, has closely, and with ardent admiration, been following Gandhiji's writings and struggles, writes to him in February 1939.

'Jews are being persecuted, robbed, maltreated, tortured, murdered,' Buber writes. 'And you, Mahatma Gandhi, say that their position in the country where they suffer all this is an exact parallel to the position of Indians in South Africa at the time you inaugurated your famous "Force of Truth" or "Strength of the Soul" (Satyagraha) campaign.' ' . . . I read and re-read these sentences in your article without being able to understand. Although I know them well, I re-read your South African speeches and writings, and called to mind, with all the attention and imagination at my command, every complaint you made therein, and I did likewise with the accounts of your friends and pupils at that time. But all this did not help me to understand what you say about us.'

Buber recalls the incidents that Gandhiji had listed in the first of speeches in regard to the treatment of Indians—an Indian's shop in one village was set on fire; elsewhere another shop had burning rockets thrown into it. Set against these two incidents, are the thousands and thousands of Jewish shops that have been burnt and destroyed, the synagogues and scrolls of law that have been reduced to ashes. 'The only other complaint you set forth there is of three Indian school teachers who were walking after 9 p.m. contrary to orders, were arrested and later let off,' Buber notes.

> That is the only incident of the kind you bring forward. Now do you know or do you not know, Mahatma, what a concentration camp is like and what goes on there? Do you know of the torments in the concentration camp, of its methods of slow and quick slaughter? I cannot assume that you know of this; for then this

tragi-comic utterance 'of almost the same type' could scarcely have crossed your lips. Indians were despised and despicably treated in South Africa. But they were not deprived of rights, they were not outlawed, they were not hostages to a hoped-for change in the behaviour of foreign Powers. And do you think perhaps that a Jew in Germany could pronounce in public one single sentence of a speech such as yours without being knocked down? Of what significance is it to point to a certain something in common when such differences are overlooked?

And you counsel *satyagraha.* 'In the five years I myself spent under the present regime, I observed many instances of genuine *satyagraha* among the Jews,' Buber tells Gandhiji, 'instances showing a strength of spirit in which there was no question of bartering their rights or of being bowed down, and where neither force nor cunning was used to escape the consequences of their behaviour. Such actions, however, exerted apparently not the slightest influence on their opponents. All honour indeed to those who displayed such strength of soul! But I cannot recognise herein a watchword for the general behaviour of German Jews that might seem suited to exert an influence on the oppressed or on the world.'

'The word *satyagraha* signifies testimony,' Buber tells Gandhiji in the idiom that is Gandhiji's own. 'Testimony without acknowledgment, ineffective, unobserved martyrdom, a martyrdom cast to the winds—that is the fate of innumerable Jews in Germany. God alone accepts their testimony. God "seals" it, as is said in our prayers. But no maxim for suitable behaviour can be deduced from that.'

And then he turns to the central point that Gandhiji has been reiterating again and again. 'But, you say, our non-violence is that of the helpless and the weak,' Buber writes. 'This is not in accordance with the true state of affairs. You do not know or you do not consider what strength of soul, what *satyagraha* has been needed for us to restrain ourselves here after years of ceaseless deeds of blind violence

perpetrated against us, our wives, and our children, and not
to answer with like deeds of blind violence . . .'

And he turns to the aspersion that Gandhiji has
unwittingly repeated to buttress his assessment that the
Jews have never accepted non-violence as a creed:

> You say it is a stigma against us that our ancestors crucified Jesus.
> I do not know whether that actually happened, but I consider it
> possible. I consider it just as possible as that the Indian people
> under different circumstances should condemn you to death—if
> your teachings were more strictly opposed to their own tendencies
> ('India,' you say, 'is by nature nonviolent'). Nations not
> infrequently swallow up the greatness to which they have given
> birth. Now, can one assert, without contradiction, that such action
> constitutes a stigma! I would not deny, however, that although
> I should not have been among the crucifiers of Jesus, I should also
> not have been among his supporters. For I cannot help
> withstanding evil when I see that it is about to destroy the good.
> I am forced to withstand the evil in the world just as the evil
> within myself. I can only strive not to have to do so by force.
> I do not want force. But if there is no other way of preventing
> the evil destroying the good, I trust I shall use force and give myself
> up into God's hands.

'"India," you say, "is by nature nonviolent,"' Buber
continues. 'It was not always so. The Mahabharata is an
epoch of warlike, disciplined force. In the greatest of its
poems, the Bhagavad Gita, it is told how Arjuna decides on
the battlefield that he will not commit the sin of killing his
relations who are opposed to him, and he lets fall his bow
and arrow. But the god reproaches him, saying that such
action is unmanly and shameful; there is nothing better for a
knight in arms than a just fight . . .'

It is a long letter. Buber writes that he has taken many
days to write it, that he has often put down his pen and
searched whether he has 'overstepped the measure of self-

preservation allotted and even prescribed by God to common humanity, and whether I had not fallen into the grievous error of collective egotism.'

SATYAGRAHA IN HITLER'S GERMANY?

Three days later, another prominent Jewish figure, Judah Magnes, a Rabbi in the United States, writes to Gandhiji. He sets each element of Gandhiji's counsel against the facts. You say what you would do were you a Jew in Germany— that you would insist that Germany is your home, and bear the consequences, the Rabbi recalls. But that is precisely what countless Jews say and feel and have been doing in Germany. Their history in Germany goes back to Roman times. They do regard it as their home . . . 'I would challenge him to shoot me or to cast me into the dungeon,' you have affirmed, he writes to Gandhiji. 'Many Jews— hundreds, thousands—have been shot. Hundreds, thousands have been cast into the dungeon. What more can *satyagraha* give them?'

'I would not wait for fellow Jews to join me in civil resistance, but would have confidence that in the end the rest are bound to follow my example,' Magnes quotes from Gandhiji's article, and asks, 'But the question is how can Jews in Germany offer civil resistance? The slightest sign of resistance means killing or concentration camps or being done away with otherwise. It is usually in the dead of night that they are spirited away. No one, except their terrified families, is the wiser. It makes not even a ripple on the surface of German life. The streets are the same, business goes on as usual, the casual visitor sees nothing. Contrast this with a single hunger strike in an American or English prison, and the public commotion that this arouses. Contrast this with one of your fasts, or with your salt march to the sea, or a visit to the Viceroy, when the whole world is permitted to hang upon your words and be witness to your acts. Has not this been possible largely because, despite all the excesses of its imperialism, England is after all a democracy with a Parliament and a considerable measure of free speech? I wonder if even you would find the way to public opinion in totalitarian Germany, where life is snuffed out like a candle, and no one sees or knows that the light is out.'

He quotes Gandhiji's counsel further: 'If one Jew or all the Jews were to accept the prescriptions here offered, he or they cannot be worse off than now.' 'Surely you do not mean that those Jews who are able to get out of Germany are as badly off as those who must remain?' Magnes asks. 'You call attention to the unbelievable ferocity visited upon all the Jews because of the crime of "one obviously mad but intrepid youth". But the attempt at civil resistance on the part of even one Jew in Germany, let alone the community, would be regarded as an infinitely greater crime and would probably be followed by a repetition of this unbelievable ferocity, or worse.'

'And suffering voluntarily undergone will bring them an inner strength and joy' Gandhiji has written. 'I wonder that no one has drawn your attention to the fact that those German Jews who are faithful to Judaism—and they are the majority—have in large measure the inner strength and joy that comes from suffering for their ideals . . . But as to the Jews—I do not know if there is a deeper and more widespread history of martyrdom . . . If ever a people was a people of non-violence through century after century, it was the Jews. I think they need learn but little from anyone in faithfulness to their God and in their readiness to suffer while they sanctify His Name . . .'

Indeed, in a manner that would give you satisfaction, Magnes tells Gandhiji, large numbers of refugees, 'who in Germany were used to wealth, comfort, culture, have without too much complaint and very often cheerfully buckled down to a new life in Palestine and elsewhere, many of them in the fields or in menial employment in the cities.'

You say that if one war would be just in the name of humanity it is war waged against Germany to prevent the wanton persecution of a whole race, but then you add that, as you do not believe in war, 'a discussion of the pros and cons of such a war is, therefore, outside my horizon and province.' But what would you then *do*? What should *we* do? Stand aside and see others die waging that just war? . . .

Gandhiji sticks to his views. Three months later, he is again confronted with the query, How can you counsel satyagraha to those in Germany? Were a Jewish Gandhi to arise, and attempt to do in Germany what you are so heroically doing in India, he would not survive five minutes. Gandhiji reproduces the argument of the critic in *Harijan*. But he stays firm in regard to the advice he has advanced to Jews in Germany.

'THE IMMOLATION OF HUNDREDS, IF NOT THOUSANDS'

'Having read the reply more than once,' Gandhiji writes, in an article 'The Jewish Question' in May 1939, 'I must say that I see no reason to change the opinion I expressed in my article. It is highly probable that, as the writer says, "a Jewish Gandhi in Germany, should one arise, could function for about five minutes and would be promptly taken to the guillotine". But that will not disprove my case or shake my belief in the efficacy of *ahimsa*. *I can conceive the necessity of the immolation of hundreds, if not thousands, to appease the hunger of dictators who have no belief in ahimsa.* Indeed the maxim is that *ahimsa* is the most efficacious in front of the greatest *himsa*. Its quality is really tested only in such cases. *Sufferers need not see the result during their lifetime. They must have faith that if their cult survives, the result is a certainty.* The method of violence gives no greater guarantee than that of non-violence. It gives infinitely less. For the faith of the votary of *ahimsa* is lacking.'[37]

Soon the Second World War has erupted. Hitler's armies are overrunning Europe. A Dutch correspondent writes to Gandhiji. He had been living in Germany for many years. He has had to leave, and makes his way to Holland. Holland is overrun. He describes what the Nazis are doing. 'Hitler aims at nothing less than the destruction of all moral values, and in the bulk of the German youth he has already attained that end . . . Through Nazism, German youth has lost all individuality of thought and feeling. And the great mass of young people has lost its heart and is degraded to the level of a machine.' 'The German conduct of the war is absolutely mechanical,' he points out. 'Machines are driven by robot men who have no qualms of conscience about crushing under the tanks bodies of women and children, bombing open towns, killing hundreds of thousands of women and children, and on occasion using them as a screen for their advance, or distributing poisoned food. These are facts, the truth of which I can vouch for.' He comes to the operational point that pertains to Gandhiji: 'I have spoken with many of your followers about the possibility of applying non-violence against Germany. A friend of mine whose work it is to cross-examine German prisoners of war in England, was deeply shocked by the spiritual narrowness and heartlessness of these young men, and agreed with me that non-violence could not be applied with any success against such robots . . .'

Recall that the War is in full swing, it has been raging for a year; that Hitler's armies are laying Europe waste; that facts about their brutalities are known in every nook and corner. Gandhiji accepts as fact the correspondent's description of Nazism, and writes:

---

[37] *The Collected Works of Mahatma Gandhi*, Volume 69, op. cit., pp. 289-90.

What, however, concerns me is not so much his characterisation of Nazism as his belief that non-violent action may have no effect on Hitler or the Germans whom he has turned into so many robots. Non-violent action, *if it is adequate*, must influence Hitler and easily the duped Germans.

Notice the conditional clause, 'Non-violent action, *if it is adequate . . .*'

No man can be turned into a permanent machine. Immediately the dead weight of authority is lifted from his head, he begins to function normally. To lay down any such general proposition as my friend has, betrays ignorance of the working of non-violence. The British Government can take no risks, can make no experiments in which they have not even a workable faith. But if ever an opportunity could be given to me, in spite of my physical limitations, I should not hesitate to try what would appear to be impossible. *For in ahimsa it is not the votary who acts in his own strength. Strength comes from God.* If, therefore, the way is opened for me to go, *He will give me the physical endurance and clothe my word with the needed power.* Anyway all through my life I have acted in that faith. Never have I attributed any independent strength to myself . . .[38]

Notice that the War and what has come to be known about Hitler and his methods have not changed Gandhiji's view about the efficacy of non-violence, and this view is based on his belief that God provides and, indeed, constitutes the strength that sees non-violent action through.

A FEW LESSONS

Gandhiji's faith in God was intense, almost intimate. On many occasions, he reported that he actually heard a voice tell him what he should do.[39]

---

[38] *The Collected Works of Mahatma Gandhi*, op. cit., Volume 72, 1978, pp. 360-61.

[39] In the very conversation with a visitor, John R. Mott, that we have encountered above, we have the following account:

It is indeed the case that Gandhiji was sustained throughout by his faith in God.

It is also possible that to do great things, one just has to have blind spots of the kind that we have encountered in Gandhiji's observations in the foregoing, that one just has to be obstinate.

We must also be very careful in drawing inferences from Gandhiji's faith in God. It never for a moment meant to him that we should sit back in the faith that God would set His world right. Gandhiji's inference was the exact opposite: that we would be doing God's work only when we are ourselves attending to the task at hand.

He certainly was no fatalist telling himself, God is repaying us for our karma, we have to wait for it to work itself out. For him, the inference was the opposite. Not that, as the past has already determined the present, I should just sit it out, but that, as what I do in the present will surely determine what happens in the future, I must strive to the utmost today . . .

He was also, as we saw in the case of the Bihar earthquake, entirely practical, entirely focused on the here

---

JM: When have you had indubitable manifestation of God in your life and experiences?

MKG: I have seen and believe that God never appears to you in person, but in action which can only account for your deliverance in your darkest hour.

JM: You mean things take place that cannot possibly happen apart from God?

MKG: They happen suddenly and unawares. One experience stands quite distinctly in my memory. It relates to my 21 days' fast for the removal of untouchability. I had gone to sleep the night before without the slightest idea of having to declare a fast the next morning. At about 12 o'clock in the night something wakes me up suddenly, and some voice—within or without, I cannot say—whispers, 'Thou must go on a fast.' 'How many days?' I ask. The voice again said, 'Twenty-one days.' 'When does it begin?' I ask. It says, 'You begin tomorrow.' I went quietly off to sleep after making the decision . . . *The Collected Works of Mahatma Gandhi*, op. cit., Volume 68, pp. 171-72.

and now: whether you agree with my views about the earthquake being divine chastisement or not, you must work to assist all who have suffered in Bihar; whether you agree with my views about the earthquake or not, untouchability is a heinous sin, and you should rid yourselves of it.

But Gandhiji's observations—on the reason for the Bihar earthquake, on why non-violence is bound to melt even a Hitler's heart—also show where a line of reasoning based on faith in God leads. For one thing, it pins the blame on the victim. As God is just, the victim *must have* done something to deserve the chastisement.

And it is manifestly circular. Non-violence is certain to melt the stoniest heart. When Hitler's heart clearly does *not* melt, that is because sufficient numbers have not offered themselves for immolation. And when someone asks, 'But aren't *six million* sufficient?' the answer clearly is, 'But they did not have love in their heart.' And how do we know that they did not have love in their heart as they entered the gas chambers? From the fact that Hitler's heart did not melt . . .

In the end, Gandhiji's unshakeable faith in non-violence rests on his unshakeable faith that God does come to the aid of those who are true.

Apart from the question whether that faith is at all tenable, that stance shuts out examination. Moreover, the observations of Martin Buber and Judah Magnes show that men equally devoted to God can and do come to contrary conclusions as to His purposes, and the possible course that His light illumines.

Whether non-violence would have succeeded against Hitler is one aspect of the matter—in retrospect few would agree with Gandhiji that it would have succeeded if only the Jews had love for Hitler in their hearts. The question that bears even more on our subject is the basic one: if nothing happens but by the will of God, did God set Hitler and the

Germans up to carry out the holocaust? Did He do so, so that Hitler, having wreaked evil, may, as chastisement, die an ignominious death in his bunker, and so that Germans may be killed in turn, and suffer the humiliation of resounding defeat?

6
Two saints, so unlike God

Baba Amte was in Delhi. He was so kind as to take time off to visit the school that had been set up for spastic children, the school which at the time Adit attended and which Anita helped run. As everyone who had met him knows, Baba Amte had presence. His work had been of the highest order. To see Anandvan, the settlement of leprosy patients that had grown up as a result of his lifelong service to them, was to see a miracle. Persons afflicted by this terrible ailment led lives of utmost dignity. They grew crops—'Everything other than tea', they used to say joyfully. They produced goods— 'Everything other than salt', they used to say in triumph. They manned a complex and extensive irrigation system. They cooked, they taught. By their earnings they had endowed an enormous college for the uncaring, ungrateful community of those like us who are 'healthy'. Their houses were spotlessly clean. When one was in the presence of Baba Amte, therefore, one was in the presence of a person who had worked a miracle. And he had done so by sheer grit, by a superhuman obstinacy. And then there was his own physical condition—because of an injury to his spine, he could not sit; when he was not walking, he had either to stand or lie down.

He had been round the school. He had planted a pipal sapling. He was now lying on a cot, talking to the children. Every word he said rang true, for he was not reciting words, he had lived them. Difficulties, and how to put them to work. Service—how to serve without expectation of

reward. Determination. Obstinacy . . . Look not at what you
don't have, the faculty you *don't* have, the limb you *can't* use,
but at what is *left*, at the limb that you *can* use, look always
at what you *have*. Faith . . .

He finished. We were properly humbled, and moved.

Alok raised his hand. Now, Alok Sikka was—and
remains—as much of a fighter as Baba Amte. He is, if I may
say so, in Baba Amte's mould. At that time he could not
walk, he had to crawl on all fours. His speech was difficult
to comprehend. He had a hundred problems. But his spirit
was—and remains—as strong as Baba Amte's was. After
Baba Amte had finished his talk, and perhaps because Baba
Amte had said something in passing about God, Alok asked,
and it took him quite a while to complete the sentence, 'But
why did your God do this to me?'

For a moment there was silence. Baba Amte looked
around at us. After a while he said, 'I will tell you what
happened once.' He recalled that one of Gandhiji's
associates had a retarded daughter. The associate and his
family, including the daughter, were staying at Gandhiji's
ashram. Upon reaching his quarters one day, the father
found the child in a most distressing condition—Baba Amte
described it. The father, who had just come from Gandhiji,
flew into a rage. He lifted up the daughter and almost ran
back to Gandhiji's room.

Gandhiji was sitting with his head bowed, silent, in
contemplation. The father as good as hurled the child into
Gandhiji's lap. 'Why has your God done this?' he
demanded.

Gandhiji was startled. He did not speak for a moment.
And then he said softly, 'He has done this to melt your heart
into kindness.'

We were all moved.

Not Alok. He said, 'But if your God wanted to make my
parents kind, why did He do this to *me*?'

Everyone was dumbstruck. Including Baba Amte.

And for good reason. After all, look at Baba Amte's own life. He was a very successful man of the world. One day he was out for his early morning walk. Perhaps the sun had not risen or there was fog, I forget the exact circumstance he recalled. But he could see for only a short distance. He heard a groan of agony. He walked over. There in the dirt on the side of the road, with nothing but a few newspaper sheets to shield him against the searing cold, lay a man—unconscious, disfigured by leprosy. Baba Amte gave up all his affairs, and with just his wife and, as he used to say, one lame cow, he set off to serve lepers for the rest of his life.

Over the years, as he served them—so many of them broken in spirit, disfigured in body—dread, revulsion, anger, frustration, all must have welled up in him. Seeing these emotions and reactions, watching them mindfully as the Buddhist masters would say, he must have overcome them. But could one therefore say that the others had been afflicted with that terrible ailment so that he—Baba Amte—might conquer fear, revulsion, rage and the rest? Obviously not.

And that is why, whenever we chanced to meet after that encounter with Alok, Baba Amte would exclaim, even before I had reached him and paid my respects, 'I am still searching for the answer to Alok's question.'

GOD'S FREEDOM

God, of course, would have no difficulty with that question. For, while in Gandhiji's response, God is projected as at least having a constructive purpose—He inflicts mental handicap on a helpless girl so as to melt the hearts of her parents into kindness—God Himself is under no constraint to put a construction of this sort on what He inflicts. He just *does* it. Thus, even as He proclaims that the sins of fathers shall not be visited upon their sons, He exempts Himself from the rule and does precisely that. Of course, this belief in double standards, one set for Himself and another set for others, can be taken to be one of His defining characteristics: how often He condemns the jealous, and yet the one sin which He will not forgive is that of putting anyone next to Him; how strongly He denounces covetousness, and yet, though He has the entire universe to Himself, He is determined to have the adulation of the last man!

But to proceed with one of the rules from which He exempts Himself—that of not visiting on sons the sins of their fathers. David is, of course, one of the most celebrated of the rulers of Israel. But he is also one who is easily tempted. As Nathan, God's own prophet, tells him, he had been given everything by God: God had anointed him king over Israel; He had delivered David from the hands of Saul; He had given David not just his master's house, He had given him the master's wives also. 'And if that had been too little, I also would have given you much more,' God tells David. But look what you have gone and done.

You saw Bathsheba, the wife of Uriah, one morning, fell for her, seduced her, and made her pregnant. Her husband had been away for long fighting a war—for you. As your seducing his wife would have got known because of the pregnancy, you conspired with the commander to have the husband killed in the melee of war. The husband out of the way, you took the woman as wife.

Not right. Clearly unpardonable in terms of laws that God has set out. So, what does God do?

'Behold,' He thunders. 'I will raise up adversity against you from your own house'—so far so good: David is going to be put to trouble because of what he has done. But God is not finished. *'And I will take your wives before your eyes and give them to your neighbour, and he will lie with your wives in the sight of the sun. For you did it secretly, but I will do this thing before all Israel, before the sun.'*

Now, David did wrong. Why are the wives being put to this mortal humiliation?

But even that is not the end. Actually, Nathan assures David that God has 'put away your sin', and so 'you shall not die.' 'However, because by this deed you have given great occasion to the enemies of the Lord to blaspheme, *the child also who is born to you shall surely die.*'

And that is what comes to pass—'*the Lord struck the child that Uriah's wife bore to David, and it became ill.*'

David pleads with God to spare the child. He lies down on the floor through the night. He refuses food. Nevertheless, on the seventh day, the child does die—exactly as God has decreed.

David gets up, washes and anoints himself, changes his clothes. He returns to his house and asks for food. It is brought.

The servants are perplexed. 'What is this that you have done?' they ask. 'You fasted and wept for the child while he was alive, but when the child died, you arose and ate food.' 'While the child was alive,' David explains, 'I fasted and wept; for I said, "Who can tell whether the Lord will be gracious to me, that the child may live?" But now that he is dead; why should I fast? Can I bring him back again? I shall go to him, but he shall not return to me.'

The end of the episode says it all: 'Then David comforted Bathsheba his wife, and went in to her and lay with her. So, she bore a son, and he called his name Solomon. Now the Lord loved him, and He sent word by the hand of Nathan the prophet: So he called his name Jedidiah . . .'

David's seducing another's wife is the sin. To us, his pragmatism too would be one. But the real question is: what had the poor child done to be put to death?[1]

---

[1] *2 Samuel*, 12.7-25. In the Quran, God makes David 'a vicegerent on earth'. He is without blemish. The slightest trace of self-importance enters his mind when he has to judge between two partners in dispute over an

Given this way of punishing a helpless infant for the sins of a wanton adult, how would God answer Alok's question?

Perhaps, as the car-sticker says? 'There is no reason for it. It is just Our policy.'

IS HE BUILDING OUR CHARACTER?

The other variant of what Baba Amte had said is more direct: 'Suffering builds character.' Apart from the fact whether an All-powerful God could not have devised some other method of instruction, the question that naturally

---

ewe. Allah admonishes him, 'So judge thou between them in truth (and justice): Nor follow thou the lusts (of thy heart), for they will mislead thee from the Path of Allah . . .' [Quran, 38.17-26]. With considerable satisfaction do the Muslim commentators differentiate the presentation of David in their text from that in the Old Testament. Hence we read in Abdullah Yusuf Ali's volume, 'As stated in [an earlier note] above, this vision and its moral are nowhere to be found in the Bible. Those who think they see a resemblance to the Parable of the prophet Nathan (2 *Samuel*, xii, 1-17) have nothing to go upon but the mention of "one ewe" here and the "one little ewe-lamb" in Nathan's Parable. The whole story here is different, and the whole atmosphere is different. The Biblical title given to David, "a man after God's own heart" is refuted by the Bible itself in the scandalous tale of heinous crimes attributed to David in chapters xi and xii of 2 *Samuel*, *viz.*, adultery, fraudulent dealing with one of his servants, and the contriving of his murder. Further, in chapter xiii, we have the story of rapes, incest, and fratricide in David's own household! The fact is that passages like these are mere *chroniques scandaleouses*, *i.e.*, narratives of scandalous crimes of the grossest character. The Muslim idea of David is that of a man just and upright, endowed with all the virtues, in whom the least thought of self-elation has to be washed off by repentance and forgiveness.' (Abdullah Yusuf Ali, *The Meaning of the Glorious Quran*, Dar Al-kitab Al-Masri, Cairo, no date, p.1223, note 4178.) Which of the two accounts, both sent down by God, should we believe? Does the fact that the Quran does not mention Nathan's parable establish that the entire sequence set out in the Bible did not occur, that the transcribers of the Bible concocted it, that they just wanted to include a salacious incident as they were interested in purveying gossip? On the other hand, does that fact that the Quran paints a very different character of David than does the original source, the Old Testament, entail that the former is a gloss?

arises is: 'Whose character?' Six million Jews are killed. Are they murdered so that the character of Hitler is built? Or that of the post-Hitler Germans? Or that of those Jews who were massacred? Or of the post-massacre Jews? Or of mankind in general? As God loves all of His creation, as He loves every element in it and every being in it equally, why should He so arrange things that millions should die so that the character of some may be built?

Whose character does a tsunami build?

What of the poor animals who are killed and eaten every day? Is their character being built? What lesson are they meant to learn as part of this character building? That they should adore God? Animals are used for medical research, and in the process they are mutilated, they are killed. Yes, we learn—we learn how to combat diseases that God has allowed or decreed should plague us. What do the animals—as much a part of His creation—learn? Or is it that the suffering of animals matters less to God than our suffering? Or is it that, as the latter doesn't seem to matter much either, the suffering of animals that we use and eat is just more par for His course?

Could He not have arranged the food chain in such a way that one species would not have to kill the other so as to survive? Could He not have planted a gene for vegetarianism in humans, for instance? In the alternative could He not have created food directly from molecules—as is going to be done using nanotechnology tomorrow? Or did He stay His hand from doing so, so that man may discover nanotechnology on his own?

If 'X' is caught in a vice of injustice, and he resigns himself to it meekly—is he submitting to God's will? If he fights it, is he then resisting God's plan? Or has God put the injustice in his way so that he fights it and smashes it? Assume he picks up the cudgels. If he fails, is God affirming His will and punishing him for his hubris? Or is God testing X's faith in

Him?' If 'X' succeeds, and the unjust are overthrown, has he succeeded because of, or in spite of God's will? As God sent Jesus; as the death of Jesus was also entirely in accordance with God's plan; was Judas who betrayed Jesus, were those who reviled and mocked him, were those who shouted that the sinner and not Jesus be pardoned; were those who drove those horrible nails into him—were they sinners or were they carrying out God's plan as His faithful instruments? Had they refused to discharge their role in God's plan would they not have been guilty of the sin of disobeying God?

To say that God's ways are a mystery—right from why he created the Universe in the first place to why things happen now; to say that Krishna destroyed the entire city of Dwarka and killed his entire clan because he had to live up to the curse Gandhari had hurled at him—to say all this is not to answer the question; it is just to push the question one step back. For then we have to explain why Krishna did what he did to invite the curse . . . and we get back into the infinite regress.

How can we be so sure that, while His motive is a mystery, His existence is a certainty?

Similarly, the disproportionality of what He inflicts calls into question either His rationality or His compassion. That Adam and Eve ate an apple, and for that reason the whole of mankind should be punished? And that it should be punished *forever*? That some of us should sin here, and God should create a torture house—Hell—in which we will be baked and drowned in boiling oil *forever*?

Author after author has pointed out that the premise that God is omniscient leads to problems of its own. Being omniscient, He knows the future. As He knows that future, He knows how Pol Pot will use free will to wreak havoc on other humans. He knows that this fiend will exterminate a third of the entire population of Cambodia. Could He, then, not have given free will to everyone except this person? Or planted something else in Pol Pot so that this 'revolutionary' would *not* misuse the potency that God was planting in him? That certainly is not beyond either His power or His design. Going by theistic beliefs, He *does* create Jesus, Ramakrishna, Ramana—who are all *incapable* of doing wrong. Even in the collective, He could have so structured us that we did not have the capacity to harm others. He did, after all, limit our capacities in various ways, O'Connor reminds us in his persuasive book: we cannot jump 20 feet, we cannot run as fast as the tiger, we are not as strong as the elephant. Why did He not impose one more limitation on us? Or, while implanting free will, add a little extra? Why did He not simultaneously impart a little more intelligence so that we would not use that freedom to harm others?[2]

OUR RELIGION'S ANSWERS

What answers does our religion, Hinduism, offer? Do those answers escape the dilemmas that we have encountered while glancing through the scriptures of other religions?

What do the great exemplars of our religion say about all this? What did they say as they consoled those who came to them as the followers were buffeted by blows? What did the followers say, what did the great exemplars themselves say as great suffering—incurable ailments, extreme physical pain—afflicted the paragons themselves?

So that we may consider the explanations on their own merit and not be influenced by our devotion or aversion for who is advancing them, let us continue our experiment of going through the explanations without knowing who the Master is who is advancing them.

---

[2] These and other questions are raised in a telling way in David O'Connor, *God, Evil and Design, An introduction to the philosophical issues*, Blackwell, Oxford, 2008.

THE MASTER'S RESPONSE

The Master is compassion, kindness, consideration, empathy personified. He is deeply moved by the plight of others. Not just of his devotees. Nor just of human beings. He is to go into town. A second-class horse carriage has been hired. The party sets off. The coachman strikes the horses with his whip. 'He is beating me!' the Master exclaims in anguish. The devotee makes sure that, henceforth, the strongest and fastest horses are sent—so that they are never to be hit when the Master is in the carriage.[3] Such is his compassion for, his empathy with every living thing.

Inevitable: And so, when individuals who have suffered a blow come to him for solace, he does not say, as our televangelists are apt to do, *'Sab maya hai.'* He acknowledges their pain, he feels it, he sees that it is real. A devotee has lost his son. He has brought his grief-stricken wife. She stays at a distance. The devotee goes up to the Master. Bring your wife, the Master says. 'Ask her to come. Let her stay here for a couple of days . . .' The devotee says, with perhaps a little too much certitude, 'Yes, sir. It would be fine if she developed intense love of God.' 'Oh, grief pushes out devotion,' the Master says with so much greater understanding of a mother's heart. 'And he was such a big boy!' The Master recounts the case of another person who lost both his sons—they were grown-up sons, and both of them had attained what was a rare distinction in those days, a university degree. And the father, *'jnani* that he was,' the Master recalls, 'could not at first control himself. How lucky I am that I have none!'

---

[3] A, p. 236. So that the reader may consider the explanations and observations per se, and not be influenced by her veneration for the saints, their names are not being mentioned just yet. For the same reason, at this stage the references also are being listed merely by alphabets.

He proceeds to recount the instance of Arjuna himself: 'Arjuna was a great *jnani;* and Krishna was his constant companion. Nevertheless he was completely overwhelmed with grief at the death of his son Abhimanyu.'[4]

But while he feels the pain of others intensely, while he regards it as real, the Master also says that it is inevitable. So long as the body is there; so long as our ego reigns; so long as the feeling of being separate from God remains; so long as our attachment to things and relationships of this world remains, so long suffering is inevitable. It is inescapable.

But why should such pain be inflicted on devotees of God? his followers ask. Yakub Khan, the amir of Afghanistan, has just been deposed, one of them reports. His empire has been snatched from his hands. And he is a great devotee of God.

'But you must remember that pleasure and pain are the characteristics of the embodied state,' the Master explains. 'In Kavi Kankan's *Chandi* it is written that Kaalvur was sent to prison and a heavy stone placed on his chest. Yet Kaalu was born as a result of a boon from the Divine Mother of the universe. Thus pleasure and pain are inevitable when the soul accepts a body.' 'Again, take the case of Srimanta, who was a great devotee,' the Master continues. 'Though his mother, Khullana, was very much devoted to the Divine Mother, there was no end to his troubles. He was almost beheaded. There is also the case of the woodcutter who was a great lover of the Divine Mother. She appeared before him and showed him much grace and love; but he had to continue his profession of woodcutting and earn his livelihood by that arduous work.' The Master gives yet another instance: 'Again, while Devaki, Krishna's mother, was in prison, she had a vision of God Himself endowed with four hands, holding mace, discus, conch shell, and lotus. But with all that she could not get out of prison.'

---

[4] B, p. 959.

Prarabdha karma: A devotee butts in, 'Why speak only of getting out of prison? This body is the source of all our troubles. Devaki should have been freed from the body.'

' . . . The truth is that *one must reap the result of the prarabdha karma,*' the Master explains, giving the classical reason of our tradition for what happens to us. 'The body remains as long as the results of past actions do not completely wear away. Once a blind man bathed in the Ganges and as a result was freed from his sins. But his blindness remained all the same.' [*'All laugh,'* records the chronicler.] *'It was because of his evil deeds in his past birth that he had to undergo that affliction.'*[5]

In a word: suffering, afflictions, loss of dear ones, their suffering are all

❑ Inevitable; and
❑ They are the results of what they and we have done in this or previous lives—deeds whose fruit we have not yet lived out.

But everything happens according to God's Will. Why does He implant sinful tendencies in man, and then put him through such afflictions for sinning? the devotees ask repeatedly.

'In God's creation there are all sorts of things,' the Master says. 'He has created bad men as well as good men. It is He who gives us good tendencies, and it is He again who gives us evil tendencies.'

But in that case, the devotee responds, we aren't responsible for our sinful actions, are we?

'Sin begets its own result,' the Master says. *'This is God's law.* Won't you burn your tongue if you chew a chilly? . . .'[6]

Darkness too is needed: But that doesn't *explain* the matter. 'Why has God created wicked people?' the devotee asks.

---

[5] B, pp. 275-76.
[6] B, p. 97.

'That is His will, His play,' the Master says. 'In His *maya*
there exists *avidya* as well as *vidya*. *Darkness is needed too. It
reveals all the more the glory of light.* There is no doubt that
anger, lust, and greed are evils. Why, then, has God created
them? *In order to create saints.* A man becomes a saint by
conquering the senses. Is there anything impossible for a
man who has subdued his passions? He can even realize
God, through His grace. Again, see how His whole play of
creation is perpetuated through lust. Wicked people are
needed too. At one time the tenants of an estate became
unruly. The landlord had to send Golak Choudhury, who
was a ruffian . . . There is need of everything . . .'[7]
     But if the power of *avidya* is the cause of ignorance, and
ignorance is the cause of the ills that befall us, the devotees
ask, why has God created it? The Master exclaims, 'That is
His play. The glory of light cannot be appreciated without
darkness. Happiness cannot be understood without misery.
Knowledge of good is possible because of knowledge of evil.
Further, the mango grows and ripens on account of the
covering skin. You throw away the skin when the mango is
fully ripe and ready to be eaten. It is possible for man to
attain gradually to the knowledge of Brahman because of
the covering skin of *maya*. *Maya* in its aspect of *vidya* and
avidya may be likened to the skin of the mango. Both are
necessary.'[8]
     'The joys and sorrows of the body are inevitable . . .' the
Master observes on another occasion when devotees press
him on the same question. 'God places one sometimes in
happiness and sometimes in misery.' He gives the example
of his favourite devotee, one they all look up to. The
devotee's father has died. The family has fallen on bad days.
They do not have enough to eat. They are, the Master tells
those who are around him at the time, in 'extreme

[7] B, pp. 97-98; pp. 250, 1013 similar.
[8] B, p. 216.

suffering'. The devotee, though attached to the Master, is in extreme distress. 'It is true,' the Master says, 'that no one starves at the temple of Annapurna in Benares; but some must wait for food till evening.'

A devotee protests, 'God is just. He must look after His devotees.'

'It is said in the scriptures that only those who have been charitable in their former births get money in this life,' the Master begins taking us back to karma and past lives. 'But to tell you the truth, this world is God's *maya*. And there are many confusing things in this realm of *maya*. One cannot comprehend them . . . There is much confusion in this world of His *maya*. One can by no means say that "this" will come after "that" or "this" will produce "that".'[9]

The purpose for which we have come: But there is another explanation too—one that comes through in the case of this disciple himself. The privation to which the family has been driven upon the death of the father is indeed extreme— some days there isn't food in the house for all of them to eat; on such days, so as not to be a burden on the rest of his family members, the devotee tells his mother that he has been invited for lunch by a friend. 'Even before the prescribed period of mourning was over,' the devotee recounts, 'I was running hither and thither in search of a job. Dizzy from lack of food, I had to go from office to office barefoot in the blazing sun, carrying my application papers. Everywhere I met with refusal. From that first experience I learnt that unselfish sympathy is very rare in this world; there is no place here for the poor and the weak. Even those who, only a few weeks previously, would have regarded it as a piece of luck if they could do me a favour, now made wry reluctant faces, though they could easily have helped me if they had wished . . .'

---

[9] B, pp. 397-98.

Days pass. Driven to even greater despair, the young man strikes upon an idea. 'God grants the Master's prayers. I shall make him pray for me so that the suffering of my mother and brothers for want of food and clothing might be removed. He will never refuse to do so for my sake.'

He goes to the Master. Sets out their condition. Beseeches him to pray to the Mother. 'My child,' says the Master affectionately, 'I cannot say such words, you know. Why don't you yourself pray? *You don't accept Mother. That is why you suffer so much.*' The disciple persists—he has no knowledge of Mother, he says, 'Please pray to Mother yourself for my sake. I will not leave unless you do so.' The Master tells him, 'I prayed to Mother many times indeed to remove your sufferings. *But as you do not accept Mother, She does not grant the prayer.* Well, today is Tuesday, a day especially sacred to Mother. Mother will, I say, grant you whatever you ask for. Go to the temple tonight, bow down to her, and pray for a boon . . .'

The disciple goes to the temple. But in presence of the idol, he forgets everything, and the prayer that comes out is not that the Mother relieve his family's suffering but that She grant him discrimination, detachment, divine knowledge, devotion.

As he returns to the Master, the latter inquires, 'Did you pray to Mother for the removal of your worldly wants?' The disciple is startled—for he had forgotten what he had gone for. So what should I do now? he asks. 'Go quickly again and pray to her,' the Master says. The disciple hurries across the courtyard. A second time, he prays for divine knowledge, for devotion. 'Well, did you tell her this time?' the Master asks as he returns. 'I was startled again,' the devotee writes. What is to be done now? The Master urges him to hurry back a third time. But as he nears the temple 'a formidable sense of shame occupied my heart.' His suffering seems so trifling a thing now. And so, once before the idol, he exclaims, 'I don't want anything else, Mother. Do grant me divine knowledge and devotion only.'

As he is returning, the disciple realizes that all this was 'certainly the play of the Master'. 'It is certainly you who made me intoxicated that way,' he remonstrates with the Master. You have to pray for us now. 'My child, I can never offer such a prayer for anyone. It does not indeed come out of my mouth,' the Master answers—words that we should remember as they will be put to the test just a few years later, and will show the integrity of the lives of these saints, an integrity that evokes reverence. 'You would, I told you, get from Mother whatever you wanted. But you could not ask her for it. *You are not meant for worldly happiness.* What can I do?'

'That won't do, sir,' the strong-minded disciple says. 'You must utter the prayer for my sake. It is my firm conviction that they will be free of all sufferings if you only say so.'

'As I kept persisting,' the disciple writes, 'he said, "All right—they will never lack plain food and clothing."'[10]

The enthralling story continues, and we will pick up fragments in a while. But for the moment, the thing that concerns us is that affirmation—that the sufferings that you and your family have to bear are inescapable as is the anxiety they will cause in you—for you are meant for other things, not for worldly happiness.

In a word, the explanations lie in

- ❏ The purpose for which God has sent us;
- ❏ Our karma;
- ❏ In particular, that committed during our past lives;

The explanations raise a host of questions, and are eventually saved only by the faith that God's ways are inscrutable.

---

[10] A, pp. 65-70.

No need to know: And I do not need to see beyond the veil, the Master exclaims in his childlike faith, his pristine innocence. And, by implication nor do we. 'Is it possible to understand God's actions and His motive? He creates, He preserves, and He destroys. Can we ever understand why He destroys? I say to the Divine Mother: "O Mother, I do not need to understand. Please give me love for Thy Lotus Feet." The aim of human life is to attain *bhakti.* As for other things, Mother knows best. I have come to the garden to eat mangoes. What is the use of my calculating the number of trees, branches, and leaves? I only eat the mangoes. I don't need to know the number of trees and leaves.'[11]

Of great value: Nor must we forget that in the Master's reckoning, suffering has great value in the scheme of things. A devotee leaves home for office. He crosses the river by boat. But because of troubles at home, his mind is very disturbed. He thinks that it would be better for him to go to the Master than to the office. So, he takes another boat and lands up at the Master's meagre quarters. As he walks up to the Master, the latter exclaims, 'What! You ran away from your office? That is not good. Live in this world like a crocodile. It lives under water, but sometimes it raises its snout above water, takes a deep breath, and again dives below the surface. People are submerged in their worldly life, and they come here only when they are suffocating at home. *Does anybody tread the path of religion without first undergoing sorrows and suffering? Misery has a great value. It helps a person find the path to God.'*

'I know you are married,' the Master continues, and asks, 'Do you have a mother?' 'Yes, my mother is still alive,' the devotee replies. The Master remains silent. After a while, he says, 'All right, now stay at home. *A little misery is good.*

[11] B, p. 161.

It helps one to make progress in spiritual life. If there is no misery, would anyone chant the Lord's name?' [12]

Pause for a moment. Consider the last few sentences again: 'A little misery is good. It helps one to make progress in spiritual life. If there is no misery, would anyone chant the Lord's name?' Would they hold for a child who is born mentally handicapped? That misery isn't 'little', of course. Does it help the child make progress in spiritual life? Does it turn him to chant the Lord's name? Assume that it does. Could the All-knowing Lord not have devised an easier way to turn the child towards Himself? As Alok told Baba Amte, *think of the child, not of the parents as you answer those questions.*

Hanging on to the power of attorney: Everything that happens, the distressing as much as the pleasant, happens by God's will, the Master teaches at every turn. And accepting whatever happens as the working out of God's will is the way to a cure for one's suffering. Give your power of attorney to God, he says. Then no burden that has befallen you is your burden. It is God's to carry. Should a man sitting in a cart carry his luggage on his head, or leave it on the floor for the cart to carry along with him?

You insist on keeping the burden on your head because your ego, your identification of yourself with your body makes you think that you are the doer. 'Suppose you are cooking rice in a pot with potato, eggplant and other vegetables,' the Master would say in his simple, direct way. 'After a while the potatoes, eggplant, rice and the rest begin to jump about in the pot. They seem to say with pride: "We are moving! We are jumping!" The children see it and think the potatoes, eggplant, and rice are alive and so they jump that way. But the elders, who know, explain to the children that the vegetables and rice are not alive; they jump

[12] A, pp. 369-70.

not by themselves, but because of the fire under the pot; if you remove the burning wood from the hearth, they will move no more. Likewise the pride of man that he is the doer, springs from ignorance . . .'

'If a man truly believes that God alone does everything, that He is the Operator and man the machine, then such a man is verily liberated in life . . . a *jivanmukta*, a free soul though living in a body . . .'[13]

'"I" and "mine"—that is ignorance,' the Master explains, pointing the way out of misery. '"Thou" and "Thine"—that is knowledge. A true devotee says, "O God, Thou alone art the Doer; Thou alone doest all; I am a mere instrument; I do as Thou makest me do. All these—wealth, possessions, nay the universe itself—belong to Thee. This house and these relatives are Thine alone, not mine. I am Thy servant; mine is only the right to serve Thee according to Thy bidding."'[14]

'One is aware of pleasure and pain, birth and death, disease and grief, *as long as one is identified with the body*,' the Master says. 'All these belong to the body alone, and not to the soul. After the death of the body, perhaps God carries one to a better place. It is like the birth of a child after the pain of delivery. Attaining Self-knowledge, one looks on pleasure and pain, birth and death, as a dream . . .'[15]

Once you see that you are not the doer, indeed that God is all, that everything is God, the problem is no more. The visitor is not satisfied. ' . . . If things happen through God's grace,' he protests, 'then I must say God is partial.'

'But God Himself has become everything—the universe and its living beings,' the Master responds. 'You will realize it when you have Perfect Knowledge. God Himself has become the twenty-four cosmic principles: the mind,

---

[13] B, p. 893.
[14] B, pp. 900-01.
[15] B, p. 257.

intellect, body, and so forth. Is there anyone but Himself to whom He can show partiality?'

The visitor does not give up. He asks, 'Why has He assumed all these different forms? Why are some wise and some ignorant?'

'*It is His sweet will,*' the Master exclaims. And breaks into song, and continues singing,

How many are the boats, O mind
That float on the ocean of this world!
How many are those that sink!

'It may be Her sweet will,' the visitor says, 'but it is death to us.'

'But who are *you?*' the Master asks. 'It is the Divine Mother who has become all this. It is only as long as you do not know Her that you say "I", "I".'[16]

Notice that

❑ Suffering is a problem that requires an explanation only if we posit a God. Otherwise, it is just what Donald Rumsfeld, the former US Secretary of Defense would say—'Stuff happens'.

❑ And the problem is resolved if we posit that all is God.

Just as important: notice that to us who do not know, both the diagnosis and the prescription seem a tautology. You say you suffer? You say your son suffers? But who are you? Who is your son? God is all—He is the one who suffers, He is the one who apportions happiness and suffering, He is the suffering itself. Where do you or your son come in? And the prescription: once you surrender fully to God, once you recognize that everything that happens is the working out of the will of God, the sting goes out of suffering—if it

---

[16] B, p. 818.

doesn't, that only means that your surrender is not complete.

But to the Master, to the one who has seen, the affirmation that all is God is self-evident truth, a truth his life bears out. The prescription is something that follows ineluctably from what he has *seen*—personally, directly.

THE MASTER AGAIN

As I wrote, 'The Master is compassion, kindness, consideration, empathy personified. He is deeply moved at the plight of others. Not just of his devotees. Nor just of human beings . . .' We must bear this trait in mind, otherwise we are likely to push several of the answers aside as they will appear callous. The point is that, far from being callous and uncaring, the Master is compassion, consideration, kindness personified. Hence, each time we are offended by an answer, we have to reflect, 'How does such a kind and compassionate saint believe all this?'

But first the nature of the Master.

Trudging across the hill, he puts his left foot near a bush. He doesn't notice that there are hornets there. They 'clustered round my left leg up to the knee and went on stinging', he recalls. 'They never did anything to my right leg. I left the left leg there for some time, so that the hornets could inflict full punishment on the leg which had encroached on their domain. After a time, the hornets withdrew and I walked with difficulty and reached [the Seven Springs], and [an associate ascetic] . . . gave me some buttermilk with jaggery which was all that he could provide by way of food . . .' A snake creeps over his body. He does nothing. It looks into his eyes. And creeps down. 'Snakes raise their hoods and look into our eyes,' he explains later when asked, 'and they seem to know when they need not be afraid, and then they pass over us. It did not strike me either that I should do anything to it.' Workers trying to get

mangoes from a tree strike it so that the fruits fall. He is
unable to bear the sight: 'Enough of this! Now go! . . . In
return for giving us fruit, is the tree to be beaten with sticks?
. . . You need not gather the fruit. Go away!' The Master's
voice which, on this occasion 'was like thunder', recalls a
devotee, 'reverberated in the ears of all who were there and
made them tremble with fear . . .' A devotee he has known
for years is plucking flowers for puja. He chides her for
doing so . . .

A snake slithers near the hall in which he and the
devotees sit. 'What kind of snake is it?' devotees shout. 'Beat
it! Beat it!' When he hears the actual beating, the Master
cries out, 'Who is beating it?' The devotees beating the snake
do not hear him. The snake is killed. The Master says,
'If these persons are beaten like that, they will know what it
means.' Indeed, he is on the best of terms with an
assortment of animals and birds. Monkeys and squirrels eat
out of his hands. Birds complain to him when an
overzealous attendant removes their nest. A peacock and a
cobra dance in front of him. His hand accidentally brushes
against a bird's nest. An egg drops and cracks. He is aghast.
He is distraught: 'Look, look,' he cries out in despair, 'what I
have done today.' He picks up the egg with the greatest
gentleness, and wraps it in a wet cloth; he places it back in
the nest; over the next few days, he beams healing thoughts;
till one day, the little birdling comes out alive. 'With gleeful
smiling face, radiant with the usual light,' writes a close
devotee, 'he takes the child in his hand, caresses it with his
lips, stroking it with his soft hand, and passes it on for all
bystanders to admire . . .' He is on the most affectionate
terms with a cow—after years of companionship, when she
is dying, he takes her head in his lap, puts one hand on her
head and one on her heart . . . She is buried as a saint . . . [17]

----

[17] Almost every eyewitness account of the Master is replete with such
instances. The leopards and the snakes: C, pp. 25-26; the hornets: D, p. 187;

He is often overcome with emotion—to the point of shedding tears—as he reads or hears the lives of saints, as he hears of the travails of his devotees, as he sees a motherless boy and girl . . . Whenever one of Gandhiji's associates is agitated, Gandhiji sends him to the Master. The Master, in turn, urges enthusiastic youth to cultivate Gandhiji's detachment, his selflessness, his devotion to God, his complete surrender to God's will of the results that would follow from his striving for the country . . .

He will not accept being served first . . . He will eat only what is served to everyone to the point that he would not even take special medicines and diet that have been prepared for him as he weakens. . . He wakes up at 2.30 a.m. every day to cut vegetables and cook for the devotees . . . In a word, in every way—compassion, humility—he is so unlike God.

An assassination: Gandhiji is assassinated. As devotees file in to the hall the next morning, the Master is reading accounts of the assassination in newspapers. A reporter rings up to get his reactions. The Master, 'his voice choked with emotion said . . .' a devotee records . . . The Master leaves the hall to walk. When he returns, the radio is broadcasting one of Gandhiji's favourite hymns, *Vaishnav jan to* . . . 'And tears fell from [the Master's] eyes . . .' In the afternoon, the ladies begin singing *Raghupati Raghava Rajaram*. 'With tears in his eyes, [the Master] signed us to continue . . .' A special aarti is offered at the Mother's

---

the snake over his body: D, p. 41; the snake that is killed: D, p. 57; the cracked egg: G, pp. 30-32; Lakshmi, the revered cow: C, pp. 328-29, D, pp. 263-64, E, pp. 178-80; plucking flowers: C, pp. 217-18; beating of the mango tree: C, p. 58; the complaint of the sparrows: F, pp. 597-98; squirrels and monkeys: C, pp. 28-29, D, various places, E, p. 44; moved to tears on reading accounts of saints: E, for instance, pp. 17, 63, 172; similarly, D, for instance, pp. 10-11, 59-60, 117, 119; weeps at seeing child of deceased devotee: D, pp. 269-70; cooking for devotees: E, pp. 70-74, 92-93; for several examples, H, pp. 98-106; and so on.

temple: 'when the sacred ash and vermillion powder were brought, [the Master] took them with great reverence . . .'

We get now to explanations. 'The day before yesterday,' the chronicler writes, 'while reading the paper, [the Master] remarked to someone sitting near him, "Look, didn't a comet appear some time ago? It is written in this paper that the death of the Mahatma was due to that. So the first result of it is now over."'

'What exactly was in [the Master's] mind when he said that?' the chronicler wonders—the words will soon acquire an ominous ring.

Meanwhile, the Master takes up another paper, and on reading it remarks—and this is what concerns us at the moment—'The person who fired the shot, it seems, came up to the Mahatma and, after bowing down, asked him, "Why have you come so late today, Sir?" The Mahatma replied that it was due to some work. The shot was fired immediately after that.' The Master, records the chronicler, then drew a parallel from the Ramayana, and remarked, 'It seems that after Rama killed Ravana, he forgot that he, Rama, had to go to Vaikuntha. So the Devatas took counsel among themselves and then sent Yama, the God of Death, to him. Yama came in the garb of an ascetic, and respectfully said, "The work for which you have come is now over: please come to heaven." This is similar: "Swaraj has been obtained; your work is over; why are you still here? Shouldn't you go back? It is already late." Thus the Mahatma seems to have been sent away.' [18]

So, as in the case of the disciple we encountered a while ago, we learn that *we come for a purpose. Other aspects of our lives suffer. And once that purpose is done, we are called back*— by illness, even by assassination.

[18] C, pp. 288-91.

THE SUFFERING OF INNOCENTS

'Why is there so much pain even for the innocent, such as children, for instance?' a visitor inquires. 'How is it to be explained? With reference to previous births or otherwise?'

'As about the world, if you know your own reality,' the Master says, 'these questions won't arise. All these differences, the pains and miseries of the innocent, as you say, do they exist independently of you? It is you that see these things and ask about them. If by the inquiry, "Who am I?" you understand the seer, all problems about the seen will be completely solved.'[19]

That is the basic position, and it is reaffirmed time and time again. But has our son Adit, suffered an injury to his brain or not? Can he stand and walk? Can he talk like others? What of the recent rupture in his eye? Have these things happened or not? Or is it just that, because my wife and I, and indeed our innocent son, have not fathomed 'Who am I?', these things appear to us to have happened when in fact they have not? The question is not, 'Are these injuries significant or not?' Maybe from some vantage point they appear trivial—maybe from space, far from seeing his disabilities, you can't see the child at all. The question is one of fact: *have the injuries occurred or not?* If they have, *why have they been visited upon this helpless child?*

The Master's answers veer between the diagnosis that we are not wearing the right spectacles all the way to the counsel that we realize that the injuries are just not significant.

In what way they are not significant will become clearer as we consider actual cases of persons who, having suffered traumatic blows, come to the Master for answers and solace.

---

[19] D, pp. 24-25.

Prarabdha again: A group has come from Bengal. One of them has recently lost a child. He asks the Master, 'Why did that child die so young? Is it his *karma*, or our *karma* that we should have this grief?'

The Master replies, 'The *prarabdha* that the child had to work out in this life was over and so it passed away. So we may call that the child's *karma*. So far as you are concerned, it is open to you not to grieve over it, but to remain calm and unaffected by it, being convinced that the child was not yours but always only God's, that God gave and God took away.'

The Master takes out a copy of *Yoga Vasishta*, and asks the diarist to read out the story of Punya and Pavana. Punya advises his brother not to grieve foolishly over the death of their parents. He points out to Pavana that he, Pavana, has had innumerable births in the past. In each of these past lives, he had a number of relatives. They have all passed away just as his previous lives are all over. In the same way, as he is not mourning the death of all those relations now, he should not mourn the death of their parents either.

The visitor asks, 'When a person dies while yet a child and another lives long, which of them is the greater sinner?'

The Master: 'I cannot say.'

The visitor is not consoled. He asks whether it is not a fact that were a person to live long, he would have greater chances to attain realization.

The Master points out that the outcome may actually be the other way round: 'The person dying young may soon be reborn and have in that life better chances of striving towards realization than the other person living long in this life.'

The Master's answer to a related question gives a clue to the general theme which we will encounter again and again as we study the Master's answers. A visitor asks about the activities which we are asked to renounce—does it mean that we should reduce our activities as much as possible? he asks. The Master points out that by giving up activities what is meant is that we must give up attachment to activities or to their fruit, that we must give up the notion 'I am the doer'. As for the activities themselves, *The activities for going through which this body has come, have to be gone through. There is no question of giving up such activities, whatever one may or may not like.'*[20]

A child's body too is worn out? One who will become an ardent devotee in the years to come reaches the ashram. He is in great distress. He has been reading the works of the Master for over two years. He has lost a son. His immediate quest, as he puts it, is therefore 'for peace and solace'. He gets to glimpse the Master in the morning in the hall. 'As our eyes met, there was a miraculous effect upon my mind,' he writes. 'I felt as if I had plunged into a pool of peace, and with eyes shut, sat in a state of ecstasy for nearly an hour . . .' He hears the Master say something about the Gita. He makes bold to ask, 'The *Bhagawad Gita* says that mortals cast off their *worn-out* bodies and acquire new bodies, just as one casts away the *worn-out* clothes and wears new garments. How does this apply to the deaths of infants whose bodies are new and fresh?'

The Master responds, *'How do you know that the body of the dead child is not worn-out? It may not be apparent; but unless it is worn-out it will not die. That is the law of Nature.'*[21]

'She has not gone anywhere': In the ensuing years, another child dies. Then the devotee's wife dies. He is distraught. As he has been doing every few months, he comes again to the Master's ashram. That afternoon, the Master sends for him. 'As I came into his presence, hanging down my head, there emanated a piercing shriek wherefrom I know not. At once all my physical faculties failed me and I collapsed.

---

[20] D, pp. 16-17.
[21] E, pp. 1-2.

When I came to myself, [the Master] called me close to him and made me sit near his feet. He spoke only a few words, but his tranquil look overflowing with Grace dwelt long upon me and most effectively healed my heart's wound.'

'The thought that she has gone,' the Master instructs him, 'must be got rid of. *She has not gone anywhere. She abides in the Self as the Self. How can she be non-existent?* Without God's existence, can we exist? Likewise, without her existence, where are the children, where is the family?'[22]

Days pass. The devotee complains that, while he used to be able to see his wife at least in dreams, now even that little solace has faded away. 'What! Do you find comfort in dream vision?' the Master asks. That night the devotee has a dream in which he encounters his wife. And is left all the sadder for that experience. 'Did you have the dream?' the Master inquires as the devotee comes into his presence the next day. The devotee acknowledges that, indeed, he had the dream, but that has left him all the sadder. 'Why do you grieve now?' the Master exclaims. 'You wanted the dream vision and you had it. You thought it would bring comfort. Instead it has produced a crushing grief. *All illusion is sorrow. Only the Real Self is happiness.'*

After a few days—days during which the devotee pens a few new poems, in particular one around the Master's *sandesam* to the devotees—the Master sends for the devotee again, and tells him: 'Yes, she has heard your message, and her reply is just what she said to you in a recent dream as recorded by yourself in verse 10, part II, that is, "Believe me, I have never gone anywhere, I am always with you." That is *her sandesam. Hitherto she appeared to be apart from you. But now she is with you and in you.* That is the truth. You need not worry about *her. She* is quite all right. Only you and the children are suffering from the *thought* of her loss.'[23]

---

[22] E, pp. 112-13.
[23] E, pp. 114-15. Italics in the original.

Is this, in fact, the case? Or has the Master told this to the devotee as this is what will console him?

Another son gone: 'A very devoted and simple disciple has lost his only son, a child of three years,' we learn in one of the most comprehensive accounts of the conversations of the Master. 'The next day he arrived at the *asramam* with his family.' The Master speaks with reference to them and their loss: 'Training of mind helps one to bear sorrows and bereavements with courage. But the loss of one's offspring is said to be the worst of all griefs.'

Notice that the Master is acknowledging that the grief is real, not phantasmagoric. That said, we are taught the proposition so often set out in the Upanishads and the Gita: 'Grief exists only so long as one considers oneself to be of a definite form. If the form is transcended one will know that the one Self is eternal. *There is no death nor birth. That which is born is only the body.*'

But the matter does not stop there. We are told next, 'The body is the creation of the ego. But the ego is not ordinarily perceived without the body. It is always identified with the body.'

And we come to the cure, and the simile that is stated often: 'It is the thought which matters. Let the sensible man consider if he knew his body in deep sleep. Why does he feel it in the waking state? But, although the body was not felt in sleep, did not the Self exist then?'

The same question could be asked the other way round: 'But, although the body was not felt in sleep, did not the *body* exist then?' We shall soon see why the question is not posed in this form, why we are almost pushed to conclude that, as the body was not felt in sleep, it is not to be taken as existing in reality. However, to continue with what is said with reference to the three-year-old who has died and his parents:

How was he in deep sleep? How is he when awake? What is the difference? Ego rises up and that is waking. Simultaneously thoughts arise. Let him find out to whom are the thoughts. Wherefrom do they arise? They must spring up from the conscious Self. Apprehending it even vaguely helps the extinction of the ego. Thereafter the realization of the one Infinite Existence becomes possible. In that state there are no individuals other than the Eternal Existence. Hence there is no thought of death or wailing.

The Master elaborates the reason and, ipso facto, the cure:

If a man considers he is born he cannot avoid the fear of death. Let him find out if he has been born or if the Self has any birth. He will discover that the Self always exists, that the body which is born resolves itself into thought and that the emergence of thought is the root of all mischief. Find wherefrom thoughts emerge. Then you will abide in the ever-present inmost Self and be free from the idea of birth or fear of death.[24]

But has the child died or not? We wonder. Or is it that what has died was so immaterial, so to say, so inconsequential, so much of a phantom of our thoughts that rectifying the thoughts is all? Not in the sense that the child will be brought back, of course, but in the sense that we grieve for that which never was.

Not exactly. Not that the child never was but that *the essence in the child which alone was/is real* remains exactly as it was/is.

A mother's faith: It is late, 11 p.m. A group from Andhra arrives at the ashram. Among them is a middle-aged woman 'with a sad but firm look'. She addresses the Master, and we can, to this day, feel the travails that she has been through, travails that so many mothers have to wade through in this world that the All-knowing, All-powerful, All-compassionate God has made:

When my son was in the womb my husband died. The son was

born posthumous. He grew up all right for five years. Then he was attacked by infantile paralysis. When nine he was bedridden. Nevertheless he was bright and cheerful. For two years he was in that condition and now they say that he is dead. I know that he is only sleeping and will awake soon. When they said that he had collapsed I was shocked. I saw in a vision a *sadhu* who appeared to pass his hands over the child's body and the child awoke refreshed. I believe that *sadhu* is yourself. Please come and touch my boy so that he may get up.

The Master inquires what the doctor said.

The mother: They say that he is dead. But what do they know? I have brought the boy all the way from Guntur to this place.

To console her, the Master says, 'If your vision be correct the boy will wake up tomorrow.'

But the mother's heart will not be deflected. She pleads, 'Please touch him. May I bring him to the compound?'

Those present protest. They persuade the party to leave. They learn the next morning that the body of the child has been cremated.

Talk turns to events of the night. Asked whether the dead can be revived, the Master replies, 'It is said of some saints that they revived the dead. They, too, did not revive all the dead. If that could be done, there will be no world, no death, no cemetery, etc.'

'The mother's faith was very remarkable,' one devotee remarks. 'How could she have had such a powerful vision and still be disappointed? Can it be a superimposition attendant on her child's love?'

The Master: She and her child not being real, how can the vision alone be a superimposition?

'Then how is it to be explained?' a devotee asks.

'No answer,' records the chronicle.[25]

---

[25] F, pp. 310-11.

Could it be that what the Master says to the mother, the conditional assurance he holds out—'If your vision be correct the boy will wake up tomorrow'—is, in fact, a way to persuade her that the son has actually died? That when the child does not wake up the next morning, she will that much more readily agree to allow the body to be cremated?

Intervention: But there is the related point, about Masters intervening or not intervening to reverse tragedies. A reader who goes through the accounts of devotees, or one who has himself gone to gurus and godmen for help will be struck by one feature. If the person we want helped, say a child who is gravely ill, gets better, we ascribe the reversal to the blessings and the miraculous powers of the godman. When the illness continues to worsen, we put the worsening to the child's karma or ours. This sequence is played out again and again in the accounts of devotees of the Master. During the period covered by a devotee's reminiscences, the devotee loses his wife and two children—in spite of his heartfelt prayers to the Master. In another instance, he sends an urgent cable and letter describing the alarming deterioration in the condition of one of the children. The cable reaches the abode of the Master and is handed over to him. It transpires that at the exact time at which the Master opens and reads the message, hundreds of miles away, the child turns the corner. And soon gets well. This sudden reversal is put to the Master's compassion and intervention.

But the Master has something much more subtle to say regarding the turn of the illness—and what he says now will become very important in understanding an infinitely more significant occurrence a while hence, and his dogged refusal to intervene.

The devotee goes to the ashram again the following Christmas. He asks the Master what the latter thought upon reading the cable he, the devotee, had sent. 'Yes, I read your message,' the Master replies, 'and also noted that the clock was then striking seven.' The devotee persists and asks,

'[Master] did you not think that you must do something to save the child?' The Master says, 'Even the thought to save the child is a *sankalpa* [will], and one who has any *sankalpa* is no *Jnani*. In fact such thinking is unnecessary. *The moment the Jnani's eye falls upon a thing, there starts a divine, automatic action which itself leads to the highest good.*' 'The conversation was in Telugu,' the devotee records, 'except the English phrase "divine, automatic action" which [the Master] himself uttered.'[26]

The words will become significant in the years to come. For the moment, let us proceed with accounts of other instances in which persons come to the Master for solace and help.

'Even now you are not born': News is brought to the Master that a person known to them at the ashram has died. The Master responds, 'Good. The dead are indeed happy. They have got rid of the troublesome overgrowth—the body. The dead man does not grieve. The survivors grieve for the man who is dead.'

The Master sets out the reason for not fearing death and not lamenting the fact that someone dear to us has died:

> Do men fear sleep? On the contrary sleep is courted and on waking up every man says that he slept happily. One prepares the bed for sound sleep. Sleep is temporary death. Death is a longer sleep. If the man dies while yet alive he need not grieve over others' death. One's existence is evident with or without the body, as in waking, dream and sleep. Then why should one desire continuance of the bodily shackles?

From this, the cure: 'Let the man find out his undying Self and be immortal and happy.'[27]

'Is there reincarnation?' a devotee inquires.

'Reincarnation can be if you are incarnate now. Even now you are not born,' says the Master.

---

[26] E, pp. 19-21.
[27] F, p. 71.

The root of all diseases and suffering: In response to another devotee, the Master says, 'The ego is the root of all diseases. Give it up. There will be no disease.'[28]

We may assert that my wife's ego and mine are the root of our son being born. But are those egos also the root of his suffering a brain injury? Or was the ego of our son when he was all of three days old the root of his suffering the brain injury? Or is it my ego and the egos of all round him who love him that are the root of *our perception* that he suffers from an injured brain?

A person working at the Benares Hindu University has lost his wife as well as children. How should I get peace of mind? he beseeches the Master. The Master's answer addresses the specific question—*how should I get peace of mind?* It does not exactly deny the reality of the tragedies. But we should study the answer—for it takes on a particular hue in the context of other affirmations of the Master in regard to blows that persons have suffered. The Master tells the professor:

> It is in the mind that birth and death, pleasure and pain, in short the world and ego exist. If the mind is destroyed all these are destroyed too. Note that it should be *annihilated*, not just made latent. For the mind is dormant in sleep. It does not know anything. Still, on waking up, you are as you were before. There is no end to grief. But if the mind is destroyed the grief will have no background and will disappear along with the mind.[29]

It is indeed the case that as far as the specific person is concerned, grief, pleasure, pain are mental states. They are feelings. Hence, they can be said to be in his mind. But, surely, in several instances, events have actually transpired that have occasioned the grief, pleasure, pain, etc. In the

---

[28] F, p. 141.
[29] F, p. 160.

case at hand, for instance, the person *has* lost his wife and children. True, the impact of the events has come through the filter of the mind—that filter may have exaggerated the injustice in them. True also that the wife and children having gone, the grief that remains is a feeling and, in that sense, can be said to 'exist' only in the mind. Truer still that, while nothing can be done about the actual events—in this case, the deaths—the gentleman has to work on his mind. And, therefore, a guide is right in directing the man to the one thing that he *can* do, that is in directing him to his mind on which he can, and must work. But, just as surely, the events that triggered them did not lie in his mind, they do not exist merely in his mind—which is what the opening words of the answer may lead one to believe.

Nor is that a one-off statement.

A gentleman, who is the Financial Secretary of the Department of Posts and Telegraphs in Delhi, loses his wife. They had been married happily for eleven or twelve years. The gentleman has read books that contain accounts of the Master and his teaching. But he does not find solace in them. In fact, he 'wants to tear them up'. Nor does he want to ask questions. He simply wants to sit in the presence of the Master. And so he has journeyed to the ashram.

The Master speaks at length about death and grief, and points the way. Grief is natural, he acknowledges, especially at the passing away of one's wife. It is said, he recalls, 'The wife is one-half of the body . . . So her death is very painful.'

That acknowledged, he emphasizes:

This pain is however due to one's outlook being physical; it disappears if the outlook is that of the Self. The *Brihadaranyaka Upanishad* says, 'The wife is dear because of the love of the Self.' If the wife and others are identified with the Self, how then will pain arise? Nevertheless such disasters shake the mind of philosophers also.

He recalls how we are happy in deep sleep. In that condition, there are neither wife nor others. In the waking state, they become apparent and thus give rise to pleasure or pain. The reason that state of bliss does not continue in the waking state is that we wrongly identify our Self with our bodies. He recalls what the Bhagavad Gita says: 'The unreal hath no being; the real never ceaseth to be . . .' 'The real is ever real, the unreal is ever unreal . . .' 'He is not born, nor doth he die; nor, having been, ceaseth he any more to be; unborn, perpetual, eternal, ancient, he is not slain when the body is slaughtered . . .'

'Accordingly,' the Master says, *there is neither birth nor death. Waking is birth and sleep is death.*'

'Was the wife with you when you went out to the office, or in your deep sleep?' he asks the distressed officer. 'She was away from you. You were satisfied *because of your thought* that she was somewhere. Whereas now you *think* that she is not. That is the cause of pain. *The pain is because of the thought of the wife's non-being. All this is the mischief of the mind.* The fellow [i.e. the mind] creates pain for himself even when there is pleasure. Both pleasure and pain are mental creations.'

There are two separate propositions involved here, and we should pause to distinguish between them. One is that what was essential about the wife continues unchanged, and therefore there is no warrant for distress. The other is that whatever has happened, that anything that happens registers on us through the filter of the mind, and, *in this sense,* 'Both pleasure and pain are mental creations.' That is an important distinction, and we shall have to return to it later on.

There is a third proposition. The Master emphasizes it often, and will do so in almost identical words in the most trying of circumstances.

'Again, why mourn the dead?' he asks. 'They are free from bondage. Mourning is the chain forged by the mind to bind itself to the dead.' To skip ahead a little, 'Mourning is not the index of true love,' the Master says. 'It betrays love of the object, of its shape only. That is not love. True love is shown by the certainty that the object of love is in the Self and that it can never become non-existent . . . Still it is true, pain on such occasions can only be assuaged by association with the wise.'

'What if anyone is dead? What if one is ruined?' the Master asks, steering the distressed towards what, from his vantage point, is the antidote. 'Be dead yourself—be ruined yourself. In that sense there is no pain after one's death. What is meant by this sort of death? Annihilation of the ego, though the body is alive. If the ego persists the man is afraid of death. The man mourns another's death. He need not do so if he predeceases them [by waking up from the ego-dream, which amounts to killing the ego-sense]. The experience of deep sleep clearly teaches that happiness consists in being without the body. The wise also confirm it, speaking of liberation after the body is given up.'

He adds words that will soon acquire a poignant ring:

Thus the sage is awaiting the casting off of the body. Just as a labourer carrying a load on his head for the sake of wages bears the burden with no pleasure, carries it to the destination, and finally unburdens himself with relief and joy; so also the sage bears this body, awaiting the right and destined time to discard it.

And then to the grieving officer once again, 'If now you are relieved of one-half of the burden, i.e., the wife, should you not be thankful and be happy about it?' Feeling relieved on this count is difficult for the uninitiated, the Master acknowledges. But, as he has said earlier, that is because of their 'physical outlook'—that is, their identifying themselves with their bodies as well as identifying the one who has departed with his or her physical body.[30]

Was the son present when you were asleep? A lady comes, seeking peace of mind. Stricken by tragedy—she has lost a young son—she is 'disgusted with life', she says, and wants to retire and take to the spiritual life. But she is not able to do so, she feels, as she is married and has a family to look after.

Retirement means abidance in the Self, the Master explains. Leaving one's surroundings is not the cure. One will only get entangled in another set of circumstances—one may leave the concrete world and get entangled in the mental world, he reminds her.

As for the tragedy, 'The birth of the son, his death, etc., are seen in the Self alone,' the Master explains. And he reiterates the argument about sleep and the waking state— the son, his birth, his death were not present when you were asleep; they come about when you are awake. What has happened between the two states? 'It is the rise of the ego,' the Master says. 'That is the arrival of the *jagrat* state. There was no ego in sleep. *The birth of the ego is called the birth of the person. There is no other kind of birth. Whatever is born is bound to die. Kill the ego; there is no fear of recurring death for what is once dead. The Self remains even after the death of the ego. That is Bliss—that is Immortality.*'[31]

'If a person dies whom we love,' a devotee says as they sit around the Master months later, 'grief results. Shall we avoid such grief by either loving all alike or by not loving at all?'

'If one dies,' the Master responds, 'it results in grief for the other who lives. The way to get rid of grief is not to live. *Kill the one who grieves.* Who will remain then to suffer? The ego must die. That is the only way. The two alternatives [which the devotee has spelled out] amount to the same

---

[30] F, pp. 170-72.
[31] F, pp. 205-08.

state. When all have become the one Self, who is there to be loved or hated?'[32]

The world and its miseries: unreal? The subject won't go away. A month has barely passed, and a devotee inquires, 'There are widespread disasters spreading havoc in the world, e.g., famines and pestilence. What is the cause of this state of affairs?'

'To whom does all this appear?' the Master asks— pointing the direction in which the questioner should look.

'That won't do,' says the devotee. 'I see misery around.'

'You were not aware of the world and its sufferings in your sleep; you are conscious of them in your wakeful state,' the Master says. 'Continue in that state in which you were not afflicted by these. That is to say, when you were not aware of the world, its sufferings do not affect you. When you remain as the Self, as in sleep, the world and its sufferings will not affect you. Therefore look within. See the Self! There will be an end of the world and its miseries.'

The reader will notice the distinction again. Is it the case that the Master sees that this particular devotee is bothering himself needlessly about the affairs of the world—he, the devotee, isn't in a position to do anything about them and the Master is, therefore, counselling him to focus on that about which he really *can* do something? Or is it the case that, from the vantage point of the Master, the world that we see as external to us, and consequently its miseries, are just not there?

'But that is selfishness,' the devotee protests, as we might.

'*The world is not external,*' the Master says. '*Because you identify yourself wrongly with the body you see the world outside, and its pain becomes apparent to you. But they are not real. Seek the reality and get rid of this unreal feeling.*'

Again, is the Master saying this so as to persuade the devotee to stop tilting at windmills and focus on what he *can*

---

[32] F, pp. 210-11.

do, or is it because, in fact, the world and its sufferings 'are not real'? Is the *feeling*—the distress of the devotee—unreal as in the last sentence? Or are the world and its pain 'not real' as in the penultimate sentence?

The exchange continues—the devotee does not give up, the Master restates his position patiently. 'What is to be done by us for ameliorating the condition of the world?' the devotee asks. 'If *you* remain free from pain, there will be no pain anywhere,' says the Master.

Put the distant and vast world aside, consider a speck of it: if a mother keeps herself 'free from pain' will the child struck by leukaemia not be suffering from leukaemia?

'The trouble now is due to your seeing the world externally and also thinking that there is pain there. *But both the world and the pain are within you.* If you look within there will be no pain'—no pain in the world or no pain for the devotee on account of the pain in the world?

The devotee frames the question in a different way: 'God is perfect. Why did He create the world imperfect? The work shares the nature of the author. But here it is not so.'

'Who is it that raises the question?' the Master asks aiming to steer the devotee back to searching his Self.

'I—the individual,' the intrepid devotee answers.

'Are you apart from God that you ask this question?' the Master asks in turn. And answers: 'So long as you consider yourself the body you see the world as external. *The imperfections appear to you. God is perfection. His work also is perfection. But you see imperfection because of your wrong identification.*'

But then why did the Self manifest as this miserable world? asks the devotee.

'In order that you might seek it,' says the Master : . . [33]

Where has he gone? Two weeks have not passed, and the matter comes up again. A lady and her companions have

---

[33] F, pp. 226-28.

arrived from UP. The Master is reading an account that suggests that a boy of four remembers his previous life, that he was married in such-and-such a village to two women. From reincarnation the conversation turns to whether one can ascertain the condition of an individual after death. 'It is possible,' the Master affirms. 'But why try to know it? *All facts are only as true as the seeker.*'

Those words seem to undercut the reality quotient, so to say, of birth and death. And so the lady says, 'The birth of a person, his being and death are real to us.'

'Because you have wrongly identified your own self with the body you think of the other in terms of the body,' the Master says. 'Neither you are nor the other is the body.'

'But from my own level of understanding I consider myself and my son to be real,' the lady responds.

Notice again, that it would be perfectly within even our limited grasp if the proposition was that 'neither you nor the other is the body alone'—there would be the mind, the life that has been lived, the experiences that have been gone through, the etchings that these have left on the mind . . . But the Master is pointing to something other than this amalgam.

'The birth of the "I"-thought is one's own birth, its death is the person's death,' he says. 'After the "I"-thought has arisen the wrong identity with the body arises. Thinking yourself the body, you give false values to others and identify them with their bodies. Just as your body has been born, grows and will perish, so also you think the other was born, grew up and died.'

'Did you think of your son before his birth?' the Master continues. 'The thought came after his birth and persists even after his death. Inasmuch as you are thinking of him he is your son. Where has he gone? He has gone to the source from which he sprang. He is one with you. So long as you

are, he is there too. If you cease to identify yourself with the
body, but see the real Self, this confusion will vanish.
You are eternal. The others also will be found to be eternal.
Until this truth is realized there will always be this grief
due to false values arising from wrong knowledge and
wrong identity.'

The Master recounts two stories. We have already come
across the first one, of Punya instructing his brother. The
second story that the Master narrates is from *Panchadasi*.
Two young men set off on a pilgrimage. One of them dies.
The other earns a little and decides to stay at the place of
pilgrimage for a while. He encounters another pilgrim from
their village. He asks him to convey the news of his friend
who has died and him to their parents. The pilgrim does so,
but inadvertently switches the names. 'The result was that
the dead man's parents rejoiced in his safety,' the Master
narrated, 'and the living one's parents were in grief.' From
this, the Master draws the conclusion, *'Thus, you see, pain or
pleasure has no reference to facts but to mental conceptions. Jiva
Srishti* is responsible for it. Kill the *jiva* and there is no pain
or pleasure but mental bliss persists forever. Killing the *jiva*
is to abide in the Self.'[34]

Surely, the story is just a simple expedient to suggest a
possibility—that, in these particular circumstances,
pleasure and pain resulted from misconception rather than
from facts. Even as we internalize the prescription—of
killing the *jiva*—does the general conclusion—italicized in
the foregoing—that is drawn, follow? After all, who rejoices
and who mourns when at last the youth who has survived
returns to the village? Do the facts when they become
apparent not cause pleasure and pain?

Where was your son before he was born? Ten years pass.
An Englishman who used to be a missionary and is at the

---

[34] F, p. 233.

time a teacher comes. 'I lost my son in the war,' he tells the Master, and inquires, 'What is the way for his salvation?'

'Your worry is due to thinking,' the Master says. 'Anxiety is a creation of the mind.' But is there not the objective fact that the son has died? 'Your real nature is peace,' the Master teaches. 'Peace has not got to be achieved; it is our nature. To find consolation, you may reflect: "God gave, God has taken away; He knows best"'—words that, given the Christian background of the visitor, are liable to find ready resonance.

'But the real remedy is to enquire into your true nature. It is because you feel that your son does not exist that you feel grief. If you knew that he existed you would not feel grief. *That means that the source of the grief is mental and not an actual reality.'* The Master then recounts the story from the *Panchadasi* that we have just encountered. *'So it is not any object or condition that causes grief,'* the Master concludes, *'but only our thought about it. Your son came from the Self and was absorbed back into the Self. Before he was born, where was he apart from the Self? He is our Self in reality. In deep sleep the thought of "I" or "child" does not occur to you, and you are the same person who existed in sleep. If you enquire in this way and find out your real nature, you will know your son's real nature also. He always exists. It is only you who think he is lost. You create a son in your mind, and think that he is lost, but in the Self he always exists.'*[35]

BUT THEN, WHY?

The responses of the Master, thus, cover two sets: the child who dies or is inflicted with an ailment, and those to whom she or he is dear and who, therefore, suffer because of his suffering. As the latter category of persons are the ones who come to the Master for relief and solace, the responses of the Master are directed more at them.

---

[35] D, p. 208.

The general theme that emerges is that they suffer because of wrong perception. And this is a dual *avidya*, so to say. First, they wrongly identify themselves with their bodies; second, they wrongly identify the child with that child's body. As a result of the first misidentification, they look upon the child as 'my child', etc., rather than as a fragment of the Self, one that is attached no more to them than to the rest of the cosmos. As a result of the second misidentification, when they see the body of the child hit by an ailment, when they see the body of the child inert—as in death—they take it that the child is suffering, that the child has gone, when, in fact, that which is essential to the child, his Self, is one that is not burnt by fire, nor wet by water, one that was never born and shall never die.

This twofold wrong identification arises because of the 'I'-thought, the ego.

But then, why have affairs been so designed that the 'I'-thought, the ego, arises to cloud our vision? the Master is naturally asked. The answer can only be inferred. 'What is the purpose of creation?' a devotee inquires. 'To know the inquirer is the purpose . . .'[36] 'What is the purpose of creation?' the Master is asked on another occasion. 'It is to give rise to this question; investigate the answer to this question, and finally abide in the supreme or rather the primal source of all, including the Self. The investigation will resolve itself into one of quest for the Self and cease only after the non-self is sifted away and the Self realized in its purity and glory.'[37] 'The object of creation is to remove the confusion of your individuality . . . If you cease to identify yourself with your body, no questions regarding creation, birth, death, etc., will arise. They did not arise in your sleep. Similarly, they will not arise in the true state of the Self. The object of creation is thus clear, that you should proceed

---

[36] E, pp. 47-48.
[37] F, p. 341.

from where you find yourself and realize your true being. You could not raise the question in your sleep because there is no creation there. You raise the question now because your thoughts appear and there is creation. Creation is thus found to be only your thoughts . . .'[38]

Thus, the answer to the question, 'Why have affairs been so arranged that the "I"-thought, the ego arises to cloud our vision?' would seem to be that affairs have been so arranged to give us the opportunity to get beyond the ego to the Self.

On occasion suffering and death, etc., are acknowledged to have a reality quotient, so to say. On these occasions, they are attributed to *prarabdha karma*—to the deeds we did or neglected to do, deeds whose fruits have commenced but ones that we have not borne to the point of exhausting them. *Prarabdha karma* will just have to be gone through, the Master affirms again and again, there is no dodging it—if your *prarabdha* is to teach, even if your knowledge is imperfect, 'it will surely be done whether you will it or not; if *karma* be not your lot, it will not be done even if you intently engage in it.' Nor should you worry about the karma that has fallen to your lot to perform. What you can do, and what you must strive to do as Janaka and Suka did, as Lord Krishna urged Arjuna to do is to give up the sense of doer-ship.[39]

But that leaves not one, it leaves two questions unanswered: why and how have affairs been so arranged that I am bound to do what my *prarabdha* binds me to do or not do, and yet I remain free to give up or not give up the sense of doer-ship?

Second, as a devotee asks, 'A person does something good but he sometimes suffers pain even in his right activities. Another does something wicked but is also happy. Why should it be so?' 'Pain or pleasure is the result of past *karma*

---

[38] F, pp. 566-67.
[39] F, pp. 46-47.

and not of present *karma*,' the Master explains. 'Pain and pleasure alternate with each other. One must suffer or enjoy them patiently without being carried away by them. One must always try to hold on to the Self. When one is active one should not care for the results and must not be swayed by the pain or pleasure met occasionally. He who is indifferent to pain or pleasure can alone be happy.'[40] The response is typical, if I may say so, in that the prescription in it—of shedding the sense of doer-ship, of bearing hardships patiently—is ever so apposite. But the response does not answer the question—*why* injustice, *why* suffering?

There are other strands in the responses that have been recorded about which we need to reflect.

His inscrutable will: The first is a melding of a standard position that we have encountered earlier—the inscrutability of His will—and of a utilitarian reason. 'Why then is *samsara*—creation and manifestation as finitised—so full of sorrow and evil?' a devotee asks.

The Master: God's will!

Devotee: Why does God will it so?

'It is inscrutable,' the Master says. 'No motive can be attributed to that power—no desire, no end to achieve can be asserted of that one Infinite, All-wise and All-powerful Being. God is untouched by activities, which take place in His presence; compare the sun and the world activities. [The Master often points out that all sorts of good and evil things are done, all sorts of benevolent and malevolent life comes into being under the sun's rays, and yet the sun can neither be held responsible for nor is it affected by what happens as a result of its having risen for the day.] There is no meaning in attributing responsibility and motive to the One before it becomes many.'

And then he gives a utilitarian argument for believing that the reason there is sorrow and evil is

---

[40] F, pp. 516-17.

God's inscrutable will:

> But God's will for the prescribed course of events is a good solution of the free-will problem. If the mind is restless on account of a sense of the imperfect and unsatisfactory character of what befalls us or what is committed or omitted by us, then it is wise to drop the sense of responsibility and free-will by regarding ourselves as the ordained instruments of the All-wise and All-powerful, to do and suffer as He pleases. He carries all burdens and gives us peace.[41]

Fate, predetermined in every way: But it is not just that this is a useful belief. And that is the second strand in the responses. On several occasions, the Master emphasizes that the tragedies that have afflicted those who have come to him have happened because they were fated to happen. A devotee who was living at the ashram yearns to go elsewhere on pilgrimages. He goes on one of these. And dies. The Master recalls, 'Acharyaswami who was there came here and died, and the one who was here went there and died. Everything moves according to fate . . .'[42] *Everything*, from death to the smallest things. The Master inquires if there is any orange pickle. Upset that there is none at the ashram, the ashram in-charge writes to a devotee to send a basket of country oranges. The Master, on reading the communication 'flares up'. 'To these people salvation seems to lie in country oranges! Otherwise why should we write to someone for them? Would they not come of their own accord if they are destined to come? . . .'[43] 'Are all important events in a man's life, such as his main occupation or profession, predetermined, or are trifling acts in life, such as taking a cup of water or moving from one place in the room to another, also predetermined?' an earnest devotee asks. 'Yes,' says the Master, 'everything is predetermined.' 'Then what responsibility, what free will

[41] F, p. 32.
[42] C, pp. 68-70.
[43] E, pp. 13-14.

has man?' the devotee asks. 'What for then does the body come into existence?' the Master asks in return. And answers, 'It is designed for doing various things marked out for execution in this life. The whole programme is chalked out. "Not an atom moves except by His Will" expresses the same truth, whether you say "Does not move except by His Will" or "Does not move except by karma." As for freedom for man, he is always free not to identify himself with the body and not be affected by the pleasures and pain consequent on the body's activities.'[44]

The question comes up again and again in different guises. The Master is explaining that one *can*, and in the case at hand, the person *should* pursue the spiritual quest even as he performs duties at his office and discharges responsibilities towards his family. 'In the early stages would it not help a man to seek solitude and give up his outer duties in life?' another devotee asks. 'Renunciation is always in the mind,' the Master explains,

> not in going to forests or solitary places or giving up one's duties. The main thing is to see that the mind does not turn outward but inward. *It does not really rest with a man whether he gives up his duties or not. All that happens according to destiny. All the activities that the body is to go through are determined when it first comes into existence. It does not rest with you to accept or reject them. The only freedom you have is to turn your mind inward and renounce activities there.*

The devotee persists: but will certain things not help, especially a beginner, like putting a fence around a young tree? For instance, do the books not counsel that pilgrimages, satsang etc., shall help? Of course, they will help, the Master replies, *'Only such things do not rest with you, as turning your mind inward does. Many people desire the pilgrimage or* satsang, *that you mention, but do they all get it?'*

---

[44] D, p. 78.

'Why is it that turning inward alone is left to us and not any outer things?' the devotee asks. Unfortunately, the diarist records the answer *he*, the diarist gave, rather than what the Master said: 'Nobody can answer that. That is the Divine scheme'—though, the answer is in consonance with what the Master has observed on other occasions.[45]

'Can I engage in spiritual practice, even remaining in *samsara*?' the Master is asked on another occasion. 'Yes, certainly. One ought to do so,' the Master counsels. But is the *samsara* not a hindrance? '*Samsara* is only in your mind,' the Master explains, and elaborates in words similar to the one we have noted above. But then why did you leave your home in your youth? he is asked. 'That is my *prarabdha* [fate],' the Master responds. 'One's course of conduct in this life is determined by one's *prarabdha*. My *prarabdha* is this way. Your *prarabdha* is that way.' Should I not also renounce? the devotee persists. 'If that had been your *prarabdha*, the question would not have arisen,' the Master concludes.[46]

When everything—from great decisions and turns in one's life to the tiniest detail—is predetermined, when the course that the body is to traverse is set down to the dot at the very time the child is born, I must, I suppose, conclude that his brain will suffer an injury too has already been determined.

Paradoxical inference: As 'the real disease is the body itself', as 'everything that happens is already ordained', an inference follows which, at first sight, is altogether paradoxical. The Master is a synonym for compassion. So many are helped by just being in his presence. And it is indeed the case that one who has attained jnana just cannot lie; he just cannot harm another—that itself is a boon to the

---

[45] D, pp. 211-12.
[46] F, p. 209.

world. Moreover, the Master explains, 'A Self-realised being cannot help benefiting the world. His very existence is the highest good.'[47] And yet a forbidding inference follows from the premises affirmed so often by the Master himself: namely, that the jnani is completely indifferent to not just what happens to his body, he is completely indifferent to, and 'immaculately aloof' from calamities that fall upon the rest of us, indeed upon the world. Of course, he does not and cannot cause calamities, but even if he did—Krishna destroying his entire clan and his city, Dwarka—he is unaffected by what he has wrought. 'For a realised man, the one who remains in the Self,' the Master explains, 'the loss of one or several or all lives either in this world or in all the three worlds makes no difference. Even if he happens to destroy them all, no sin can touch such a pure soul.' The Gita itself states, the sage recalls, 'He who is free from the notion of ego, whose intellect is unattached, though he annihilates all the worlds, he slayeth not, nor is he bound by the results of his actions.'[48] 'There were *rishis* like Vishwamitra who could duplicate the universe if they wished,' the Master says later. 'They lived during the lifetime of Ravana who caused agony even to Sita and Rama among others. Could not Vishwamitra have destroyed Ravana by his occult powers? Though capable, he kept still. Why? The occurrences are known to the sages, but pass away without leaving an impression on their minds. Even a deluge will appear a trifle to them; they do not care for anything.'[49] 'So many pictures pass over the cinema screen,' the Master explains, using a favoured simile, 'fire burns away everything; water drenches all; but the screen remains unaffected. The scenes are only

---

[47] F, p. 177.
[48] F, pp. 12-13.
[49] F, p. 389.

phenomena which pass away leaving the screen as it was. Similarly the world phenomena simply pass on before the jnani, leaving him unaffected.'[50]

If the destruction of the three worlds will not move the jnani, how can we hope that the travails of a mother, the suffering of an infant will move him? And yet it is also a fact that jnanis *do* intervene on occasion—Krishna at Kurukshetra, Rama in Lanka, acts of deep compassion of the Master recorded by so many devotees. How then is one to reconcile the inference that follows from the propositions that the Master advances so often with what the jnanis themselves do on occasion?

In the way made familiar to us by the Gita—the jnani acts but without the sense of doer-ship. It is in this sense that the jnani can live without the mind although living and acting require use of the mind, the Master explains. 'The potter's wheel goes on turning round even after the potter has ceased to turn it because the pot is finished . . . The *prarabdha* which created the body will make it go through whatever activities it was meant for. But the *jnani* goes through all these activities without the notion that he is the doer of them . . . He knows that he is not the body and is not doing anything even though his body may be engaged in some activity . . . The fact is that any amount of action can be performed, and performed quite well, by the *jnani* without his identifying himself with it in any way or ever imagining

---

[50] F, pp. 439, 468 similar. The Upanishad is cited: 'For one who knows, where all beings become the Self, there what is the illusion, what is the grief, for one who sees the oneness?' And in the explication to which the Master often directed devotees who sought answers, the commentator states, 'By this *mantra* of the Upanishad in the *Samhita*, it is explained that for a person who knows, all these beings appear in the true form of the Self. The knower of the Self who has turned away his activities from the dispersal of the mind sees oneness everywhere. It is stated that he is devoid of grief and delusion . . .' (I, pp. 160-61).

that he is the doer. Some power acts through his body and
uses his body to get the work done.'[51]

So that He may have something to do: The third strand
bears on the nature of God, and not just His will. The Master
is explaining the centrality of thoughts and the mind, and
how one must annihilate them. He sets out various methods
that aspirants may use, and warns that the mind shall not
give way without a struggle, that one must persevere. 'The
thoughts are the enemy,' he tells the devotees. 'They amount
to the creation of the universe. In their absence there is
neither the world nor God the Creator. The Bliss of the Self is
the single Being only.' But that when we seek to quell it,
mighty forces will strive to deflect us—for their own sake!
He recalls how, when Prahlada was in samadhi, Vishnu
Himself became apprehensive:

> This *asura* being in *samadhi,* all the *asuras* are in peace. There is no
> fight, no trial of strength, no search for power, nor the means of
> gaining power. In the absence of such means for power—*yaga,*
> *yajna,* etc., the gods are not thriving; there is no new creation; nor
> even is any existence justified. So I will wake him up; then the
> *asuras* will rise up; their original nature will manifest itself; the
> gods will challenge them; the *asuras* and others will then seek
> strength and adopt the means for its acquisition. *Yajnas,* etc., will
> flourish; the gods will thrive; there will be more and more of
> creation, more and more of fight and I shall have enough to do.

'So Vishnu awakened Prahlada,' the Master recounts,
'blessing him with eternal life and *jivanmukti. Deva/asura*
fight was resumed and the old order of things was restored
so that the universe continues in its eternal nature.'

That is a typical story from our Puranas. And it triggers
the obvious question. The devotee asks, 'How could God
Himself wake up the *asura* element and bring about

---

[51] D, pp. 189-90.

constant warfare? Is not Pure Goodness the nature of God?' *'Goodness is only relative,'* the Master instructs. *'Good always implies bad also; they always co-exist. The one is the obverse of the other.'*[52] In a word, the very nature of God—perfect goodness—inextricably contains, indeed it *implies* evil and the suffering that results.

The good from suffering: The fourth strand is that suffering is not just for a purpose, it is for good purposes. First, it hones devotees, it tests and sifts them. The Master recalls the song that has been sung by a saint who lived on the hill earlier: 'God proves the devotee by means of severe ordeals. A washerman beats the cloth on the slab, not to tear it, but only to remove the dirt.'[53] Second, suffering turns men's minds to God: 'Suffering is the way for realisation of God,' the Master tells a yogi who will soon become well known in the West.[54] To a devotee who complains that from the day of his birth he has never had happiness, that his mother too suffered from the time she conceived him, that he has not sinned in this life, and yet he suffers, and asks why this is so, the Master, after urging the questioner to reflect on who suffers, to whom do the questions arise, remarks, 'if there were no suffering how could the desire to be happy arise? If that desire did not arise, how would the quest of the Self be successful?'

Alzheimer's disease entails unspeakable suffering. Does it induce in the patient the desire to be happy? Having eaten away the mind, what mind does it propel towards a quest for the Self?

'Then all suffering is good?' the devotee asks. 'Quite so,' says the Master. And goes on to ask in turn, 'What is happiness? Is it a healthy and handsome body, timely meals

---

[52] F, p. 290-92.
[53] F, p. 416.
[54] F, p. 103.

and the like? Even an emperor has troubles without end though he may be healthy. So all suffering is due to the false notion "I am the body." Getting rid of it is *jnanam*.[55]

THE INTEGRITY OF THEIR LIVES AND EXPERIENCE

So that we may consider the explanations they offered independently of who was advancing them, I did not mention who the Masters were. But, of course, anyone with the slightest acquaintance with accounts of Sri Ramakrishna Paramhamsa and Sri Ramana Maharshi would have at once recognized that they are the Masters that we have been reading about; that the disciple whose family was driven to penury and want was none other than the young Narendra who would soon be known the world over as Swami Vivekananda.[56]

Sri Ramakrishna and Sri Ramana were saints, without a doubt. Every word they uttered, every gesture of theirs rings true through the decades. That their mystic experience was

---

[55] F, p. 593-94.

[56] As explained earlier, for the same reason, the accounts from which the instances have been taken were referred to merely by alphabet. The books are as follows: (A) Swami Chetanananda (ed. and trans.), *Ramakrishna as We Saw Him,* Advaita Ashram, Calcutta, 1990/1993; (B) 'M' [Mahendranath Gupta], *The Gospel of Sri Ramakrishna,* Swami Nikhilananda (trans.), Sri Ramakrishna Math, Madras, 1981/1986; (C) Suri Nagamma, *Letters from Sri Ramanasramam,* D.S. Sastri (trans.), Sri Ramanasramam, Tiruvannamalai, 1970/1985; (D) A. Devaraja Mudaliar, *Day by Day with Bhagavan,* Sri Ramanasramam, Tiruvannamalai, 1968/1989; (E) G. V. Subbaramayya, *Sri Ramana Reminiscences,* Sri Ramanasramam, Tiruvannamalai, 1967; (F) *Talks With Sri Ramana Maharshi,* Sri Ramanasramam, Tiruvannamalai, 1955/1984; (G) T.K. Sundaresa Iyer, *At the Feet of Bhagavan,* Duncan Greenlees (ed.), Sri Ramanasramam, Tiruvannamalai, 1980; (H) Arthur Osborne, *Ramana Maharshi and the Path of Self-Knowledge,*Sri Ramanasramam, Tiruvannamalai, 1970/1997; (I) *Sri Ramana Gita, Being the Teachings of Sri Ramana Maharshi composed by Sri Vasishtha Ganapati Muni, with Sanskrit commentary Prakasha of Shri T.V. Kapali Sastriar, English rendering S. Sankaranarayanan,* Sri Ramanasramam, Tiruvannamalai, 1998/2006.

authentic, on that there cannot be the slightest doubt. That they had extraordinary powers was experienced by so many directly that the fact cannot be in doubt: so many persons of such extremely diverse backgrounds, even a rebellious, sceptical and pugnaciously independent-minded youth like Narendra, the future Swami Vivekananda, soared into an indescribable effulgence at the mere touch of Sri Ramakrishna; so many of equally diverse backgrounds were transported into the same bliss and radiance by the gaze and silent transmission of Sri Ramana that the experience just has to be taken to have been genuine.

I remember to this day, Madhava Ashish describe what happened to him and to so many when they went up to see the Maharshi at Arunachala. Learned persons would go with a bundle of questions they had compiled, questions that they were certain would expose the inconsistencies in the Maharshi's teaching. But once they entered the hall where Sri Ramana Maharshi would be sitting, and the Maharshi's benevolent gaze met theirs, they would be transported, the questions would just evaporate from their awareness; if remembered, they would seem trivial, the answers manifest.[57] The compassion of Sri Ramakrishna, of the Maharshi, their utter simplicity and austerity, their

---

[57] So it was no surprise to read the following account: 'Somerset Maugham, a well-known English author, was on a visit to Sri Bhagavan. He also went to see Maj. Chadwick [an earnest devotee of Ramana Maharshi who gave up everything and lived for many years at the *Ramanasramam*] in his room and there he suddenly became unconscious. Maj. Chadwick requested Sri Bhagavan to see him. Sri Bhagavan went into the room, took a seat and gazed on Mr. Maugham. He regained his senses and saluted Sri Bhagavan. They remained silent and sat facing each other for nearly an hour. The author attempted to ask questions but did not speak. Maj. Chadwick encouraged him to ask. Sri Bhagavan said, "All finished. Heart-talk is all talk. All talk must end in silence only." They smiled and Sri Bhagavan left the room.' *Talks With Sri Ramana Maharshi*, op. cit., p. 517. The mesmerizing effect that Sri Ramakrishna had on Keshab Chandra Sen,

complete mastery over their minds, emotions, to say nothing
of the five senses, take one's breath away even to this day.

But in regard to the subject at hand we have to confine
ourselves to the explanations they gave for suffering, to
what they told devotees who had suffered blows, to what
they read into their own pain and illnesses. Did these
ring true in the earlier part of this chapter when we did
not know who the Master was? Or did they sound
commonplace, the sorts of things that every self-styled guru
repeats day in and day out? And did they suddenly ring
true when we learnt that these great sages had delivered
them?

PUT TO THE EXTREME TEST

What they had been telling others, the explanations that
they had been giving for suffering, the cure that they had
been urging were all put to the test in their own lives. Each
had the usual array of ailments that afflict us ordinary
mortals. Sri Ramakrishna broke his arm. Sri Ramana's
shoulder bone cracked as he slipped. His back and his sides
were afflicted by eczema. He had severe rheumatic pains
from his feet to his knees to his back. He came to find
walking very difficult. His eyesight deteriorated . . . So much
so that once when a young man, who had brought an elder
to Sri Ramana, approached him and said that the elder had
lost his eyesight, Sri Ramana 'nodded, as usual'. 'Soon after,
Bhagavan got up [for his walk] and told us,' the diarist

---

the head of Brahmo Samaj, is well known, and was of immense
consequence. Missionaries and those interested in saving Indians by
drawing them into Christianity had put great store by Keshab Chandra Sen
and his Brahmo Samaj. As Max Müller's letters show, Keshab Chandra was
going to be the beacon who would finish Hinduism as it was known and
bring millions into the light of Christianity. [I have set the matter out in
Missionaries in India, ASA, New Delhi, 1994.] Alas! Upon coming into contact
with Sri Ramakrishna, Keshab Chandra fell under his spell, and that put
paid to the hopes and plans of Max Müller and others!

recorded, "'He says he has lost his eyes. I have lost my legs. He comes and tells me. To whom am I to go and complain!'" Nor was this the first time, the diarist noted, that Sri Ramana had said, 'All of you come and complain to me. To whom am I to go and complain?'[58]

In the end both of them were stricken by cancer—Sri Ramakrishna by cancer in his throat, Sri Ramana by a ferocious tumour on his arm. Both of them died extremely painful, indeed harrowing deaths. Just a few months into the ailment, Sri Ramakrishna could not swallow solid food. He used to get tired after speaking just a few sentences. He had to communicate by whispers and often just by gestures. The young devotees, led by Narendra, who were trying to look after him during those terrible days could not bear to look at him, in such agony was he. While he bore the illness and pain with incredible fortitude, always solicitous of those who had come to call on him—even those who were rude and querulous—and even though his face was always bathed in his angelic, guileless, childlike smile, he was compelled by the pain to often plead with the doctors that they cure him, that they ease the pain.[59]

In Ramana Maharshi's case, the final days were prolonged into even greater pain, and even greater distress for the devotees. By 1948, he had begun losing weight at a rate that alarmed those who had not seen him for a few months. By June 1949, the tumor 'was blood-red and of the size and shape of a small a cauliflower . . . [with] frequent oozing of blood'. Towards the end of June, the Maharshi tottered and fainted . . . The growth turned septic . . . An operation had to be performed and the growth removed . . .

---

[58] A. Devaraja Mudaliar, op. cit., p. 31. Mudaliar adds, 'This is quite consistent with his teaching, that there is nothing but the Self and that he is That!'

[59] For instance, 'M' [Mahendranath Gupta], *The Gospel of Sri Ramakrishna*, op. cit., pp. 844-45, 932, 938.

Soon, a new tumour appeared above the old wound and
grew rapidly . . . That too had to be removed surgically . . .
Then one appeared below the shoulder joint. It soon grew to
'the size of an orange' . . . A third operation . . . The damned
tumour sprouted again. This time, it became 'the size of a
coconut' . . . A fourth operation. The Maharshi's condition
becomes heart-rending: blood keeps oozing out; the cancer
keeps growing, with overgrown pieces falling off; only *kanji*
can be taken; terrible pain wracks his hand, and his back all
the way up to his neck, this morning he fell down—so run
the accounts of devotees who were present.[60]

As those mishaps and ailments struck these saints, as that
final, excruciating turn came, what did their close devotees
read into the suffering of these saints? What did they
themselves say about the causes on account of which they
had been struck such a terrible blow?

The first thing to remember, of course, is the patient
detachment with which they viewed the pain and ailment,
at times from so great a distance as if the pain was battering
someone else. Their smile, their humour, their concern for
others did not leave them even in what for others would
have been unbearable pain. The total control of their minds
to which this bore testimony was superhuman. Sri
Ramakrishna's throat was in agony, the pain was
excruciating—everyone who has attended on a relative
stricken with cancer knows how very painful and
disheartening it can be even today; a hundred years ago
there were hardly any ways of either treating it or
alleviating its searing pain. In the course of assessing his
condition and administering medicine, one of the doctors
who attended on him, would prod and squeeze his throat,
he would have Sri Ramakrishna stretch his mouth open to

---

[60] For instance, G.V. Subbaramayya, op. cit., pp. 194-210; Suri Nagamma,
op. cit., pp. 457-463; Arthur Osborne, op. cit., pp. 167-76.

examine the insides. One day, as he touched the throat, the pain became unbearable. Sri Ramakrishna recoiled, and asked the doctor to pause for a minute. Now you can proceed, he said in a moment: he had shifted his awareness, the pain did not register. The doctors would tell him not to talk, to desist from samadhi. But he would keep on answering questions of his devotees who kept streaming in, till his throat would just not allow him to utter a sound—so as not to hold back anything from them, so as not to disappoint them. Even when he could scarcely get up from bed, he would force himself to greet and bless the devotees who came for the final darshan . . . Sri Ramana's final months and days were filled with the same concern and solicitude for others. He could no longer sit in the hall. He was lodged in a small room. Devotees would be allowed to pass by him in this small room. Soon he could not sit up in bed. Someone would support him and his head so that devotees could have their darshan. In the end, devotees could not be allowed even into the tiny room—a window was then kept open so that they could have darshan through a bathroom. Even this proved such a strain that the doctors and attendants closed the window. On learning that this had been done and seeing that many would have to go away disappointed, Sri Ramana—unable to sit, unable to eat even semi-solid food, in excruciating pain—refused to drink even a drop of water till the window was opened and the people could have their final fill . . .

These traits—solicitude and compassion—are the first things that strike one as we read accounts of the final days of these saints, and they are so unlike what we see of God through His deeds: as totally unlike is the humility of these sages. The second feature that strikes one is how the life and teaching of these saints were one. Throughout they had taught that the enlightened being is totally indifferent to

what happens to his body, that, indeed, the body is to be
discarded when the purpose for which it has been assumed
has been accomplished. The body itself is the disease,
Ramana Maharshi said so many times; this is just a disease
on that disease. The body is like banana leaves, he would
say. You put tasty dishes on them at the feast. But once the
guests have eaten, do you keep the soiled leaves? You throw
them away. The body is like a burden being carried by a
coolie, the Maharshi used to say. With this heavy burden on
his back, trailing behind the master, he looks forward to the
moment when they will reach the master's house, and he
will be able to get the burden off his back. As the final
illnesses struck them, as they became weaker, as pain
became more and more intense, the devotees implored them
to ask the Divine Mother in the case of Sri Ramakrishna, to
ask God in the case of the Maharshi to cure them. The
devotees implored them to use their own power—remember
that in both instances the devotees looked upon them
as incarnations of God—to reverse the disease. Both
absolutely refused to do either. On occasion, they rebuked
the well-wisher who suggested that they do so.

When a pandit, learned in the scriptures, urged him to
cure his throat by concentrating his mind on it, and recalled
that scriptures declare that yogis have the power to cure
themselves in that way, Sri Ramakrishna 'rebuked' the
person, writes Swami Nikhilananda: 'For a scholar like you
to make such a proposal! How can I withdraw the mind
from the Lotus Feet of God and turn it to this worthless cage
of flesh and blood?' 'For our sake at least,' begged Narendra
and the other disciples. 'But,' replied Sri Ramakrishna, 'do
you think I enjoy this suffering? I wish to recover, but that
depends on the Mother.' 'Then please pray to Her,'
Nikhilananda has Narendra imploring the Paramahamsa.
'She must listen to you.' 'But I cannot pray for my body,'
Sri Ramakrishna said. Narendra was not to be deflected:

'You must do it, for our sake at least,' he insisted. 'Very well,
I shall try,' Sri Ramakrishna told him. 'A few hours later,'
Nikhilananda writes, 'the Master said to Narendra, "I said
to Her: 'Mother, I cannot swallow food because of my pain.
Make it possible for me to eat a little.' She pointed you all out
to me and said: 'What? You are eating enough through all
these mouths. Isn't that so?' I was ashamed and could not
utter another word."'[61] Later, when the subject turned to
his illness, the pain he was having to bear and how the
Mother naturally could and would abate it if only he prayed
to Her to do so, Sri Ramakrishna exclaimed, 'I cannot tell the
Mother about my illness. I feel ashamed to talk about it.'[62]
Later still, when his pain and torture had worsened a
great deal and a devotee asked him repeatedly to do so, Sri
Ramakrishna reacted sharply: 'Leave me alone. I can't
say these things. I can't ask the Divine Mother to cure my
illness.'[63]

In a subsequent exchange, he gave a reason for not doing
so. 'Yes, people lay ailing children down on the ground
where men chant the name of God, in order that they may
be cured, or people cure disease through occult powers,'
he said. 'All this is miracle-working. Only those whose
spiritual experience is extremely shallow call on God for
healing the disease.' Continuing to explain with his usual
patience and concern to the doctor—an argumentative
one—Sri Ramakrishna set out why even the desire to cure
himself had waned. 'As long as there is the body, one should
take care of it,' he told the doctor. 'But I find that the body is
quite separate from the Self. When a man rids himself
entirely of his love for "woman and gold" [his catchwords
for attachments to things of the world], then he clearly

---

[61] Swami Nikhilananda, 'Introduction' to The Gospel of Sri Ramakrishna,
op. cit., pp. 69-70.
[62] 'M' [Mahendranath Gupta], The Gospel of Sri Ramakrishna, op. cit., p. 834.
[63] Ibid., p. 842.

perceives that the body is one thing and the Self another.'
'When the milk inside the coconut is all dried up,'
Sri Ramakrishna said giving one of his inimitable similes,
'then the kernel gets separated from the shell; you feel the
kernel rattling inside when you shake the coconut. Or it is
just like the sword and its sheath. The sword is one thing
and the sheath is another. Therefore, I cannot speak to the
Divine Mother about the illness of my body . . .'

'Once, a long time ago,' he continued, 'I was very ill. I was
sitting in the Kali temple. I felt like praying to the Divine
Mother to cure my illness, but couldn't do so directly in my
own name. I said to her, "Mother, Hriday asks me to tell
You about my illness." I could not proceed any farther.
At once there flashed into my mind the Museum of the
Asiatic Society, and a human skeleton strung together with
wire. I said to Her, "Please tighten the wire of my body like
that, so that I may go about singing Your name and glory."
It is impossible for me to ask for occult powers.'[64] The cancer
continued its relentless assault. The pain continued to get
more and more intense. Sri Ramakrishna continued to
weaken by the day . . . But he never budged from his
absolute refusal to pray that he be cured.

Sri Ramana's refusal was as final. The jnani is unaffected
by, he is indifferent to what happens to his body, he had
often said to his devotees. Fourteen/fifteen years before the
final illness was to strike the Maharshi, we find him telling a
visitor who is going on asking whether in life or upon death

---

[64] 'At first Hriday asked me—I was then under his control—to pray to the
Mother for powers,' Sri Ramakrishna continued. 'I went to the temple.
In a vision I saw a widow thirty or thirty-five years old, covered with filth.
It was revealed to me that occult powers are like that filth. I became angry
with Hriday because he had asked me to pray for such powers'
[Ibid., pp. 870-71]. Hriday was a distant nephew who looked after Sri
Ramakrishna for long and bore witness to his ecstatic mystic states,
but eventually became very possessive of his uncle. For a misdemeanour,
he was expelled from the temple in which Sri Ramakrishna was serving as
a priest.

the body can be made to disappear, 'These are only physical
matters. Is that the essential object of our interest? Are you
not the Self? Why trouble about other matters? Take the
essence; reject other learned theories as useless . . . If you
melt a gold ornament before testing it to be gold, what
matters it how it is melted, whole or in parts, or of what
shape the ornament was? All that you are interested in is if
it is gold. The dead man sees not his body. It is the survivor
who thinks about the manner in which the body is parted
from. The realised have no death with or without the body,
the realised man is equally aware and sees no difference.
To him the one state is not superior to the other. To an
outsider also the fortunes of a liberated man's body need not
be of any concern; mind your own business. Realise the Self;
after realisation there will be time to think of what form of
death is preferable to you . . .'[65]

He would recall a verse from the *Yoga Vasishtham:* 'The
jnani who has found himself as formless pure Awareness is
unaffected though the body be cleft with a sword.
Sugarcandy does not lose its sweetness though broken or
crushed.'[66] Not just to what strikes his body, the jnani is
indifferent to life and death themselves, he would say:
'A *jnani* is indifferent to death as to life. Even if his physical
consideration [condition?] should be most wretched, even if
he be stricken with the most fell disease, and die rolling on
the ground and shrieking with pain, HE remains
unaffected, HE is still the *jnani*.'[67] Sri Ramana recalled a
sloka from the *Hamsa Gita,* 'Just as a man blinded with
drunkenness sees not the cloth that he has on, so the Self-
realised *Siddha* knows not whether the perishable body is
existent or non-existent, whether by force of *karma* it has

[65] *Talks With Sri Ramana Maharshi,* op. cit., p. 41.
[66] *Ramana Maharshi and the Path of Self-Knowledge,* op. cit., pp. 168-69.
[67] *Reminiscences,* op. cit., p. 30. Caps in the original.

gone from him or come to him.'[68] Once, when a devotee countered by recalling that even Sri Ramakrishna had felt the pain that cancer was causing him, the Maharshi explained that a jnani struck by pain may feel it 'in the beginning, due to long association [with the body?] or habit. But afterwards it will pass off.'[69] The jnani knows that he is the Self, the Maharshi would explain. He—as the Self— remains the same whether his body continues or falls off. Therefore death makes no difference to him: 'Death is also another name for us. For what is death but giving up the body? Our real nature is to be without the body.'[70]

One night not long before the accursed tumour would appear, Mudaliar was to record, 'The talk turned to various recipes suggested by various people about *kaya kalpa*. Bhagavan mentioned a few *kalpas* based on camphor, a hundred year old *neem* tree, etc., and said, "Who would care to take such trouble over this body? As explained in books, the greatest malady we have is the body . . . [the disease of birth], and if one takes medicines to strengthen it and prolong its life, it is like a man taking medicine to strengthen and perpetuate his disease. As the body is the burden we bear, we should on the other hand feel like the coolie engaged to carry a load, anxiously looking forward to arrival at the destination when he can throw off his burden.'[71]

As the excruciating tumours swelled, as they were cut out, and appeared again, these affirmations were put to the test. The devotees read into the terrible sequence, the lessons that the Master had been trying to drive into them. Throughout, Ramana Maharshi remained calm and aloof from the eruption and removal of the deadly tumours.

---

[68] Ibid., pp. 97, 143-44.
[69] *Day by Day With Bhagavan*, op. cit., p. 20.
[70] Ibid., pp. 86-87, 97.
[71] Ibid., p. 93.

As one treatment after another was proposed—allopathic, ayurvedic, homeopathic, eventually surgery after surgery— he would let the devotees do as they pleased. 'Yes, yes'—he would say to every proposal, as if knowing what the outcome would in any case be. The only thing he did not allow the doctors to do was to amputate the arm, something that is forbidden in the texts. And as the final end approached, he waved away the attempt of a doctor to give him oxygen.[72]

Do not worry, he would tell the distressed and helpless devotees, 'As it came, so it will go.' At that moment, some of the devotees would find solace in this. They would read a reassurance into what the Maharshi was saying. Later they were left wondering as to what it was that the Maharshi meant by 'it would go as it had come'. What would go? The tumour? The cancer? The body? Life itself?

He had long taught the devotees not to look upon his body as him. One day he was asked what changes had come in him since he had come to the Arunachala hill. He answered, 'I am ever the same. There is neither *sankalpa* [will] nor change in me. Till I reached the Mango Grove, I remained indifferent with my eyes shut. Afterwards I opened my eyes and I am actively functioning. Otherwise there is no change whatsoever in me.' But we do note many outward changes, a devotee remarked. 'Yes,' the Maharshi said, 'that is because you see me as this body. So long as you identify yourself with your body, you cannot but see me as an embodied being. So long as the doubter is there, the doubt persists.'[73] But, proximity to the Maharshi notwithstanding, it was as difficult for the devotees who lived and moved with him to dissociate him from the

---

[72] On these painful particulars, *Letters from Sri Ramanasramam*, op. cit., pp. 457-63; *Ramana Maharshi and the Path of Self-Knowledge*, op. cit., pp. 167-171; *Reminiscences*, op. cit., pp. 190-219.

[73] *Reminiscences*, op. cit., p. 31.

physical presence that they saw before them as it is for us sixty years later. And so, as the cancer took its toll, there was a pall of sorrow and foreboding over the ashram. 'They take this body for Bhagavan and attribute suffering to him,' he said watching the disconsolate devotees. 'What a pity! They are despondent that Bhagavan is going to leave them and go away—where can he go, and how?'[74]

Given this uncompromising conviction, like Sri Ramakrishna, the Maharshi steadfastly refused to either appeal to God or to use any power within himself to cure his disease. In typical passages, Arthur Osborne was to record the fate of entreaties that he cure himself:

> It was hard to give up hope that even if the doctors failed he might still put aside the sickness by his own power. A devotee begged him to give but a single thought to the desirability of getting well, as this would have been enough, but he replied, almost scornfully, 'Who could have such a thought!'
>
> And to others who asked him simply to will his recovery he said, 'Who is there to will this?' The 'other', the individual that could oppose the course of destiny, no longer existed in him; it was the 'non-existent' misery that he had got rid of.[75]

WHAT THE DEVOTEES SAID

In both instances, the devotees were bewildered by the grave illness and pain that had struck the saints—we have to bear in mind, after all, that for the devotees both Sri Ramakrishna and Sri Ramana were avtaars, they were God incarnate. The devotees could think back and recall the numerous cases where persons they were certain had got well—often from the brink of death—only by the grace of these two. They could not but conclude that either the disease was just another play that the Master himself was

---

[74] *Ramana Maharshi and the Path of Self-Knowledge,* op. cit., p. 170.
[75] Ibid., pp. 172-73.

staging for some purpose, or that it was just a passing cloud that would soon blow away—most certainly if only the Master would direct it to do so.

Swami Nikhilananda writes that three groups formed among the young devotees who were serving Sri Ramakrishna during his last illness. One group felt that 'The Master had willed his illness in order to bring his devotees together and promote solidarity among them. As soon as the purpose was served, he would himself get rid of the disease.' The second group argued that 'the Divine Mother, in whose hand the Master was an instrument, had brought about this illness to serve Her own mysterious ends.' The third group led by Narendra 'refused to ascribe a supernatural cause to a natural phenomenon. They believed that the Master's body, a material thing, was subject, like all other material things, to physical laws. Growth, development, decay, and death were laws of nature to which the Master's body could not but respond.'[76] 'How can any illness afflict the great doctor who cures the disease of birth?' a devotee of Sri Ramana wrote to a fellow-devotee.[77]

While a few, like the young rationalists led by the future Swami Vivekananda, ascribed the illness to the natural course of aging and decay, most believed that there were causes other than these, and that, in particular, there was a definite purpose—of God, or, which was more or less the same thing, of Sri Ramakrishna and Sri Ramana—on account of which the illnesses had struck the saints.

Sri Sarda Devi, the Mother to the devotees, who had been nominally married to Sri Ramakrishna, attributed the Paramahamsa's cancer to a curse, a curse that arose from a trifling thing he did and one that was hurled inadvertently.

---

[76] Swami Nikhilananda, 'Introduction' to *The Gospel of Sri Ramakrishna*, op. cit., pp. 67-68.

[77] *Reminiscences*, op. cit., p. 191.

'*Karma* alone is responsible for our misery and happiness,' she said.

> Even the Master had to suffer the effects of *karma*. Once his elder brother was drinking water while delirious. The Master snatched the glass out of his hand after he had drunk just a little. The brother became angry and said, 'You have stopped me from drinking water. You will also suffer likewise. You will also feel such pain in your throat.' The Master said, 'Brother I did not mean to injure you. You are ill. Water will harm you. That is why I have taken the glass away. Why have you, then, cursed me in this manner?' The brother said, weeping, 'I do not know, Brother. Those words have come from my mouth. They cannot but bear fruit.' At the time of his illness the Master told me, 'I have got this ulcer in my throat because of that curse.' I said to him in reply, 'How can a person possibly live if such a thing can happen to you?' The Master remarked, 'My brother was a righteous man. His words must come true. Can the words of anyone and everyone be thus fulfilled?'[78]

The proposition has several of the ingredients which we find in our mythology. The curse. Even if uttered inadvertently. Especially if uttered by a good man. Krishna destroys his entire clan and his own city because of a curse of Gandhari. He dies of an arrow released mistakenly by a hunter because of another curse. In the myths, just as many tragedies and catastrophes have resulted from curses hurled by evil persons as by saintly ones. It is of course ironic that rishis who, after all, have mastered their senses through long and severe austerities, fly off the handle at the slightest provocation or an even slighter mistake of someone, even someone dear to them. Those who give primacy to controlling the mind would naturally look askance at such flying off into a rage. But for the moment our concern is the sincere belief of Sri Ramakrishna himself, and that of the Mother. A curse triggered by a trifling thing done, even by

---

[78] *Ramakrishna as We Saw Him*, op. cit., pp. 27-28.

as saintly a person as Sri Ramakrishna, and done in the
belief that it was for the good of the other person.

The second dominant theme among the devotees was
that the illness was 'vicarious penance' for their deeds, or
those of devotees who used to visit Sri Ramakrishna for
blessings and relief. Sri Ramakrishna himself said as much
on several occasions. 'The Master used to say, "I have been
suffering for all of you,"' Sri Sarda Devi recalled. '"I have
taken upon myself the miseries of the whole world." The
Master suffered as he had taken on himself the sins of
Girish.'[79]

Most accounts describe him taking the sins upon himself
of his own volition. Swami Ramakrishnananda recorded
how Sri Ramakrishna would himself walk over to someone
who had travelled a long distance to seek his blessing but,
finding the room full of people, would shrink away into a
corner, 'and touch him, and in a moment he would be
illumined'. 'By that touch, Sri Ramakrishna really
swallowed ninety-nine percent of the man's karma,' the
Swami wrote. 'Taking others' karma was the reason he had
his last illness. He used to tell us, "The people whose karma
I have taken think that they are attaining salvation through
their own strength. They do not understand that it is
because I have taken their karma on me."'[80] Swami
Abhedananda also recalls his telling them, 'The Divine
Mother has shown me that people are getting rid of their
sins by touching my feet. I am absorbing the results of their
sinful action, so I am suffering from this terrible cancer.'[81]
On occasion, however, it seems that he felt that the sins of
others had been thrust on him against his will. Sri

[79] *Sri Ramakrishna as We Saw Him*, op. cit., p. 27. Girish Chandra Ghosh was
a rakish stage actor. Sri Ramakrishna was most indulgent towards him.
[80] Swami Ramakrishnananda in *Sri Ramakrishna as We Saw Him*, op. cit.,
p. 157.
[81] Swami Abhedananda in *Sri Ramakrishna as We Saw Him*, op. cit., p. 222.

Ramakrishna had been shifted to a house in Cossipore during his final illness. 'One day when I went to see him,' a devotee wrote later, 'he got up and told me, "Ramlal, my hands and feet are burning. Please bring some Ganga water and sprinkle it on me." He was extremely restless. I asked, "What happened?" He replied, "I came into this world secretly with a few close devotees, and now Ram [Ram Chandra Datta] is spreading my name. He brings all sorts of people here and asks me to touch and bless them. How much burden can I carry? I got this disease by taking the sins of these people upon myself. Look, I shall not stay in the world any longer" . . .'[82]

Sri Ramana does not seem to have attributed—it would have been out of character for him to do so—his fatal illness to the sins of others though there is a typically elliptical remark that is often quoted. As he lay ill and in such severe pain, a Parsi lady-devotee, Mrs Taleyarkhan, said to him, 'Bhagavan! Give this sickness to me instead. Let me bear it!' Sri Ramana responded, 'And who gave it to me?'[83] In any case, the devotees believed as much as the devotees of Sri Ramakrishna that he had taken their sins upon himself, that he had 'drunk the poison of the karma of others,' and that his doing so is what had brought on the terrible ailment. They too concluded that he was undergoing 'vicarious penance'.

He was always accessible to all, a devotee recorded. They came to him with their suffering and pain. As he was compassion personified, the moment he saw the pain of another, 'automatic rescue operations would start'. 'Was there a simultaneous transfer of a portion of the bad karma of the devotees on Ramana's body? It seems so quite clearly

---

[82] Ramlal Chattopadhyay in *Sri Ramakrishna as We Saw Him*, op. cit., pp. 55-56.

[83] *Ramana Maharshi and the Path of Self-Knowledge*, op. cit., p. 173.

if we look at the evidence of events which tell their own tale.' In a typical instance, a person suffering from pain or some severe ailment would come to the ashram; while the patient would have said nothing, Sri Ramana would start massaging the very part of his own body which was ailing in the visitor's body; as he did so, the pain in the latter would subside. Kapali Sastri, a well-known scholar—and devotee of both Sri Ramana and Sri Aurobindo—is reported to have described the case of Jagadeeshwara Sastri— another scholar, and the author of *Ramana Sahasranama*. Jagadeeshwara had developed cancer of the abdomen. He was given only a few days to live. He wrote eight verses appealing to Sri Ramana to cure his cancer. Sri Ramana's 'usual position,' a devotee recalled, 'used to be that the divine law would take its course: "What can we do? That is the law."' But nor could he refuse to help because of his compassion. Jagadeeshwara was saved. The devotee writes, 'Did it have a toll on Ramana's body? One wonders.'

The various ailments which afflicted the Maharshi—from eczema to the crack in the collarbone to the rheumatic pains and eventually the cancer—'were all perhaps due to the transference of the *karma* of devotees to the Maharshi's body,' the devotee writes. Nor was this any cause for surprise to the devotee: after all, the devotee noted, 'Had he not imposed the limitation of the human body, in the first place, to protect humanity?'[84] He has 'drunk the poison of our *karma*,' the devotees told each other. 'It is only our *prarabdha* which is afflicting his body,' they wrote to each other. 'How can any illness afflict the great doctor who cures the disease of birth? It must be our offence . . .'[85]

---

[84] A.R. Natarajan, *Insights Into the Ramana Way*, Ramana Maharshi Centre for Learning, Bangalore, 1992, pp. 100-02.

[85] *Reminiscences*, op. cit., pp. 181, 191, 193. See, also *Letters from Sri Ramanasramam*, op. cit. pp. 457-63, and *Ramana Maharshi and the Path of Self-Knowledge*, op. cit., pp. 167-71.

258 DOES HE KNOW A MOTHER'S HEART?

That devotees would reason thus is but natural. In both instances they were convinced that their idols were indeed God incarnate. Therefore, the Master was immaculate— nothing that *he* had done could visit such a terrible ailment on him. As the ailment had nonetheless erupted, it must have been the bad karma of others that had caused it. For the same reason, their idol, by definition, had the fullest power to reverse the disease. When he did not do so; when the disease kept worsening—recall that Sri Ramana had said that though the jnani does not will a cure, the moment he sees suffering or hears of it 'divine automatic rescue operation starts'—he must have withheld his power and the 'divine automatic rescue operation' for a purpose. One purpose that was read into the extreme and prolonged suffering which the two underwent was that they were preparing the devotees for their inevitable departure. In a passage typical of such readings, Arthur Osborne writes, 'There was also a deeper sense of inevitability, far beyond the medical: that Sri Bhagavan knew what was appropriate and sought to give us strength to endure his body's death. Indeed, this long, painful sickness came to appear as a means of preparing us for the inevitable parting which many had first felt they would not be able to endure . . .'[87]

And the way to strengthen the minds of the devotees so that they would not be overwrought by the death of his body was to drive into them the conviction that he was not the body. The devotees read this too as the purpose for which Sri Ramana let the ailment go on. 'Ramana would sometimes say,' a devotee writes, 'that the disease which wracked his body with pain would bring home to the devotees the truth that he was not the body. Its purpose was to establish in their minds the certainty of his continued existence even after his body dropped off. Ramana said so

[87] *Ramana Maharshi and the Path of Self-Knowledge*, op. cit., p. 170.

specifically to Dr Ananthanarayana Rao, the *ashram* physician. Ramana's purpose was to remove the illusion of body-consciousness by a practical demonstration of heart-based life. In what better way could it be demonstrated than by Ramana exuding joy while his body was subject to the ravages of a fatal and malignant disease?'[87]

'EVERYTHING THAT HAPPENS, HAPPENS FOR A PURPOSE'

For Sri Ramakrishna, God was a direct, immediate, palpable presence. He talked to Her. She talked to him. He had seen Her as the fan in his hand, he said. He had seen God with form as well as without form, he often said.

For him, everything that happened was by Her will. And She made things happen for a definite purpose. His arm had broken now, as his tooth had broken earlier, 'in order to destroy my ego to its very root. Now I cannot find my ego within myself any more. When I search for it I see God alone. One can never attain God without completely getting rid of the ego . . .'[88] Hence, for Sri Ramakrishna, even run-of-the-mill injuries were by design; they were for a definite purpose. And the purpose had long ago been achieved.

As the ego had long ago been erased—and it is entirely true that it is impossible to imagine a more egoless person than Sri Ramakrishna: ever so completely humble, his surrender to what he perceived as Divine will so totally complete—the final illness could not have been for erasing the ego even further.

As the cancer in his throat advanced, as the pain became more and more intense, it would seem that at some moments Sri Ramakrishna himself wondered why a fatal illness and such intense pain had been brought to bear on him. He is talking to 'M'. He asks 'M' how long it will take for him to get well.

---

[87] *Insights into the Ramana Way*, op. cit., p. 100.
[88] *The Gospel of Sri Ramakrishna*, op. cit., p. 459.

'*M*': 'Perhaps five to six months.'

Sri Ramakrishna: 'So long? What do you mean?'

'*M*': 'I mean, Sir, for complete recovery.'

Sri Ramakrishna: 'Oh, that! I am indeed relieved.'

And then he asks '*M*', 'Can you explain one thing? How is it that in spite of all these visions, all this ecstasy and *samadhi*, I am so ill?'

Of course, it is entirely possible that Sri Ramakrishna asked '*M*' only to test how much the latter had understood. But it is just as possible that, wracked by that extreme pain, he was himself puzzled.

'Your suffering is no doubt great,' '*M*' replied, 'but it has deep meaning.'

'What is it?' Sri Ramakrishna inquired.

'A change is coming over your mind,' '*M*' replied. 'It is being directed towards the formless aspect of God. Even your "ego of knowledge" is vanishing'—Sri Ramakrishna used to use this expression to indicate the faculty that a few realized souls like Adi Shankara deliberately retain so as to teach others.

'That is true,' Sri Ramakrishna agreed. 'My teaching of others is coming to an end. I cannot give any more instruction. I see that everything is Rama Himself.'

'There is yet another purpose in this illness,' '*M*' continued. 'It is the final sifting of disciples. The devotees have achieved in these few days what they could not have realized by five years' *tapasya*. Their love and devotion are growing by leaps and bounds.'

'That may be so,' Sri Ramakrishna observed, not saying anything definite about the first part of '*M*'s observation— that about sifting disciples. On the second part—of the love and devotion of the disciples growing by leaps and bounds—Sri Ramakrishna, anxious as he was that the small band of young disciples continue as a team for the task for which he was convinced the Divine Mother had sent them, observed, 'but Niranjan went back home . . .'

As the conversation continued, Sri Ramakrishna became abstracted, and soon went into samadhi. On regaining consciousness, he told 'M', 'I saw everything passing from form to formlessness . . . Well, this tendency of mine toward the formless is only a sign of my nearing dissolution. Isn't that so?'

'M': 'It may be.'

Sri Ramakrishna: 'Even now I am seeing the Formless Indivisible *Satchidananda*—just like that . . . But I have suppressed my feelings with great difficulty.'

He returns to that matter of sifting disciples. 'What you said about the sifting of disciples was right: this illness is showing who belong to the inner circle and who to the outer. Those who are living here [the house that had been taken on rent in Cossipore], renouncing the world, belong to the inner circle, and those who pay occasional visits and ask, "How are you, sir?" belong to the outer circle . . .'[89]

This was a matter of utmost importance to Sri Ramakrishna as he had been imploring the Divine Mother to send him a band of youngsters who would carry forward the task. Even when he was well, while he gave freely of his time and energy to everyone, Sri Ramakrishna would often complain of the numbers who would flock to him, often seeking, through his blessings, to attain some worldly goal. Talking to 'M' during this final illness, he described the mystical states through which he passed, and said that he had earlier also appealed to the Divine Mother to bring about a vital transformation in him so that only genuine seekers would stay, and She had done so. ' . . . Therefore I feel that it is the Divine Mother Herself who dwells in this body and plays with the devotees. When I first had my

[89] Ibid., pp. 932-33.

exalted state of mind, my body would radiate light. My chest was always flushed. Then I said to the Divine Mother: "Mother, do not reveal Thyself outwardly. Please go inside." That is why my complexion is so dull now. If my body were still luminous, people would have tormented me; a crowd would always have thronged here. Now there is no outward manifestation. That keeps weeds away. Only genuine devotees will remain with me now. Do you know why I have this illness? It has the same significance. Those whose devotion to me has a selfish motive will run away at the sight of my illness . . .'[90]

The illness could have another objective, Sri Ramakrishna felt—to prevent him from giving too freely of himself and the teaching. 'Perhaps there is a meaning in what has happened to my throat,' he told 'M'. 'This has happened lest I make myself light before all, lest I should go to all sorts of places and sing and dance.'[91] He returned to this proposition later. The close band of devotees is sitting around him. Sri Ramakrishna tells them, 'I see that it is God Himself who has become the block, the executioner and the victim for the sacrifice.' The same God is now hastening his end. 'If the body were to be preserved a few days more many people would have their spirituality awakened,' 'M' tells him, perhaps to give him reason to make an effort to live longer. After a while, Sri Ramakrishna says to the assembled devotees, 'But this is not to be. This time the body will not be preserved. Such is not the will of God. This time the body will not be preserved, lest, finding me guileless and foolish, people should take advantage of me, and lest I, guileless and foolish as I am, should give away everything to everybody. In this *kaliyuga*, people are averse to meditation and *japa*.'[92]

---

[90] Ibid., pp. 831-32.
[91] *The Gospel of Sri Ramakrishna*, op. cit., p. 826.
[92] Ibid., p. 942.

The illness would also serve as consolation for others who suffer. 'People will not have the courage to approach you unless you resembled them in all respects,' 'M' told Sri Ramakrishna. 'But they are amazed to find that in spite of such illness you don't know anything but God.'

Sri Ramakrishna smiled, 'M' records, and observed, 'Balaram also said, "If even you can be ill, then why should we wonder about our illnesses?" Lakshmana was amazed to see that Rama could not lift His bow on account of His grief for Sita. Even Brahman weeps entangled in the five elements.'[93] But on another occasion, he made light of the suggestion that his illness was meant to teach others. Upon being told that 'M' had told another devotee that 'your illness is for teaching men', Sri Ramakrishna remarked, 'But that's only his guess.'[94]

In the end it was surrender, it was acceptance of the Divine Mother's will. The illness by now is far advanced. The devotees are sitting around him. They say that they hope he will not go and leave them behind. Sri Ramakrishna says, 'A band of minstrels suddenly appears, dances, and sings, and it departs in the same sudden manner. They come and they return, but none recognizes them.'

After a few minutes he adds, 'Suffering is inevitable when one assumes a human body.'[95]

PURPOSE AS DISTINCT FROM RESULT

There are half a dozen reasons that suggested themselves to the devotees of Sri Ramakrishna and Sri Ramana as explanations for the fatal illness that struck them and for the extreme pain that they had to go through. They themselves gave expression to some of these: taking on the karma of

---

[93] *The Gospel of Sri Ramakrishna*, op. cit., pp. 837-38.
[94] Ibid., pp. 969-70.
[95] Ibid., p. 943.

others; to erase the ego; the curse of a brother; sifting devotees; preparing devotees for the inevitable parting; to remove from the minds of devotees the illusion that they are the body; God's inscrutable will; turning the mind towards the formless; being a consolation to others . . . But there was a common thread: everything that happens, happens for a purpose.

That their life conformed so uncompromisingly to their teaching—their resolute refusal to divert their minds to heal their bodies, for instance—evokes veneration and astonishment. The equanimity with which the painful and fatal illnesses were borne by these sages is, of course, a lesson and an example to us. But, their own averments notwithstanding, I just cannot bring myself to believe that they were afflicted with such searing pain just *so that* they may leave us an example of how even extreme pain and tribulation ought to be borne.

In her last two years, my mother—true to her name, Dayawanti, an ocean of kindness; truly the centre of so many lives; a mother to so many more than us three, her children—suffered a series of strokes, transient ischaemia, the doctors labelled them. She lost her kind voice. Her kind eyes lost most of their sight . . . She bore each blow with serenity. My father, himself near ninety by then, would seat her in a chair, and sit next to her for hours, holding her hand and talking to her of the sixty-five years they had spent together. He would recite the first words of some Urdu poem or couplet they had known over the years. He would goad her, cajole her, he would insist that she complete the poem or couplet. Even though she would just sit mute, he would go on doing so. 'But why are you doing this?' I would remonstrate. 'Each time you try to get her to say the words you are only reminding her that she can't speak. Why are you doing this, Daddy?' '*Kaakaa tainu kuch pataa ee nayeen aenaa cheezan da*'—'My dear boy, you just don't understand these things,' he would reply, and go on coaxing my mother. I would leave in silent, but exasperated helplessness. But over the weeks, she would start responding. First just with her eyes. Then by moving her lips. Then by mumbling something. Then by speaking a syllable or two of the words. Eventually by completing the verse. This sequence was repeated three or four times. I was surely taught several lessons—in devotion, in patient striving, in nursing, quite apart from the fact that I did not know about these things, as my father would say. But could anyone in his right mind believe that my mother was subjected to the strokes, *so that* my father would have the opportunity to nurse her, and that opportunity was created *so that* their children would learn these lessons?

In the end there was a massive haemorrhage. With an attendant holding her arm, she was making her way to her bed. I had just come into the room. I saw her subside. I rushed over and slowly lowered her into the bed. Within minutes, we wheeled her into the car—we had, and have a number of wheelchairs in the house because of Adit. I drove her to the nearest hospital. The CAT-scan showed a large bleed. On the doctors' advice, we shifted her to a hospital better equipped to handle such cases. Her brain lost its faculties.

Our mother was in intensive care for five days. My sister, Nalini, my brother, Deepak, others and I would attend on her by turns. As she was loved by everyone who knew her, several relatives would come, pray, stand silently by the bed, tears in their eyes as they saw the tubes stuck into her. I slept at the hospital. Late one night the doctors told us that she had lost all awareness, that there was no point in keeping the life-support systems going. They sought our consent. What could we say? The doctors said that they would remove them at 4 a.m., that her heart and other organs would cease functioning around six. All of us gathered around her bed in the unit. Nalini stroked her forehead. She applied the bindi on her forehead—a large bindi that our mother always wore. She combed her hair. Deepak stroked and massaged her arms. I massaged her feet. We kept doing so till a little after six when the machines showed that her heart and pulse had ceased completely. That is how she passed away—her face serene; her forehead with the large bindi that had sheltered us so long; her hair as they always had been, neatly combed; Nalini stroking her forehead and moving her fingers through her hair, Deepak holding her hand, and I gently rubbing her feet.

Am I to believe that the strokes that robbed her of balance, voice, sight, that the final haemorrhage were for a purpose? That they were to hold out for us an example of serenity? That they were to teach us forbearance? That they were to teach us how to go through the final days? That the final hours were designed to bond the three of us to each other?

The illnesses *could have that result*. It may even be that we could, that we did *wrest those lessons* from those illnesses. But can one really believe that someone high up contrived them *so as to achieve those results?* I find it as impossible to believe that the illnesses that wracked saints like Ramakrishna Paramahamsa and Ramana Maharshi could have been designed by some super power for instilling equanimity in those who witnessed the Masters in the final days, as I do to believe that my mother's strokes and final haemorrhage were designed to instill some lesson in us, her children.

7

As everything, including the world, is 'unreal', How is karma real? How does it stick?

Yudhishthira is distraught. In spite of what Bhishma had explained to him earlier,[1] he is weighed down by guilt—the guilt of having brought about the catastrophe on them, in particular for having reduced Bhishma to such a piteous condition.

Bhishma consoles him. No one is free to follow his will, Bhishma says. Why then do you hold yourself responsible for good or evil deeds? The question of what causes that which happens is very subtle indeed, it is beyond the knowledge of the senses. We are all instruments in the hands of destiny. Neither you nor Duryodhana could have avoided what was destined to happen. Destiny is all-powerful, he says, its ways are elusive. And, therefore, neither you nor Duryodhana is personally responsible for the tragic events that have transpired.

To drive home the moral, Bhishma recounts the ancient parable of Gautami, her son and the snake.

*

Gautami is elderly, a good person. She remains immersed in contemplation and prayer. Her only son is bitten by a snake. The son dies. Arjunaka, a fowler, catches hold of the snake, ties it up, and brings him to Gautami. 'Here is the wretched snake that has killed your dear son. Tell me, quick, how do you want me to execute him? Should I throw him in the fire? Should I cut him to pieces?'

---

[1] Mahabharata, *Shantiparva*.

Gautami hesitates. Is the snake really the one who has caused my son to die? Will we be taking on a sin if we kill it? Will my son come back to life by our killing the snake? If not, will we, by taking the life of a living thing, not hurtle ourselves into the vice of Yamaraja, the Lord of Death? We are not supposed to give in to anger. Then, how can we, out of anger, kill this snake? Should we not have mercy on the snake and pardon it?

At each argument and doubt, the fowler grows more and more impatient. He argues: Did Indra not kill Vritra? Did Mahadeva not destroy a sacrifice? The snake must be killed, he says. Just as it has killed your son, if left alive it will kill others. He declares, 'I will not let this contemptible thing survive.'

Hearing the argument, the snake speaks up. O innocent, Arjunaka, it says. What is my crime? I am not free. Far from it, I am an instrument. Death compelled me to bite the boy. If there be any crime in what has happened, the one who is responsible is Death, not me.

O snake, Arjunaka answers. If we were to go by your reasoning, no thief or murderer is guilty. In that case, sin and its punishment will be in vain. Stop your nonsense. Even if you bit the child on the command of someone else, you *did* bite him. And so you too are a cause, you too are a culprit—even as, in the making of earthen vessels, the tools that the potter uses are reckoned among the causes. By what you have yourself said, therefore, you are a murderer. I shall not spare you.

But, exactly so, the serpent responds. Just as, in the making of those vessels, the tools are slaves of the potter so was I a mere bondsman of Death. If you are going to fix responsibility, the whole concatenation of circumstances and actors has to be held responsible, not just me. Just as in the yagya, priests and other participants put the *aahuti* but the benefit accrues only to the *yajmaan* and not to them; so also the responsibility cannot be pasted on a mere instrument like me.

Alerted by the disputation, Death comes down and addresses the serpent. It is not on my own that I directed you to bite the boy. I did so because I was directed by Destiny to do so. As the mighty wind buffets the clouds, so am I sent hither and thither by Destiny. The *gunas*, animate and inanimate objects, the earth and the heavens, the sun, moon, water, wind, fire, the rivers, the sea, waxing and waning—each and every one of them is in the grip of Destiny. Knowing this, how do you hold me responsible for the death of the boy?

I am not holding you responsible, the serpent tells Death, nor am I exonerating you. All I am saying is that, in biting the boy, you are the one who propelled me. I am not interested in holding you or Destiny responsible. All I am interested in is that *I* am not the one who is responsible.

'You have heard Death, haven't you?' the snake asks the fowler. Having heard it, it is not right for you to continue to hold me in the snare.

I have heard both of you, Arjunaka replies. But what the two of you have said exonerates neither of you. It only shows that both of you are responsible for the death of this boy. I shall *not* spare you.

Hearing the tussle, Destiny enters. I am not responsible either, it explains. The serpent, Death, I—none of us is the impeller or the contriver of the boy's death. The karma that this boy had done, that is what has caused his end. The boy has died of his own karma. All of us are under the reign of karma. In the world, it is karma which accounts for happiness and sorrow. As karma impels everyone in the world, so we too are impelled by karma. As the potter fashions such vessels out of mud as he wants, so does karma. As sunlight and shadow remain conjoined to each other, so do karma and the doer of karma. In this way,

neither the snake, nor Death, nor indeed Me, Destiny, is
responsible. This boy has gone to his death by his own
deeds.

Gautami, pious as she is, accepts what Destiny has said
without so much as fleeting doubt. Yes, my son has gone to
his death by his own karma, she says. Arjunaka, I also must
have done some evil karma by which it is my son who has
died. Let Destiny and Death go forth to their respective
places, and you let go of this serpent.

And so, Bhishma concludes, Destiny, Death and the
serpent returned to the stations from which they had come,
and Arjunaka's anger and Gautami's grief were allayed.
And so, my lord, be at peace, shed your grief. All beings get
deserts according to their karma. Neither you nor
Duryodhana did anything. Think of all that has happened
as but the doing of Destiny.

Having heard this exposition, the worries of Dharmaraja
Yudhishthira abated, and he proceeded to the next
question . . . [2]

*

How convenient, the exculpation!

Who would let Yudhishthira off, and Duryodhana of all
persons, on such reasoning?

And which mother, I have long wondered, would give in
to the reasoning of the trio—the serpent, Death, Destiny?
And that too without so much as a murmur? And blame her
own son for his death?

One of three kinds.

One who has been thoroughly conditioned by our
presuppositions.

One who is desperate to believe—that there must have
been some *reason* why such a blow has fallen on her son
and her.

---

[2] Mahabharata, *Anushasanaparva*, I.15-83.

One who is exhausted by the struggle. Speaking of the mind, and so as to encourage the aspirant to work at it, the *Chhandogya Upanishad* uses a simile that, in the context of life, of looking after a handicapped child day after day, or an ailing companion year after year, has always seemed to me to be as cruel as it is true: tethered to the breath, the mind will eventually give up its wandering and settle down on the breath itself, says the Upanishad, as the bird, fastened with a string, flaps around, flies in this direction and then in that, trying to break away, but ultimately, exhausted, gives up and settles down on the string itself with which it is fastened . . .[3]

Having struggled day in and day out; having tried every device to make sense of what has happened; having rushed from one godman to the other; having tried this remedy and the other; having been on pilgrimages; having kept fasts; having pleaded with this god and that; at last, worn-out, exhausted, the mother is willing to believe anything, even the reasoning of that self-serving trio. And blames the victims—her beloved son, herself . . .

PROPOSITIONS AND THEIR IMMEDIATE CONSEQUENCE

Notice that four distinct propositions are involved:

- ❑ 'X' has happened; therefore, there must have been a cause;
- ❑ The cause must have been some deed of the individual himself;
- ❑ As we cannot think of some deed that he has done in this lifetime which may merit such recompense, he must have done something evil in some past lifetime;
- ❑ As what has happened to him is the result of his own deeds, it is justified: 'Everything has a cause' becomes 'Everything that happens is justified', as

---

[3] *Chhandogya Upanishad*, VI.8.2.

what has befallen us is merely punishing or rewarding us for what we have done.

One immediate consequence of this is that God is let off the hook. Karma is 'a convenient fiction' thus, not just in 'explaining' what has happened to an individual but also in getting God off the hook.[4]

THE SAME CONUNDRUMS HIT US AS WELL

Of course, in Hinduism, we have the entire range of opinions and beliefs—from atheism to the indescribable, attributeless Brahma. But the overwhelming proportion of us believe in God.

We believe in a God with attributes. Indeed, the God we worship is the embodiment of all conceivable, auspicious attributes.

And not just that. We believe in a personal God. Both in the sense that He is personal to us, the worshippers: so many speak of 'our family deity'; so many speak of a God specific to our profession or work—the Goddess of learning, of wealth, the God of workmen, the God who protects travellers, the Goddess who protects fishermen . . . And He is a personal God in the sense of being anthropomorphic, more or less a person Himself or Herself. He is pleased if we do certain things—for instance, if we perform certain rituals, if we keep certain fasts, if we go on specified pilgrimages. And He is angered if we don't. He is All-knowing, All-powerful, full of mercy, the Dispenser of

---

[4] The expression is used by Eliot Deutsch in 'Karma as a "Convenient Fiction" in the Advaita Vedanta', *Philosophy East and West*, Volume XV, number 1, 1965, pp. 3-12. Deutsch lists the six methods of proof that are accepted in Advaita Vedanta and argues that karma and its effects over a series of lives cannot be established by any of them, and the notion thus is a convenient fiction that is set up to explain and interpret what cannot otherwise be demonstrated.

justice, the Keeper of ledgers of our good and bad deeds, the Embodiment of love, of beauty . . . Obviously, if God were merely the impersonal, indivisible, transcendent/immanent Brahma, He wouldn't have these attributes and preferences. A disembodied Force wouldn't be keeping ledgers.

Not just that, we believe in a God that intervenes in human affairs. Ever so often, He descends to earth as an avatar to fight evil, to restore good, to set the balance right. From his very first days when he has to fight Kansa, to his very last day when he destroys his entire clan and city, Sri Krishna is fighting evil. And in verses that are oft recalled, he assures us that he shall come down to do so whenever the situation demands:

> *Whenever there is a decay of righteousness, O Bharata!, and exaltation of unrighteousness, then I create Myself;*

> *For protection of the good, and destruction of the evil-doers, for the sake of firmly establishing righteousness, I am born from age to age.*[5]

The lives of Sri Rama, of Parashurama exemplify the same trait—of intervening in human affairs to put down evil. Indeed, we believe in a God who does not just intervene on the big issues—destroying the evil, restoring the good, and the like. We believe in a God who attends, every moment, to the petitions of His devotees.

And we petition Him all the time—to ensure that our children do well in exams; to ensure that a sick relative gets well; to ensure success in our professions and businesses. 'What a delight to meet you,' I say on encountering a friend. 'How are things?' 'God is kind,' he says. 'Business is really looking up.' Perhaps that is why things are the way they are, I tell myself. God is so busy ensuring that everybody's business prospers, how can He have time for climate change? . . .

---

[5] Bhagavad Gita, IV.7-8.

Not only do we petition God, not only do we believe that God will attend to our petitions. We petition His representations. We believe that His representations—idols, pictures—will act on our petitions.

In a word, whatever our seers may have seen as The Truth, whatever they may have said is The Singular Reality, in our day-to-day practice, we act more or less on the same premises on which believers of other religions act. They go on pilgrimages to Mecca and Medina, we go on pilgrimages to Badrinath and Kedarnath; they circumambulate the Kaaba, we circumambulate the idol in every temple; they pray at the graves of saints, we visit the shrines of Jnaneshwar and other saints; they wear taaweez, we treasure articles given to us by our godmen; they keep fasts during Ramzan, we do so on several occasions; they sacrifice animals to please God, we have given up doing so . . . That is why, 'we act *more or less* on the same premises on which . . .' But more rather than less . . .

And so we end up with the same conundrums as we have seen erupt from the texts of other religions.

It is, of course, stated that worship of or meditation on a personal God, on a God with attributes is but a stage in meditating on the God without attributes, on the *nirguna* Brahma. And it has been the distinguishing feature of our religion that it has provided a gradation of means, its teachers have taught a variety of paths so that each devotee may traverse the one that is best suited to his particular capacity and aptitude.

But that does not dilute the conundrums. The adjectives used to describe Brahma too, eventually gravitate to making Him out to be one who intervenes—Creator, Preserver, One who oversees, Omniscient, Omnipotent, Omnipresent, Immanent, Transcendent, *Antaryamin*, the Inner Ruler . . .

The same conundrums, therefore, erupt. *Why*, for instance, did Brahma, all-pervasive, completely self-sufficient, create? 'It willed to create the world . . .' we are told. ' . . . Prajapati, who desired "May I be more, may I have progeny" . . .' we are told. ' . . . That non-existent created Mind with the thought "let Me be" . . .' we are told. 'Prajapati, desirous of progeny, practised *tapas* . . .' we are told. 'In the beginning this was Atman alone in the form of Purusha,' we learn. 'He [being alone] found no pleasure; He desired to have a second . . .' we are told. ' . . . He, desirous of producing beings of various types from His body . . .' we are told. 'In the beginning this world was Being, only one, without a second. It bethought itself, "Would that I were many! Let me procreate myself!" It emitted heat . . .' we are told. 'In the beginning this world was just the Self. He wished, "Would that I had a wife, then I would procreate. Would that I had wealth, then I would offer sacrifice" . . .' we learn.

But when even the ordinary mortal, on attaining knowledge of the Self shall remain content and fulfilled forever, desirous of nothing, why should Brahma have felt lonely? Why should He have yearned for a wife and progeny? Why should He have yearned to make sacrifices?

There is the related difficulty that arises at creation. The doctrine of karma asserts that a person receives birth in accordance with his karma in previous lives. This is how differences in natural endowments, in predispositions, and in circumstances are explained. But at the moment of creation, there had been no previous lives. Hence, how did differences in natural endowments and circumstances arise at that point? How did those who were to subsequently sink commit the first evil deed? How did those who were to subsequently ascend higher commit the first good deed which then engendered predispositions in them to go on committing good deeds in the subsequent rounds?

That this is a problem that has to be got around became apparent to our seers long ago—both Shankaracharya and

Ramanuja devote considerable energy to tackling it. What they say shows the knots the doctrine entails.

The adversary charges God with partiality—for He pastes unequal endowments on individuals—and with cruelty—for He ever so often inflicts such extreme infirmities on so many of us. The sutra states in response, 'No partiality and cruelty (can be charged against God) because of (His) taking other factors into consideration. For so the Vedas show.'

The Vedantin explicates this: 'No fault attaches to God, since this unequal creation is brought about in conformity with the virtues and vices of the creatures that are about to be born.' God is to be compared to rain, we are told. Rain is the common cause for the growth of paddy, wheat, barley, etc. The differences that arise between the crops and plants are caused by the varying potentialities of the different seeds. 'Similarly, God is the common cause for the birth of gods, men, and others, while individual fruits of works associated with the individual creatures are the uncommon causes for the creation of the differences among the gods, men, and others.'

Shankara then cites three statements from the Upanishads and the Gita—which actually work at cross purposes. 'It becomes virtuous through good acts,' he cites the *Brihadaranyaka Upanishad* saying, 'and vicious through evil acts'.[6] God's dispensation is contingent on the merit or otherwise of what is done by the specific individual, he says, on the authority of Sri Krishna affirming in the Gita, 'In whatever way men worship Me, in the same way do I fulfil their desires.'[7] But he also cites the *Kaushitaki Upanishad*: 'This one, truly, indeed causes him whom he wishes to lead up from these worlds to perform good actions. This one, indeed, also causes him whom he wishes to lead downward, to perform bad action . . .'[8]—an

---

[6] *Brihadaranyaka Upanishad*, III.ii.13, IV.iv.5.

[7] Bhagavad Gita, IV.2.

[8] *Kaushitaki Upanishad*, III.8.

affirmation that would seem to fly in the face of the other two.

The next two sutras have to contend with the manifest problem with this formulation: 'If it be argued that it is not possible [to take karma—merit and demerit—into consideration in the beginning],' the sutra reads, 'since the fruits of work remain still undifferentiated, then we say, no, since the transmigratory state has no beginning.' 'Moreover, this is logical, and (so) it is met with (in the scriptures).'

How do we know that transmigratory existence has no beginning? Shankara says that must be so, 'for had it emerged capriciously all of a sudden, then there would have been the predicament of freed souls also being reborn here, as also the contingency of results accruing from non-existing causes, for the differences in happiness and misery would have no logical explanation'.

Surely, that is circular. How do we know that transmigratory existence is without beginning? Because if it were not so, souls would have emerged and been reborn capriciously. If it were not so, happiness and misery would have no logical explanation. And how do we know that the souls did not emerge and are not reborn capriciously? How do we know that there is a logical explanation for happiness and misery? Because transmigratory existence is without beginning!

And the Vedas and smritis state that creation was without beginning. So it was without beginning. Passages are quoted to this effect.[9]

The problem does not go away, and the sutras turn to it again later.

For, in the scriptures, God affirms again and again that *He* is the Inner Ruler who directs us. Thus in the Gita, Sri Krishna declares, that it is 'an eternal portion of Mine own

---

[9] *Brahma-Sutra Bhasya of Sri Sankaracharya*, Swami Gambhirananda, [trans.], Advaita Ashram, Calcutta, 1972, pp. 362-65.

Self' that, 'transformed in the world of life into a living spirit, draweth round itself the senses of which the mind is the sixth . . .' That 'When the Lord acquireth a body and when He abandoneth it, He seizeth these and goeth with them, as the wind takes fragrances from their retreats.' That it is He, 'enshrined in ear, eye, skin, tongue and nose, and in the mind also', who enjoys the objects of the senses. That the unintelligent and untrained do not perceive Him, deluded as they are, but 'the wisdom-eyed perceive.' That the splendour in the sun, the moon, in the fire is from Him. That He is the One who nourishes all plants, He digests all food. That 'And I am seated in the hearts of all, and from Me memory and wisdom and also negation. And that which is to be known in all the Vedas am I; and I indeed the Veda-knower and author of Vedanta.'[10]

The consequence is inescapable: 'O son of Kunti!, bound by thine own duty, born of thine own nature, that which from delusion thou desirest not to do, even that helplessly thou shalt perform.' 'The Lord dwelleth in the hearts of all beings, O Arjuna!' Sri Krishna declares, 'by His elusive-Power, causing all beings to revolve, as though mounted on a *maya* machine'.[11]

Then, how is the individual responsible? Why is he punished for what Brahma/the Cosmic Principle/God has made him do? 'The individual soul must be the agent,' the *Brahma Sutras* say, 'for thus alone the scriptures become purposeful'—if it were not the agent, then all the injunctions enjoined in the scriptures would be meaningless. A circularity again: the scriptures lay down injunctions because the individual soul is the agent; the individual soul must be the agent because, if it were not, the injunctions would be meaningless!

---

[10] Bhagavad Gita, XV.7-12, 15.
[11] Ibid., XVIII.60-61.

Further reasons are given in the same strain: the individual soul must be the agent because the scriptures speak of the soul roaming about; because had it not been so, the scriptures would have given a contrary indication . . . Some 'reasons' ring better than the others. But agentship is not innate to the soul, it is 'a superimposition of the attributes of the limiting adjuncts' . . . And this is shown to be the case on the same sort of reasoning. And this adventitious characteristic of agentship 'is derived from God, for that is what is stated in the Vedic texts.' But that immediately puts God on the spot: He is now open to the charge of partiality and cruelty, as we saw earlier. Hence, the next sutra: '(God is), however, dependent on efforts made, so that injunctions and prohibitions may not become meaningless and other defects may not arise.' 'God acts merely as a general instrumental cause,' Shankara explains, 'dividing the resulting fruits of works unequally in accordance with the inequality of merit and demerit acquired by the individual beings, even as the rain does.' The rain analogy we encountered earlier is reiterated: 'It is seen in the world that rain becomes the common instrumental cause of long and short creepers etc. or of rice and barley etc. which grow in accordance with their own seeds, and yet unless there be rainfall, they can have no differences in sap, flower, fruit, leaves, etc., nor can they have these in the absence of their own seeds; so also it stands to reason that God ordains good and bad for the individual beings in accordance with the efforts made by the beings themselves.' 'Although the individual's agentship is dependent on God,' Shankara says, 'still it is the individual who really acts. God directs him just as he himself would proceed with his work. Moreover, God directs him in accordance with what he did previously, and He directed him earlier in accordance with what he had done still earlier.'

And how do we know that God directs him in accordance with what he had done earlier? 'The answer,' says the Vedantin, 'is contained in, "so that the injunctions and prohibitions may not become meaningless and other defects may not arise".'[12]

The injunctions and prohibitions are prescribed because the soul is an independent agent. The soul must be an independent agent because otherwise the injunctions and prohibitions would become meaningless . . .

But that gets us back the original problem: how did God ordain unequal capacities and predispositions at the moment of creation for at that moment there were no prior good or bad deeds that had been committed by individuals? And we get back into the loop we have been through earlier.

Ultimately, it is always: 'And this is so because the scriptures say so.' The scriptures say this because it is thus. It must be thus because the scriptures say so.

Nor is the defence very different to this day. Writing on the doctrine of karma, in his monumental study, *History of the Dharmasastras*, P.V. Kane, the then National Professor of Indology, observes:

> The doctrine of Karma is not a mechanical law; it is rather a moral or a spiritual necessity. It cannot, however, be said that this doctrine is an induction from observed facts nor can it be asserted that it is experimentally verifiable, but it is only a hypothesis or supposition; *it is, however, far better than other naïve and childlike theories. In the absence of the theory of karma and rebirth it would have to be assumed that the world is arbitrary, that the Creator is not bound to regard the nature of men's actions but may distribute rewards as he pleases or by caprice.*

---

[12] *Brahma-Sutra Bhasya of Sri Sankaracharya*, op. cit, sutras II.iii.33-42, pp. 494-506. Ramanuja's commentary is similar at least on these sutras. Cf., *Vedanta-Sutras with Ramanuja's Commentary*, Part III, George Thibaut, *Sacred Books of the East*, Volume XLVIII, Oxford University Press, London, 1904, Motilal Banarsidas, Delhi, 1962/1971, pp. 477-79, 552-58.

But why is chance more naïve or childlike as a hypothesis or supposition? Kane has a reason: Under the doctrine of Karma there is no such thing as chance or luck.

> When we use those words they correspond to no reality and are a tacit confession of our ignorance or inability to state the cause or causes of what has happened.[13]

But in my reckoning, it would be just as accurate to say, 'When we use the word Karma it corresponds to no reality and is a tacit confession of our ignorance or inability to state the cause or causes of what has happened.' Especially, when the word is conjoined with past lives.

Later on, Kane observes,

> The doctrine of Karma and transmigration accounts for apparently unmerited misery and suffering of many people, while some enjoy undeserved happiness or a good life. Our sense of fairness and justice would be shocked by the inequalities in the world, if such a doctrine were not there.

That without this 'explanation' our sense of fairness and justice would be shocked is no proof of the validity of the hypothesis—any more than it is a reason for swallowing any other soporific.

The hypothesis is useful in another way—that it 'would act as an urge to continual effort for goodness in this life and is likely to deter men from vice and cruelty.' That is, of course, true—as in some cases is the hypothesis of an All-knowing, All-seeing, Merciful God.

Having posited it no higher than a hypothesis that is neither derived from empirical observation nor can be subject to verification, Kane soon raises its status to that of being an explanation. He writes:

---

[13] P.V. Kane, *History of Dharmashastra, Ancient and Mediaeval Religious and Civil Law*, Volume V, Part II, Bhandarkar Oriental Research Institute, Poona, 1977, p. 1561, and 1572-73.

This doctrine of Karma not only offers *an explanation* about the varying degrees of happiness and unhappiness among human beings, but also *accounts for* differences in material well-being and unhealthy bodily conditions. It offers *a solution* of the problem of evil in the world and explains precocious abilities in mathematics, music and arts among children and grown up men . . . It also *explains* sudden accession of prosperity or high position such as, for example, a poor man's son being adopted by a prince or queen and then becoming an enlightened and famous ruler as was the case with the late Sayajirao Maharaj Gaikwad of Baroda.

Explains? Accounts for? It does so any better than randomness and chance?

Similarly, another great scholar, R.N. Dandekar, turns to the question we have seen being dealt with by the *Brahma Sutras*—of how individuals could have been created unequal in the first instance as, before creation, they had not existed and they could certainly not have done some good or bad karma. 'Such a question is philosophically inadmissible,' Dandekar begins. Pause just there for a moment: why is it 'philosophically inadmissible'? Even if it is inadmissible in philosophy, why is it inadmissible in life? The sentences that follow in Dandekar's exposition exhibit the same circularity of reasoning that we have encountered above. He writes:

According to Hindu thought, the *samsara* is beginningless (*anaadi*). It is impossible to visualize an individual without antecedents. For, strictly speaking, individuality is itself the product of antecedents. If the essential self is unaffected by any antecedents, it does not become liable to be born at all and so to assume any individuality.[14]

What is here termed 'Hindu thought' is proved on the basis of assumptions that are made in that thought—that the

---

[14] R.N. Dandekar, *Insights Into Hinduism, Select Writings, Volume II*, Ajanta Publications, Delhi, 1979, p. 63.

universe is 'beginningless'. Similarly, the proposition that an 'individual' must have 'individuality' seems self-evident at first sight. But that is because of the similarity of the words—'individual' and 'individuality'. Would the matter seem as self-evident if we said an *infant* or a *person* must have individuality, and then drew the conclusions that follow? The proposition that follows is of the same class: that this individuality can only come from antecedents— why not from the random play of genes, and subsequently from nurture?

THE INFINITE SERIES

That this sort of reasoning leads to a string of problems has been manifest, and a matter of considerable concern to our thinkers and seers. The doctrine has had to be modified, it has had to be stretched to provide for each dilemma: as the privations could not be explained in terms of what the person had done in this life, what he had done in previous lives was introduced. And as the calamities may be so severe that they could not all be assigned to what the person may have done in one previous life, the proposition was advanced that what a person may have done in an infinite series of previous lives would cause his present condition. And it is on this basis that karma is said to ensure justice in the long run. Here is how the noted scholar, Arvind Sharma, puts the proposition:

> To an Australian aborigine, the operation of the boomerang could well symbolize the operation of karma. In other words, what you give is what you get; what you send out is what you receive back; the way you treat others is the way you get treated. One might protest that this is not the way the world is, where the virtuous suffer and the wicked prosper. In the face of this *immediate* fact the doctrine of karma asserts the *ultimately* just nature of the universe. The expression 'ultimate' is important. We say, for instance, that justice prevails in the state of Quebec. Does it mean that no theft or

robbery, no crime is committed in Quebec? Quite obviously crime is committed in Quebec. What it really means is that when crime is committed the criminals are apprehended and brought to book. The principle of justice implies not the absence of violation of law but the principle of its ultimate assertion after a phase of its apparent lapse. So is it with karma. Karma is payback.[15]

Notice, first, that this run is longer than even the economists' Long Run—that 'never, never land of unrealized tendency' as Professor Robertson had called it. High-grade opium! As the poet, Agha 'Shayer' Kizilbash, put the matter:

Hashr mein insaaf hoga, bas yahee sunte raho
Kuchch yahaan hotaa rahaa hai, kuchch vahaan ho jayegaa

Just as Arvind instructs us, 'The expression "ultimate" is important' in the sentence 'In the face of this *immediate* fact the doctrine of karma asserts the *ultimately* just nature of the universe', in my reckoning, the word 'asserts' is the important one. After all, how do we know that ultimately the good prosper and the wicked suffer? That is just an assertion, or an assumption, if you like—for we know nothing about what happens 'ultimately'. Even assuming that this life is followed by other lives, how do we know that the series is not unidirectional? How do we know that the wicked do not always keep ascending and the good do not keep forever going down? How do we know, in the alternative, that the series does not just keep bouncing around at random—both in direction and amplitude?

Second, notice that there have been a variety of assertions of how exactly this happens: whether one is punished or rewarded for each deed separately or the reward or punishment is meted out in accordance with the, so to say,

---

[15] Arvind Sharma, *Hinduism for Our Times*, Oxford University Press, Delhi, 1996, p. 24.

net balance on the ledger; whether karma of its own accord and by its own potency produces effects or God weighs the good and bad deeds and thus apportions good or bad births:

> Having described at length 'those born with demoniacal properties', the Lord declares, ' . . .These haters, evil, pitiless, vilest among men in the world, *I ever throw down into demoniacal wombs.'*

And that is just the first step, so to say,

> 'Cast into a demoniacal womb, deluded birth after birth, attaining not to Me, O Kaunteya!, they sink into the lowest depths.'[16]

Is it the soul itself which destroys the body and fashions a better one as in the *Brihadaranyaka Upanishad*?

> . . . Just as a leech (or caterpillar) when it has come to the end of a blade of grass, after having made another approach (to another blade) draws itself together towards it, so does this self, after having thrown away this body, and dispelled ignorance, after having another approach (to another body) draw itself together (for making the transition to another body).

> And as a goldsmith, taking a piece of gold turns it into another, newer and more beautiful shape, even so does this self, after having thrown away this body and dispelled its ignorance, make unto itself another, newer and more beautiful shape like that of the fathers or of the *gandharvas,* or of the gods or of *Praja-pati* or of *Brahma* or of other beings.[17]

Or is it that some higher, ledger-keeper does so; whether the self that leaves is unalloyed consciousness or an amalgam of consciousness and of psychological tendencies and the elements as in the following:

> That self is indeed Brahman, consisting of (or identified with) the understanding, mind, life, sight, hearing, earth, water, air, ether, light and no light, desire and absence of desire, anger and absence of anger, righteousness and absence of righteousness and all

---

[16] Bhagavad Gita, XVI.19-20.
[17] *Brihadaranyaka Upanishad*, IV.iv.3-4.

things. This is what is meant by saying, (it) consists of this (what is perceived), consists of that (what is inferred) . . .[18]

Whether karma adheres to the soul as a viscous substance or actually pours into it; whether karma stays in the soul for a relatively short period or—and this may be an infinite length of time—till it is fully burnt up; the duration for which karma stays in the soul; the ways by which the soul proceeds; the stations on the way at which it passes time; the time it will pass at each station; the world to which it goes—the moon or some other; whether it will work through a part of the recompense for its karma in one of these worlds or whether all of the karma it has accumulated will have to be worked out when it returns to earth; the ways by which the soul proceeds; the stations on the way at which it passes time; the time it will pass at each station; the worlds to which it goes; the interval after which it returns; the path it shall follow as it re-enters this world, in particular the womb; which specific womb it shall enter—that is, what kinds of karma result in what kind of rebirth.[19] On one and each of these questions, the texts—all equally sacred, all having been composed by seers—offer a very wide range of answers. These differences and ambiguities need not detain us. But we should note two facts, and draw one lesson.

First the two facts:

❑ Several elements have not been explained at all, and they certainly are not self-evident by any stretch. How does karmic dust adhere to the soul as it transits from one body to the next? And, mind you, the adhesive is such that it does not let the dust fall away literally through hellfire and high water. After all, here is an entity that is 'not wet by water, not

---

[18] Ibid., IV.iv.5.
[19] The monumental study of Surendranath Dasgupta, *A History of Indian Philosophy*, Cambridge, 1922, Motilal Banarsidass, Delhi, 1975, contains a large enough sample of the divergent answers.

burnt by fire'—how is it that something sticks to it? As the soul is identical with the undifferentiated universal soul, how is it affected separately by an individual's karma? Does past karma determine only the pleasure and pain a person shall feel in this life, or also the capacity of the person to do good or evil in this life? Does it determine the capacity or also the strength of will and the direction towards which it will be inclined?[20]

❏ As each variant has been set out by a seer, by an eyewitness, so to say, how come they have seen such different sequences, such different 'facts'?

From these follows the lesson. As so many of the entities that are at the heart of the construct—like the soul, like past and future lives; as every step is unverifiable, we must not set up walls, we most certainly must not enter into disputes over these things: how bewildering, and also how lamentable it is to read that '. . . Indeed, it is not unreasonable to say that the basic social distinction between Jainas and their Hindu neighbours derives mainly from the disagreement of these communities over the period of time required for transmigration to occur . . .'; that as the Hindus believe that it takes quite some time for the soul to transit to a new body, and to other worlds, they observe the *shraadha* so as to provide for the journey their ancestor would be making from one birth to the next; on the other hand, the Jainas, certain that rebirth is instantaneous, do not observe *shraadha*, as 'a soul which goes to its next body in one moment cannot be fed, propitiated, or dealt with in any other way by those left behind'[21]; indeed, they hold the

---

[20] Again, Dasgupta's *A History of Indian Philosophy, op. cit.*, contains a wide range of answers.

[21] Padmanabh S. Jaini, 'Karma and the problem of rebirth in Jainism,' in *Karma and Rebirth in Classical Indian Traditions*, Wendy Doniger O' Flaherty [ed.], Motilal Banarsidass, Delhi, 1983, pp. 233-34.

practice in some derision. Aren't these what Lenin called quarrels over how many angels can perch on the head of a pin?

NECESSARILY CIRCULAR

The third fact that is apparent is that the reasoning here has been and remains circular. Because he is suffering in this world, we must believe, he *must* have done something evil in his previous birth. How do we know that he must have done something evil in some previous life of his? Because he is suffering in this life.

The proposition is made unverifiable, and, therefore, irrefutable—in two ways. It is often stressed that, while the primary impulse for what happens to us is the result of what we had done, we should not look for a one-to-one correspondence: what happens will also be influenced by a host of other factors—the analogy is given of the harvest that the farmer gets: it will greatly/primarily be influenced by the labour that he puts in, the decisions he makes during the crop cycle, etc., but it will be influenced also by the climate, the rains. 'No *thing* causes any other thing, for causality resides not in things but in the whole,' Sri Krishna Prem and Madhava Ashish write.[22] Hence, if manifest evil done by a person does not result in the consequences that any reasonable man would expect, well, maybe the outcome that was to befall him has been deflected by the totality of circumstances. Similarly, as we noticed, because one previous life could not be made to bear the entire burden of explaining what the person was going through, what he must have done in a series of infinite previous lives is brought into the calculus. The circularity is

---

[22] Sri Krishna Prem and Madhava Ashish, *Man, the Measure of All Things*, Theosophical Publishing House, Wheaton, 1969, p. 210; cited in V. Hanson, R. Stewart, S. Nicholson, (eds), *Karma, Rhythmic Return to Harmony*, The Theosophical Society Publishing House, 1975, Motilal Banarsidass, Delhi, Reprint, 1975, p. 12.

manifest: 'If one accepts the view, as most Hindus do,' writes Arvind Sharma, 'that we continually undergo reincarnation, then the question arises: what determines where we will be reincarnated and what will befall us in that incarnation? The answer to this question in a word is: karma!'[23] May one not with equal justification say, 'If one accepts the view, as most Hindus do, that we are governed by our karma, then the question arises: how can one hold this to be the case when we see inequality, injustice, suffering around us? The answer in one word is: reincarnation!'

An example will indicate how the reasoning here necessarily has to be circular. So many must have suffered from Parkinson's disease for millennia. The discovery, as recently as the 1960s that dopamine was the chemical that had to be supplemented and thereby the development of L-Dopa made a world of difference to patients being able to cope with the symptoms of the ailment, at least for a while. Was it the karma of the ones who suffered and died before the 1960s that L-Dopa had not been discovered till then? Or consider those who suffer from this terrible, degenerative disease today. Anita, my wife, has had Parkinson's disease for almost twenty-two years. She has it to a heartbreaking degree today. Ten years from now, drugs or therapies would have been discovered to reverse this disease. Is it her karma that a therapy will be discovered next year, and thereby the quality of her life will be restored to what it used to be? Or is it her karma that she will miss the cure? The answer will be given only in retrospect.[24]

---

[23] Arvind Sharma, *Classical Hindu Thought, An Introduction*, Oxford University Press, 2000/2003, p. 98.

[24] And that makes it unassailable! My niece, Ratna, all of ten years old, and her eight-year-old brother, Sukaran, had come to see their grandparents and us. I found Ratna reading to her little brother the astrological forecast for the week from one of the papers. Better cure her of this before it

Through this specious and circular reasoning a devastating effect is ensured: it is not just that God is let off, the blame is put on the victim of *His* design and *His* doing. And, as thinkers like Erich Fromm might point out, this is the ineluctable result of an entire sequence:

❑ Unable to comprehend much that is happening to him and around him, man creates God in his own image.

❑ He endows his invention with everything he wished he had but does not have: absolute power, total knowledge, unalloyed, unlimited compassion. In a word, with perfection.

❑ As fidelity comes to be gauged by the extent to which he 'believes', he holds on to the propositions in the face of overwhelming evidence to the contrary,

---

becomes a habit, I thought. 'But Ratna, that is all nonsense,' I said and fetched four/five other papers that were lying about the house. 'Now read out each of them,' I told her. She read the forecasts out aloud. 'See?' I said triumphantly. 'See, one says one thing and the other its opposite.' 'But you don't understand, Arun Mama,' she said. 'That is why we have to read them all. One of them is bound to come true.' The same sort of thing happened in a grander setting. V.P. Singh was the Prime Minister. He had chosen his classmate, Vinod Pande, to be the Cabinet Secretary. A large-hearted, open, garrulous person, Vinod was better known as a poet and an astrologer and for colourful expressions. I was editing the *Indian Express* at the time. We got to know each other well. V.P. Singh's government started floundering. I was with Vinod in his office for some other work. During a lull, I asked him what astrology indicated about the longevity of the government. 'No, no, nothing to worry about,' he said. 'Difficulties will increase for the next two and a half months, but the government will get over them, and everything will be all right by February.' Soon, the government fell. While talking to him over the phone one day, I said, 'Pandeji, just two weeks ago you said everything would be all right by February, but the government has fallen.' 'When did I say that?' he demanded. 'Not even two weeks ago when I had come to your office,' I said. 'Not two weeks ago, you fool. *What was the day* when I said that?' Holding the phone, I looked up the desk calendar. 'Wednesday, the . . .' 'No wonder,' Vinod said. 'Every forecast I made that day just *had* to come out wrong. That was a very inauspicious day for me.'

evidence that is hurled at him day in and day out. Thus, to take one instance from the context of karma, he continues to believe simultaneously that God is Compassion and that the same God continues to let him go on doing things which are certain to invite condign pain and suffering.

But as Fromm points out in his succinct and lucid essay, the more he does this, the smaller he feels. The more dependent he becomes, the more *he* is responsible for things that go wrong—with the world, of course, but even more so with himself. Not just suffering but also guilt and blame—these become his lot.[24]

ELEMENTS

That our deeds will boomerang and affect us—there can be no difficulty with that proposition. Especially so when, as is the case in our scriptures, 'deeds' are taken to include not just deeds that we actually execute but in addition 'deeds' of the mind—our thoughts, desires, intention, will: that is, all the mental formations that precede the carrying out of the deed. Indeed, there can be no doubt that mental formations so construed have effects on us even if they are not followed by an actual 'deed'. Thus, a person given to depressing thoughts will eventually end up as a depressive, and, even if that does not result in any overt deed, that condition itself would have been enough of a consequence of that particular set of mental formations. Thoughts, desires, etc., deepen grooves that similar thoughts, desires, etc., have etched on/in the mind. These, in turn, predispose us to act in a particular way, they predispose us to react to a new

---

[24] For a telling account of this sequence, Erich Fromm, *Psychoanalysis and Religion,* Yale, New Haven, 1950: In particular his sketch of 'authoritarian religions', pp. 49-53.

situation in a particular way. And that increases the chances of our hurtling along in a particular direction, and thereby inviting a set of consequences on ourselves.

The problems arise, as we have seen, when this proposition is stretched in two directions. One, when our deeds are made the sole or even overwhelming determinant of what happens: as we have seen in the case of a child who is born with handicaps, as we have seen in the case of thousands who get killed by natural disasters, chance often is the major determinant. Second, when the notion of reincarnation is tagged so that, when our condition is manifestly not attributable to our deeds here and now, that condition is 'accounted for' by asserting that the person *must have* committed deeds in his past lives which merit his present condition.

Once we shear away these two extensions, and make karma shoulder a lighter explanatory burden, there are several elements that are valuable indeed.

The doctrine has been stated so often over the millennia, and elaborated so much that we hardly need to devote much energy into recounting it: after all, it is the staple of every Indian's everyday beliefs. A few well-known passages from the *Brihadaranyaka Upanishad* will suffice to set out the principal elements—including one of those that cause difficulties!

Artabhaga is questioning the great sage Yajnavalkya about what happens to man when he dies. Yajnavalkya enumerates the elements and the places to which each organ and faculty go—the speech into fire, the breath into air, the eye into the sun, the mind into the moon, hearing into the quarters . . . Artabhaga then asks, after each of these organs and faculties have gone to these respective places, 'what then becomes of the person?' Yajnavalkya takes him by the hand, and says, 'We two alone shall know of this, this is not for us two [to speak of] in public.'

AS EVERYTHING, INCLUDING THE WORLD, IS 'UNREAL' . . .

293

'The two went away and deliberated,' the Upanishad
records. 'What they said was karma and what they praised
was karma. Verily one becomes good by good action, bad by
bad action . . .'[25]

A little later, the Upanishad states almost the complete
doctrine in a nutshell: ' . . . According as one acts, according
as one behaves, so does one become. The doer of good
becomes good, the doer of evil becomes evil. One becomes
virtuous by virtuous action, bad by bad action.'

Then follows the vital extension:

Others, however, say that a person consists of desires. As is his
desire so is his will; as is his will, so is the deed he does; whatever
deed he does, that he attains.

On this there is the following verse: 'The object to which the mind
is attached, the subtle self goes together with the deed, being
attached to it alone.'

And then the extension that occasions problems:

'Exhausting the results of whatever works he did in this world
he comes again from that world to this world for (fresh) work.'

And then the invaluable guide pointing the way out:

This (is for) the man who desires. But the man who does not desire,
he who is without desire, who is freed from desire, whose desire is
satisfied, whose desire is the self; his breaths do not depart. Being
Brahman he goes to *Brahman*.

On this there is the following verse: 'When all the desires that
dwell in the heart are cast away, then does the mortal become
immortal, then he attains *Brahman* here (in this very body).' Just as
the slough of a snake lies on an anthill, dead, cast off, even so lies
this body . . .[26]

---

[25] *Brihadaranyaka Upanishad*, III.2. 1-13; the quotation is from III.2.13.
[26] Ibid., IV.4.5-7.

The principal elements thus are five:

- ❑ Our deeds determine what we become;
- ❑ 'Deeds' include desires, will, and other mental formations;
- ❑ Deeds have to be paid for; if the payment is not exhausted in this lifetime, one has to come back and continue bearing the consequences in a subsequent life;
- ❑ There is, therefore, a clear way to liberate oneself from the consequences of one's karma: perform the deeds without desire for the fruit; attain knowledge of the Self.

Several ways are enumerated by sages that will enable one to perform deeds and yet not have consequences stick to one. Do not perform acts for one's selfish ends. While performing duties and tasks that the welfare of all requires, surrender the results of karma to God, give up all concern for the fruit of one's efforts; that is, give up the sense of doership; and ipso facto give up all pride or feeling of superiority or of being special that usually arises from doing work for the welfare of others. Attain knowledge of the Self . . . And for performing deeds in this fashion, for attaining knowledge of the Self, a slew of suggestions is offered. The practices are of inestimable value—based, as they are, on what persons of utmost perspicacity, diligence, perseverance and insight have verified by their own striving.

- ❑ Once this attitude of detachment is attained, once actions are done without any hankering after results, once knowledge of the Self is attained, karma lose their potency to produce further consequences 'as seed that have been burnt cannot yield plants'.

Several inferences of these elements are manifestly valuable—even to one who is afflicted by grave circumstances.

First, once we confine ourselves to the here and now, and once we keep in mind the broader implication of the word 'deeds', the notion is manifestly true. What we do comes back to us by the reactions it sets among others. Even more directly, it comes back to us in the way it affects our minds. Dr S. Radhakrishnan puts the point succinctly. In his introduction to the Upanishads, he writes, 'The law of karma is not external to the individual. The judge is not without but within. The law by which virtue brings its triumph and ill-doing its retribution is the unfolding of the law of our being.'[27] This is all the more so when we consider the change that comes about once we commence the practices that the seers have prescribed. As we condition our minds to be watchful, as we become 'mindful' about what we do and think, our minds become more and more receptive. Even slender events, even the slight rustling in our circumstances registers on our minds, and thereby alters our preconceptions and predispositions. That is why, for instance, karma is said to leave no karmic residue in or on the mind of the jnani—as he acts without any selfish motive or any hankering after reward, what he does leaves no scratches on his mind.

And that leads us directly to the next feature: the notion enshrines great optimism. But that is so only if we do not overburden it—if we do not conclude, for instance, that the outcome will correspond exactly to what we do; similarly, if we do not conclude that what we can do and will do is completely predetermined by what we have done in the past: recall the remark of the sage in the preceding chapter when he tells a devotee that every detail—whether he would pick up a particular glass or not, whether he would move from one part of the room or not—was predetermined. Shorn of these extremes, the notion of

27 S. Radhakrishnan, *The Principal Upanishads*, 'Introduction', George Allen and Unwin, UK, 1953; HarperCollins, India, 2009, p. 114.

karma makes each of us a major participant in fashioning our world. We can, for instance, change predispositions through meditation, introspection, through reflection, in a word through 'mindfulness', to use the Buddhist expression, and thereby alter our course. Changing course is always within our capacity. This is tempered by recognizing that the outcome will depend on a host of other factors also. But the result on what is nearest to us, and what is the principal instrument we have for the future—our mind—is certain, here and now. That is of the greatest importance by itself: even for perception and interpretation of what we observe through our senses, or how we interpret what happens to us and thereby how we should react to it. For, the world and events do not register on us 'in their pristine form' so to say. They are filtered through the predispositions that we have formed. Hence, by altering these, we can affect the behaviour that an event will trigger in us. We come to look at the event or person or situation through an unconditioned mind, 'through a child's eye'.

Emphasis on the fact that the mind and what happens in it are as much a part of karma as the overt deed is important in another sense also. As we shall see later on, one lesson that serving a stricken child or friend, or indeed grappling with insurmountable odds in any setting teaches us is autonomy. We have to strive to be autonomous not just in the sense that the outcome—the happiness of the child— should depend as little on the efforts of others around us as possible. In addition, we have to be autonomous in the sense that *the goal towards which we are striving should be as independent of others as possible.* Inner growth is the most autonomous among such goals. The efforts that dealing with the child's condition necessitates then become not an occasion for self-pity. They become a ready, and relentless stream of occasions for the next step in our inner growth. Mahatma Gandhi's life is the great lesson in this as in other respects. At every turn, he had to face impediments. At every turn, men who were not, as General Smuts put it in his own case, worthy to untie his shoelaces could, and did derail what he was striving to accomplish. They would ensnare his projects in conspiracies. They would throw him in jail. They would let loose calumnies. Each of these would have felled a man who was obsessed with the goal—say, swaraj—a goal that was as much in the hands of others as of Gandhiji. But as he had made inner growth his objective, each setback, each hurdle, every perverse conspirator became an aid. Confronted by these, he would not just do what he could to deal with them, he would watch his own reactions, and thereby take another step in controlling his mind.

Even when God is admitted into the equation, and he certainly was very firmly in the equation in Gandhiji's case, the doctrine need not necessarily cause helplessness: if God's role is confined to that of a mere keeper of the ledger of our good and bad deeds, then, while He may be the One who is meting out our deserts, He does so strictly in accordance with our own deeds. So, we remain the architects of our lives. Of course, even in the most activist of texts, for instance the Gita, God says at every turn that the outcome is in His hands, and so, going by the texts, one cannot present Him as a mere ledger-keeper. Why not substitute 'the rest of circumstances' for the word 'God' wherever the latter occurs. That is, we must put in our best, always bearing in mind that the outcome will depend, not just on our efforts but on 'the rest' also—encompassing in 'the rest' everything and everybody other than us and our individual effort. That will induce humility as much as the notion that the final outcome depends on 'God'.

Notice that from the very beginning, even as some texts stressed that one's karma could not but cause consequences, it was assumed that one *could* alter the outcome. Even in the earliest texts, various methods were prescribed by which the effects of past deeds may be alleviated—rituals, sacrifices and the rest. In any case, it was always stressed that just as our present condition had been affected by what we had done in the past, the future was ours to shape. The Gita is, of course, the prime example of such texts: every syllable of Sri Krishna is an argument for and an exhortation to act. And the result of the entire sequence is not that Arjuna sits down and waits for past karma to work itself out. He casts aside the doubts that had paralysed him and fights. A while earlier, Draupadi and Bhima exhort Yudhishthira to rise and act. In a devastating fusillade, Draupadi first blames God for being capricious and unfair—that one so devoted to virtue as Yudhishthira should be hurled into such a woeful condition while the sinful Duryodhana should be enjoying to the full. Yudhishthira admonishes her for talking the language of atheists, for blaspheming God. Draupadi reframes her attack somewhat—saying that the outcome is not dictated by God out of capriciousness alone but is the compound of Divine providence, chance, our past karma as rewarded by God, and by our own efforts. She doesn't say, 'You are right, let us sit and wait for our karma to work itself out.' She says, therefore, get up and act. Bhima, 'sighing in wrath', reinforces the message in much harsher words.

That such an activist notion—karma—came to be associated with fatalism, that it became the rationalization for passivity shows two things. First, that life determines text, text does not determine life. As the people were beaten down into helplessness over millennia, they came to read passivity into the notion. Second, that the drift to fatalism was spurred by persons who made extreme statements into which fatalist resignation could be read, whatever they may have themselves meant to convey.

As conditions began to change, a different meaning began to be read into the same texts and verses. The reformulation was assiduously furthered by leaders. And it resonated better with the people at large than it would have in the conditions that had held them in thrall for millennia. Our past karma determines only the general circumstances in which we are placed, we were now taught. It only circumscribes the ambit of opportunities that we have, it only lays down the general handicaps we have to carry. How we avail of those opportunities, how we stretch them, the extent to which we strive in spite of the initial handicaps is up to us.[28]

That an activist notion should have become the rationalization for fatalism also shows that group-think is group-karma. It has consequences for the group just as much as an individual's mental formations do for the individual. As the people at large internalized defeat, they

---

[28] Among others, Dr S. Radhakrishnan in his *Hindu View of Life* advanced this reformulation eloquently. Swami Vivekananda, Lokmanya Tilak, Gandhiji, that entire phalanx which stood us on our feet, did not just advance a reformulation. They lived it. On all this see the fine accounts of Arvind Sharma in *Hinduism for Our Times*, OUP, Delhi, 1996; *Classical Hindu Thought*, OUP, Delhi, 2000/2003; and *Modern Hindu Thought, An Introduction*, OUP, Delhi, 2005. The well-known philosopher Giddes MacGregor draws attention to this feature of karma—that karma determines the general circumstances in which one is placed rather than the specific acts that one will do—as the way to reconcile the Christians' resistance to the Law of Karma and the apprehension that it limits the power of Jesus to save Christians through his death and resurrection. He observes, 'What, according to Christian teaching, does Christ do for the Christian? What is the nature of his redemptive work? The answer, however formulated, is essentially this: he puts the Christian in the right way, providing the conditions that make possible his or her salvation. Through faith in Christ the Christian is "justified", that is, "put right", so that it is now possible for him or for her, as before it was not, to be "sanctified", that is, to get out of the bind and make progress in spiritual development. It is the discovery of the aid that Christ provides in this undertaking that causes the Christian to be, in C.S. Lewis's felicitous phrase, "surprised by joy".' Giddes MacGregor, 'The Christening of Karma,' in *Karma, Rhythmic Return to Harmony*, V. Hanson, R. Stewart and S. Nicholson, (eds), Theosophical Publishing House, 1975, Reprint, Motilal Banarsidass, Delhi, 2001, p. 88.

began to read passivity into the texts. And as they read passivity into the texts, the texts reinforced defeat.

Nor is it just a question of putting forward an argument—that we *can* determine our future—for taking matters in hand. The notion also puts *responsibility* squarely on the shoulders of the individual. And not just on the individual. As has been pointed out by scholars, several texts, in particular the large number that dealt with matters medical, placed responsibility on the community by emphasizing that the outcome—from harvests to epidemics—was influenced by what the community as a whole did. Mutual interdependence enhances collective responsibility. Indeed, it has been stressed that the karma of all of us taken together shall have consequences for us even if as individuals we are opposed to what the community is doing. That places a dual responsibility on each of us: we must not just be mindful of our own conduct; we must actively work to ensure that the community does what is right. We must actively nudge humanity at large today in regard to, say, climate change. Similarly, the fruit of a mother's care and love for her impaired child will shrivel if the attitude of society at large towards the handicapped does not improve. So, in addition to serving her child, she must do every little bit she can to change society's attitude towards the handicapped.[29]

One of the most fertile extensions of this notion, of course, is the one advanced so incisively—his word was 'cautiously'—by Jung—that of 'psychic heredity'. He wrote of 'inherited psychic factors' that are 'not confined either to family or to race,' and are instead 'the universal dispositions of the mind . . . in accordance with which the mind organizes its contents'. These are as uniform across mankind as the uniformities of the body, he wrote. 'They are

[29] On karma in the medical texts, see, for instance, Mitchell G. Weiss, *'Caraka Samhita* on the doctrine of karma', in *Karma and Rebirth in Classical Indian Traditions,* op. cit., pp. 90-115. Several of the essays in *Karma, Rhythmic Return to Harmony* stress group-karma and its implications.

eternally inherited forms and ideas which have at first no specific content. Their specific content only appears in the course of the individual's life, when personal experience is taken up in precisely these forms.' Jung's reflection and direct experience with his patients had led him to observe that these 'dynamic, instinctual complexes . . . determine psychic life to an extraordinary degree.' 'That is why I have called them *dominants* of the unconscious,' he wrote, and that 'the layer of unconscious psyche which is made up of these universal dynamic forms I have termed the *collective unconscious.*' In a word, we experience and react to events and relationships in part through the filter of archetypes that have formed over millennia as a result of the experiences that our ancestors went through and the ways in which they reacted to those experiences, and, in turn, the experiences we go through and the ways we deal with them shape these dynamic forms.[30]

Even on the surface, we see the influence of 'psychic heredity'—from the differential ways in which we react even to words that may strike someone else as synonyms: Gandhiji would say that the word 'God' does not fill and stir his being the way 'Ram' does; to so many of our beliefs and perceptions: 'memories of past lives' seem to be so culture-specific. Jung's extension, therefore, seems especially productive: collective karma generating the collective unconscious and its archetypes, and these in turn predisposing us to perceive and react in particular ways and thereby remoulding the collective unconscious.

WHAT SORT OF KARMA?

As we shift the focus from lives in the past and in the future

---

[30] C.G. Jung, *Psychology and the East*, R.F.C. Hull (trans.), Princeton, Bollingen Series, 1978, pp. 67-70. In a sense, the point was the theme of much that Jung wrote in regard to religion and myths. The expressions in the text are taken from Jung's discerning introduction to *The Tibetan Book of the Dead*.

to the here and now; as we concede a major role to chance; as we recognize that the outcome will be affected by what all of us do collectively; as we internalize the principal lesson—that the most consequential effect that our deed shall have is on our mind, we will come to see rituals, pilgrimages, visiting temples, worshipping idols, and similar practices in a different light.

To the extent that these practices help, they do so not by pleasing God but by reconditioning our minds, and thereby equipping us to better deal with the situation. In this sense, the practices are valuable: they contain potions derived from eons of experimentation by seers. The rituals that a son has to perform at the cremation of his father, for instance— right up to bursting the skull when the body is being consumed by fire—are carefully devised to drive in the finality of what has happened. It is because they contain the experimental heritage of a culture in dealing with distressing circumstances that the rituals are valuable, but only in this sense.

The same holds, for say, the steps enumerated in Patanjali's *Yoga Sutras*, or the doctrine of abandoning the fruit of action in the Bhagavad Gita. We should heed them, strive to the utmost to live by them, not because they are from God but because they are inherently right; because they appeal to reason; because they have been verified by persons of the subtlest perspicacity; because they have been devised and verified by them through experimentation and reflection over millennia. This has been one of the great strengths of our religions—especially of Hinduism and Buddhism: as new evidence, new knowledge has become available, there has been no reason not to embrace it, and adjust what we have believed hitherto. And it is this capacity and openness that are weakened when rituals substitute for substance.

THE REAL 'RITUAL' THAT IS REQUIRED

We must always bear in mind that, basically, the deed that is required to overcome the effects of karma and chance is not a havan or a pilgrimage, but one that unweaves the consequences of our original deed and of chance, here and now. Abandoning everything to serve and love the child, not running from one holy place to the other.

How well the Buddhist elder sisters put the lesson.

A cold, winter morning. The maid, Punnika, has gone down to the river to fetch water. She sees a Brahmin knee-deep in the cold river—shivering, performing ablutions with water. I am a water-carrier, she tells the Brahmin. I have to come here always 'from fear of my mistresses' beatings, harassed by their anger and words'. But why do you come down and stand here doing all these things 'with shivering limbs, feeling great cold'?

Do you not know, the Brahmin asks, that you are asking one who is doing skilful karma that will ward off evil? Whoever has done evil is set free from evil karma by water ablutions.

Who taught you this—that through water ablutions one is set free of karma? Punnika asks. Some ignorant one teaching another ignorant one? Were this the case, would not all the frogs, turtles, serpents, crocodiles and every other being that lives in water be set free? Would butchers and thieves and fishermen and trappers and executioners and all others doing evil karma not be able to free themselves by performing some rituals with water? Moreover, if these rivers could carry away your evil deeds, would they not also carry away your good deeds as well? What then? Whatever you fear, at least don't punish your skin by the cold.

If you are afraid of pain, if you dislike pain, desist from evil karma. If you do evil, you will get no freedom from

the consequences 'even if you fly up and hurry away'.
'If you are afraid of pain, if you dislike pain, go to
the Awakened One for refuge, go to the Dhamma and
Sangha . . .'

The Brahmin heeds her counsel, goes to the Awakened
One for refuge . . . 'Before, I was a kinsman to Brahma;
now, truly a Brahman. I am a three-knowledge man,
consummate in knowledge, safe and washed clean.'[31]

---

[31] 'Punnika and the Brahman,' *Therigatha*, 12.1, 236-251, translated
from the Pali by Thanissaro Bhikku, *Access to Insight*, http://
www.accesstoinsight.org/tipitaka/kn/thig/thig.12.10.than.html.

8
As unreal as it seems?

In what Sri Ramakrishna and Ramana Maharshi told their devotees as the latter came to them in distress, *prarabdha karma* was one recurring theme. Two other themes recurred. We must now see what implications these have, and how, at our midgets' level, we may cope with the teaching.

The first, of course, is the one that is set out in the oft-quoted passages of the Gita, for instance. As Arjuna sinks into 'the slough of despond' at the prospect of fighting and slaying his brothers and uncles, his elders and teachers, Sri Krishna assures him that he—Arjuna—grieves for those who should not be grieved for. The reason is not that the latter have committed sins that merit execution—that calculus does not enter the picture at this juncture. The reason why 'The wise grieve neither for the living nor for the dead,' is much deeper. Neither I, nor you, nor indeed these princes and the rest did ever not exist, nor shall we ever cease to be in the hereafter, Sri Krishna declares. Going over to another body is no different from the change that the body experiences as we proceed from childhood to youth to old age, he tells Arjuna. 'The unreal hath no being; the real never ceaseth to be,' he declares—the sense in which one thing alone is real and the rest, our bodies, the world we perceive, are all unreal is something we shall glimpse in a moment. That which has spread all this out, that which pervades all this is indestructible, it is imperishable. The bodies you are focusing on are mere finite entities: 'The one who regardeth him as slayer [that is the Arjuna who is

weighed down with the guilt that he will end up slaying his
elders and relatives], and he who thinketh He [that is the
essence that pervades all] is slain, both of them are ignorant.
He slayeth not, nor is He slain.' And then the vital verses
that we see printed in advertisements every time a relative
dies:

> He is not born, nor doth he die; nor having been, ceaseth he any
> more to be; unborn, perpetual, eternal and ancient, he is not slain
> when the body is slaughtered.

> Who knoweth him [as] indestructible, perpetual, unborn,
> undiminishing, how can that man slay, O Partha!, or cause to be
> slain?

> As a man casting off worn-out garments, taketh new ones, so the
> dweller in the body, casting off worn-out bodies, entereth into
> others that are new.

> *Weapons cleave him not, nor fire burneth him, nor waters wet him, nor*
> *wind drieth him away.*

> *Uncleavable he, incombustible he, and indeed neither wetted nor dried*
> *away; perpetual, all-pervasive, stable, immovable, ancient.*

> *Unmanifest, unthinkable, immutable, he is called; therefore, knowing him*
> *as such, thou shouldst not grieve.* [1]

Two inferences follow. First, what we perceive as suffering
occurs to that which is superficial, if not phantasmal. The
victim feels it, and we who love the victim feel it because he
and we erroneously identify ourselves with our bodies and
him or her with his or her body.

And why have things been so arranged that we
erroneously identify him and ourselves with our respective
bodies? That is one of the mysteries that God has kept with
Himself, say some. That is because of a culprit, Sri Ramana

---

[1] Bhagavad Gita, II.14-30. Sri Krishna goes on to say, of course, that,
even if Arjuna regards them as being born and dying, he should not
grieve—for death is inevitable for all who take birth, that He, the Lord, has
already slain them.

says: the ego. The Self does not have any sense of separateness, he points out. By itself the body is inert, he points out; so it too does not have any sense of separateness. Between the two, the ego interposes itself. With its interposition, the sense of separateness arises, and from it all the consequences like suffering and joy. The question naturally arises: Why have things been so arranged that the ego interposes itself? So that we may seek the essential Self behind the veil of phenomena like the body, says Ramana Maharshi.

Soon after birth, an infant develops a blood disorder. Because of his ego? Or is it that the infant does not suffer, and the suffering is limited to those who love the helpless child? Are only *their* egos which are at play there? Is it that all that is happening as the infant wastes and dies is that they suffer because they wrongly identify the infant with his body and themselves with their bodies? Or has everything been arranged in this way so that the infant may seek its essential Self behind the veil of phenomena like the body?

But we are getting ahead of the story.

The second theme that recurs repeatedly is that the world is 'unreal', that it is all in the mind, that it is just a mental projection. Naturally, were this so, there would be no point in worrying about suffering—in the unreal world the unreal child would be having an unreal disorder of his unreal blood and the unreal relatives would be going through an unreal agony.

That sounds so far out that we are forced to look for the sense in which the great teachers, and indeed so many of our scriptures, could possibly have meant the proposition. After all, Adi Shankara who, with his unalloyed non-dualism, is said to have been most emphatic on this score, wrote hymns of devotion that are sung to this day. He wrote extensive and complex commentaries on the *Brahma Sutras*, the Gita as well as the principal Upanishads—indeed, the principal ones are regarded as being the 'principal' ones on the ground that Shankara wrote commentaries on them. He traversed the entire country. He set up centres of pilgrimage. He debated the opponents and worsted them in cerebral jousts in the presence of large audiences. Would he have done any of these things if the objects of devotion, if the hymns, if the religion and country, if the centres he was setting up, if the opponents and their doctrine, if his own commentaries and his teaching were all unreal meant for people who were unreal in a world that was unreal?

Even before him, while many texts we hold sacred declare that this world is unreal, the very same texts, as Kane notes, prescribe rituals that we should perform for relief in this very world. In the very texts, the sages pray for physical health. Manu castigates those who seek to resort to sanyas prematurely. Moksha is to be sought after the three stages have been traversed, and duties pertaining to them have been discharged. Indeed, we are instructed that the final goal—of knowing Brahman—can be 'attained only by him who already has become tired of the world of senses'.[2] Where would the occasion be for any of this if the world and everything in it—our bodies and senses, the fourfold goals, rituals and the lot—were unreal?

Hence, what exactly did sages like Ramakrishna Paramhamsa and Ramana Maharshi say in this regard? What may we make of what they said? In what sense may we cope with it?

WHAT THEY SAID

Read by themselves—even paying due regard to the context in which these revered figures made the statements—their averments do seem puzzling.

The devotee has been seeking to learn about the 'I' that the Maharshi urges everyone to seek. 'Who is this "I"?' the

---

[2] For a quick glance at representative passages, P.V. Kane, *History of the Dharmashastras, op. cit.,* Volume V, Part II, pp. 1508-13.

devotee asks. 'It seems to be only a continuum of sense-impressions. The Buddhist idea seems to be so too.'

'The world is not external,' the Maharshi responds. 'The impressions cannot have an outer origin. Because the world can be cognised only by consciousness. The world does not say that it exists. It is only your impression. Even so this impression is not consistent and not unbroken. In deep sleep the world is not cognised; and so it exists not for the sleeping man. Therefore the world is the sequence of the ego. . .'

The exchange continues. The visitor remarks that it is the world that sends impressions and he awakens—a reference to the simile that the Maharshi often gives about the absence of difference between the waking and dream states, an allusion to which we shall soon turn.

'Can the world exist without someone to perceive it?' the Maharshi asks.

Pause for a second. It is only now that we have begun to get glimpses of the farthest reaches of the universe—through space probes like the Hubble telescope, *Chandra* and *Galileo*. Can we, therefore, say that those stars and gaseous formations that we are now seeing did not exist ten years ago? Clearly, when a seer asks, 'Can the world exist without someone to perceive it?' we have to inquire earnestly, 'What meaning does he want us to read into the word "exist"?'

But to continue with what the Maharshi said.

'Can the world exist without someone to perceive it?' he asks. 'Which is prior? The Being-consciousness or the rising-consciousness? The Being-consciousness is always there, eternal and pure. The rising-consciousness rises forth and disappears. It is transient'—a vital point whose importance for the question at hand—the reality or unreality of the world—we shall soon see.

'Does not the world exist for others even when I am asleep?' the intrepid devotee asks.

'Such a world mocks at you also for knowing it without

knowing yourself,' the Maharshi admonishes. 'The world is the result of your mind. Know your mind. Then see the world. You will realise that it is not different from the Self.'

'Is not the Maharshi aware of himself and his surroundings, as clearly as I am?' the devotee persists.

'To whom is the doubt?' the Maharshi counters. 'The doubts are not for the realised. They are only for the ignorant.'[3]

A few months later, another devotee is seeking to learn about the 'heart' that Sri Ramana sometimes refers to as the seat of the Self, and sometimes as the Self itself—not the physical heart on the left side of our chest but the notional one in 'a cavity' on the right side. The devotee inquires how it is that one should realize the heart.

'There is no one who even for a trice fails to experience the Self,' the Maharshi says. 'For no one admits that he ever stands apart from the Self. He is the Self. The Self is the heart.'

'It is not clear,' the devotee says.

'In deep sleep you exist; awake, you remain,' the Maharshi continues. 'The same Self is in both states. The difference is only in the awareness and the non-awareness of the world. *The world rises with the mind and sets with the mind.*' The Maharshi goes on to state that that which is transient, that which rises and sets is not the Self. 'The Self is different, giving rise to the mind, sustaining it and resolving it. So the Self is the underlying principle.'[4]

Similar exchanges continue to take place. The Maharshi reiterates the proposition on several occasions. One day a year later, he is explaining that there is really no difference between those who assert that maya is the shakti of illusion

[3] *Talks with Sri Ramana Maharshi*, Sri Ramanasramam, Tiruvannamalai, 1955/1984, pp. 56-57.
[4] Ibid., pp. 92-93.

that is premised in Shiva and has no independent existence, and others who say that maya manifests itself as the display of the cosmos 'on account of her independent will'. 'Her manifestation is the display of the cosmos on pure consciousness, like images in a mirror,' he explains. 'The images cannot remain in the absence of a mirror. So also the world cannot have an independent existence.' Both sides agree that the display is not real, the Maharshi explains. 'The images of the mirror cannot in any way be real. The world does not exist in reality . . .'[5]

We should bear each of these expositions in mind—for they contain allusions that will enable us to discern the sense in which the expressions, 'The world does not exist in reality,' 'The body is nothing but a projection of the mind,' etc., should be understood. It is then that we will be able to discern their import for the suffering that we ordinary folk experience.

Later, a lady seeks to know how she may remain free of thoughts. The Maharshi takes her through the answers: 'Only remain still. Do it and see' . . . The lady says that as one does so, thoughts rise more and more. Then ask 'Who am I?' Should one do so as each thought arises? she inquires, and asks the question that is relevant to our present concern: 'Is the world our thought only?'

'Leave this question to the world,' the Maharshi responds. 'Let it ask, "How did I come into being?"'

'Do you mean that it is not related to me?' the lady asks.

'Nothing is perceived in deep sleep,' the Maharshi points out. *'All these are seen only after waking; only after thoughts arise the world comes into being; what can it be but thought?'*[6]

Another year passes. A European has come. He asks, 'Why should individuals remain caught up in the affairs of this world and reap troubles as a result? Should they not be

---

[5] Ibid., pp. 247-48.
[6] Ibid., p. 285.

free? If they are in the spiritual world they will have greater freedom.'

The Maharshi answers, *'The world is only spiritual.* Since you are identifying yourself with the physical body you speak of this world as being physical and the other world as spiritual. Whereas, that which is, is only spiritual.'[7]

Recall the case we came across in a preceding chapter— the mother who has brought the dead body of her son to the Maharshi in the conviction that his touch will bring her son back to life. She and her companions are persuaded to go away. The next morning the body is cremated. Recall the exchange the next morning. 'The mother's faith was very remarkable,' a person remarks in the presence of the Maharshi. 'How could she have had such a hopeful vision and still be disappointed? Can it be a superimposition attendant on her child's love?'

'She and the child not being real,' the Maharshi says, *'how can the vision alone be a superimposition?'*[8]

We are in January 1938. The Maharshi is explaining the import of a stanza in one of his compositions. 'The mirror reflects objects; yet they are not real because they cannot remain apart from the mirror,' he observes. Pause for a second: true, the reflections cannot remain without the mirror; but do the objects that are reflected also cease to exist when the mirror is not there? But that question may be arising only because of inadequacies of similes in explaining the matter.

The Maharshi continues: 'Similarly, the world is said to be a reflection in the mind as it does not remain in the absence of mind.' Does it not remain for the person in question or does it not remain intrinsically?

The question naturally arises, the Maharshi acknowledges, that, as the universe is a reflection in the

---

[7] Ibid., pp. 293-94.
[8] Ibid., pp. 310-11.

mind, there must be a real object known as the universe in order for it to be reflected in the mind. 'This amounts to an admission of the existence of an objective universe. *Truly speaking, it is not so.'*

Sri Ramana compares the universe to the world we see in our dreams—the dream world has no objective existence, he reminds us. It is created by *vasnas* that are latent in our mind—'*Just as a whole tree is contained potentially in a seed, so the world is in the mind.'*

But the seed is a product of the tree. So, the tree must have existed for the seed to be produced—the Maharshi articulates the question that will arise in our minds. 'So [for the *vasnas* to have formed in our minds] the world also must have been there for some time.' 'The answer is, No!' he says with emphasis, and accounts for the *vasnas* in much the same way as the *Brahma Sutras* account for *prarabdha* karma. That is, in terms of previous existences of the mind: 'There must have been several incarnations to gather the impressions which are remanifested in the present form. I must have existed before as I do now.'

'The straight way to find an answer,' he continues, 'will be to see if the world is there. Admitting the existence of the world I must admit a seer who is no other than myself. Let me first find myself so that I may know the relation between the world and the seer. *When I seek the Self and abide as the Self there is no world to be seen. What is the Reality then? The seer only and certainly not the world.* Such being the truth the man continues to argue on the basis of the reality of the world. Whoever asked him to accept a brief for the world?'[9]

A visitor points out that the illustration of the mirror relates only to the sense of sight, but that we perceive the world by other senses also. 'Can the unreality be established in relation to the other senses as well?'

---

[9] Ibid., pp. 412-13.

'*A figure on the screen in the cinema show appears to watch the world,*' the Maharshi says and asks, '*What is the reality behind the subject and the object in the same show?*' and answers, '*An illusory being watches an illusory world.*'

'But I am the witness of the show,' the devotee exclaims.

'Certainly you are,' the Maharshi responds. '*You and the world are as real as the cinema figure and the cinema world.*'[10]

A professor of philosophy has come. He has a doubt, the kind that we, though far from being professors of philosophy, will have. 'How can the world be imagination or thought? Thought is a function of the mind. The mind is located in the brain. The brain is within the skull of a human being, who is an infinitesimal part of the universe. How then can the universe be contained in the cells of the brain?'

So long as the mind is conceived of in that way, the Maharshi concedes, that sort of doubt will arise. 'But what is the mind?' he asks. And answers:

The world is seen when the man wakes up from sleep. It comes after the 'I'-thought. The head rises up. So the mind has become active. What is the world? It is objects spread out in space. Who comprehends it? The mind. Is not the mind, which comprehends space, itself space (*akasa*)? The space is physical ether (*bhootakasa*). The mind is mental ether (*manakasa*) which is contained in transcendental ether (*chidakasa*). The mind is thus the ether principle, *akasa tattva*. Being the principle of knowledge (*jnana tattva*) it is identified with ether (*akasa*) by metaphysics. Considering it to be ether (*akasa*) there will be no difficulty in reconciling the apparent contradiction in the question. Pure mind (*suddha manas*) is ether (*akasa*). The dynamic and dull (*rajas* and *tamas*) aspects operate as gross objects, etc. Thus the whole universe is mental.

The Maharshi turns to the man who dreams. He has gone to sleep, locking all the doors so that nothing can come in. He

---

[10] Ibid., pp. 412-13.

closes his eyes also so that he doesn't see anything either. Yet, whole regions appear in his dream in which people, including him, live and move about. Through what did the phenomena enter? It has been simply unfolded to him by his own brain. 'How does it [the sleeper's brain] hold this vast country in its tiny cells?' the Maharshi asks. 'This must explain the oft-repeated statement that the whole universe is a mere thought or a series of thoughts.'

Not everybody seems convinced. Rather, we may say that not everyone has understood. A swami sitting nearby says, 'I feel toothache. Is it only a thought?'

The Maharshi: 'Yes.'

The swami: 'Why can I not think that there is no toothache and thus cure myself?'

The Maharshi: 'When engrossed in other thoughts one does not feel the toothache. When one sleeps toothache is not felt.'

'But the toothache remains all the same,' the swami points out.

'Such is the firm conviction of the reality of the world that it is not easily shaken off,' the Maharshi says. 'The world does not become for that reason any more real than the individual himself.'

'Now there is the Sino-Japanese war,' the swami says— the conversation is taking place in February 1938. 'If it is only in imagination, can or will Sri Bhagavan imagine the contrary and put an end to the war?'

'The Bhagavan of the questioner is as much a thought as the Sino-Japanese war,' the Maharshi says to the laughter of devotees.[11]

A few days later, a lady narrates her troubles. She says that she has tried to get the benefit of being in proximity to Sri Ramana, but that has not happened. The time for her to

[11] Ibid., pp. 426-27.

leave is drawing close. She says that she finds others in the
hall attaining peace through meditation. She is unable to
obtain peace. That fact is depressing her.

The thought 'I am not able to concentrate' is the obstacle,
the Maharshi tells her. That you are not able to sit for
hours—the 'hours' in that thought are also just a thought.
That your health does not permit you to meditate, the
depression that results—all these thoughts have their origin
in the fact that you identify yourself with your body. 'The
disease is not of the Self. It is of the body. But the body does
not come and tell you that it is possessed by the disease.
It is you who say it. Why? Because you have wrongly
identified yourself with the body. *The body itself is a thought.*
Be as you really are. There is no reason to be depressed . . .'[12]

As this line of exposition—that the body is just a
projection of the mind—recurs again and again, we should
pause once more and, even though doing so takes us ahead
of the story, try and discern the sense in which the
expression is meant, and why it is put forth with such
persistence.

A person who has come—in this case at Gandhiji's
urging—has asthma—actually the person is none other
than Dr Rajendra Prasad. When the matter is put to
Ramana Maharshi, and Jamnalal Bajaj asks him why a
person like Rajendra Prasad who has sacrificed his all for
the sake of our country should be weighed down by such an
ailment, the Maharshi's response goes through the
following steps:[13]

❏ There is asthma;
❏ The Self is not asthmatic;

---

[12] Ibid., pp. 435-37.
[13] I am summarizing the steps. The response to Jamnalal Bajaj's
observation is reported in two versions: in one, the Maharshi just smiles; in
the other he says, 'The body is the disease. This is the disease of the disease.'

- ❑ The disease is of the body;
- ❑ The body does not say, 'I have asthma';
- ❑ You say;
- ❑ That is because you wrongly identify yourself with the body;
- ❑ Hence, 'The body is just a thought'—that is, without the identification-via-thought, from the viewpoint of the Self, the body would be as if it were not;
- ❑ Similarly, 'The body is a mental projection' in the sense that the identification of oneself with the body instead of with the Self is the mischief of the mind. The mind itself is just a bundle of thoughts;
- ❑ Once the mind, to use the Maharshi's word, is 'annihilated', the identification is ended and the body, in the sense relevant to the discourse, is ended.[14]

But it is not just the body that is a projection of the mind in this sense. All objects are.

February 1938: the Maharshi is explaining the mind to devotees. It is something mysterious, he says. It is 'like *akasa* (ether). Just as there are objects in the *akasa*, so there are thoughts in the mind. The *akasa* is the counterpart of the mind and objects are of thought.' One cannot hope to measure the universe and study the phenomena, he tells the listeners. 'It is impossible. *For the objects are mental creations.* To measure them is similar to trying to stamp with one's foot on the head of the shadow cast by oneself. The further one moves the farther the shadow does also.' What then should be done? He gives an arresting simile. A child is trying to hold the head of his shadow. He bends, and stretches his arm to hold the head—the head moves away. Seeing this,

---

[14] The sequence is evident at many places. The instance we considered before turning to asthma, illustrates it. Cf., Ibid., pp. 435-37.

the mother makes him touch his own head, and look at the shadow—the shadow-head is now in the shadow-hands. 'Similarly for the ignorant practiser to study the universe. *The universe is only an object created by the mind and has its being in the mind.* It cannot be measured as an exterior entity. One must reach the Self in order to reach the universe.'

The Maharshi moves on to urge self-inquiry rather than to calm the perturbations of the mind—a matter that need not detain us here. He avers that once objects are eliminated, misery will be eliminated. And how will objects cease to be? *'The shrutis and the sages say that the objects are mental creations. They have no substantive being. Investigate the matter and ascertain the truth of the statement. The result will be the conclusion that the objective world is the subjective consciousness. The Self is thus the only Reality which permeates and also envelopes the world . . .'*[15]

Again, there is an allusion in the passage that will help us discern the sense in which we may comprehend averments like this one: namely, 'Similarly *for the ignorant practiser* to study the universe.' The statements have a definite purpose, one that we shall see soon stated explicitly: their purpose is not to set out a theoretical framework, it is to steer the beginner.

Such a person, a young English lady, comes in May 1938. She inquires about the use of Self-Realization: Does it remove discontent? 'I am in the world and there are wars in it,' she says. 'Can Self-Realisation put an end to it?'

'Are you in the world?' the Maharshi asks. 'Or is the world in you?'

'I do not understand,' the lady says. 'The world is certainly around me.'

'You speak of the world and happenings in it. They are mere ideas in you,' the Maharshi says. *'The ideas are in the mind. The mind is within you. And so the world is within you.'*

---

[15] Ibid., pp. 462-64.

'I do not follow you,' says the lady, as we might. 'Even if I do not think of the world, the world is still there.'

'*Do you mean to say that the world is apart from the mind and it can exist in the absence of the mind?*' the Maharshi asks.

Yes, the lady answers.

'Does the world exist in your deep sleep?' the Maharshi asks.

It does, the lady avers.

Do you see it in your sleep?

No, I don't but others who are awake see it.

The Maharshi points out that this knowledge—that others see the world while she is asleep—is something she has learned upon waking up. It is not something she has experienced while she was asleep. 'So you speak of waking knowledge and not of sleep-experience,' he continues. 'The existence of the world in your waking and dream states is admitted because they are the products of the mind. The mind is withdrawn in sleep and the world is in the condition of a seed. It becomes manifest over again when you wake up. The ego springs forth, identifies itself with the body and sees the world. So the world is a mental creation.'

How can it be? the lady asks.

'Do you not create a world in your dream?' the Maharshi asks in turn, and adds, '*The waking state is also a long drawn out dream.*'

The Maharshi explains that the fact that there are dream and waking experiences implies the existence of a seer. The body and the mind cannot be this seer. The seer remains even in deep sleep. That seer alone remains from one state to the other, the states themselves are transient. When one is asleep, does the world say that it exists? he asks.

'No,' responds the lady. 'But the world tells me of its existence now. Even if I deny its existence, I may knock myself against a stone and hurt my foot. The injury proves the existence of the stone and so of the world.'

So central is the notion to the Maharshi's way that he reiterates the position. 'Quite so,' he acknowledges. 'The stone hurts the foot. Does the foot say that there is the stone?'

'No—"I",' answers the lady.

'Who is this "I"?' the Maharshi asks. 'It cannot be the body nor the mind as we have seen before. This "I" is the one who experiences the waking, dream and sleep states. The three states are changes which do not affect the individual. The experiences are like pictures passing on a screen in the cinema. The appearance and disappearance of the pictures do not affect the screen. So also, the three states alternate with one another leaving the Self unaffected. The waking and the dream states are creations of the mind. So the Self covers all . . .'

To realize that Self is happiness, it is perfection, it is Realization, the Maharshi concludes.

But how can the realized man be happy when there are wars going on?

'Is the cinema screen affected by a scene of fire or sea rising?' the Maharshi asks. 'So it is with the Self.'

And then comes another proposition, one that is as puzzling, and yet as crucial to grasping the way in which we may cope with the teaching.

'The idea that I am the body or the mind is so deep that one cannot get over it even if convinced otherwise,' the Maharshi allows. 'One experiences a dream and knows it to be unreal on waking. *Waking experience is unreal in other states.* So each state contradicts the others. *They are therefore mere changes taking place in the seer, or phenomena appearing in the Self,* which is unbroken and remains unaffected. *Just as the waking, dream and sleep states are phenomena, so also birth, growth and death are phenomena in the Self, which continues to be unbroken and unaffected. Birth and death are only ideas. They pertain to the body or the mind . . . Mortality is only an idea and cause of misery. You get rid of it by realising the immortal nature of the Self.'*

The exchange is resumed the next day. Is there no difference between the dream and waking states? the Maharshi is asked. *'The standards of time differ in the two states,'* he answers. *'That is all. There is no other difference between the experiences.'* You go to sleep and dream a dream in which fifty years of your life are condensed into five minutes. As in the waking state, the dream also gives the sense of being continuous. *'Which is real now? Is the period of fifty years of your waking state real or the short duration of five minutes of your dream?'*[16]

A visitor seeks to learn about 'this gigantic world illusion', the Maharshi's devotee, S.S. Cohen records. 'We speak of the world as illusion,' the visitor remarks, 'yet everything in it follows rigid laws, which proves it to be well-planned and well-regulated.'

'Yes,' the Maharshi answers, 'he who projected the illusion gave it the appearance of order and sound planning.'[17]

Another visitor asks about the difference between the waking and dream states. Is there any genuine difference between the two? he asks the Maharshi.

'None,' the Maharshi responds unambiguously, 'except that the *jagrat* appears to be more enduring than the other to the person who is in *jagrat*, though not so to the dreamer himself. The person in *jagrat* relates his dream to have sometimes covered hundreds of years, hence he calls it transitory, *whereas actually there is not the slightest difference between the nature of the two states.'*

But there is this difference, the visitor persists: each time we return to the waking state, we come to the same place,

---

[16] Ibid., pp. 465-69.
[17] S.S. Cohen, *Guru Ramana, Memories and Notes*, Sri Ramanasramam, Tiruvannamalai, 1980, p. 61.

we meet the same people, we engage in the same activities, we have the same interests which is not the case when we go into the dream state.

The Maharshi is unmoved. 'This is because things move very rapidly in dreams, as they appear now to you in *jagrat*. But each time you go into the dream world do you feel a stranger in it? Do you not feel thoroughly at home with the people and places as you do here? . . . The dream is as real then to you as *jagrat* is now. *Where is the difference? If you call the dream illusion, why do you not do so to jagrat also?'*

The visitor persists: Arjuna saw the Divine Form of Krishna, he remarks alluding to the Gita. Was that vision true? Ramana Maharshi first disposes of the vision-argument—in terms of the Gita itself. In Chapter Two, Krishna says 'I have no form . . .' In Chapter Nine, that He transcends the three worlds. Later that He is time. Does time have a form? 'The solution to these apparent contradictions,' the Maharshi observes, 'lies in His statement to Arjuna: "See in Me all you desire to see . . ." which means that His form varies according to the desires and conceptions of the seer.'

'Men speak of divine visions, yet paint them differently with the seer himself in the scene. Even hypnotists can make one see strange scenes and phenomena, which you condemn as tricks and jugglery, whereas the former you extol as Divine. *Why is this difference? The fact is that all sights are unreal, whether they come from the senses or the mind as pure concepts. THIS IS THE TRUTH.'* [18]

Major Chadwick, a long-time devotee of Ramana Maharshi and resident of Tiruvannamalai, takes the opposite route to ascertaining the reality quotient of the world. He remarks, 'The world is said to become manifest after the mind becomes manifest. There is no mind when I sleep. Is the world not existent to others at that time? Does it

---

[18] Ibid., pp. 64-65. Caps in the original.

not show that the world is the product of the universal mind? How then shall we say that the world is not material but only dream-like?'

'The world does not tell you that it is of the individual mind or of the universal mind. It is only the individual mind that sees the world. When this mind disappears the world also disappears.' The Maharshi then narrates one of his engaging parables:

There was a man who saw in his dream his father who had died thirty years earlier. Furthermore he dreamt that he had four more brothers and that his father divided his property among them. A quarrel ensued, the brothers assaulted the man and he woke up in a fright. Then he remembered that he was all alone, he had no brothers and the father was dead long ago. His fright gave way to contentment. So you see—*when we see our Self there is no world, and when we lose sight of the Self we get ourselves bound in the world.*[19]

Notice that from the Maharshi vantage point, the ordinary waking state in which we do not see the Self is no different from the dream state. In what sense may we bring the affirmation within our comprehension?

'How can we deny the world and the people therein?' asks a British Lady. 'I hear some music. It is sweet and grand. I recognise it as Wagner's music. I cannot claim it to be mine.'

'Does Wagner and his music exist apart from you?' the Maharshi asks in turn. 'Unless you are there to say that it is Wagner's music, can you be aware of it? *Without being aware of it, can it be said to exist?* To make it more clear—do you recognise Wagner's music in your deep sleep? And yet you admit that you exist in sleep. So it is clear that Wagner and music are only your thoughts. They are in you and not out of you.'[20]

---

[19] *Talks with Sri Ramana Maharshi*, op. cit., p. 518.
[20] Ibid., pp. 565-66.

Two things become evident:

❑ Ramana Maharshi leaves no quarter: the universe, the world, our body, all objects, all sensations, all experiences—these are one and all 'mental projections', they are one and all products of our minds;

❑ If what is said by the Maharshi is taken literally, all suffering is defined away; it is as phantasmagoric as ourselves, at the least as phantasmagoric as the conception of ourselves that we commonly have.

And yet the Maharshi's own life was one of intense engagement with the world. Like Shankara, he taught. He composed hymns. He revered the hill, Arunachala. He had disciples—for whom he cared intensely. He loved birds and animals and had the most loving relations with them—with none more so than with the cow, Lakshmi. All this when each and every one of these entities was just a projection of thoughts?

In what way may we then understand the position that he stated so often, so unambiguously and so emphatically?

That the world is not just what we perceive with our senses—there is no difficulty in accepting that: we do not see microbes, but they can be lethal; we cannot see far into the universe without powerful aides to our senses and yet there is an infinitude there. Similarly, that the world is not entirely what it seems to our senses—that also is easy to grasp: the laptop on which I type, the table on which it rests, appear solid and yet are aggregations of swirling electrons, protons and neutrons, entities that I cannot perceive with any of the five senses.

All this is readily comprehensible. But wholly 'unreal'? Entirely a projection of our minds?

NOT AS UNREAL AS IT SEEMS

The first reassuring thing that emerges from reflecting on the Maharshi's statements is that the world is not as unreal as it might seem at first sight!

A good place to start is to see how Sri Ramana deals with the criticism that is levelled at Shankara in this regard. The tantriks accuse Shankara of *mayavad* without understanding him, the Maharshi says. Shankara made not one but three statements, he recalls: (1) Brahman is real; (2) the universe is a myth; (3) Brahman is the universe. He did not stop at the first. As Brahman is the universe and as Brahman is real, how can the universe be unreal?

Read harmoniously, the three statements imply that the universe conceived apart from Brahman is unreal; the universe conceived as Brahman is real. There are some misconceptions that evaporate the moment we are apprised of the truth: in dim light, the coiled rope seems to be a snake; we get a fright; the friend picks it up; the next day, the rope may still look like a snake in the dim light, but it no longer evokes fright—'After the truth of the rope is known, the illusion of the snake is removed once for all.' But other perceptions persist, even though we no longer turn to them or away from them: a mirage still appears to contain water even after we realize that it is just a mirage; but we no longer turn to it to quench our thirst. The world is a myth like the mirage: 'Even after knowing it, it continues to appear. It must be known to be Brahman and not apart.'[21]

When objects are seen by themselves, as so numerous and so varied, they are unreal, the Maharshi says. When they are seen as Brahman, they are real—*they derive their reality from the substratum, Brahman.*[22]

---

[21] Ibid., pp. 277-78.

[22] Ibid., p. 269; similar statements occur at several other places in this collection.

Asked, 'What is meant by saying that the world is false?' the Maharshi says, 'It means that the world is real,' and goes on to quote a Sanskrit verse that says, 'The world seen as world through ignorance is false, but the same world seen as Brahman through knowledge is real.'[23]

That knowledge, of course, is also that the Self is Brahman. And so, the Maharshi often puts the same perception in terms of the 'Self' rather than 'Brahman'. The seer is said to be real, a seeker says. The seen is said to be unreal. But the seer and the seen are said to be the same. How then is the seen unreal? 'All that is meant,' the Maharshi explains, 'is that the seen *regarded as an independent entity, independent of the Self, is unreal.* The seen is not different from the seer. What exists is the one Self, not a seer and a seen. *The seen regarded as the Self is real.*'[24]

A visitor asks, 'Sri Aurobindo says the world is unreal and you and the Vedantins say it is unreal. How can the world be unreal?'

'The Vedantins do not say the world is unreal,' the Maharshi responds. 'That is a misunderstanding. If they did, what would be the meaning of the Vedantic text, "All this is Brahman"? They only mean that the world is unreal as world, but it is real as Self. If you regard the world as not-Self, it is not real. Everything, whether you call it world or *maya* or *lila* or *sakti*, must be within the Self and not apart from it. There can be no *sakti* apart from the *sakta.*'[25]

Both statements—that the world is an illusion and that the world is real—are true, the Maharshi says in response to another set of questions. 'They refer to different stages of development and are spoken from different points of view.'

---

[23] G.V. Subbaramayya, *Sri Ramana Reminiscences,* Sri Ramanasramam, Tiruvannamalai, 1967/1979, p. 10.

[24] A. Devaraja Mudaliar, *Day by Day With Bhagavan,* Sri Ramanasramam, Tiruvannamalai, 1968/1989, pp. 2-3.

[25] Ibid., p. 233.

'The aspirant starts with the definition, that which is real exists always; then he eliminates the world as unreal because it is changing . . . The seeker ultimately reaches the Self and there finds unity as the prevailing note. Then, that which was originally rejected as being unreal is found to be a part of the unity. Being absorbed in the reality, the world is also Real. There is only Being in Self-Realisation, and nothing but being . . .'[26]

Notice the subtle differences in the terms that the Maharshi uses to indicate the sense in which the world is not real—the world *apart from* Brahman; the world as seen apart from its *substratum*, Brahman; the world *independent of* Brahman; the world *in* Brahman. The variations, and their purpose will lead us a step further.

The Maharshi used to sometimes say *'mithya* means *satyam'*, Mudaliar records, and, so, one day he asked Sri Ramana what the expression was meant to signify. 'Yes, I say that now and then,' Ramana Maharshi said, and asked in turn what Mudaliar understood *'satyam'* and 'real' to mean. After Mudaliar had given the standard answer—that which is permanent and unchanging alone is 'real'—Sri Ramana replied at some length. The reply contains a clue that will take us towards comprehending what exactly is regarded as 'real' and why the rest turns out to be unreal—in discourse.

The Maharshi replied as follows: 'These names and forms which constitute the world always change and perish. Hence they are called *mithya*. To limit the Self and regard it as these names and forms is *mithya*. To regard all as the Self is reality . . .'

Notice that the matter turns on *the way the word is used*: it becomes *a matter of what is meant by* 'reality' and 'unreality', a matter of definition so to say. And the reason why this

26 *Talks With Sri Ramana Maharshi*, op. cit., pp. 41-42.

definition is taken as apposite and not the one we would commonly associate with 'reality', is the felt experience of the jnani. The Maharshi continued:

> He who sees the Self, sees only the Self in the world also. To the *jnani* it is immaterial whether the world appears or not. Whether it appears or not, his attention is always on the Self. It is like the letters and the paper on which the letters are printed. You are wholly engrossed with the letters and have no attention left for the paper. But the *jnani* thinks only of the paper as the real substratum, whether the letters appear on it or not.[27]

Two factors are mentioned again and again. First, objects of the world cannot exist without the spectator; hence, they are not different from the Self. Second, that they do not affect the Self; hence, relative to the Self, they are not real. To gauge the sense in which these statements may be taken, and to gauge the consequence they have for an experience like suffering, consider a statement or two in which the Maharshi affirms these aspects of the matter.

People do not understand, they do not even want to understand 'their every day, ever-present and eternal experience,' he says during a discussion with Paul Brunton, 'whereas they are eager to know what lies beyond—heaven, hell, reincarnation. Because they love mystery and not the bare truth, religions pamper them—only to bring them round to the Self. Wandering hither and thither you must return to the Self only. Then, why not abide in the Self here and now?'

'The other worlds require the Self as a spectator or speculator,' he continues. 'Their reality is only of the same degree as that of the spectator or thinker. *They cannot exist without the spectator, etc. Therefore they are not different from the Self.*'

That, of course, is not self-evident. You and I cannot exist

---

[27] *Day by Day With Bhagavan*, op. cit., p. 266.

without food; are we, therefore, the same as food? The earth is surely the substratum on which we stand, by which we exist. Are we, therefore, the earth? Or, for the reason that we cannot exist without it, are we the air? True, the images in the mirror cannot exist without the mirror. But from that does it follow that the images and the mirror are the same? We cannot pick up the images and hurl them across the room; we certainly can the mirror. Or does the statement mean that the images do not exist even as we see them?

And not just that. The point is pushed further: the world being to Absolute Consciousness what the images are to the mirror, we are told, the world does not exist in reality. Is it just that the simile is inadequate? Or is the basic proposition difficult to accept?

The reason the matter is not evident to us, the Maharshi explains, is that we confuse ourselves with the body, the senses and 'the plays going on in the world'. For the realized man, 'Subject and object—all merge in the Self. There is no seer nor objects seen. The seer and the seen are the Self. There are not many selves either. All are only one Self.'[28]

The second reason that the Maharshi gives often is that the entities of our common perception and discourse—the individual, the world and its objects, even God—'are all conceptions of the "I".' They are not present during deep sleep—as they should be if they had an independent existence. 'They arise only after the advent of the "I"-thought.' Nor do those entities say, 'I am the world,' 'I am the body.' We do. 'So these are only your conceptions. Find out who you are and then there will be an end of all your doubts.'[29]

One way in which such averments can be read is that what is being talked of is the *mental conception* of the world,

---

[28] *Talks With Sri Ramana Maharshi*, op. cit., pp. 127-28; on the mirror and the images on it: pp. 247-48.

[29] Ibid., at several places; for instance, pp. 163-64.

the *mental conception* of the body, etc. As this mental
conception does not exist in deep sleep, that *conception* is the
creation of the mind. Hence, it is not real on its own.

Could there be a reason why a sage like Ramana is
always focusing only on the *conception* of the world rather
than on the world per se? We shall see.

The same consideration suggests itself when we are told
that *'The thoughts are the enemy. They amount to the creation of
the universe. In their absence there is neither the world nor God
the Creator. The bliss of the Self is the single Being only.'*[30]
One way to comprehend such unequivocal and emphatic
statements is to think of them as being made *from the point of
view of the individual seeker*—the rising of thoughts in him is
what gives rise to the universe of names and forms *for him.*
When the thoughts subside, there is no universe *for him.*

Could there be a reason on account of which a sage like
Ramana is always formulating the matter from the point of
view of the seeker? Is there a clue there? We shall soon see.

The third reason on account of which the world and its
phenomena are talked of as unreal is that they do not affect
the Self. They affect it no more, Sri Ramana says often, than
fire in the cinema scene burns the screen or the floodwaters
wet it or the tools in the scene harm it.[31] To us, the matter
turns on the fact that the Self is *defined* as an entity
that never changes—that, therefore, is not affected by any
thing. To the jnani, that is the definition of the Self *because
that is its nature.*

THREE ANSWERS

The first reason on account of which the world is spoken of
as 'unreal' in the scriptures and by sages like Ramakrishna
Paramahamsa and Sri Ramana, it turns out, really lies in the
way 'reality' is defined.

---

[30] Ibid., pp. 291-92.
[31] For instance, Ibid., p. 416.

The Maharshi is explaining the path to yoga-liberation: one has to persevere, he instructs—'Success begets success. If one distraction is conquered the next is conquered and so on, until all are finally conquered. The process is like reducing an enemy's fort by slaying its man-power—one by one, as each issues out.'

What is the goal of this process? the devotee asks.

'Realising the Real.'

What is the nature of the Reality?

And here we come to the answer that enables us to comprehend the statements: the Maharshi says,

'(a) Existence without beginning or end—eternal.
'(b) Existence everywhere, endless, infinite.
'(c) Existence underlying all forms, all changes, all forces, all matter and all spirit.

'The many change and pass away (phenomena), whereas the One always endures (noumenon).

'(d) The one displacing the triads, i.e., the knower, the knowledge and the known. The triads are only appearances in time and space, whereas the Reality lies beyond and behind them. They are like a mirage over the Reality. They are the result of delusion.'[32]

From our worm's point of view, the matter turns on how the word is defined. After all, we could have gone by Dharmakirti's definition: whatever has the potential of causing consequences in this phenomenal world is 'real'— the rock is 'real' as, when it is hurled, it can break a

---

[32] Ibid., p. 29. At several places, for instance, ibid., p. 123. The foregoing discussion is confined to what Sri Ramana said. Corresponding statements of Ramakrishna Paramhamsa can be gleaned from several accounts of devotees who moved with him. For instance, that the world is unreal because it is transitory and only that is real which does not change: 'M', *The Gospel of Sri Ramakrishna*, Swami Nikhilananda (trans.), Sri Ramakrishna Math, Mylapore, Madras, 1981/1986, pp. 91, 325. The world is not as we perceive it: ibid., p. 325. It cannot exist without Brahman: ibid., p. 395. And so on.

windowpane; a thought is likewise 'real' as it can trigger an overt act which may help or hurt someone. Or, indeed, why not the Buddhist position that, in fact, there is nothing, that is 'real' in as much as there is nothing unchanging; that there is no 'being'; that all there is, is ceaseless 'becoming'; and that, therefore, the only reality is impermanence; that the notion of an unchanging absolute is itself the result of the deeply dualistic habits of the mind—a mind that, conditioned as it is, pictures itself as distinct from an idealized conception of itself. Such alternatives would be as justified; they have been testified to by as many jnanis— though they happen to be Buddhists—as the alternative which Sri Ramana has seen and set out; they turn out to be as therapeutic: as there is no core to anything or being; as everything is forever changing; as everything, every phase is marred by an irreducible unsatisfactoriness, why fret at what has happened? Were we to internalize these notions, we would be as relieved of our sorrows as we would be if we internalized the notions we have been encountering. But as reality *is defined* by our sages as having the sorts of marks we saw enumerated above, the world, our bodies and emotions, the three states of waking, dreaming, and deep sleep, etc., all turn out to be 'unreal'. From the peak from which the sage sees, reality is defined as having these features *because that is how it is*.

And that is the second clue. When we read of the rapturous states into which Sri Ramakrishna was ever so often transported, when we visualize the exalted and steady bliss in which Sri Ramana remained, we see that that beatific experience is so overwhelming that after it nothing short of it seems as being the real thing. It is as if we were to travel and see the Himalayas—their silent majesty, their shimmering loftiness—and then, when we came back and were going out of Delhi, someone were to exclaim, 'Ah, ha, here come the Aravali mountains.' Would we not respond,

'What did you say? The Aravali *mountains?* These are not mountains, they are mounds, they are molehills. To see *mountains*, you should go to Kausani and look at the Himalayas.'

Similarly, the mystic experience must be so overwhelming that by comparison everything else must seem so trivial as to be next to nothing. Several accounts of Sri Ramakrishna have him describing the transported state, and how things seem from that vantage point. In a typical instance, while deriding mere scholarship, the Paramhamsa remarks, ' . . . I go into a strange mood while thinking of the Lotus Feet of God. The cloth on my body drops to the ground and I feel something creeping up from my feet to the top of my head. *In that state* I regard all as mere straw . . .'[33] Sri Ramana says as much many times over.

A visitor inquires, in what sense is the world a dream? He says he sees friends in a dream; when he wakes up and asks them, they cannot corroborate what they did together with him in the dream. But when all of them do things together while awake, they can corroborate what they did. Hence, the two states are not the same. Sri Ramana turns the matter aside with characteristic humour: for corroboration of things done in the dream, he tells the visitor, you have to ask persons in the dream during the dream! 'The main point is'—and this is what is relevant to our present concern—'are you prepared when awake to affirm the reality of any of your dream experiences? Similarly, *one who has awakened into* jnana *cannot affirm the reality of the waking experience. From his point of view, the waking state is a dream.'*[34] The three states—of waking, dreaming, and deep sleep—are unreal because they come and go, and only that—pure consciousness which underlies them—is real as it does not change. And then he adds,

---

[33] *The Gospel of Sri Ramakrishna,* op. cit., p. 689.
[34] A. Devaraja Mudaliar, *Day to Day With Bhagavan,* op. cit., p. 3.

'However much one may explain, the fact will not become
clear till oneself attains Self-realisation and wonders how he
was blind to the self-evident and only existence so long.'[35]
The same fact is affirmed in the *Ramana Gita*. The jnani is so
totally immersed in the Self, we learn, that he does not
perceive anything else—rather that everything else seems to
him to be nothing but that Self. 'Just as to a man who is
awake when he is thinking about one thing one-pointedly,'
the scholar Kapali Sastri remarks in his Introduction to the
Ramana Gita, 'at that time he has no concept of existence or
non-existence of other things, as he has no occasion to
remember and take note of other things, likewise, as the
person established in the form of the Self is aloof from the
universe, for him it can be said that the world is false . . .'[36]

The third answer, or at least the third clue to learning
why these sages are so insistent that the world and body,
etc., are just projections of the mind becomes evident at
several turns.

Are the *jiva* and God one? Are they separate? Will they
become one at death or upon realization? Sri Ramana
recounts the different averments, and remarks, 'However it
may be at the end, let us not trouble ourselves about it now.
All are agreed that the *jiva* is. Let the man find out the *jiva*,
i.e., the Self. Then there will be time to find out if the Self
should merge in the Supreme, is part thereof, or remains
different from it . . .'[37]

Can a yogi know his past lives? asks a visitor. 'Do you

[35] Ibid., pp. 90-91.
[36] *Sri Ramana Gita, Being the Teachings of Bhagavan Sri Ramana Maharshi
composed by Sri Vasishtha Ganapati Muni with Sanskrit Commentary Prakasha
of Sri T.V. Kapali Sastriar*, Sri Ramanasramam, Tiruvannamalai, 1998/2006,
p. 40. Ganapati Muni was the 'premier disciple' of Sri Ramana. After the
Ramana Gita had been composed and gone over, often, when a question
was asked, Sri Ramana would ask the seeker to look up the answer in this
book. Kapali Sastri was a well-known scholar in his days—he was equally
devoted to Sri Ramana and Sri Aurobindo.
[37] *Talks With Sri Ramana Maharshi*, op. cit., p. 69.

know the present life so well that you wish to know the past?' the Maharshi responds. 'Find out the present life, then the rest will follow. Even with our present limited knowledge we suffer so much. Why do you wish to burden yourself with more knowledge and suffer more?'[38]

Visitors are questioning him about Sri Aurobindo's teaching, and how it compares with his own. 'Aurobindo advises complete surrender,' the Maharshi observes, adding, 'Let us do that first and await results, and discuss further, if need be, afterwards and not now. There is no use discussing transcendental experiences by those whose limitations are not divested. Learn what surrender is . . .' 'What about Aurobindo's claim to start from Self-Realisation and develop further?' a devotee asks. 'Let us first realise and then see,' the Maharshi replies. Sri Ramana dilates on different theories about Realization and the paths to it, and then remarks, 'The fact is: there is Reality. It is not affected by any discussions. Let us abide as Reality and not engage in futile discussions as to its nature.'[39]

What happens to man after death? asks a devotee. 'Engage yourself in the living present,' the Maharshi tells him. 'The future will take care of itself. Do not worry about the future . . .'[40]

Meditation of the God of Immanence is hard to understand, a devotee says. 'Leave God alone. Hold your Self,' the Maharshi advises.[41]

How long does it take a man to be born after death? asks a devotee. Is it immediately after death or does rebirth take some time? 'You do not know what you were before birth, yet you want to know what you will be after death,' the Maharshi says. 'Do you know what you are now?'[42]

---

[38] Ibid., p. 144.
[39] Ibid., pp. 167-69.
[40] Ibid., pp. 191-92.
[41] Ibid., p. 194.
[42] Ibid., p. 235.

February 1938: Europe is hurtling towards war. Two ladies from London and one from New Zealand have come. They ask the Maharshi, 'What is the best way to work for world peace?' The Maharshi's answer reveals his approach to all such queries. 'What is world?' he asks. 'What is peace, and who is the worker? The world is not in your sleep and forms a projection of your mind in your *jagrat*. It is therefore an idea and nothing else. Peace is the absence of disturbance. The disturbance is due to the arising of thoughts in the individual, who is only the ego rising up from pure consciousness . . .'[43] Why are you worrying about working on the world and wars in it—things about which you can do little? he is telling them in effect. Work on what you *can* rectify—your own minds.

Scores and scores of such examples can be given—responses to questions about the nature of God, of the state of Realization, of the kind of karma whose fruit one can enjoy after death, and so on. Ramana Maharshi's responses run to a definite pattern: every time visitors or devotees seem set on pursuing questions that do not relate to what they should be doing themselves, the Maharshi brings them back to their own task vis-à-vis themselves, indeed to the next step that they have to take in their own practice.

This is the crux of the matter. At one level, when these great sages talk of the world, and therefore our experiences in it like joy and suffering being unreal, they are reflecting their experience—in that, having not just glimpsed but living in a continuous heightened state, to them all the rest seems trivial to the point of unreality. At another level, they keep reaffirming that the rest is unreal so as to turn the devotees away from it, to turn them inwards. Writing of Ramana Maharshi, Arthur Osborne makes this point with his customary lucidity and directness: Sri Ramana was not

---

[43] Ibid., p. 428.

interested in setting up a theoretical system, he writes; his concern was to steer devotees towards practice.[44] Indeed, often it wasn't even to chart out the course of practice in the abstract: his focus was what the particular devotee conversing with him at that moment should be doing next. Often, therefore, we find him stressing one aspect of a matter, and to another visitor stressing something altogether different—much as Sri Krishna in the Gita.

As devotees and visitors were caught up in the affairs of the world, sages like Ramakrishna and Ramana were always berating the significance of the world. This they were doing so as to turn the listeners away from the world and to a search within.

We find confirmation of this in words of the Maharshi himself. In her unpretentious, simple *Letters from Sri Ramanasramam*, Suri Nagamma records a telling observation of Ramana Maharshi. It deserves to be read at length for it sets the entire matter in proper perspective, and reveals the intent behind so many of the statements that seem so completely far out to ordinary folk like us. The Maharshi says:

> The question arises: It is said that Brahman is real, and the world an illusion; again it is said that whole the universe is an image of Brahman. How are these two statements to be reconciled? *In the sadhak stage, you have got to say that the world is an illusion.* There is no other way, because when a man forgets that he is the Brahman, and deludes himself into thinking that he is a body in the universe which is filled with bodies that are transitory, and labours under that delusion, *you have got to remind him that the world is unreal and a delusion.* Why? *Because, his vision which has forgotten its own Self is dwelling in the external material universe and will not turn inward into introspection unless you impress upon him that all this external, material universe is unreal.* When once he realizes his own Self, he will come

---

[44] At several places; for instance, *The Teachings of Ramana Maharshi*, Arthur Osborne (ed.), Rider and Co., London, 1962/1975, p. 13.

back to look upon the whole universe as Brahman. There is no universe without his Self. *So long as a man does not see his own Self which is the origin of all, but looks only to the external world as real and permanent, you have to tell him that all this external world is an illusion. You cannot help it.* Take a paper. We see only the script, and nobody notices the paper on which the script is written. The paper is there, whether the script on it is there or not. To those who look upon the script as real, you have to say that it is unreal, an illusion, since it rests upon the paper. The wise man looks upon both the paper and script as one. So also with Brahman and the universe.[45]

REASSURING CONCLUSIONS

Hence, affirmations that the world is unreal are not as fatal to the reality of our suffering as might have seemed at first sight:

- ❑ To some extent the affirmations are a device—to draw us back from what is outside us to that which is inside, especially to what goes on in our mind;
- ❑ In part, the matter turns on how 'reality' is defined;
- ❑ Statements that the world, our bodies, our pain are all 'mental projections' are intended not to deny their reality as much as to continually focus our attention on the principal instrument at hand, namely, our mind;
- ❑ The sages and our scriptures reiterate this perspective—of what is real and what is just a projection of the mind—incessantly because, as Osborne notes, their objective is not to set up a theoretical system but to steer us to what must be done here and now;
- ❑ From the mystics' vantage point, of course, everything seems trivial, almost inconsequential;

---

[45] Suri Nagamma, *Letters from Sri Ramanasramam*, Sri Ramanasramam, Tiruvannamalai, 1970/1985, p. 94.

but, as exemplified in the lives of Sri Ramakrishna and Sri Ramana, and in spite of what they tell devotees who are still lower down in the plains, even they felt deeply the pain of others, and did an enormous lot to comfort them.

Even when all this is taken as read, a foundational point remains—that there is a 'Self/soul', which, as Sri Krishna declares in the Gita, is never-changing, everlasting, which is not wet by water nor burnt by fire.

What can we say about the soul today? What do psychologists and neuroscientists say about the effulgence that mystics report experiencing, and which is what the mystics are said to see?

It is to these questions that we shall now turn.

9

Removing the props

'Buddhist cosmological theories,' the speaker said, paused, looked around, and continued, 'a disgrace.'

Some tittering across the hall—a bit uncertain, a bit embarrassed, quite a bit surprised.

'A disgrace,' the speaker continued. 'Must throw them out.'

He laughed—his gurgling, infectious laugh.

And he went on to elaborate what he often says: 'Buddhism must face facts. If the new discoveries of science contradict what some ancient scripture says, the scripture must make way.'[1]

We were at the Ashoka Hotel in Delhi. The Dalai Lama was giving discourses on Kumarshila's text on meditation.

The result is that the Dalai Lama has not just opened Buddhism to science. He has sought to incorporate the scientific attitude into Buddhism. As Sogyal Rinpoche reports, on hearing the case of a child remembering her or his previous life, the Dalai Lama's reaction is to send a team to examine the case.[2] The Dalai Lama has introduced science as a subject in Buddhist monasteries. I learnt the other day from his physician that he has now enabled the physician and other scientists to minutely study cases in which a great practitioner dies, and yet for days his body

---

[1] For an account of comments by the Dalai Lama to the same effect, see Sharon Begley, *Train Your Mind, Change Your Brain*, Ballantine Books, New York, 2007/08, pp. 11, 18, an account to which I shall soon turn.

[2] Sogyal Rinpoche, *The Tibetan Book of Living and Dying*, Random House, London, 1993, pp. 86-88.

shows no sign of decomposition—the physician said that he had himself been present throughout the thirteen days when a great master having died, his body remained in perfect condition even though the season was one of heat and humidity.

The Dalai Lama has collaborated in setting up the Mind and Life Institute. Among other activities, the Institute has been organizing a running dialogue between leading scientists and Buddhist scholars and savants, including the Dalai Lama. The leading scientists—front-line researchers in physics, neuroscience, and other disciplines—report the latest advances in their respective fields, and the Buddhist authorities and practitioners report what implications they see in those advances for what was experienced by Buddhist masters and is enshrined in authoritative texts. In spite of their reluctance, the Dalai Lama has encouraged Tibetan meditation masters to make themselves available to neuroscientists so that the effects of intense and prolonged meditation on the physiology and functioning of the brain may be examined and documented.[3]

'Buddhism is not a religion,' he has said so as to drive home the point and the change in perspective that he is convinced is necessary. 'It is a science of the mind.'

Isn't there a lesson in that? We are so defensive about our

---

[3] Sharon Begley's book referred to above gives an account of what transpired at the meeting of the Dalai Lama, Buddhist scholars and neuroscientists in Dharamshala in 2004. Similarly, Pier Luigi Luisi with Zara Houshmand, *Mind and Life, Discussions with the Dalai Lama on the Nature of Reality*, Columbia Series in Science and Religion, Columbia University Press, New York, 2009, describes interactions of biologists and physicists with the Dalai Lama and Buddhist monks and scholars. In November 2010, the Dalai Lama's Foundation for Universal Responsibility and the Mind and Life Institute jointly organized the meeting in Delhi. Leading practitioners from Hinduism, Jainism and other Indic religions attended. The Dalai Lama encouraged them to urge masters of yoga and meditation, etc., in their own traditions to collaborate with neuroscientists and physicists to study the effects of these practices on the brain, mind and consciousness.

ancient texts. Few study them. But everyone insists that they
contain the truth, nothing but the truth, the whole truth.

Indeed, our basic scriptures do contain profound insights.
But they also contain much that is dated—notions and
explanations that were believed at the time the texts were
composed or added to. One of the strengths of our religion
has been that, at every turn, reformers and commentators
have looked at the texts afresh. Even in recent times, Swami
Dayanand, Swami Vivekananda, Sri Aurobindo, and
others read entirely novel meanings into the texts. In the
process, they winnowed much—sometimes by making a
big issue of doing so, as in Swami Dayanand's case, and
sometimes just doing it. That freshness continued even
till Gandhiji's time. Read the introduction of Dr
S. Radhakrishnan to his translation of the principal
Upanishads or that of Sri Rajagopalachari to his
characteristically austere and brief compilation of select
passages from the Upanishads. In Gandhiji's case, of course,
he was like the algebraist who leaves the expression within
the parentheses unchanged but changes the sign outside!
He inferred completely new meanings from the text of the
Gita, for instance: 'sacrifice' became not the sacrifice of an
animal but of one's ego; 'prayer' became not the pleadings
to some external entity but a device to imbibe humility,
to learn how puny we are compared to the circumstances
that will determine the outcome of our efforts; Kurukshetra
was no longer a place in which a sanguinary war took place
but one's heart in which the tussle between right and wrong
is forever taking place; Krishna's call to violent war became
the call to non-violent satyagraha . . .

All of these great men were open to new knowledge—on
matters that were outside the traditional ambit of religion,
of course, but even on matters that were strictly religious.

Nor have this openness and eagerness been a hallmark
only of the great reformers and exemplars. The openness is
germane to our religion as such. The Upanishads are

not posited as unalterable words from God-on-high. They record exchanges—between the earnest seeker and the one who has traversed the path earlier. Nor are the disciples submissive: they go on questioning; in fact, they go on cross-examining their teachers—even when, as in the *Katha Upanishad*, the teacher is Yama, the Lord of Death himself. In Christianity, the final touchstone is the person of Jesus—the 'Word made flesh' as my friend Arvind Sharma reminds me. In Islam, it is the Word of God, that is the text of the Quran as lived and exemplified in the life of one man, the Prophet, that is the final arbiter. But in our case, in the end, the only test is one's direct, personal experience.

That open-mindedness, not just the willingness but the eagerness to embrace every advance in knowledge, is hardly evident in the religious sphere these days. Several factors have conspired to bring about this clamming up. Faced with an assault by exclusivist traditions, even an open, inquiring tradition tends to assert certainties in turn. When religion is yoked to politics, one cannot afford to admit tentativeness. Similarly, when religion is converted into big business— several of our evangelists charge astronomical sums for their *pravachans*—one must be seen to be conveying not just the eternal and ultimate truths but possessing miraculous *siddhis*.

Minds must be shut. And they have been.

But that will not stop the advance of knowledge. And one day those advances will breach the dam, and the props that we have come to rely on, will be washed away.

How much better that we open ourselves to every advance, that we reformulate whatever has to be reformulated in the light of new knowledge, or, if that is what is necessary, we recast our understanding of the questions that our ancients dealt with.

THE 'SOUL' AND THE MYSTIC EXPERIENCE THAT TESTIFIES TO IT

In forming a view about the world, and as a guide to one's

quest, in our tradition the testimony that is most highly regarded is that of mystics.

On the testimony of mystics whom we revere, the mystical experience suffuses one with an ecstatic experience. 'Highs' occasioned by drugs or by some other agent or exposure are evanescent. Unlike these, the ecstatic experience that one gains through spiritual realization is deep, indeed all-consuming, as well as enduring.

That itself makes the experience incomparably superior to any other, and, therefore, worth all the effort we can put in. But this subjective state is not the primary reason on account of which the experience is esteemed. That reason is the belief that the mystical experience opens an aperture through which we see the transcendental, the Real Thing so to say.

What this transcendental reality is, is encapsulated in the four *mahavakyas,* each taken from one of the principal Upanishads. One of them affirms that the soul is the Brahman—*ayamatma brahma,* 'This *atman* is Brahman.' Two of them identify this soul as the one inhering in each of us— *tat tvam asi,* 'You are That;' *aham brahmasmi,* 'I am Brahma.' And one of them speaks of the identity of consciousness and Brahman—*prajna brahma,* 'Consciousness is Brahman.' Notice that 'God', at least as conventionally conceived, does *not* figure in any one of the *mahavakyas,* while soul or its synonym—'You', 'I', 'consciousness'—appears in each. In a word, our religion is not dependent on 'God'. But it *is* on the soul. The soul, consciousness, Brahman and their identity— that is the very core of our religion.

This is 'The Truth' to which the mystical experience is taken to bear testimony. And in that, in the eye of our religion, lies its principal function as well as its inestimable value.

There is no doubt that the experience is overwhelming for the one who has it: the testimony of mystics through the ages down to recent times as in the cases of Sri Ramakrishna and Ramana Maharshi just cannot be doubted. But the question is: Does the experience testify only to what is happening within the mystic or does it, in addition, testify to a reality that inheres in but also transcends the mystic?

In other words, is it that, when he is transported into that state, the mystic sees something 'out there'? Or is it that, wittingly or unwittingly, she or he has learnt how to trigger a sequence within his body and brain and mind which transports him to that state, and that transportation is all that is happening?

That the answer to this question has the farthest-reaching consequences for our religion is manifest. If God goes, little happens. But if the soul is found to be non-existent, the entire edifice of our religion crumbles, and has to be reconstructed. The significance of these alternatives even for the narrow question that is our present concern is evident. If all that is happening is that the mystic is triggering a sequence within his brain and body that transports him into that ecstatic state, the moral can only be: one way to deal with suffering is to learn to trigger that sequence so that we just don't feel the condition and pain any longer. But if the report of the mystic is true about our essence—the soul— and about the nature of reality—Brahman and its identity with our soul—then in a real sense the suffering we experience is just a scratch on the surface, something so superficial as to be trivial, as is implicit, and ever so often explicit, in the responses of Ramana Maharshi that we have encountered earlier.

The idea that there is a 'soul' thus is the very foundation of the structure that our religion builds. And the mystic experience is said to testify to its existence as an independent, that is a non-contingent, enduring entity.

Now, consider four types of facts.

A FEW FACTS AND FINDINGS

What is the experience that is being described when the

person writes of his or her self as having 'blended into the eternal flow . . .'; of having come to rest in 'a silent mind and tranquil heart . . .'; of 'the dramatic silence that had taken up residency inside my head'; of the fact that as he or she was now 'Unencumbered by any emotional connection to anyone or anything outside of myself, my spirit was free to catch a wave in the river of blissful flow'; of how 'I felt like a genie liberated from its bottle. The energy of my spirit seemed to flow like a great whale gliding through a sea of silent euphoria. Finer than the finest of pleasures we can experience as physical beings, this absence of physical boundary was one of glorious bliss . . . I morphed from feeling small and isolated to feeling enormous and expansive . . .'; of the state as being one in which 'All I could perceive was right here, right now, and it was beautiful . . . I was no longer isolated and alone. My soul was as big as the universe and frolicked with glee in a boundless sea . . . I was consciously alert and my perception was that I was in the flow. Everything in my visual world blended together, and with every pixel radiating energy we all flowed *en masse*, together as *one*. It was impossible for me to distinguish the physical boundaries between objects because everything radiated with similar energy . . . I experienced people as concentrated packages of energy . . .'

A mystic describing a mystical experience? In fact, the sentences are from the account of a neurologist, Jill Bolte Taylor, describing the stroke she suffered and the feelings that came over her in its immediate aftermath.[4] She had suffered a massive haemorrhage in the left hemisphere of her brain—the one that is primarily responsible for analytic functions, including the awareness of oneself as distinct from what lies beyond our body. The perception of boundaries—of space and time—had got impaired. As a

[4] Jill Bolte Taylor, *My Stroke of Insight, A Brain Scientist's Personal Journey*, Viking, New York, 2008.

result, her perception of her self as distinct in space and as situated in a particular time had got blurred—a characteristic feature of the mystic experience.

Similarly, while the two are poles apart, at least some of the constituents of the mystical experience are also felt by those who ingest drugs—the oft-mentioned out-of-body experience; a becalmed floating; visions of celestial beings, and the like. These are not the experiences that everyone has with every drug: different drugs, different doses of different drugs lift different persons into varying states—including states that are frightening, etc. The point that is relevant for our present concern, however, is that these altered and heightened states have nothing to do with either access to some divine force or intervention by some such force. They are triggered simply by electrochemical changes in the brain as a result of ingesting the drugs.

Next, recall the great excitement with which books of Raymond Moody and Elisabeth Kubler-Ross describing near-death experiences were received in India when they came out. Even at that time, by pooling research into the functioning of the brain, Susan Blackmore and others showed that every element of the experiences—the tunnel; the white light at the end of that tunnel towards which the subject said she or he had rushed; the rapid life-review; the reporting of what had been said or done during the period when the person was supposedly dead or unconscious; the out-of-body experience; the ineffable peace and the extreme reluctance to be revived back into 'life'; the absolute certainty that accompanies the experience; the evaporation of the fear of death in the person who has 'returned'—they showed that each element could be explained as a consequence of the processes through which a dying brain passes. These processes and the sequence in which the brain extinguishes were adequate to explain the 'core' constituents of the experience. The particular variations could often be traced to the sort of experiences that the person had earlier had in her or his life, and, most significantly, by the cultural milieu—including in that the religious milieu—in which the person had lived.[5]

The first fact that we have to keep in mind, therefore, is that it is possible to trace several of the constituents that we associate with mystical experience to 'natural' factors and to account for them without recourse to anything beyond them.

Nor is the matter confined to elements glimpsed in heightened or altered states. While neuroscientists are the first to say that they are far, very far from fully understanding the brain—'The human brain is the most complicated material object in the known universe,' says a leader of the field[6]—they have made enormous progress towards understanding its structure and functioning. It is already possible to explain by perfectly this-worldly factors several of the states and experiences that were mysteries till the other day, states and experiences that were taken as proof of the existence of a controller/witness. The differences in awareness that mark waking, sleep with dreams and the dreamless sleep states; the fact that I can 'witness' myself—including what is going on in my mind; and so on, were, as we have seen in the remarks of Sri Ramakrishna Paramhamsa and Sri Ramana Maharshi, taken to prove the existence of this separate witness. As were turning points: how does the material brain

---

[5] Even though the review is by now many years old, Susan Blackmore's *Dying to Live, Science and the Near-death Experience*, Grafton, HarperCollins, London, 1993, is a most instructive account—all the more so for persons like us in India who, conditioned as we are by what our religion and culture and grown-ups have weaned us on, are more than apt to latch on to accounts that 'prove' the existence of a soul, the continuance of life after death, and the associated bundle of beliefs.

[6] Gerald M. Edelman, *Wider Than The Sky, The Phenomenal Gift of Consciousness*, Yale, New Haven, 2004, p. 14.

generate a non-material thought, to say nothing of the entire and equally non-material mind? How does mind result in consciousness . . . Each of these was taken as proof of the existence of a 'soul'—much as the question of how life first formed from or in the original chemical soup was taken as proof of God's hand.

But just as it has since been possible to create life ab initio in a lab, neuroscientists are able to explain almost all the conditions and factors that had so mystified us earlier by unravelling just the structure of the brain, the interconnections of its neural networks, the electrical and chemical signals that neurons send and receive along axons and via synapses. They have been able to account for many more states than just the three that figured in the expositions of our saints—not just waking, sleep with dreams and the state of dreamless sleep; but, in addition, the condition of awareness when there is a sudden interruption of oxygen to the brain as in cardiac arrest; when one is under general anaesthesia; when one has been overtaken by diseases like Alzheimer's; when one transits through stages like the vegetative state to coma; when some specific segment of one's brain has suffered an impairment, and countless other states and conditions. Neurologists are able to account for several experiences—including wholly non-material feelings, memory, strategies for acting and reacting to external sensory inputs—by the ways in which one or several regions in the brain are activated by sensory input—including in the 'senses' the Buddhist notion of the mind, with our memories and predispositions subsumed in it, as yet another sense.

They have been able in a similar way to account step by step and 'from the bottom up' for the appearance of different constituents of the human brain as well as the different abilities that it has acquired over the eons purely in terms of evolution—from the unicellular entities that functioned purposively but had no brain all the way to the brains of humans; from 'unconscious' activity to consciousness to higher consciousness including the consciousness of being conscious. At no step of development of the brain or any of its parts in successive species, at no stage of explaining the nature and extent of consciousness in any of the conditions of the brain and body have they had to invoke either the intervention of a 'God' outside or to posit the existence of some abiding entity like the governing and directing 'soul' or a Krishna-like charioteer inside the brain or body. The mind and consciousness turn out to be not entities by themselves but, as the phrase goes, 'emergent phenomena' that are located in no particular part of the body or brain. Instead, they turn out to be, as Edelman puts the matter, 'works in process' that come into being at that moment through several components of the brain cooperating and activating simultaneously several neural circuits across many regions of the brain and integrating the signals to and from them.

Given the attributes on which our religious literature and authorities most base their belief in the existence of a 'soul', we should note in particular that neuroscientists are today able to advance perfectly credible evidence and reasonable hypotheses to account for the appearance of the 'self' and consciousness in terms of evolution and Darwinian determinants alone—the stubborn determination to survive and the continuous adaptation through trial and error to the environment and the changes in it.[7] Even though what neuroscientists take the 'self' and 'consciousness' to mean

---

[7] The relevant literature is vast indeed, and I would hesitate to give even the briefest reading list. But the following five books will give a fair idea of what neuroscientists have already discovered and of its implications for beliefs such as ours in a 'soul': Francis Crick, *The Astonishing Hypothesis, The Scientific Search for the Soul,* Touchstone, Simon and Schuster, New York, 1994/1995; Gerald M. Edelman, *Wider Than The Sky, The Phenomenal*

are in significant ways different from what mystics imply by these terms, the fact that neuroscientists are already able to account for the former by these processes and variables takes us so much closer to the stage when they will be able to account for the mystic's 'self' and 'consciousness' also by the same processes and variables.

The third set of facts that has an immediate bearing on the question at hand is documented beyond doubt by now. And that is the plasticity of the brain. While it used to be believed till even a few decades ago that the human brain stops 'growing' once one reaches adulthood, it is a commonplace now that the brain keeps changing, and can be made to change literally till we die. Nor is it just the way the brain functions that changes, the very structure of the brain changes. The interconnections between its components, the 'cubic space' devoted to particular functions, the ability of components to take over the functions of other parts—for instance, the areas devoted to receiving and processing visual inputs taking over the function of 'hearing'—in each of these and many other ways, the brain remains plastic.[8]

Findings on five counts are particularly significant for

Gift of Consciousness, op. cit.; V.S. Ramachandran, *The Emerging Mind, The Reith Lectures 2003*, BBC with Profile Books, London, 2003; V.S. Ramachandran, *The Tell-tale Brain, Unlocking the Mystery of Human Nature*, Random House India, 2010; Antonio Damasio, *Self Comes to Mind, Constructing the Conscious Brain*, William Heinemann, London, 2010. And for the philosopher's formulation that builds on the work of neuroscientists, Daniel C. Dennett, *Consciousness Explained*, Viking, Penguin, London, 1993.

[8] Even lay persons like us can follow three arresting accounts that report findings in this regard. We have already encountered Sharon Begley's *Train Your Mind, Change Your Brain*, Ballantine Books, New York, 2008; similarly, Jeffrey M. Schwartz and Sharon Begley, *The Mind and the Brain, Neuroplasticity and the Power of Mental Force*, Harper Perennial, New York, 2002, reports a host of relevant findings; and Norman Doidge, *The Brain that Changes Itself, Stories of Personal Triumph from the Frontiers of Brain Science*, Viking, Penguin, New York, 2007.

what the mystical experience may signify. Not just the mind, but the brain—its structure, its interconnections, its functioning—is altered:

- ❑ By what we do; in particular by what we do repeatedly, over time;
- ❑ By what happens to us, and how we react to it;
- ❑ The 'doing' and 'happening' includes not just overt acts but also bare mentation—that is, thinking, mere activity within the mind alters the brain;
- ❑ Among the factors that affect the brain is the intensity of the emotion or motivation that accompanies the doing or thinking;
- ❑ The changes can be produced in a very short span of time—even within just a few weeks.

Taken together, these findings are certainly suggestive of a possibility: the peak religious experiences that mystics report may well be the result of processes that are happening within the brain and mind. In a word, the mystic may have unwittingly learnt to trigger processes that simultaneously activate several regions in the brain that result in that heightened experience.

There, of course, are instances of spontaneous, unbidden experiences of this kind: Ramana Maharshi's description of the sudden fear of death that seized him as he was sitting alone in a room in his uncle's house is well known—of how he watched it with perfect calm; of how it led him to realize that he was not the body that had 'died', that he was in fact 'the deathless Spirit'; of how, from then on, the fear of death vanished; of how the experience left him with absolute, permanent, unshakeable certainty; of how from then on he was absorbed in the 'Self' . . .

But, in general, the mystic's experience is preceded by long periods of austerities, of practices such as deep meditation, and an intense longing. Sri Ramakrishna put the matter in his customary, electrifying way. 'How wonderful Narendra's state of mind is!' he told disciples one day as he lay ill. 'You see, this very Narendra did not believe in the forms of God. And now see how his soul is panting for God! You know that story of the man who asked his *guru* how God could be realized. The *guru* said to him: "Come with me. I shall show you how one can realize God." Saying this, he took the disciple to a lake and held his head under the water. After a short time he released the disciple and asked him, "How did you feel?" "I was dying for a breath of air!" said the disciple. When the soul longs and yearns for God like that, then you will know that you do not have long to wait for His vision. The rosy colour on the eastern horizon shows that the sun will soon rise.'[9]

In view of what is today known about the plasticity of the brain, the prolonged austerities, the meditative practices, this intense longing, and the cultural-cum-religious conditioning throughout our upbringing are together certainly capable of re-forming the brain and mind to trigger experiences of the kind that our mystics report. Even in instances such as that of Ramana Maharshi, we must bear in mind the intensely religious milieu in which he was brought up—a milieu which would predispose one to proceed in a particular direction—and the fact that, over millennia, culture in this broad sense is known to alter not just the mind but also the brain, and, in fact, the very genes: an example that is often given is the way lactose tolerance developed among peoples that domesticated milk-yielding animals and thus began drinking milk regularly. The culture in which we in India are weaned—the tales that we imbibe with our mothers' milk; the exhortations of our texts and gurus; the practices we grow up venerating—all place a heightened value, indeed the highest value on the mystical

---

[9] 'M' [Mahendranath Gupta], *The Gospel of Sri Ramakrishna*, Swami Nikhilananda (trans.), Sri Ramakrishna Math, Mylapore, Madras, 1981/ 1986, p. 937.

experience. They are the very core of our cultural inheritance. They are embedded in our 'collective unconsciousness', and through that deep inside our individual unconscious. They would subconsciously steer a sensitive child and adolescent towards that goal.

None of this is meant to suggest that the mystical experience is not real. It is. It is overwhelming. It transforms the life of the one who has it. The question is whether it is to be taken as testifying to an abiding 'soul' within, or to a particular conception of reality within and outside.

The reason we should be concerned about this matter is that if, fifty years from now, the question is settled and it really turns out, as seems more and more likely, that such experiences are triggered by processes within the brain, the entire foundation on which our religious beliefs are built will have been swept away. We will then be left either with little on which to base our beliefs, and contrive solace, or to enter a state of acute denial—much like the American creationists today.

The better course would be for us to encourage our adepts to collaborate with neuroscientists, as the Dalai Lama has encouraged the Tibetan meditation masters to do, so as to ascertain the nature of the singular experience on which we rest our core beliefs. Second, for the rest of us, ordinary folk, to begin to keep abreast of progress in neurosciences and, at every turn, reflect on the implications that the successive findings have for our beliefs. Third, we should jettison the expository excesses that, for instance, denigrate the body, the mind and the mundane self; and replace the statements with rational arguments for going beyond them. Finally, and most important, we must learn to reverse our habit of mind: instead of latching on to some supernatural 'explanation' the instant we are confronted with a phenomenon we cannot understand, we should get into the habit of first looking for a 'natural', mundane explanation that could account for it.

'But if we jettison the soul, the belief that there *is* something that will endure, that there *is* an entity that fire cannot burn nor water decay, from where can we derive the least solace?' That an idea provides solace does not establish its veracity. It does not even provide any reason to believe that it will continue to provide solace in times to come. On the contrary, it may become the very trigger for despair if subsequent knowledge shows it to be untenable. And consider the Buddhists: they derive solace from the completely opposite belief—from the notion that absolutely nothing abides unchanged, that everything is always changing, that 'You cannot step into the same river *once*', for it is not the same river from one instant to the next. They derive solace from the fact that as everything is forever changing, not just good times but bad times too will not last; that as everything is always changing, there is no reason to lament the change that registers at death. Solace comes not from the notion that there is *some* thing that never changes, or that there is nothing that remains the same; solace comes from *internalizing* either notion.

What holds for the 'soul' holds as much for the other key notion, 'God'. That notion is less central to our religion than the 'soul'. But it is far more central to our religious beliefs and our religious practices.

QUESTIONS THAT HAVE BEEN ASKED OF GOD FOR CENTURIES, EVERY DAY

- ❑ If a word does not have a meaning to begin with, commencing it with a capital letter—'god' with a capital 'G', 'God'—or writing it in all-caps does not suddenly endow it with meaning.
- ❑ Writing it in Latin or Arabic or Sanskrit doesn't do so either.
- ❑ Nor does using a substitute word explain anything. Each of those substitute words invites questions of its own that have to be answered.

○ God is the 'Ultimate Cause', that he is the 'Uncaused Cause', we say—but then one must explain why, let us say, 'nature' or 'this universe' or 'the multi-verses that exist' are themselves not the 'Ultimate Cause', the 'Uncaused Cause'? In this sense, God turns out to be just a definition: we insist that everything must have a cause, and that the one entity that does *not* have a cause is 'God'.

○ Why not the Devil? asks Peter Cave in his book of thought experiments. Actually, the Devil *is* the One who created the universe from scratch, everything from nothing, Cave asks us to think. Being the shy and retiring kind, and hating intrusions of adulating mobs, He has fooled us into believing that His subordinate, God, who is all the time yearning for veneration in any case, is the one who has created it. Furthermore, the Devil has created the scriptures to confirm us in ignorance about Himself and His powers. He has thrown in good and beauty and love for good measure as part of His maya so that we get even farther from the truth, and so as to make people jealous of the ones who prosper by doing good and being beautiful, and thereby eventually increasing the misery of the good and beautiful. But by now He is quite upset, Cave informs us, because, in spite of the clear evidence He has thrown in our way in the form of evil and suffering, we have actually started believing that that subordinate of His, God, is the one who is the Creator, Sustainer, Destroyer. So, He is about to set us right by inflicting such suffering and pain that our eyes will at last see His dark light.[10] Why is this any less plausible than the supposition that the Uncaused, Original Cause is God?

○ God is 'Undifferentiated', 'Attributeless' 'Oneness', we say. Again, just a definition. Moreover, if He is that, how do we get from this 'Undifferentiated', 'Attributeless' 'Oneness' to a God that is All-knowing, All-powerful, Compassionate—each of which is an attribute? How does that Oneness become a ledger-keeper? A judge? One who doles out ghastly punishments and not just rewards? As Steve Eley and the websites devoted to the religion of their special God, the true God, would ask, aren't we talking here of the one who actually created the universe, the Invisible Pink Unicorn—the one who, given the extraordinary spiritual powers he has, is both invisible and pink at the same time?[11]

○ God is shakti, 'undifferentiated pure energy'? 'Energy' keeps ledgers? 'Energy' knows? 'Energy' dispenses justice? 'Energy' hears and answers our prayers?

---

[10] Peter Cave, *Can a Robot be Human? 33 Perplexing Philosophy Puzzles*, One World, Oxford, 2007, pp. 12-18.

[11] On behalf of adherents of the religion of the Invisible Pink Unicorns, Steve Eley maintains that 'Invisible Pink Unicorns are beings of great spiritual power. We know this because they are capable of being invisible and pink at the same time. Like all religions, the Faith of the Invisible Pink Unicorns is based upon both logic and faith. We have faith that they are pink; we logically know that they are invisible because we can't see them.' Quoted in Jack Huberman, *The Quotable Atheist*, Nation Books, New York, 2007, p. 103.

'Undifferentiated pure energy' *has preferences*—that you join religion 'X' and I join religion 'Y', that you eat pork and I shun it?

○ The same goes for 'God is Truth', 'God is Love'. For we then have to explain what we mean by 'truth' and 'love' in this context. Capitalizing the first letter endows them with no more meaning than does capitalizing 'g' in 'God'.

❑ Ever so many of the 'explanations' merely shift the question one step further back. Krishna exterminates his entire clan. He entirely destroys his city, Dwarka. To say that he did so as fulfilment of the curse that Gandhari had hurled at him thirteen years earlier does not 'explain' his act. It merely shifts the question: we have then to explain why Gandhari hurled that curse, why Krishna allowed his kinsmen to become so irremediably sinful that the only way out was to destroy all of them . . . Ultimately, we have to explain the original question: why did Krishna-that-is-God not so arrange matters that they would not eventually result in his having to exterminate his entire clan, and to erase his city from the face of the earth?

❑ That question holds not just for the past but also for what we make-believe shall come to pass in the future. When we tell ourselves, 'But the evil will be punished in the next life. Everyone will be brought to book on The Day of Judgement,' we are just pushing the problem to an indefinite future. After all, we must then explain why it is that God postpones justice to the next life or The Day of Judgement. Moreover, many have asked, if The Day of Judgement is one after which the world comes to an end, what is the point of dispensing justice then? Who would be there to experience it?

❑ For centuries, and with immense glee, philosophers have been pointing out that the attributes we paste on Him entangle God in contradictions. He is compassionate, we say. How then, McCall Smith's Isabel Dalhousie wonders, does He create a torture chamber in which people are boiled in oil, held to the fire, dismembered and skinned *forever*?[12] Not only does He devise and fabricate such an eternal torture chamber, He has people do such deeds that He can keep it well stocked. Compassionate? Is He per chance deficient in what we are taught is a divine virtue—forgiveness? Or is that the problem lies in His very strength? Is it that, as the car-stickers say, 'Power corrupts. Absolute power corrupts absolutely. God has absolute power'?

❑ He is omnipotent, we say. Can He then create an entity that *no one, including Himself* can lift? If He can't create such an entity, He is not all-powerful. If, having created it, He can't lift it, He is not all-powerful. He is all-good, and all-powerful? Can He send little children to the gas chambers? If He can because He is all-powerful, He is not all-good. If He cannot because he is all-good, He is less powerful than a mere Hitler. He *can* but *doesn't?* And yet allows others to do so. That is all-goodness? As He is omniscient, He knows everything that is going to happen in the future—including the fact that the free will that He is giving man will be used to torture others. But that aside, can He introduce such truly random shocks into the stream of time so that no one

[12] Alexander McCall Smith, *The Comfort of Saturdays*, Little, Brown, London, 2008, p. 70.

can anticipate what the future will be? If He can't, there are limits to His capacities. If He can, He is not all-knowing. He has limited our capacities in so many ways, observe philosophers: we can't jump twenty feet, for instance; why did He not limit our capacity to harm others? If He did not want to put yet another limit on the capacities of the acme of His handiwork, man, surely He could have added to our intelligence a bit so as to ensure the same result . . .[13]

❑ But that is the point, philosophers say: 'God is unknowable, in fact indescribable, indeed inconceivable,' we exclaim to all such questions. If so, how are we always pasting shapes and attributes and preferences on Him? And all that with certainty? And killing each other for what we insist can be neither known nor described? If He is unknowable, inconceivable, etc., how do we know, for instance, that He likes us to adhere to truth? Or that He does not want us to be mass murderers? Maybe He wants us to be like Him, philosophers say! He tricks and misleads people, after all—the holy books that He has Himself sent down inform us in great and triumphal detail. He kills wholesale . . .

❑ Is there a threshold? Will we be justified in concluding that there is no one there when suffering and evil exceed that limit? After all, what has been the experience over eons?

---

[13] For centuries, questions such as these have been the staple of books on God, and they remain unanswered. As representative of recent accounts, see, for instance, Bart D. Ehrman, *God's Problem, How the Bible Fails to Answer Our Most Important Question, Why We Suffer,* HarperCollins, New York, 2008; David O'Connor, *God, Evil and Design, An introduction to the Philosophical Issues,* Blackwell, MA., 2008; Victor Stenger, *God: The Failed Hypothesis, How Science Shows that God Does Not Exist,* Prometheus, New York, 2008; Andre Comte-Sponville, *The Book of Atheist Spirituality,* Bantam Press, London, 2008.

Hazaaron tareh apnaa dard hum usko sunaate hain
Magar tasveer ko har haal mein tasveer paate hain . . .[14]

❏ He has come as avatars, He has sent His Son, He has
sent His messengers time and again to redeem the
world. Why has He been so 'spectacularly
unsuccessful'? And why does He not come now?
Was the world on those occasions in a worse state
than it is today? Was man more in need of
correction? Only He knows!

❏ 'He sets the great laws in motion. He cannot be
bothered by every trifling thing that gets hurt as they
work out any more than a man, walking down the
road, can be bothered by every ant that might get
trampled,' we are told. 'He would be paralysed
forever if He stopped at the prospect of any little
collateral damage.' But He is no ordinary man
walking down a street, to say nothing of the fact that
even some women and men *are* bothered by the ant
they might step on—the Jain nuns and monks, for
one! As for being paralysed at the prospect of
collateral damage, why is He in such hurry? His
seconds are eons. He has all the time in the world.
How does His hurry to get going with His laws sit
with His compassion? In any case, how is it that, in
one breath, we say, 'Having set His laws in motion,
He cannot be bothered by every trifling thing that
gets hurt as they work out,' and, in the next, we
make ourselves believe, 'He will answer our
prayers'? Indifferent in one breath, and a call centre
in the next?

❏ 'The very fact that it is nearly impossible that
precisely this combination of conditions should have
come about which would enable life on earth shows

---

[14] Asi Uldani.

that someone has brought them about deliberately.' First of all, few today think that the earth is the only place with that precise combination of conditions. Second, we do not even know if this is the only universe—the larger the number of universes, the lesser this argument works. But, third, so many combinations are so improbable and yet they come to be—without the hand of God. In his delectable little book, *Irreligion*, the mathematician, John Paulos shows up the error of inferring probability in retrospect. Shuffle the deck of 52 cards, he instructs us. Lay them out. One particular combination has appeared. Paulos points out that the probability of this particular combination appearing is 1 in 10 to the power 68—that is, 10 with 68 zeros following it. That is the number of ways in which 52 cards may be ordered: any of 52 may be the first; any of the remaining 51 may be the second, and so on. As the probability of the cards appearing in this particular sequence is so minuscule, has God's hand been needed to bring it about? With infinite time being available for combinations of basic conditions to form, why is God required to bring about a particular combination than mere chance? Paulos recalls Voltaire on how well suited everything is for the purpose for which it is meant: Look at the nose, he recalls Voltaire observing, how well it has been formed to hold spectacles![15]

---

[15] John Allen Paulos, *Irreligion: A Mathematician Explains Why the Arguments for God Just Don't Add Up*, Hill and Wang, New York, 2008, pp. 17, 28-29. Paulos's analogy about miracles is equally telling: 'Any particular bridge hand of 13 cards has a probability of one in 600 billion of being dealt. It would nevertheless be beyond silly to look at the 13 cards dealt to you and proclaim them to be a miracle, or, worse, say that the hand's very improbability was evidence that you were not really dealt it. Even our specific personal genetic make-up is an extremely improbable

The fact that our conception of God has changed over time is a clue in itself: the conception originated from our needs; and it changed as our needs and knowledge changed. We couldn't understand natural phenomena. We were frightened of them. We concluded that there was someone behind them—an entity ordering and executing them. Apart from 'explaining' things that we did not understand, as Daniel Dennett has pointed out, this instinct—of attributing events to an agent—was helpful, indeed necessary for survival: through the corner of our eye, we saw a bush stir; it was infinitely safer to assume that the bush had stirred because hidden in it was a predator that was about to lunge at us, than to assume that it had just moved on its own; if there was no predator, all we got was a false scare, but if there was one, and we had not taken that possibility into account, we would be his meal in little time.

The anthropologist, Stewart Guthrie had pointed to the same usefulness as being behind our tendency to 'anthropomorphize' what we sense: we see faces in clouds, in shadows on the wall, in the weave of a carpet. This tendency formed as it was most useful in locating a predator in the bush, he explained. And that very tendency led us to personify forces that jostled us round.[16] Today, neurologists point to the fact that the 'social brain'—the part of the brain that is engaged in reading the mind of others, something necessary for ensuring that they do not catch us by surprise—remains active even when other parts of the brain have quietened down. This overactivity of this part of the brain, they suggest, and the proclivity to 'mentalize', that is to 'read the mind of another,' may well explain our tendency to anthropomorphize, to see minds and their

---

accident. A different sperm might have united with the same or different egg, and we wouldn't have been . . .' (Ibid., p. 85).

[16] Stewart Guthrie, *Faces in the Clouds*, Oxford University Press, 1993.

possessors where none exist, as in inanimate objects and behind events and 'forces'.[17]

As we began to understand more and more of what was occurring around us, the things we attributed to God contracted. As His sphere has shrunk, He has become more and more impersonal and He has receded farther away—from being a person just behind the clouds to an abstraction in the unknown yonder.

Different phenomena were attributed to different gods. The importance that a phenomenon had in the life of a particular group affected the significance that a particular god acquired in the pantheon of a particular group—gods who were taken to be behind what happened out in the sea naturally became more important among seafaring peoples than among landlocked ones.

The gods jostled for rank as communities came in touch with each other. When they came to be so close together as to impinge on each other all the time, jostling among the communities caused perennial disorder and violence. An overarching authority had to be established. One tribe had to be conceded dominance. A nascent State was being born. And so among gods. In some instances—as among us in what is today India, Gurudev Rabindranath Tagore pointed out long ago—this was ensured through incorporation: entities that others venerated were not annihilated, they were incorporated in the darbar, so to say. You venerate the elephant? He is incorporated as the head of Ganesha. You venerate the mouse? He becomes the vehicle of Ganesha—and very aptly, too: Ganesha is the one who gets us around impediments; his mount must be one that is always able to find a way around obstacles. You worship snakes? They

---

[17] Jason P. Mitchell, 'Watching minds interact,', in *What's Next, Dispatches from the Future of Science,* Max Brockman (ed.), Vintage, Random House, New York, 2009, pp. 78-88.

become the adornments of the ascetic Shiva. You are fair, I am dark? Some of our gods become fair, some blue, some green . . .

In the Middle East, ascendancy was established by vanquishing. As an exercise, count the latitudes and longitudes within which the Jewish prophets, and Jesus and Muhammad moved and taught. In this constricted space, much of it barren, even small bands would impinge on each other. Skirmishes, raids, 'wars' were the perpetual consequence. The need arose for an overarching authority. On the other side, some tribe or group would have in the natural course proved more successful than the others in raids, wars and the like. That group would feel the need to legitimize and fortify its ascendancy. A single, jealous God—Yahweh, Allah—was the natural product. A God who would countenance almost everything, but not one thing: if you put anyone at par with Him, there was no saving you. In a word, the State: the one unpardonable crime in its view is allegiance to some other State or entity.

The 'nature' of God too changed as the fortunes and needs of the group changed: full of wrath in one phase or region, the embodiment of tolerance and compassion in another. As did that of His commands: jihad is mandatory, said Sir Syed Ahmed, when one is in power; it is prohibited when one is weak. We see this happening in front of our eyes today: look at the way religions are adjusting their view of women as times are changing. Life determines scripture so much more than scripture determines life.

Freud, Jung and other psychologists and psychoanalysts have shown correspondingly how our deep, personal needs have accounted for the origin and development of deities and religions and notions that we associate with religions. The trauma at the loss of ones dear to us; the dread of our own death; the inability to explain or accept injustice and privation that we experience and see all round us—these lead us to invent notions of an afterlife, of heaven and hell, of a God who will see to it that justice is done eventually, of a next life in which justice will be done at last . . . In our little world, Adit illustrates to us every single day the origins of these notions. His Nani was his life. She passed away three years ago. Twice or thrice a day, he insists that we put on the tapes she recorded for him. *'Nani kahaan hain?'* he demands. We try to deflect the question: *'Tumhaaraa matlab ki Nani ka tape kahaan hai?'* *'Naheeeen,'* he corrects us, *'Nani.'* *'Woh doosari duniya mein hain,'* we say. *'Woh hamara intezaar kar rahin hain. Dada aur Dadi aur Nana ke saath. Kuchch hi dino mein hum sab un sab se milenge, saath honge . . .'* As he is clearly not consoled, we elaborate the fiction, bringing it down to a place he knows: *'Jaise hum yahaan baithe hain. Kya hum unko dekh sakte hain jo Goa mein hain? Isi tareh hum abhi Nani ko nahin dekh sakte . . . Nahin, Raja, phone bhi doosri duniya tak nahin pahunch sakta . . .'*

In his book cited earlier, Andre Comte-Sponville puts the point precisely. The belief in God is 'so strikingly congruent with our longings,' he writes, that it seems to have been invented to fulfil them. 'Given an alleged reality that nothing attests but which corresponds to our most powerful wishes,' he continues, 'we have every reason to suspect it of being the expression of those very wishes, and indeed (as Freud says) directly derived from them—to suspect it, in other words, of having the structure of an illusion.' An illusion, he reminds us, 'is not a particular type of error; it is a particular sort of belief. To be deluded is to believe that something is true because one wants it to be true . . .'[18]

Of course, the springs lie deeper than our surface needs. Freud, Jung and other thinkers have shown, to pluck expressions from Jung, how 'Many of the early gods developed from "persons" into personified ideas, and finally into abstract ideas;' how 'The beginning, where everything is still one, and which therefore appears as the

[18] Andre Comte-Sponville, *The Book of Atheist Spirituality,* op. cit., pp. 125-29.

highest goal'—notice the literal relevance of the words to the 'reality' that our mystics report—'lies at the bottom of the sea, in the darkness of the unconscious . . .'[19]

Having created God to meet our needs, we have used Him for more than our basic needs. We have used Him to inflate our vanity—man, we have concluded, is the acme of His creation. Furthermore, we have used Him to rationalize suborning every other species, and nature itself to subserve our greed and lust: God has created the earth and everything in it for your enjoyment, our prophets have assured us.

'But across the ages, across peoples and nations, people have spontaneously arrived at the concept of God. How could all of them have been wrong?' In fact, they have *not* come up with the same concept of God, His ways, His preferences—indeed, for just as long they have been killing each other to enforce their particular concept of God and their particular version of His commands on to the victims. Almost all of them have indeed shared one belief: that those who do not subscribe to their conception of God and His preferences are (a) misguided, (b) perverse, and/or

---

[19] The expressions are taken from C.G. Jung, *Psychology and the East*, op. cit., pp. 25, 37. By now, there is a mountain of literature that explains the origins and evolution of religious impulses without the intervention of God, so to say, and in terms of evolution and our inner needs. The few paragraphs in the text are meant for a limited purpose—to urge that we in India open our minds to alternative, non-divine explanations for our religions and religious beliefs—and are in no way a survey or even a summary of this vast literature. The reader would like to see, to begin with, Sigmund Freud, *The Future of an Illusion*, Doubleday, New York, 1964; C.G. Jung's extensive writings on the subject; Daniel C. Dennett, *Darwin's Dangerous Idea, Evolution and the Meanings of Life*, Simon and Schuster, New York, 1995; Richard Dawkins, *The Selfish Gene*, Oxford University Press, London, 1976; Richard Dawkins, *The Blind Watchmaker*, Longman, London, 1986; Pascal Boyer, *Religion Explained, The Evolutionary Origins of Religious Thought*, Basic Books, 2001; Daniel C. Dennett, *Breaking the Spell, Religion as a Natural Phenomenon*, Penguin, 2006; Robert Wright, *The Evolution of God, The Origins of Our Beliefs*, Little, Brown, New York, 2009.

(c) propelled by Satan. Most of them have believed that some subgroups among their own group—members of sects other than their own, women, the lower castes—are inferior, in fact, deficient. Do such convictions become correct because almost all have held them—across the ages, across peoples and nations?

'But if we shed the concept of God, from where do we derive notions of ethical conduct?' That sort of an argument does not prove the existence of God. On the contrary, it suggests that the concept of God has been invented to ensure compliance with what societies, and those who controlled them, have come to conclude was necessary for their survival and aggrandizement. As societies—or those who steered them—came to feel that other rules would better serve their purpose, God saw to it that the rules people were commanded to obey changed. Many rules fell into disuse. Many were explicitly revoked—the Satanic Verses in the Quran are representative of the *genre*, so to say. Many were so completely reinterpreted that they were as good as new: look at the way our seers have endowed completely novel meanings into the word 'sacrifice' over the centuries: from the sacrifice of humans to that of animals to that of craving and attachments to that of one's ego to that of one's 'self' . . .

The hand of God in all this? Or the changing needs of society, and its expanding knowledge? But as philosophers and historians point out, even if we grant that rules of ethical conduct grew out of a belief in God, that does not prove the existence of God any more than the fact that astronomy may have grown out of astrology proves the validity of astrology; or that chemistry and metallurgy grew out of alchemy, and history as we know it today out of mythology would prove the validity of the methods of getting at gold in one case and the chronologies and feats in myths.

In any case, look at two great examples close at hand— Buddhism and Jainism. They are firmly grounded in ethical norms. Yet they have no concept of God. And today—what with newspapers being full of the abuse of children by Christian priests, of the abuse of female devotees by our godmen, of the excesses of mullahs—we do not need anyone to remind us that those believing in God, those acting in His name are no more moral than the rest of us.

The moment such cases burst into the press, the defence is, 'But they weren't really religious. Otherwise they could never have done anything like this.' Till their deeds were discovered, they were exemplars of the piety that belief in God creates. The moment their deeds became known, they turned out to have not been really religious. Another tautology: those devoted to God do not do such things because, if someone does such things, he is not truly a devotee of God.

'Frankly, do you need to believe in God to be convinced that sincerity is preferable to dishonesty, courage to cowardice, generosity to egoism, gentleness and compassion to violence and cruelty, justice to injustice, love to hate?' asks Andre Comte-Sponville in his fine and dispassionately argued book.[20]

And what of other species, to whom, presumably, God has not revealed Himself or given scriptures? Observers of species ranging from ants to baboons have carefully documented how members of the group obey rules, how meticulously they carry out specific tasks, how they sacrifice themselves for the group.[21]

Similarly, since the pioneering work of Giacomo Rizzolatti and his associates, neuroscientists have detected

[20] Andre Comte-Sponville, *The Book of Atheist Spirituality*, op. cit., p. 22.

[21] The findings and arguments that Matt Ridley's sparkling account, *The Origin of Virtue*, Penguin, 1997, contains should be sufficient to convince anyone that neither the origin of ethical notions nor adherence to them requires the notion of God. See also, Daniel C. Dennett, *Darwin's Dangerous Idea*, op. cit. For those who, to believe, would rather see than read, one of the most widely watched amateur videos, 'Battle at Krueger

what they term 'mirror neurons' in our brains. The neurons that are activated when we do something or something is done to us—we reach out to a dish, a hand is placed on our shoulder—get activated in the same way when we observe another person doing the same thing or the same thing being done to another person. These mirror neurons have led neuroscientists to wonder whether we are not altruistic by nature: the hunger and suffering of another may be triggering empathy in us because that is how evolution over millennia has constituted us.[22] And there is good reason why such reflexes would aid in survival: groups whose members respond to the danger or pain impinging on another member of the group and, thereby, rush to his aid, are more liable to survive and flourish than groups in which members are unaffected by the danger or pain afflicting another; indeed, in an important sense, it would be difficult to think of the latter as a group at all.

A pile of such investigations is able to explain the origins of ethical norms without invoking God, and even more so the way these norms have transformed over the centuries. And in that the findings hold the general lesson we

---

Park' [http://www.youtube.com/watch?v=LUDDYz68kM]—between the time it was put up in 2007 and the end of 2010, it had been viewed by over 58 million viewers—is a breathtaking portrayal of a 'dumb' species risking their life to rescue a member of the group. A herd of Cape buffaloes ambles across to a watering hole. A pride of lions that has been lounging nearby rushes at them. A calf is isolated, and seized by the lions. The calf and the lions gripping it tumble into the water. The struggle to subdue the calf continues. Two crocodiles emerge from the water. The lions and crocodiles engage in a fierce tug of war—each side tugging at the calf. The lions win. They drag the poor calf onto the bank. As they ready themselves to devour it, the herd returns. The buffaloes butt the hell out of the lions—isolating them, tossing one high into the air, chasing them away one by one. The calf is saved. The best of humans would risk no more than the buffaloes do in the sequence. By every norm the conduct of the buffaloes is ethical, indeed altruistic in the extreme.

[22] Cf., V.S. Ramachandran, *The Emerging Mind*, BBC, The Reith Lectures 2003, Profile Books, 2003/2005, and *The Tell-tale Brain, Unlocking the Mystery of Human Nature*, Random House India, 2010.

encountered earlier in the chapter: whenever we encounter
a trait or event or phenomenon, we should first see whether
it can be explained by non-divine, 'mundane' factors. Those
committed to God will, of course, not change their opinion:
they will insist that it is God who implanted those mirror
neurons in us in the first place. But in the case of the rest of
us, the non-divine explanation will open our minds—
especially as it is but the latest in a series of explanations that
have successfully accounted for phenomena which we
could not earlier comprehend without invoking God—and
thus nudge us towards relying on ourselves than pinning
our hopes on some unknown.[23]

The contrast itself is instructive. Those who are most
zealous in their belief in God are also the most fearful of
opening God, His books—rather, God's Book in the singular,
for each set among them insists that there is only one Book
that God has sent down—His prophets and the like to
examination. Does this show confidence? Or does it betray
nervousness?

But, more important for our present concern—that of
handling suffering—should one make oneself dependent on
a prop about whose stability and strength one is so
doubtful? Indeed, on a prop about whose existence we are
so totally uncertain? Should we rest our hopes on a
phantom reed?

EXERCISES

□ As man has created God in his own image—only
larger, wiser, more powerful—God must be held to
the ethical standards that our experience has taught
us are worthy. Would you gouge out the eyes of your
child if she misbehaved? Would you maim her? Why
then is God justified in doing so?

---

[23] Of course, the believers have a ready response to that also: it is God,
they will say, who has told us that He helps those who help themselves!

- ❑ Why should He not require proof? Why should His deeds and His creations for us—Heaven and Hell—not require evidence and justification?

- ❑ Why is proof required for anything that is outside the ambit of religion but not for what can be claimed to fall within the circumference of religion? In particular, why do we require proof for the propositions and claims advanced by the religions of others, but insist that propositions on which our religion rests are 'matters of faith' and are, therefore, beyond scrutiny?

- ❑ The same holds for actions that we insist are religious. Over the centuries, we have come to accept that I can claim immunity from oversight or intervention only for acts that do not affect others—that is, only for actions that are strictly self-regarding. Thus, the way a husband treats a wife, the methods by which he may divorce her are no longer regarded as beyond scrutiny and censure—the actions of the husband injure the wife. But as it is now evident that even thoughts on which we do *not* act affect our predispositions, our minds so to say, and thereby affect the way we are liable to act later, for what sort of acts can we claim total autonomy on the ground that they are what our religion requires us to do? As our religious beliefs trigger the way we act towards others—women, non-believers, members of other sects—are they not as much open to scrutiny as beliefs and acts that arise in the non-religious spheres?

- ❑ When confronted by something that seems inexplicable, first look for possible scientific, physiological, non-divine, non-religious explanations for the event or phenomenon.

- ❑ Make a list of views and positions that were held till a few years ago to be absolutely, non-negotiably true—to the point that anyone who did not subscribe to them was branded a heretic or, at the least, as one who has 'crossed the barricades' and gone over to the other side—and which have since been abandoned, quietly.

❑ Make a list of events and phenomena that till just a few years ago used to be attributed to God and His associates, and are today entirely explained by current knowledge. Project the likely advances in the sciences in the next fifty years. Which of the phenomena that are currently inexplicable will be explained by new knowledge by then? What will be left as the impenetrable empire of God?

❑ We depend on God as a prop. God depends on organized religions, their scriptures and custodians as props. Examine these.

❑ In any statement that seeks to 'explain' a phenomenon by attributing it to God's will, actually His *inscrutable* will, substitute the words 'The Rest, that is everything apart from me'; or, as the websites say, the words—after Steve Eley—'The Invisible Pink Unicorn' or—following Bobby Henderson—'The Great Flying Spaghetti Monster'. Does the statement 'explain' any less of the phenomenon?

❑ Here is a variant of an experiment that J. Krishnamurti prescribed once. On your next walk, look for a stone that has some shape that appeals to you—round, smooth, dark. Pick it up with reverence. Bring it home. Wash it. Place it on the mantelpiece, in your *puja-ki-almaari* if you have one. You will soon begin to see its many estimable attributes. It is hard and yet smooth. It remains unruffled—a *sthitpragyan*—in rain, in cold, in heat. Not much later, you will come to look upon it as a symbol of the One Who Originated Everything. Endow it with virtues. Contemplate those virtues as you look at the stone. Watch carefully as the light falls on it every morning—this will vary depending on whether the sun is shining at that hour or whether it is hidden by a cloud. Does the stone look brighter? Do the shadows in it make some pattern? Close your eyes. Recreate the precise image the stone has made—shadows, the pattern embedded in it, and all. Pray to it. See how the day goes. When you come home in the evening, review how the day has gone. Discern how the way that the day turned out reflects the way the stone seemed that morning. You will soon begin to feel that the stone is not just any odd stone—after all, you picked this one when you could just as well have picked some other one. This one, you will begin to infer, was lying there to be picked up especially by you—as it had a message for *you*, as it had a potency meant especially for *you*.

Are we not the ones who are endowing the stone and any other notion or act—with meaning, with potency? Are we not then beginning to see that the thing or act had that meaning and potency all along, and thus becoming dependent on it?[24]

❏ As only a very minuscule portion of what we know about the lives of the founders of each of the religions can be taken as verifiable fact; indeed, as much of it is manifestly affected by the adoration of those who had come to be in awe of him or who had everything

---

[24] Krishnaji's experiment did not require us to even leave the house! And, as was always the case with him, his admonition was brutally direct. He was speaking in Madras in 1968 on 'The Sacred'. 'Take a piece of stick,' he said 'put it on the mantelpiece and every day put a flower in front of it— give it a flower—put in front of it a flower and repeat some words— "Coca-cola", "Amen", "Om", it doesn't matter what word—any word you like—listen, don't laugh it off—do it and you will find out. If you do it, after a month you will see how holy it has become. You have identified yourself with that stick, with that piece of stone or with that piece of idea and you have made it into something sacred, holy. But it is not. You have

to gain—everything to gain in *this* world: power,
influence, hegemony, following, wealth—we should
go by the teaching and not the 'life' and miracles that
are attributed to the founder.

❏ In examining the scripture, (i) so as to glean the mind
that the text creates, so as to discern the mind that
those who insist they are the custodians of the text—
the Church, the clergy, the televangelists—seek to
foment in the community of the faithful, look at the
whole text, not at isolated expressions that the latter
and their apologists keep projecting; (ii) look at the
plain meaning of the text, not the convenient
interpretation that apologists contrive to inveigle
from it as time and circumstance demand; (iii) to
discern the behaviour that the text foments, look at
the conduct of believers, in particular of the
custodians and controllers, not when they are
beleaguered minorities but when they are in power.
In little time, it will become obvious that all books are
man-made, and that what is projected as 'the real
meaning of the Message' is not something that
someone high-in-the-sky has sent down. It is but the
compulsion that the moment has dictated or the
opportunity that the moment has opened up. Each
text reflects what was known at the time it was
composed, it contains what was thought would best
preserve the community and comfort individuals.
And, therefore, there is no reason to exempt these

given it a sense of holiness out of your fear, out of the constant habit of this
tradition, giving yourself over, surrendering yourself to something,
which you consider holy. The image in the temple is no more holy than a
piece of rock by the roadside. So it is very important to find out what is
really sacred, what is really holy, if there is such a thing at all.'
(J. Krishnamurti, *The Awakening of Intelligence*, Victor Gollancz Ltd.,
London, 1973, pp. 214-15.)

texts from the rules by which we would study and assess other texts.

❏ The openness or otherwise to examine the scripture or the teaching is one of the best gauges of the intrinsic insights of a religion, and the confidence of its custodians in its scriptures, teaching and founder.

❏ The moment attention is drawn to a command or passage that is clearly indefensible or inconvenient given the norms that are accepted today, the response is 'But that was revealed in a particular context. You are quoting it out of context.' Till that moment, the authorities of that religion have been insisting that the commands are eternal, that the Book is context-less. At such times, we should request the authorities to provide a list of passages and commands that are confined to contexts in which they were revealed or written. Second, we should request them for the criteria by which such passages and commands can be identified and segregated from the ones that are eternal and context-less. Third, we should request them to show where the text itself authorizes such segregation. The reaction of the custodians to these simple requests will speak for itself.

❏ The same goes for the occasions on which we are told that the passages and accounts are not meant to be taken literally. Which are the ones that are to be taken only metaphorically, only symbolically? Which contain eternal truths? Where in the text does it sanction such segregation?

❏ As for custodians, keep an eye out for, and make a compilation of evidence that surfaces about what Marxists used to call their 'social practice'. How is it that, while they preach *aparigraha*—non-possession—to us, they charge astronomical sums for staging their discourses? How have their establishments amassed such enormous mundane empires? How is it that their devotion to the texts and deities has not kept them from exploiting female devotees and children? How is it that, to take the case of our own country, we have so many godmen, and yet our moral condition is what it is?

❑ Make a careful list of what you pray for. Review it. How often is our prayer just a plea for a bargain? Get me 'X', get me 'Y'; in turn, I will do 'Z' for You . . . Second, compare what happens about the matter subsequently with what you sought. Is the outcome due to perfectly comprehensible factors or to the incomprehensible God? Has prayer nudged God to intervene? Or did it work by strengthening your own mind and thereby equipping you better to deal with the situation?

❑ In particular, with utmost care write down the assurances that the godman in whom you have faith gives you, and compare what transpires with what he had said would happen. What is said ex post facto to explain away the discrepancy? 'No, no. You see, but for his blessing, things would have been much worse.' 'No, no. But Bhagvan always says that he is not here to turn back our karma. You have to go through that in any case. He just gives you the strength to face up to the consequences of what you had done.'[25]

❑ Study the congregation around you. In regard to the

---

[25] In the same vein, banter with my friend, Arvind Sharma, brings out the secret of the success of many a palmist and astrologer. Hold the palm/horoscope. Study it. After a thoughtful while, say, 'You have achieved a great deal, most certainly more than what even those closest to you expected of you. But you have yet to realize your full potential.' That always strikes them as proof of your acuity. Everyone wants to believe

powers of the godman, you are heavily influenced by their word. But they are a biased sample. In the case of a few, things may indeed have turned around. Their experience is what is broadcast. But what fraction of the total are they? Are there no normal explanations for the remission? The others, the newcomers, are desperate to believe. Their testimony consists of what they have heard from others. As they are desperate to believe, they retain memory only of cases in which they have heard the godman work a miracle. The rest of the cases, they blot out of their minds—a trait all of us share with them even if it be in a lesser degree: that of latching on to evidence that confirms what we want to or need to believe. The one set that is missing from the

---

that he has exceeded the expectations of others, especially of those closest to him. And everyone wants to believe that he has been kept from realizing his true potential! To convince the person even more of your insight, add, 'Two persons are coming in the way. Behind your back, they always do something to trip you up. One of them has even convinced you that he is your true well-wisher.' Everyone wants to believe that he is being held back by secret enemies, most can be got up to begin suspecting someone whom they have come to particularly trust. And to drive the nail home, add, 'You see, you trust others too readily. You take them at face value, you believe too readily the sob stories they come and tell you about their lives. As a result, while you put yourself out to help others, because you trust everyone, they take advantage of you.' Everyone wants to believe that he is too simple, too gullible, that he is being taken advantage of by others! And to ensure that the person comes back to you for business, add an *upaaya:* 'But don't worry. Just be careful. That is all that is required at this stage—your basic horoscope is strong. X will transit out of the house of Y in three months. After that, sailing will be much smoother. If some residual problem still persists, do let me know, and I will study and tell you what has to be done to counter the baleful designs of your so-called friends. In the meantime, wear an emerald ring . . . ' He will come back for sure: you have inflated his self-image; you have given him 'reason' to believe what he wants to believe—that he is a victim, that he is just a simple, trusting soul whom others use for their own ends; and 'reason' to believe even more—that things will be better soon . . .

sample is of persons who waited and waited for the
miracle to transpire, and it did not. It is their
testimony that you never get to hear when you join
the congregation for they have left. 'But that is
precisely the point,' say the faithful who remain.
'That they left shows that they lacked faith. They
were the ones who thought that Bhagvan owed
them to solve their problems for them. How does
Bhagvan owe them anything?'

❑ Our religion teaches that the same soul inheres in
each of us, that it is the same as the Universal Soul,
etc. And yet, over the centuries, by gross perversion,
we have come to view some as superior and some
inferior merely because of their birth. Similarly,
every godman preaches that we are all one, that we
are all equally dear to him, that each of us has the
same potential to improve, etc. And yet, observe the
hierarchies that have developed in the congregation
around him—depending on whose presence he
acknowledges as he makes his way to the pedestal,
on who gets to sit near him, who gets to touch him,
to bring his food, to feed him, to whom he gives some
miraculously produced prasad or trinket, to whom
he 'appears' in a vision . . . Does the godman foment
such hierarchies or does he erase them?

How well I remember an aunt, very dear to all of
us. A simple soul, she had been wronged by many in
her life. She had been ardently devoted to a great
and distant godman. 'What I can't understand,
Arun,' she said to me once as I went to visit her in
her straitened circumstances, 'why Baba is always so
kind to his rich followers, and why he refuses to help
helpless persons like me. These rich people fly in.
They go to the ashram in their big cars. They
immediately get a private audience. They receive

prasad and watches . . . And persons like me, we suffer away. If we ever get a chance to travel to his place, he doesn't even look at us.'

Of course, the devotees would not be short of an answer. 'See, the very fact that your aunt was having this doubt about Baba is itself the answer. She lacked the total faith that is necessary. She had not surrendered totally to Baba's grace . . .'

Yes, they would not be short of an answer. But, knowing the simple soul that my aunt was, and how much she had been wronged, and knowing the sincerity and depth of her faith, I can never reconcile myself to an answer that, as we have seen ever so often while reviewing the texts, puts the blame on the victim. Most certainly not after I saw her die of cancer, still believing that He would come to her rescue . . .

❑ Even in India, for decades rationalists have been issuing challenges to godmen who attract the gullible by working 'miracles'. Materialize something bigger than your hand—a pumpkin, they said. We will tear a currency note, they said; you take half of it; we will keep the other half; now produce the half that would complete the note. Produce something *we* request you to produce rather than something of your own accord . . . Not one godman took up or has taken up a single one of their challenges. The rationalists have been demonstrating the 'miracles' for which the godmen are famous, and showing that these are the usual tricks that magicians stage. They have been showing that anyone of us can perform the same 'miracles' using elementary chemistry, that we can execute them with sleights of hand which we can master with just a little practice. We should heed them, and

be particularly wary of looking for help from persons
to whom we feel drawn not so much because of their
piety but because of the 'miracles' they perform. As a
beginning, make a list of 'miracles' that seized public
imagination in your own memory, and list the
normal explanations by which they were accounted
for subsequently. Similarly, make a list of the
godmen who suddenly acquired huge following
and find out what happened to them or came to be
known about them a while later. And what
happened to the organizations which they, with
their divine hand and foresight, had set up. The
same disputes over succession? The same tussles
over controlling property?

❏ List the questions over which religions differ and
claim superiority over each other, and even fight.
Which of these can ever be settled by evidence? If
they are such that they can never be settled, why are
we breaking heads over them? Or even wasting any
time over them? And how do we claim superiority
over some other group because of the 'answer' we
have alighted upon in regard to a question that we
ourselves say is unanswerable?

❏ List the questions over which sects have formed
within our own religion. What is the significance of
these questions for making us more humane, for
improving our conduct towards each other?

❏ As we are culturally conditioned and, therefore, do
not see through the religion in which we have been
brought up and by which we are enveloped, one
good way to start is to begin by examining the
practices, custodians and scriptures of religions
other than our own. In fact, almost the most
productive place to start is the religion that you or
your community particularly despises or fears, the

one with which your own religion has been at odds for the longest while.

❑ After you have carefully noted down the explanations that the texts of other religions offer for phenomena that seem to be so childish in the light of what we know today; after you have noted down the commands and passages from the texts of other religions that seem so manifestly indefensible; after you have noted down the superstitions and rituals of other religions that seem so manifestly meaningless to you; after you have made a full file of the evidence that has broken out about the doings of the custodians of other religions, write down the beliefs, passages, commands from the texts you have been taught to revere that correspond to those; write down the rituals that you have been brought to believe will ward off the problem; collect news reports of evidence that surfaces of the doings of the custodians of your own religion. Do the latter stand on any better footing than the former set? In the north, the auspicious time for our wedding rituals turns out to be at night. In the south, or, even in the north among the Sikhs for instance, the auspicious time turns out to be in the mornings. How is the notion of us northerners about which hours are auspicious any more defensible than the notion of those in the south? In the south, tasks are not begun in *rahu kaalam*. In the north, we are happily ignorant of *rahu kaalam*. Do more of our ventures flounder for that reason?

❑ Pause and notice how you respond to new information. To go back to my niece and the astrological columns in our papers and magazines, ask someone to cut out the names of astrological signs, and *then* read each entry. Which entry, which

'analysis of character' applies to you most and
which least? Are they any less apt than what the
astrologer-columnist has written against your 'true'
sign? What is your reaction when you learn that
there is no 'Peter Vidal' under whose name ever so
many papers publish astrological forecasts for the
coming week? And what of the report that news
agencies released on 16 January 2011—that 'the
earth's wobbly orbit means that it is no longer
aligned to the stars in the same way as when the
signs of the Zodiac were first conceived'; that as a
result 'most people go back a sign'; and that,
therefore, you have been reading the wrong
horoscope; not just that, it turns out that, in fact,
there is another long forgotten Zodiac sign,
Ophiucus, that everyone born between 29
November and 17 December falls under this sign
and that she or he just has had no horoscope to go by
till now and has, hence, been going by an altogether
fictitious one?[26]

---

[26] AFP and other agencies on 16 January 2011, about the 'Astrology
chaos' that broke out when the *Star Tribune* of Minneapolis wrote up a
story reporting the finding—a story that was itself based on accounts that
had been published in *LiveScience* earlier in 1996 and 2007. The reaction to
the disclosure will perhaps be no different from that of wine connoisseurs
who make such an ostentatious performance of sniffing and tasting wines
at restaurants to the scandals that break out periodically in the
wine trade—that the vintages have been mixed, that wines from different
areas have been sold under wrong labels, that the wines have been
artificially 'aged' by using wood chips, that acid and other substances have
been added to alter the 'bouquet' and taste of the wine: and all this turns
out to have been done by some of the most famous vineyards and labels
in regard to some of the dearest and most prized vintages. Unshaken
in their faith, unfazed in their demeanour, the connoisseurs continue
their performance! Hence, all that may happen in response to the report
of signs having shifted and a new one having been added is that readers
may now detect even greater accuracy in the 'true' horoscope of their
'real' sign.

❑ At the least, let us stop doing things by proxy. Assume that the mantras and vows that are chanted and the rituals that are gone through when we marry have been honed over the eons because they have deep psychological effect. But what effect can the mantras have if we get the priest to recite them and we don't even know their meaning? How can the rituals penetrate into our minds if we don't even know what they signify?

❑ Think up and circulate additional exercises to liberate yourself and your friends from dependence.

It is when we have removed the props one by one— God, inerrant scriptures, the authority of intermediaries, godmen and other intercessors—that we will have equipped ourselves to take the first step towards dealing with the suffering that we have to confront.

10
Each of us can be, at the least,
the servant of servants

Suffering is real. To urge anything that dismisses it as 'unreal' is to mock the pain of another.

*

So many questions have been asked of God for centuries. The answers that theists have given do not stand up. We do not have to take a final, conclusive position on the matter. But one thing is clear. Even as there are a host of other arguments for setting aside the notion of God as one who is All-knowing, All-powerful as well as Compassionate, and who, on His own telling, intervenes in human affairs, the existence of suffering—of evil in general—and that too on such a massive scale, is the most elementary and also perhaps the initial reason for excluding that notion—just as it might have been the reason on account of which mankind conjured up the notion in the first place.

For dealing with life and what it sends us, in particular for persons like us who are unlikely to pursue the higher truths of the mystics, the Buddha's position is the most helpful.

One evening, Malunkyaputta, a venerable disciple of the Buddha, comes to him and declares that if the Buddha does not tell him whether the world is eternal or not, or it is both eternal and not-eternal; whether it is finite or infinite, or both finite and infinite; whether the soul is the same as the body or not, or it is both the same and not the same; whether after death a Tathagata exists or ceases to exist, or whether he both continues to exist and ceases to exist, he, Malunkyaputta, will abandon the religious life and return to the low life.

The Buddha chides him. Did I tell you to lead the religious life on the promise that I will declare these things to you? the Buddha asks. 'No, venerable Sir,' the disciple admits. Were a person to take that attitude, the Buddha says—that I shall not lead the holy life unless the Blessed One declares to me whether the world is eternal or not or both . . ., he would be dead and the Blessed One would still not have declared those things to him.

As was his wont, the Buddha explains the point with a parable. Suppose, Malunkyaputta, an arrow, thickly smeared with poison has pierced a man, and his friends and relatives rush a surgeon over to take out the arrow and treat him; and suppose he were to insist, 'I will not let the surgeon pull out this arrow until I know whether the man who released this arrow is a nobleman or a Brahmin or a merchant or a worker . . . until I know his name and the clan from which he comes . . . until I know whether he is short or tall . . . dark or brown or of golden skin . . . until I know whether he lives in a village or town or city . . . until I know whether the bow from which the arrow was released was a long bow or a crossbow . . . until I know whether the bowstring that wounded me was made from fibre or reed or sinew or hemp or bark . . . until I know whether the shaft that wounded me was wild or cultivated . . . until I know what kind of feathers with which the shaft that pierced me was fitted—of a vulture or a crow or a hawk or a peacock or a stork . . . until I know the kind of sinew with which the shaft was bound—of an ox or a buffalo or a lion or a monkey . . . until I know what kind of an arrow it is that has wounded me—hoof-tipped or curved or barbed or calf-toothed or oleander.'

'All this would still not be known to that man,' the Buddha says, 'and meanwhile he would die . . .'

And there is a reason on account of which he had not given answers to the sorts of questions with which the disciple is obsessed, the Buddha explains. Whether the world is finite or infinite or both; whether it is with beginning and end or not; whether the Tathagata survives after death or not . . . 'there is birth, there is ageing, there is death, there are sorrow, lamentation, pain, grief, and despair.' They have to be dealt with, and it is the way to deal with them that I have set out, the Buddha says.

So, remember what I have left undeclared, he teaches: I have not declared answers to the questions you pose as these are unbeneficial; they do not lead to disenchantment, to dispassion, to cessation, to peace, to direct knowledge, to enlightenment, to nirvana. Remember what I have declared. 'And what have I declared? "This is suffering"— I have declared. "This is the cessation of suffering"—I have declared. "This is the way leading to the cessation of suffering"—I have declared.' And these I have declared because they are beneficial, they lead to disenchantment, to dispassion . . . to the cessation of suffering . . . to nirvana . . .[1]

*

It is indeed true that individuals will find solace and sustenance in different notions—some in God, some in a godman—and different practices—some in going on a pilgrimage, some in meticulous performance of rituals. It is also the case that each of these may indeed work at

---

[1] 63 *Culamalunkya Sutta, The Shorter Discourse to Malunkyaputta,* in *The Middle Length Discourses of the Buddha, A new translation of the Majjhima Nikaya,* original translation by Bhikku Nanamoli, edited and revised by Bhikku Bodhi, Wisdom Publications, Boston, 1995, pp. 533-36.

particular moments and see us through specific crises.[2] But just as often they will betray us—recourse to them will not allay the crisis. Our hopes will be raised, and then dashed against the rocks of dejection and demoralization.

One criterion for adjudging the efficacy of God, guru, ritual, place of pilgrimage is, 'Does the notion or person or action make us dependent or self-reliant?' In almost all cases, we will discern that the notion or person or action makes us look upon others to solve our problem. That way lies eventual disappointment. Contrast the notions they insinuate into our minds with the Buddha's last words— 'Work out your salvation with diligence'—in which the responsibility is placed on us alone. He warned others about his own teaching—do not take the finger pointing towards the moon to be the moon itself. He warned disciples that his teaching was like a snake—one that had to be handled with utmost care and skill. At every step, in every discourse, he throws us back on ourselves. Listening to discourses, reading volumes, going on pilgrimages—none of these is a substitute for the work that we have to do by ourselves, on ourselves. At every turn he instructs us not to take what is written in texts, including his own teaching as final till we have verified it by our own experience—that makes it

---

[2] And many, even ones with profound insight, would regard that as a sufficient test for a touchstone. That was Jung's stance, for instance. He remarked, 'One should not be deterred by the rather silly objection that nobody knows whether these old universal ideas—God, immortality, freedom of the will, and so on—are "true" or not. Truth is the wrong criterion here. One can only ask whether they are helpful or not, whether man is better off and feels his life more complete, more meaningful and more satisfactory with or without them.' C.G. Jung, 'The Art of Living', 1960. Reproduced in, C.G. Jung, *Psychological Reflections, A New Anthology of His Writings 1905-1961*, selected and edited by Jolande Jacobi in collaboration with R.F.C. Hull, Routledge and Kegan Paul, London, 1953/ 1979, p. 326. But the conclusion that I report in the next few sentences is based precisely on this test—whether the notions will or will not leave us feeling better off in the long run.

incumbent on us to make the effort on the one hand, and, on the other, it raises our own experience to be the ultimate touchstone. In a word, teachers such as him make us rely on our own efforts and experience. As against many a godman today, who skilfully makes us dependent on the godman himself, there is a Zen saying to keep in mind. So that our conception of the Buddha does not become a fetish; so that our ideas about what the Buddha would have thought or done at this turn do not congeal into preconceptions and predispositions and thus rob us of experiencing the situation ourselves, of thinking ourselves, so that they do not rob us of spontaneity, the Zenists say, 'If you meet the Buddha on the road, kill him.'

*

As we have seen, the explanations that scriptures proffer for the occurrence of pain and suffering do not stand up to the slightest examination.

*

On occasion things that we have done—not in that unknown sojourn, some previous life, but in this very life— may account for what has befallen us. But just as often, those two demons—time and chance—alone are the culprits.

Often, we conclude that those demons have singled us out. That is not so. We conclude that we have been singled out simply because we do not know enough about the traumas to which others have been, and are being subjected. When we learn to listen to the pain of others, we realize that, as *Ecclesiastes* teaches, ' . . . time and chance happeneth to them all.'

    Ram gayo Ravan gayo
    Jaake bahu parivaar . . .

*

Accordingly, the condition to which the one dear to us has been reduced by the blow is no judgement on us. It most certainly is no judgement on the poor child.

*

As we are dealt a blow, we would do well to recall Plutarch's test. Their daughter had died. His wife was distraught. Plutarch urged her to ask how many would 'gladly choose your fate, even including our present upset'. If many would, the very blow that has occasioned our pain should 'bring you to the realization of how much we have to be grateful for in what we still have'.[3]

*

No cosmic purpose is served by our suffering or that of those dear to us—just as no cosmic purpose is served by our being born or by our dying; and that for the simple reason that there is no 'cosmic purpose'.

*

It is indeed true that in many instances the suffering is so intense, so final that one can do little with it.

*

But just as often, suffering can be put to work—sometimes even by the person who has been struck the blow. One stricken by cancer can spend his last days cursing and writhing. Or he can bear the dreadful and wholly unmerited illness with forbearance, with quiet dignity as, to recall the instance we have encountered earlier, Ramana Maharshi did—and thus teach those around him how one may face up to even so terrible and unjustified a blow.

*

In any event, those that serve someone who is in distress can

---

[3] Plutarch, *In Consolation to His Wife*, Penguin, Great Ideas, London, 2008, p. 8.

put the suffering to work. The condition to which the illness has reduced the one dear to us is, after all, the first of the four 'heavenly messengers' that propelled the Buddha to seek the origin and cure of suffering: while the condition—of dependence, of inability to walk and eat, the slurred speech—may have been brought about by a particular ailment in the ones we are serving, it is the condition that we will have to contend with in our own case soon enough. Even if one demon—chance—spares us, the other one—time—by itself will see to that. The condition of the ones we love and serve thus presages our own. In assisting them we learn what we ourselves will require. Nor is it only for some distant time that their suffering is a teacher, an aid, an invaluable occasion to help ourselves. The despair, the feeling of helplessness that the blow brings in its wake is an even greater affliction than the blow itself. The surest antidote to despair is to transform that condition into an occasion to do something, any little thing to alleviate the calamity.

*

The first requisite for putting suffering to work is to begin right here and now, to shun postponing the effort. The Buddhist texts put the point precisely: death is absolutely certain; the manner and time of death are absolutely uncertain. That is why, they say, we should not postpone to tomorrow the prescribed practices. There is a corollary: good fortune may itself be the thing that turns into ill fortune; correspondingly, ill fortune itself can be the compost that can be used to yield succulent fruit. A Tibetan text narrates an arresting parable. Two bees, one golden, the other turquoise, deeply in love with each other, chance upon a sage. He gives them precious instruction. They say that they will put it to practice. But they postpone practising the dharma, and sometimes they give in to passing

pleasures. It is a wonderful day. One of them is flying
around in the fragrant breeze. The other is deep into a
flower—drinking its sweet nectar. Suddenly, a cloud floats
over the plain. The sun is obscured. The flower gathers up.
The bee that was inside is caught in it—the soft petals which
were a bed of down till a moment ago become a prison; the
stems become bars of a cell. Her companion rushes from the
raven to the chief of sparrows; to the frog, to the serpent, to
the marmot, to the cuckoo, to the wild horse, to the black
spider, to the kite. It beseeches each of them to use the
powers he has to persuade the cloud to move away so that
the sun will shine again, the flower open, and his beloved be
rescued. Each of them affirms that he does indeed have the
requisite power, and promises to work the magic. Alas! The
cloud becomes even darker. Thunder, lightning, torrential
rain ensue. The garden is devastated. The petals of that
particular flower close even more tightly. The little bee
suffocates to death. 'I am an example of a person who
intended to practice the *Dharma* but was unable to
accomplish it immediately,' laments the devastated
companion . . .[4] That is, of course, not the end of such
stories.[5] The wife conceives. The would-be mother and
father are joyous. The child is born and is growing well. She
is but nineteen months old and a disease
hits her. It leaves her blind and deaf. The parents' joy turns
to ashes . . . The child grows up and overcomes her
handicaps. She, Helen Keller, becomes a beacon of hope to
the world . . .

*

Practice is the requisite. And commencing that practice is
the imperative. One of the most persistent diversions that

---

[4] Paltrul Rinpoche, 'Holy *dharma* advice, A drama in the lotus garden', in
Enlightened Living, Teachings of Tibetan Buddhist Masters, Tulku Thondup
(trans.), Harold Talbott (ed.), Shambhala, Boston, 1990, pp. 44-97.
[5] The Tibetan parable itself continues much beyond this lament, of
course.

keep persons like us from commencing it is the 'search for ultimate answers'. Every time such questions tempt us we should recall the Buddha's sermon to Malunkyaputta that we have encountered earlier.

The second requisite for us to put suffering to work is to keep at the effort of transforming it into a teacher. The key is 'to keep at the effort'.[6] Through unremitting practice, we have to fashion a new way of looking, a new pair of spectacles, so to say. The Tibetan masters speak of this as thought training, thought transformation. We begin with the smaller inconveniences. Someone abuses us. Is there something in our conduct that justifies that abuse, we ask ourselves. If so, we regard the critic as our benefactor, and rectify our conduct. If it is unmerited, we look upon it as a warning bell—alerting us to what we will invite if we transgress. The calumner does more than merely alert us to a potential danger in the future. He provides us an occasion to look at the condition of our mind. How have we reacted to the unmerited abuse? Have we gone off the handle? Or have we heard the abuse, and let it brush past us like the breeze? The Tibetan masters recall the image of Milarepa, the revered ascetic and teacher. He has his hand cupped to his ear—everything he hears, he hears as counsel. We begin with the minor setbacks, and persevere till the new way of looking becomes our habit. Indeed, we persevere further till we come to look upon the setback or the tragedy as not only something that can be put to work, but as something that is necessary for us to ascend the next step.[7]

---

[6] Exactly as Josh Malihabadi put it:

Karti hai gauhar ko ashkbaari paida
Tamkeen ko mauje-bekaraari paida
Sau baar chaman mein jab tadapti hai naseem
Hoti hai kali par ik dhaari paida . . .

[7] See, for instance, Lama Zopa Rinpoche, Transforming Problems Into Happiness, Wisdom Publications, Boston, 1993, pp. 15-16. Several Buddhist texts set out step-by-step practices for transforming problems and adversities into opportunities for purifying the mind. Contemporary

The third requisite for putting suffering to work is deep reflection. Of course, reflection is not to wait till practice is finished; the two alternate, they intertwine, they fortify each other. The reflection is not about, 'Why has this happened to me?' but about, 'How may I put even this to work—for others as well as for myself?' The answer will come only upon deep, iterative reflection over a long period. 'Perseverance' is the word that is invariably used when prescribing practices like meditation. It is just as relevant to reflection.

*

To begin with we have to ascertain our own attitude: 'Have I perchance become accustomed to this condition? Have I become "addicted to suffering"? Do I really want to get out of the quicksand?' Just as commitment to a cause does not mean merely that we are prepared to shout a slogan, but that we are prepared to undergo the consequences that follow from embracing that position; 'want to' does not mean a mere desire. It must mean that we are prepared to do what it will take to reverse the mental trough into which we have descended as a result of the blow. Next, we must own responsibility for the circumstance. We may not be responsible for what has befallen the child. But we have to grasp in our own hands what has befallen: we must drill it into our being that no one else is going to assume responsibility for dealing with the situation—*we* have to do so. Many may help. In all likelihood, many *will* help. But in

---

Buddhist masters have elaborated the often-cryptic texts for us to understand. As representative of a vast number, see, for instance, The Dalai Lama, *Healing Anger, The Power of Patience from a Buddhist Perspective*, Snow Lion, Ithaca, 1997; Thich Nhat Hanh, *Transformation and Healing, Sutra on the Four Establishments of Mindfulness*, Parallax Press, Berkeley, 1990.

the end, it will be up to us to help our dear one, and to cope with what has happened.

*

But even that will not be enough. The goal that we channel the suffering to subserve must itself be of a particular kind. After all, in answer to the question 'How may I put even this to work for myself?' one can just as well conclude that the suffering of one's child can be put to use for garnering sympathy for oneself! Hence, reflection. Deep and sustained reflection. Excavating a purpose from that debris. A purpose of a definite kind.

*

Of what kind? In his memorable and intense work, *Man's Search for Meaning*,[8] Viktor Frankl points to the contrast he observed first-hand as a prisoner in the Nazi death camps. Many of the inmates would just be found dead in their bunks the next morning—they had just given up. But ever so many, though they knew as well as anyone that they had little chance of surviving, stayed alive, their spirits intact— even to their last breath as they were trooped into the gas chambers. The latter had endowed their suffering with meaning: even when this was no more than the stubborn conviction that their deaths would testify to what the Nazis were about . . .

Unko sholon ke rajaz apnaa pataa to denge . . .
Door kitni hai abhi subeh, bataa to denge . . .

'Finding a meaning' more often than not means not just discovering, but *extracting, excavating,* even *imposing* a

---

[8] Viktor E. Frankl, *Man's Search for Meaning*, Simon and Schuster, New York, 1959.

meaning, Frankl observed in the death camps. On occasion, even keeping an eye on oneself and one's fellow prisoners so as to discern the ways in which they were changing became a purpose—in that the attempt at objective observation put a distance, ever so slight though it was, between what was happening and oneself.[9] It was from this experience that Frankl initiated an entire school of therapy—*logotherapy*, of restoring and rehabilitating patients by re-endowing their lives with a sense of purpose. To work, the purpose must be one that transcends our personal needs and interests, a purpose that stretches our capacity, our endurance, our limits. Often we do not have the freedom to dodge the blow, Frankl taught. But we do have the freedom to choose the attitude that we shall have towards it. The freedom we have

---

[9] See, for instance, the essays of another trained psychoanalyst, Bruno Bettelheim, about those horrible camps: Bruno Bettelheim, *Surviving and Other Essays*, Vintage Books, Random House, New York, 1952/1980. Others have come upon the same lesson in other, 'extreme situations'. We find almost the same words in the memoirs of Solzhenitsyn about his years in the slave-labour camps, and about the years he spent warding off the Soviet regime. Contrary to the conclusions that I report in the text, the accounts of both Frankl and Bettelheim record that those who had a religious outlook coped much better, they discovered a purpose more often than those who did not. Solzhenitsyn records that during the extreme travails to which he was subjected, he always felt that a higher power was steering him to his real mission in life; that the obstacles had been put in his way to foreclose the easier options: see, for instance, A. Solzhenitsyn, *The Oak and the Calf*, Harper and Row, New York, 1979, pp. 111, 146. In recalling these books, I am only recalling persons representative of ones whose works have had deep impact on me—in a sense, enormous therapeutic impact. I am most, *most* certainly not implying that the tragedies that strike our ordinary lives are comparable to the terrible, unspeakable horrors that Hitler and Stalin and Mao inflicted on millions. Not in the slightest. Literature about those horrors should be read in its own right—so that we always bear in mind what villainy man—whom 'God created in His own image'—is capable of. And it should also be read to steel ourselves by Plutarch's test—we think we have been struck a terrible and unmerited blow; yes, we have; but there are millions who would with the fullest justification exchange our condition for theirs.

is restricted, he wrote. It is not freedom *from* conditions; it is freedom to take a stand *towards* the conditions.[10] Frankl called this 'the last of human freedoms'—the freedom to 'choose one's attitude in any given set of circumstances, to choose one's own way'. 'And there were always choices to make,' Frankl wrote, recalling his days in the concentration camp—as there are in serving a helpless child. 'Every day, every hour, offered the opportunity to make a decision, a decision which determined whether you would or would not submit to those powers which threatened to rob you of your very self, your inner freedom; which determined whether or not you would become the plaything of circumstance, renouncing freedom and dignity to become molded into the form of the typical inmate'.[11]

And choose we must—for there is nothing intrinsic in man's nature which automatically drives him to higher and better conduct.[12] 'Caught in a hopeless situation as its helpless victim,' Frankl wrote, 'facing a fate that cannot be changed, man still may turn his predicament into an achievement and accomplishment at the human level. He thus may bear witness to the human potential at its best,

---

[10] *Man's Search for Meaning*, op. cit., p. 130.

[11] Ibid., pp. 65-66.

[12] Ibid., pp. 98-100. To be human is to assume responsibility, Frankl wrote. Concluding his penetrating work, he noted, 'A human being is not one thing among others; *things* determine each other, but man is ultimately self-determining. What he becomes—within the limits of endowment and environment—he has made out of himself. In the concentration camps, for example, in this living laboratory and on this testing ground we watched and witnessed some of our comrades behave like swine and others behaved like saints. Man has both potentialities within himself; which one is actualized depends on decisions but not on conditions. Our generation is realistic for we have come to know man as he really is. After all, man is that being who has invented the gas chambers of Auschwitz; however, he is also that being who has entered those gas chambers upright, with the Lord's Prayer or the *Shema Yisrael* on his lips.' Ibid., pp. 134-35.

which is to turn tragedy into triumph.'[13] But for this one must be 'oriented towards the future, toward a goal in the future, toward a meaning to fulfill in the future'.[14]

The one who is dear to us and has herself suffered a blow provides us the opportunity to endow our own lives with meaning, and she does so with a directness and an immediacy that little else could have afforded—she immediately and directly endows our life with a sense of purpose, and immediately and directly teaches us to look not at the blow that has been struck but at the way it may be overcome in the future. She teaches us to be patient. Looking after my mother after she suffered strokes and helping her recover became the very purpose of my father's life, ninety though he was at the time, and fully occupied helping others through the one-man organization that he ran, Common Cause.

*

That does not, of course, mean that we should become masochists looking forward to suffering ourselves, or sadists looking forward to others being dealt a blow so that we may serve them. As Frankl pointed out, what is at issue is *irreducible suffering:*[15] and the lesson is that even this can be put to work—especially if one has reoriented oneself so that one's goal is inner growth.

*

To ascend to a vantage point from which we can endow our lives with meaning, the task that the situation throws up, apart from being one that stretches us to our limits, must be unique to the person, Frankl wrote. That is, for the pain of another to transform itself into meaning for us, for it to

---

[13] Viktor E. Frankl, *Man's Search for Ultimate Meaning*, Perseus Publishing, Cambridge, Mass., 2000, p. 123.

[14] Ibid., pp. 134-35.

[15] Ibid., p. 142.

endow our life with purpose, it must yield a task, or we must extract from it a service, that only we can perform. If we serve our child in a way, and to a degree that can be just as well handled by a servant, the little we do for our child will not endow purpose and meaning. What we do for him must be of an intensity and have the quantum of love that only we as his parents can give him.

*

Most emphatically, what we have to provide is not pity. Not even sympathy. Empathy is the word that is used—not feeling sorry for; not even feeling for. But getting into the skin of, and *feeling like* the person must feel. That is easily prescribed, and almost never attained—except by a mother in the case of her child. Even though I am with Anita almost all our waking hours, I was jolted out of complacence some years ago as we were walking. She said, 'Sometimes I feel as if I am wading through mercury.' I had been confident that I knew every inflection of her condition and mood. In fact, I had been ignorant of even that elementary sensation. The other day, we were eating. The previous day, Anita had fallen for the eighth time in the last few months. The left side of her face had taken the maximum impact. As a result, it was swollen and part of the face was beginning to turn blue. Her legs flayed. She began sweating. Her kurta became quite drenched. She had barely eaten a chapati. She began panting. She said, 'I feel I have run half a mile . . .' I was seeing her legs shake—they were hitting the table. I was seeing the difficulty she was having manoeuvring the spoon. But I had no idea of how much exhaustion that effort of eating just a chapatti had caused her.

That is why the Tibetan meditation of 'exchanging selves' is literally invaluable. And even more so the much more demanding *tong-len*—giving and taking: giving everything satisfactory in one's condition to another and

taking on, not verbally but with full feeling, the suffering
and condition of the other.

*

Nor is this a switch that can be turned on once, and shall
emit light forever. Quite the contrary. One of the truest
teachings in this regard is in the *Dhammapada:* 'As the
silversmith removes impurities from silver so the wise man
from himself—one by one, little by little, again and again.'[16]
For us who are given to quick fixes, to allopathic pills, to be
reminded of that *'again and again'* is perhaps even more
important than to be reminded of the other two clauses.
Self-pity, anger, lust, greed can go underground, so to say:
look at so many of the rishis in our mythology—how,
though they had mastered their senses through years and
years of penance, they flew into rage at trifles, and hurled
curses that triggered calamities. As even they could fly off
the handle, surely, we need that admonition, 'again and
again' all the more.

*

And, of course, it is not necessary that someone really close
to us should be the one who has suffered the blow. Doing
good work is so difficult in our country—so many put
impediments in the way; so many paste motives. For that
reason those who are doing good work require all the help
we can give them. Even if our circumstances prevent us
from serving those who are in pain, we can serve those who
are serving them: all of us have the wherewithal to be the
servants of servants. I well remember the early days of the
school for spastic children in Delhi, the difficulties those
who were running it faced every day, and the ones who
helped them out. Their example teaches us that we can help
with whatever skill we have. An artist helped the Spastics

---

[16] *The Dhammapada,* 239.

School children to try painting. She introduced different media to the school—watercolours, oils. Soon, the children began to turn out the most bewitching paintings—paintings that have what only they can gift: the innocence, the absolutely unexpected colour to depict the sky, the lake which the child may never have seen, the optimism and joy for life that you and I only read about in books.

But what of the children—and there are so many of them, our son among them—who cannot quite hold a paintbrush, their hand functions being so gross that they cannot grasp so fine a thing as a brush? Another artist introduced block printing in the school: a motif would be etched on to a small block; the child pressed the block on to a sort of stamp pad of one or more colours, and then pressed it on to thick, handmade paper. That little thing opened an entire world for so many children: for now they were making the most exquisite wrapping paper.

But the problem was that their hands could not be directed to fall in an orderly way on the paper. An engineer designed a simple grid with strings and wires. The child would now get the block into the right space, and press. But once the squares had been filled, the child had great difficulty in lifting the entire grid, taking out the paper and putting in the new sheet. So the engineer divided the grid into two, each side was affixed to hinges. Now, upon completing the printing of one sheet, the child could lift one half of the grid to the left, the other to the right, and replace the sheet.

But replacing that sheet was still a problem, so unsteady were the hands of so many of the children. The paper was therefore put on a roller. The child, having completed the printing of one portion, would now just pull, and the next 'sheet' would be ready for him to continue his work.

But what if we are not artists, and cannot teach others how to paint? What if we are not engineers? To this day

I remember my friend, the late P.R. Rajagopal. He had been the Inspector General of Delhi Police. He had been head of the Border Security Force. He had been Secretary of the Shah Commission. After he retired from such high positions, he would travel in the noonday heat in buses, and get persons he knew to buy cards that the children had made. He would go from office to office to get a shop or a telephone booth allotted for a handicapped person to man. It was the greatest problem to take the children to hospitals and doctors from the school. That was specially so when the children had to be taken to equip them with aids, etc., that they would need for sitting in examinations, and the parents were not or could not be present. So the consultant, the counsellor, the doctor who held even a weekly or fortnightly clinic in the school itself, made an enormous contribution.

Or take an even simpler problem. Because of visual impairments children like our son are not able to read. Yet they yearn for information, for news, for stories, poems, jokes, riddles. They cannot read, but they can hear. Therefore, each one of us who can read can help. We can go to such institutions or to the homes of such children and read to them. If we cannot do that, we can, in our own homes, record the stories or lessons into a tape recorder. The tapes become the child's library, they bring the world to him. A lady had a car and a driver. Twice every week she would visit one of the children at his home, and take him for a joy ride to whichever place he wanted. Those outings became the life of the child.

And we can scarcely imagine the difference which St Mary's School in Delhi made in those days to the lives of such children: it opened its gates to the graduates of the Spastics School, it welcomed them, it made them feel fully at home, it made them live that impossible dream—to feel normal. And so did St Stephen's College.

Every other week the Spastics Society used to be hobbled by some stone which had been deliberately, callously thrown in the way. An inflated, fraudulent bill would arrive from a government department: unless you pay up forthwith, your electricity will be cut off, they would be threatened. Every year these children, after a struggle that you and I just cannot imagine, would prepare themselves for Board examinations—and every year there would be the same problems. All sorts of difficulties would be put up, to take an instance, for enabling them to have writers—as they could not hold a pencil, the children would have to have someone to whom they could dictate their answers, and these writers would have to be from among persons who had been trained to work with such children for, often, the speech of the children was difficult to follow. But our heartless regulations had been framed with no heed to such needs. And so, even getting so elementary and necessary a permission would become a major struggle. When, in spite of these difficulties, the children would pass the exams, most schools for normal children would not take them in for further studies. When they passed out of schools and colleges, few employers would be prepared to engage them, and so all those years of struggle would seem to have been for nothing.

That persons who are engaged in service of such an order have to spend their time waiting outside the offices of petty officials, that it should have become so difficult to do even simple good work today is a shame for our country, it is a curse. But it is also an opportunity. It gives us—those who do not have that dedication or perseverance to serve the children directly—to serve and help indirectly. We can find out what obstacle shackles the institution that is nearest us, and we can take the burden off those running the institution by helping remove that obstacle. Often just a phone call will clear the way for them, often a mere visit to the officer concerned. It isn't that the officers are any less caring than the rest of us. Often it is just the system, those interminable procedures and requirements that have been devised to check the dishonest, but which in fact just serve to make the world so cruel for the straightforward. When the matter is brought to the attention of the official, he or she is helpfulness itself. But someone has to get to them. And so, even those of us who are at a distance, who merely stand and stare, can be of assistance.

The point is that each of us has *some* skill, *some* contact, some decision lies in our hands which can facilitate the tasks of such institutions. Each of us, therefore, has an ability which can enrich the life of such a child. Even if we do not yet have it within us to put a tragedy to work, we can put that skill, that contact to work. The great reformer, Pandurang Shastri Athawale set an example we should emulate. When devotees first came to him and offered donations of money, he would not accept the donations. For a year, sometimes for even longer, he would want them to donate their time and the skill they had in furtherance of one of his reform projects. You are an accountant? Help maintain accounts. You are a teacher? Teach the tribals. You are a doctor? Help cure those who are ill in our project areas. You are an engineer? Help design and build a better boat for the fishermen . . .

*

One sure way to alleviate pain is to transmute it into service of others. As every psychotherapist observes, one of the effects of an intractable illness, one of the effects of a blow to someone who is dear to us is that it makes us feel helpless. That feeling of helplessness may well be justified—the illness, our own or that of the one dear to us, may well be incurable. But when we transmute it into service of others, we immediately regain control—the illness is beyond our reach, but the quality of love we pour into that service, the extent to which we put ourselves out to serve the one we love *is* in our control. Instead of submitting to the circumstance, we replace it: the circumstance remains; but what fills our mind now is not that circumstance, it is the thing that we have to do for the one dear to us. For that replacement to actually occur, we must not think that we can bring it about by flipping a switch. We must put in deliberate and sustained effort. How full of insight the remark of the Dalai Lama that Jack Kornfield, the American Buddhist teacher and writer, recalls: 'If you want to be truly selfish, help someone.'

*

If I may add a footnote to that precious aphorism of the Dalai Lama: 'If you want to be truly selfish, help someone who cannot do anything for you in return.' One reason for doing so is that of the Gita. If the person is one who *can* do something in return for us, we may expect him to feel grateful for what we have done for him and thus keep looking out for what and when he will do something for us. But when we *know* that the person cannot do anything for us in return, we have the perfect situation for the kind of karma that the Gita prescribes: the service we do in such a context just has to be *nishkaama!*

*

Help how much? The answer was best given by Mother Teresa: 'Love—till it hurts.' For by then, we would have reached a point past being hurt. In addition, there are the most practical of reasons for following this stratagem—of doing more than the situation demands. One person after another who has survived long terms of incarceration and long bouts of brutality has reported that one of the things that helped him get through the years was to do something—any one thing—which was even more onerous

408 DOES HE KNOW A MOTHER'S HEART?

than the punishments that were being enforced by the guards and brutalizers. That extra bit sustained the conviction that he was still in control. It sustained the sense of self-worth.

*

But we have to actively seize the opportunity—never for a moment thinking what we are doing for the one who has been dealt the blow, thinking only of what she or he is doing for us. As the years go by, we will ourselves come to see that, while we may not have been able to stem her decline, that while we may not have been able to improve his condition, she or he would have transformed us. We don't have to go off to forests and caves looking for a dharma teacher. He is right in front of us! This is what Gandhiji meant when he told doctors that we are not doing a favour to the patient who has come to us for treatment; *he* is doing *us* a favour— by giving us the opportunity to serve him.

*

One of the ways in which he will do so, and we had seen this at the very beginning of this account, is by imparting a sense of proportion. Ever so often, we are buffeted by setbacks in our careers. Ever so often, calumny and worse are hurled at us. The extreme condition of the one we love, and the cheer and freshness with which he faces each day in spite of the affliction, enable us to see what a trifle our little setback is. He and his condition make us see our pursuits—that Award, that accolade—as the momentary excitements that they are.

He does more. His condition forces us to *subordinate* our pursuits to his needs, to subjugate our heart to his whim. Every monastery requires obedience. It prescribes rules and restrictions and rituals to *break* our routines, our habits.[17]

---

[17] For accounts from dissimilar traditions see, for instance, Abbot Christopher Jamison's description of a Benedictine monastery, *Finding*

The needs of the child compel obedience as surely as any regimen of a monastery could. In this way, his condition disciplines us. He compels us to continually strive against our natural inclinations, to continuously row against the current. And this subjugation and obedience and discipline have the virtue that they are freely chosen by us.

Every spiritual teacher asks us to pare away our fancies, our wants. The stricken child, the ailing parent or companion leaves no option in the matter.

Where we were projecting and marketing ourselves to others, he restricts us to essentials. He turns us inwards—to observe the inner workings of our minds.

He becomes a mirror—but of a very special kind: every time he turns to look at us, he makes us see *behind* our face, to see what is going on behind the mask.

He changes, indeed he overturns 'the measure of man'.

That itself is a priceless corrective. Where our eye used to alight like lightning on the shortcomings in another, we now see that our child is so much more than his incapacities. And so are others, we learn as he changes our way of seeing.

He sifts skills. Cunning, cleverness, casuistry, pretence, intrigue, the flamboyant gesture, the Napoleonic pose, the marketer's dexterity, eloquence on a public platform, even book learning, to say nothing of slick power-point presentations—these advance many a career in today's world. Of what avail are they before a helpless child?

Sanctuary, Monastic Steps for Everyday Life, Phoenix, London, 2006; and almost any description of life in Wat Ba Pong, the forest monastery founded by Ajahn Cha in Thailand. Of the Rules of St Benedict that Abbot Jamison recalls, one bears directly on what is said above: 'Earnestly competing in obedience to one another, no one to pursue what he judges better for himself but instead what he judges better for someone else.' *Finding Sanctuary,* op. cit., p. 71. For what is stated in the text see, in particular, pp. 71-76.

He tunnels our vision—to the here and now. We learn to put comparisons out of view. Nothing is to be gained, and much bitterness accumulated by imagining 'what might have been', by comparing our child to others, by recalling how things used to be before our companion was hit by this blow. Accepting that suffering is real entails your accepting that, if I contract a degenerative illness, I will just not be able to do things that others in your circle or organization do; that if I am able to do a thing, I will do it only partially; that I will take longer doing it. 'Doing things' not just as in picking up a spoon. That, of course, but also as in 'processing information', and, therefore, in answering your question—even if all you have asked is what I would like to do. As the years proceed, these faculties may get better. They may get worse. Either way, we will have to deal with things as they are at that time.

He hones the quality of attention we bring to bear, the quality of service we render. As he is our child, as he is our love, we learn to minister to his condition, and to our own reactions to his condition as gently and with as much attention as the Buddhist masters prescribe—'as a feather touching a bubble'.

As he becomes that special mirror—when his look shows us what is behind our face—we scarcely need another teacher to tell us how far we have progressed. Our reactions to his condition and needs; our reactions to the demands that his condition and needs make on our time and energy; the extent to which caring for him has awakened us to the suffering of others, and sown the seed of kindness in our hearts; the extent to which this circumstance has changed our day-to-day dealings with others—these bare the progress or lack of it as well as any teacher would.

*

Several reorientations will aid the transformation. The first of these is to realize that one key to happiness is autonomy.

So long as we are obsessed with worldly success, with acclaim and fame and office, so long are we mortgaged to others; to their opinion of us and of our work; to their benefaction. But if our goal is inner growth, we are liberated of them. 'Success' and 'failure'; ease and hardship; relief and ailment; approbation and calumny; being carried on shoulders and being ignored—all become instruments for watching our reactions, for getting to know ourselves better. All of them thereby become occasions for inner growth.

*

But for that to happen, one must be prepared to do *everything*, to do *whatever* serving the person requires— household chores if the person is no longer able to do those chores; feeding if that is what is needed; toileting when that is necessary. And to do them *whenever* they are needed. Your child has to be toileted at night, then that is when you must get up and do so.

All this was brought home to so many of us one evening. The Spastics School was having its annual fund-raising function. One of India's great classical singers was going to sing. Before the recital, a child from the school spoke. Everyone in the audience was moved to tears. And then an elderly gentleman came on to the stage. He was Colonel Vidya Sagar Nehra. He was *eighty-nine* years old at the time, and as such he was the oldest living officer of the Corps of Engineers of our Army. Seeing him itself humbled us in the audience: his back had been bent by that demon, time. Tall, with a strong voice, he looked like a question mark from afar. He told us that his back hurt at every step. But every single day he walked from his house to the school to work. He did not say a word about what he did for the children— except one to which I shall come in a moment. He spoke of what working for the children did for him. Helping them in their Herculean struggle helps him give meaning to his own life, he said. 'Yes,' he said in a voice and words that I shall

412   DOES HE KNOW A MOTHER'S HEART?

never forget, 'Yes, volunteering is selfish.' Disability is no
handicap in serving others, he said. Age is no handicap.
Quite the contrary. It is having this opportunity to serve
others that keeps me going, he told the audience. 'I know,'
he said, 'if I stop, I am finished.' And then he told us
the priceless guru mantra that I have just recalled.
'Volunteering means that you must be prepared to do
everything, to do *anything* that is required or asked for,' he
said. He himself was an embodiment of that maxim. At the
school, you would find him fetching water, you would find
him counting envelopes, you would find him completing all
sorts of tasks.

As he walked off the stage, his figure bent but his spirit
tall and soldierly, he became the teacher of us all.

So, a tragedy is no disability, it too can be put to work—
the ladies who set up and ran the Spastics Society teach us.
Age is no disability—Colonel Nehra at eighty-nine
taught us.

*

Hence, each of us can serve. But we must do whatever is
required by the person we serve, whenever it is required.
And we must go on doing so for as long as we and those we
serve live. A cardinal error is to start expecting that there
will be an end to these chores. Little triggers resentment and
frustration as the expectation that the demands placed on
us by the circumstance will end. And so, we must guard
against what Frankl called, 'the delusion of reprieve'.

*

And we must expect no recompense—no sympathy, no
recognition, no special privileges. That would be commerce,
not service. Moreover, it isn't just that we will then be
setting ourselves up for disappointment. The service will not
then be an aid to inner growth. Gandhiji put the point with
his usual precision: to 'sacrifice' is to make sacred, he said;

we do not make anything sacred if we are doing it as part of a trade for returns.[18]

*

There is pain and suffering around us, true. But so are joy and laughter. To take just the instance we are considering in this book—a helpless child. That he is with us, that he laughs and loves—are these not things to celebrate? First and foremost, we must not let our unhappiness dampen the spirit of the one who is battling the affliction. And we must do the chores that we have to in good cheer—first kissing the child as you, being roused from sleep to toilet him, lift him into his wheelchair, and then kissing him again and thanking him for helping you as you lay him back in his bed. As Gandhiji would have said, 'Service and a long face go ill together.'[19]

*

---

[18] Jung said exactly that—from a different perspective. 'If I know that I am giving myself, forgoing myself, and do not want to be repaid for it, then I have sacrificed my claim, and thus a part of myself. Consequently, all absolute giving, a giving which is a total loss from the start, is a self-sacrifice. Ordinary giving for which no return is received is felt as a loss; but a sacrifice is meant to be like a loss, so that one may be sure that the egoistic claim no longer exists. Therefore the gift should be given as if it were being destroyed. But since the gift represents myself, I have in that case destroyed myself, given myself away without expectation of return. Yet, looked at in another way, this intentional loss is also a gain, for if you can give yourself it proves that you possess yourself. Nobody can give what he has not got.' C.G. Jung, 'Transformation Symbolism in the Mass', (1942/1954). Reproduced in C.G. Jung, *Psychological Reflections, A New Anthology of His Writings 1905-1961*, selected and edited by Jolande Jacobi in collaboration with R.F.C. Hull, Routledge and Kegan Paul, London, 1953/1979, p. 332. Of course, the adept would think poorly of us if, while giving, we were so self-conscious—that I am giving without expectation of return, that I am therefore giving of myself, etc.!

[19] He actually said that while referring to young men who claimed to have or imagined that they had sacrificed much in service of their parents, institutions or causes—giving up lucrative careers and the rest. 'No sacrifice is worth the name unless it is a joy,' Gandhiji wrote. 'Sacrifice and a long face go ill together. Sacrifice is "making sacred". He must be a poor

And that is a crucial point: far from making us cheerful,
suffering does not automatically make us empathetic.
Unless we are watchful, suffering of those near us and our
own suffering can just as readily make us *less* mindful of the
pain of others. 'He has just been discovered to have the
beginnings of Parkinson's? What is the big deal? My wife
has had it for twenty-two years . . .' True, we are reminded
every day of how much we owe those who help us take care
of our dear ones in their need. But that does not result
automatically in gratitude. It can just as readily ignite
resentment—resentment at the fact that we are in bondage
to these helpers, resentment at the fact that they know that
we are dependent on them and are, therefore, taking us for
granted. Yes, at times one is fatigued; one feels harassed by
the myriad things that have to be done to get through the
day. But we have to be watchful, mindful, as the Buddhist
teachers would say, even of our fatigue, our exasperation.
Am I showing it because I really *am* that fatigued? Or am I
showing it to make the one I serve feel guilty? To see the
strain I am bearing for his or her sake? Has the worm of
resentment entered our mind—has the thought crept into
our minds that our child or companion is depriving us of
diversions that we would otherwise have enjoyed? If so,
have we not become like God and His votaries—who

---

specimen of humanity who is in need of sympathy for his sacrifice . . .' His
point was that our very nature must become such that we cannot but
forsake. He gave examples of what he had in mind: 'Buddha renounced
everything because he could not help it. To have anything was a torture to
him. The Lokmanya remained poor because it was painful for him to
possess riches. Andrews regards the possession of even a few rupees a
burden, and continually contrives to lose them if he gets any. I have often
told him that he needs a care-taker. He listens, he laughs and repeats the
same performance without the slightest contrition . . .' *Young India*,
25 June 1925. 'Sacrifice' is too big a word when parents serve their children,
or later, when children serve their parents. But Gandhiji's counsel holds as
well for service.

always blame the poor victim? It is but natural that at times we *will* feel exasperated at the fact that the demands that our circumstances are placing on us just don't end. At such times, it is absolutely essential that we think of the one who is actually ailing: if this is what I am driven to just by attending to his condition, what must the poor child be going through? Instead of wallowing in what time and chance have inflicted on us, we should comprehend, that is, feel in the marrow of our bones, what they have inflicted on the poor child.[20]

In the same way, we have to be watchful of acquiring a martyr complex on the one hand, and of despair, on the other. Suffering—in the form of illness, for instance—makes our attitude negative. We see difficulties in every option. Every morning our mind latches on to the disaster of the day, to the bad news in the newspaper. The one who is ill or suffering for some other reason has to make a conscious effort to locate the cheerful. The caregiver has to do so all the more: if he too sinks into negativity, he will deepen the negativity that has seized his companion, and he will render himself that much less able to serve the latter. But he has to do more than merely ward off this latching on to what is

---

[20] Birbal puts the point well in one of Adit's storybooks. Akbar wakes up, goes to the balcony. Looks across to the bank and the river. He sees a washerman pounding clothes on a rock. The washerman looks up. Realizing that the one on the balcony is none other than the emperor himself, he drops the clothes, presses his palms together, and bends low in salutation. Later in the day, Akbar trips, and breaks his leg. He is livid. He shouts for Birbal. As Birbal arrives, he tells him to have the washerman executed that very day. 'It is because he showed me his face first thing in the morning that I broke my leg.' Birbal agrees: 'Your Majesty is absolutely right. The man must be executed. Such impertinence, causing such grave injury to Your Majesty deserves the severest punishment. And what punishment should be decreed for Your Majesty?' 'For me?' Akbar asks in astonishment. 'What wrong did I do?' 'Majesty, you saw his face, and your leg broke. He saw your face, and he is going to lose his life.'

negative. For, in addition to falling into despondency, he is liable to subconsciously begin blaming the one who needs his help. Therefore, each expression of despair or negativity by the one who needs her or his help should be transformed into what Thich Nhat Hanh calls 'the bell of mindfulness'— a reminder to check one's own frame of mind, one's outlook and pattern of reactions: are they negative and despairing? Am I compounding the negativity that the affliction is naturally imparting to the one I am to serve?

*

Nor does service automatically make us nobler. Indeed, it can insinuate pride. 'He does so much for his child,' we hear others say, and feel ever so satisfied with ourselves.

*

Often there are cures for the blow. Just as often there aren't. It may be that a cure will be found within our lifetimes. It may be that it will not. Once again, those two demons— time and chance—rule. In any case, there are no miracles contrary to the laws of nature, as Gandhiji would say, and it is worse than useless to keep waiting for them, or to keep running around for them. By repeatedly dashing our hopes, a condition that cannot be allayed conditions us to shed, first, unattainable fancies—that position, that acclaim, that girl; and soon, impractical expectations—about a cure materializing from nowhere, about a relative suddenly deciding to stay with us and helping out. We learn to transform these unattainable longings into prisms. Each time the fantasy springs up, we take note of it. We compare it to how things actually turn out. And we learn how unwarranted, even absurd that spiral of wishes was. Eventually, as the years go by, we learn not just to observe, but in addition, to shun unrealistic expectations—and not just about the condition of our loved one, but about other aspects of life as well. We thereby immunize ourselves against preventable frustration.

*

So, it may well be that nothing can be done that will undo the primary cause of suffering—about the brain injury, about the fact that the brain has stopped producing sufficient Dopamine. But the fact is that most of us build seven-storey structures on that primary occurrence. These superstructures are constructs of the mind.

And it is in dismantling these seven-storey structures of rage and resentment and bitterness that the great teachers—the Buddha, foremost—are sure guides. One's foes are as unlimited as space, Shantideva explains. They cannot all be overcome. But if one overcomes hatred, that will be as if one has overcome all foes. There is not enough leather to cover the entire earth. But were one to wear leather sandals, it would be as if one has covered the entire earth with leather. We see this every other day. Chores weigh us down. We think of escaping to some scenic resort, some exotic place in the south. But we carry our circumstances with us. Our reactions to them remain the same. The chores have to be done there too. They exact the same weariness. In any event, we have to return from the vacation all too soon. The object that has to be transformed, therefore, is the mind, the masters have taught—'Irrigators channel water; fletchers straighten arrows; carpenters fashion wood; the wise master their minds . . .'[21] And the instrument with which it has to be, and *can* be tamed and transformed is the mind, they have shown.

One key is to see that, while the mind can think of a million things one after another, it can think of only one

---

[21] *The Dhammapada*, 82, 145.

thing *at a moment.* When we see the helplessness of our child, we are filled with anger and bitterness and with a hundred other emotions. But when we *observe* the emotions that have welled up, the thought that those emotions have erupted in us replaces the emotions themselves. That is one way to think of the 'third eye of Shiva'. It is the eye that reduces all else to ashes—observing the thought that has arisen does that to the thought that has arisen: it 'reduces it to ashes'. Emotions like anger or dejection swell and go out of hand as bitter thought follows bitter thought. Noticing the thought—being 'mindful' of it—cuts the spiralling, and thereby prevents the emotion from going on swelling.

The techniques that are prescribed—focusing on the breath, on each step that we take, on the sensations that cover our body as we sit for long periods, on not adjusting our posture in the slightest without forethought—all these aim at conditioning our mind to look at itself. Every thing, every occurrence can be made into a device for this purpose. Indeed, as the masters so often point out, we need no other teaching materials than what happens around us and to us all the time.

And, most certainly, suffering can be that teaching material—our own as much as that of the ones we serve. For all the familiar emotions well up even when we do no more than sit next to them. When we try and eat alongside a person whose legs shake uncontrollably as he attempts to eat, or a child who drools and has difficulty in swallowing his food, we soon learn to detach ourselves from the dyskinesia of our companion, and to either assist him or, if that is what is needed, to go on eating our own food as if nothing unusual was happening. In either case, the process will have to commence by our first becoming aware of, and 'reducing to ashes' our own reactions to that cruel flailing or drooling. And it is entirely likely that the person bearing the affliction will be pleased—with your concern in one case and with your show of detachment in the other. But it is also possible that either alternative—of rushing to assist or of going on as if nothing unusual is happening—may trigger resentment in the one who is actually suffering. If we rush to help, we may end up reminding the victim that his illness is all too noticeable. If we continue as if nothing unusual is happening, the person may conclude that we are neglecting him, that we do not care for him. As that resentment can in turn ignite exasperation in us—'I just can't understand what he wants me to do in the circumstances'—the occasion becomes yet another learning moment.

There is another way in which service can be an aid to catching hold of the mind. In monasteries, great emphasis is put on doing daily chores—tending the garden, cleaning the toilets, cooking . . . Some of these help overcome aversion. Some instill humility. All of them help focus the mind on the 'here and now'. One dear to us who needs our help provides that occasion automatically, continuously, insistently. He provides us the occasion to focus on the deed alone that has to be performed at that moment. The masters point out that so long as we are doing something, performing some service, say, and are thinking, 'By doing this, I will attain . . .', the activity is 'covered by the self'. It is when we are totally immersed in the activity that 'the self'—that 'bundle of preconceptions and expectations and hopes and fears'—is forgotten. We are in that moment, in that activity alone. We have 'emptied our self'. By immersing ourselves in this way repeatedly, we get into the habit of being continuously present in the moment. With 'the self' forgotten, they teach, we receive each event/object/ experience as just that event/object/experience. We become spontaneous. Everything, every occurrence becomes a vehicle of learning.[22] Now, the dearer the person is to us, the more likely that we will focus not on the fact that we have been awakened to toilet our child, but on the toileting alone; or to wipe his lips as he drools while being fed. The more likely it is that 'the self' would have been forgotten in the deed—exactly as the masters—Dogen in the *Genjo Koan* in this case—prescribe:

> To study the Buddha Way is to study the self.
> To study the self is to forget the self.
> To forget the self is to be enlightened by the ten thousand dharmas.

And she or he forces us to forgo what we would be normally hankering after, and thereby breaks us out of our habits—a first step in spiritual practice. She forces us to work against our natural inclinations till they subside and lose their hold—another step in spiritual practice. She forces us to exert beyond what we had hitherto considered to be our limit—a precondition of spiritual progress. As we are repeatedly taught, it is for a reason that the four who turned the young Siddhartha to seek—the one bent by age, the one felled by illness, the corpse, the serene monk—are called 'the four *heavenly* messengers'. The sine qua non, as Ajahn Chah, one of the greatest exemplars of the Thai forest tradition in recent times, would say, is 'steadfastness and patient endurance'. To be 'calm like the earth that endures', to be 'steady like the pillar that is firm', to be 'like a lake that

---

[22] Every teacher sets this out. To cite two authorities from completely different disciplines, see, on the one hand, Taizan Maezumi Roshi, *Appreciate Your Life, The Essence of Zen Practice*, Shambhala Classics, Boston, 2000; and the writings and teaching of the celebrated yoga master, B.K.S. Iyengar. As long as we are thinking, 'O, that is good. I can hold this asana for twenty minutes even though I am seventy . . . O, they will be really impressed when they see me do this . . . By doing this, I will get the blocked artery to open up . . .' the session will not yield its potential benefit. That will sprout only when we are so immersed in it that we are aware of nothing but the asana.

is pure . . .'[23] There is no greater spiritual practice, Shantideva taught, than forbearance.

We are taught to continue those exercises in meditation till observing our minds becomes a habit, till it becomes our second nature. The effort must be unceasing. It is like rubbing dry sticks to light the fire, Ajahn Chah reminds us. If you take a break, all you get are cold sticks. The one who is dear to us and who is caught in the vice of prolonged suffering, provides us the occasion and the impetus not to just serve. He causes us to ensure that our service is both unbroken and unending.

'Let go', we are taught. But let go *of what?* The condition that confronts us is not curable; it is not going to go away. So, it is not that condition that we can 'let go'. In the end we learn that it is *the reactions to that condition* that we have to let go. The condition lasts. The need for serving lasts. The reactions invade our mind again and again. As we observe them over the years, observing the mind becomes a habit. And we are transformed.

*

And that is how those we serve, serve us.

Indeed, they do infinitely more than we do. We just steady them as they walk. We just lift them out of bed and into a wheelchair. They, on the other hand, transform us.

*

Everyone struck a blow will find his own ways to cope—if it works for the person concerned, each of them is valid. In the foregoing, I have listed a few of the lessons that ring true to me in the light of my own limited experience. Moreover, I have sketched *possibilities.* No reader will think that I have learnt the lessons fully, and I hope that no reader will think that I think that I have learnt even a fraction of them.

---

[23] *The Dhammapada,* 95.

11
Epilogue

By the time I began work on this book, in the winter of 2009, we had moved out of Delhi to Lavasa: I had lost interest in what I had been doing in Delhi; and each passing winter had become more and more difficult for Anita—her symptoms would get worse as the weather turned cold. Lavasa has a more equable climate all the year round. We have put a large part of our life-savings and a great deal of our emotions into the house we have built there: apart from other things, it has been designed especially for Anita's needs and Adit's.

At that time, Anita would walk on her own, even though on occasion she fell down. She would eat on her own, even though her legs would shake uncontrollably. Just a few months later, as I was nearing the end of the book, an unimaginable dip occurred. She began to just freeze—even with two of us helping her, she just could not put one foot ahead of another . . . The flailing of her legs became so very severe that she had to give up eating on her own—one person had to hold her legs down while another fed her . . .

In the event, the condition eased as the medication was adjusted. But was it just the effect of the medicines that had been added, or was it the foreshadow of things to come? In any case, her condition settled down a bit.

But then a mighty blow descended. It had been a perfectly normal day. She and Adit were lying down after lunch. I was working across a courtyard. Suddenly, I heard Anita calling out to me. I rushed. Adit was shaking all over.

I sat him up, clutching him in my arms. The shaking became violent, extreme . . . 'He is having a seizure,' Anita said, alarmed by what she saw.

The convulsions lasted twenty minutes . . . The most frightening twenty minutes that either Anita or I had lived through.

I rushed him to the local hospital in Lavasa. Anita followed. The doctors stabilized Adit. You must take him to Pune, they said . . .

But taking him in the bus-ambulance over a two-and-half hour journey was unimaginable . . . He was helicoptered out. Anita followed in the car . . .

ICU . . . Days in the hospital . . . CT scan . . . EEG . . . An entirely new diagnosis . . . Another string of new words added to our vocabulary: 'Agenesis of corpus callosum with paraventricular ischemic changes . . .' The skill and calm and kindness of the neurologist . . .

No, you can't take him back to Lavasa just yet, the kind doctor said as he came to discharge Adit. I realize how difficult it is for you to give up your new home, but you just can't risk going back yet. You must either stay here in Pune or take him back to Delhi. He will have to be observed . . .

A demon that we thought had been exorcised thirty-three years ago through Ayurveda has broken out again. Adit is now on anticonvulsants. We are back in Delhi having had to leave the house that we have built specially for his needs and Anita's, and for our joy.

Talk of Adit teaching us to subjugate our longings . . .

Talk of focusing only on the task at hand, of not brooding over the past or working up dreads about the future . . .

Talk of learning to give up attachments . . .

Talk of remembering that just shifting to another place is not going to make the problem disappear, that our circumstances will accompany us wherever we go, that, instead of running from one place to another, we have to stand wherever we are, and work on our mind . . .

Talk of not getting taken in by 'the delusion of reprieve' . . .

Just twenty minutes, and all the lessons that Adit has been teaching us are blown to bits . . .

Faiz would have seen it coming:

> . . . *Ubal pade hain azaab saare*
> *Malaale-ahvaale-dostaan bhi*
> *Khumaare-aagoshe-mahvashaan bhi*
> *Ghubaare-khaatir ke baab saare*
> *Tere hamare*
> *Sawaal saare, javaab saare*
> *Bahaar aayi to khul gayen hain*
> *Naye sirey se hisaab saare* . . .

Index